STRATEGIES and TACTICS of
HUMAN BEHAVIORAL RESEARCH

STRATEGIES and TACTICS of HUMAN BEHAVIORAL RESEARCH

JAMES M. JOHNSTON
H. S. PENNYPACKER
University of Florida

LAWRENCE ERLBAUM ASSOCIATES, PUBLISHERS
1980   Hillsdale, New Jersey

Copyright© 1980 by Lawrence Erlbaum Associates, Inc.
All rights reserved. No part of this book may be reproduced in
any form, by photostat, microform, retrieval system, or any other
means, without the prior written permission of the publisher.

Lawrence Erlbaum Associates, Inc., Publishers
365 Broadway
Hillsdale, New Jersey 07642

Library of Congress Cataloging in Publication Data
Johnston, James M
    Strategies and tactics of human behavioral
research.

    Bibliography: p.
    Includes indexes.
    1. Psychological research.   I. Pennypacker,
H. S., joint author.   II. Title.   [DNLM:
1. Behavior.   2. Research—Methods.   BF76.5 J72s]
BF76.5.J63   150'.72   80-22612
ISBN 0-89859-030-2

Printed in the United States of America

to Gwen and Susanne

Contents

Preface

This volume originated from a desire to provide both those who conduct human behavioral research and those who interpret and apply its findings with a thorough strategic and tactical exposition of the best behavioral research methods. We feel that those fields of investigation variously labeled social or behavioral sciences have generally not made sufficient progress in fulfilling the promise of their self-designated status as a science in that they have not accumulated an extensive, highly reliable, and general body of behavioral facts that support an effective array of technological solutions to social and behavioral problems. The limitations on such progress seem not to lie with a special place in nature for human behavior as a subject matter but with the methods by which its experimental study is approached. Although the peculiar personal, cultural, and linguistic histories we all have regarding human behavior may ultimately be at fault, our only hope of loosening these bonds depends on applying proper and effective scientific methods. It is toward this end that this work has been created.

This desire has been occasioned by a range of personal experiences that overwhelm the bearing of the usual intracollegial squabbling characteristic of academe. We have each been involved for several years in basic behavioral research and technological innovation related to that research, and we have on several occasions found ourselves embattled and outnumbered in the sociopolitical arena that must be entered if sound technological innovations are to be widely disseminated through policy reformulation. It was through such encounters that we realized the extent of major misconceptions concerning the very nature of a science of behavior and its accompanying technologies and that these misconceptions pervade all levels and segments of the social and behavioral science/technology enterprise.

It has, therefore, not seemed appropriate to in any way restrict the audience to whom this volume is addressed; accordingly, we have taken great care to tailor its content to the widest possible range of experimental inquiry in the social/ behavioral sciences. In one sense, this has been easy to accomplish, since this spectrum of behavioral research shares far more communalities than it exhibits differences. In general, technical terms unique to our field of behavioral psychology or to other specialties have been avoided, examples have been phrased for a variety of problems and settings, and discussions are conducted in the broadest possible context. While special techniques and procedures may be required for the study of behavior occurring in certain situations, the guiding scientific strategies and their implementing tactics remain remarkably consistent for *all* experimental investigations of human behavior.

What formal training is offered in behavioral research methods usually occurs in the context of post-graduate instruction, and it is at this level that this volume is probably most appropriate. Although it may be read with varying degrees of thoroughness and many will find it ideal for advanced undergraduate courses, its maximum potential will probably be realized at the graduate level. The methodological traditions directly or indirectly inculcated in prior undergraduate and graduate coursework (especially in the area of statistics) will normally constitute adequate background for the reader; indeed, many of those traditions have in a negative sense created the need for this effort. On the other hand, the reader who lacks extensive background in statistics but who has training in one or more of the natural sciences should feel at home with most of the material and may properly regard the discussions of statistical traditions as curious digressions.

This volume is intended to have even greater relevance beyond the classroom. The multitude of researchers and practitioners whose daily concerns include the need for answers to specific questions about human behavior will surely find in these pages an approach to meeting those needs that may depart materially from the content of their formal training, but is nevertheless extraordinarily functional.

In order to appreciate fully the nature of this volume, it is important to be keenly aware of a number of distinctions. First, as the title indicates, we have confined ourselves to considering methods of behavioral *research* as opposed to methods of behavioral *technology*. In other words, we assume the reader's interest is primarily in learning more about the lawful determinants of behavior in all settings rather than in modifying behavior for educational or social gain in particular settings. This is not to imply that effective technologies are methodologically dissimilar from their parent sciences; they share extensive empirical geneology and, ideally, maintain methodological equivalence at many vital points (e.g., measurement). Therefore, most of this volume is of enormous value to behavioral technologists, although we have not oriented discussions exclusively in such a direction. Second, the question may be raised as to whether this can properly be characterized as a volume on research methods. On the one hand, it raises and discusses all the issues underlying methodological decisions and directs the reader toward some and away from other procedures. On the other hand, it is not a manual of research technique in that it does not provide extremely detailed, step-by-step instructions for conducting experiments and analyzing data. We feel that such specific skills cannot be adequately transmitted through the written word, but must be acquired through the natural contingencies experienced while conducting actual research projects.

Consequently, we conceive of the volume as being more than a conventional methodological treatise. We have tried to convey a complete perspective on the phenomena of human behavior to guide the reader through the idiosyncrasies of any research endeavor. To do this, we have found it necessary to provide brief historical background for certain contemporary practices because often the best way to understand the function of a procedure is to discover its original purpose. We have also made brief excursions into areas traditionally reserved for works on logic and the philosophy of science because these topics have direct bearing on both the understanding and practice of many facets of method. At other times, we have had to break new ground when we found ourselves considering in depth issues that have either been ignored or treated perfunctorily by other writers in the area. We hope readers will share our excitement when they encounter evidence of such excavations.

However the reader finally decides to classify this work on the basis of his or her unique personal perspective, it should be clear that this is not a methodological cookbook. We are adamant in our conviction regarding the inappropriateness of such simplistic treatments of behavioral research methods for any level of student or researcher. The quality of both scientific and technological investigations of human behavior will not improve until our understanding of the methods by which we approach discovery is sufficient to overcome our clinging to special cultural preconceptions about the subject matter. To encourage continued support for the view that the investigator need only apply a few formularized rules of method to any research problem furthers a tragic misconception that has subtle but pervasively unfortunate consequences for a science of behavior. Instead, the goal of this volume is to facilitate a thorough and integrated understanding of behavioral research methods at strategic and tactical levels so that the experimenter is in an informed and flexible position to design procedures that are ideally suited to particular experimental circumstances and that will also yield reliable and general statements about human behavior.

In keeping with the above goal, one of the organizing themes of this book rests on a denotative and heuristic distinction between *strategies* and *tactics*.

Analogous to military usage, strategies in this context refers to the overall plans, principles, or goals of scientific investigation. In the most general sense, a strategy of the science of behavior is the experimental elucidation of functional relations between organisms and environment. However, there are many strategies that can be phrased for each of the major components of scientific method. For example, considering dimensional quantities and units of measurement (Chapter 7) highlights the strategic importance of standard and absolute units in measuring behavior.

Tactics, on the other hand, refers to the general methods and procedures necessary to implement the guiding strategies. In the above example, tactics would include the prescriptions by which various dimensional quantities are actually defined and measured. It must be pointed out, however, that the strategies/tactics distinction is not absolute, but relative, and no efforts should be expended in developing formal and exhaustive lists for either level of scientific activity or in deciding whether a particular consideration is primarily strategic or tactical in nature. In addition to its literary benefits, the distinction is valuable in forcing an honest and unambiguous definition of methodological goals so that the enormous range of unique experimental circumstances may be approached with a flexible and effective but strategically consonant tactical repertoire.

A related term may now be defined. *Techniques* refers to those detailed procedures necessary to implement methodological tactics in unique experimental siutations. Whereas tactics have wide generality from one circumstance to another, techniques are less transferable, since they must suit idiosyncratic combinations of research questions, experimental environments, and subjects. Because this volume is intended to apply to the broadest range of human behavioral research, its discussion of methodological strategies and tactics necessarily stops short of considering techniques, so that the appropriate audience will not be diminished. Technique-level decisions must invariably be made in the context of specialized areas of behavioral research, although any particular technique must be consistent with its related tactics and strategies in order for scientific activities to be designated as good behavioral research.

Considerable thematic substance is further implied by the parts and chapters into which the content of this book is divided. Experimental method is often regarded as a single, amorphous undertaking when, in fact, a truer perspective may be obtained by clearly distinguishing measurement from design and both from interpretation—the strategies involved are quite different. However, even more importance atttaches to chapter-level distinctions. For instance, we have differentiated the typical holistic consideration of measurement into five chapters. Separating the extensive discussion of response definition (following an earlier chapter on behavior as a subject matter) and of dimensional quantities and units of measurement from the more common topic of observation and recording facilitates important strategic and tactical discriminations. The other chapters in the book have been similarly differentiated following our conviction that it is both didactically and functionally valuable to do so.

That some of these chapter distinctions are somewhat arbitrary must, of course, be acknowledged. All of the chapters across all five parts are closely related, and we have carefully attempted to accentuate this. Furthermore, even though the chapters have been ordered in a crude chronology of experimental activities and decisions, the sequence is at some points debatable, further necessitating a considerable integration across chapters that we hope has been achieved. Finally, we have found it impossible to adhere to the convention established by most other writers who discuss the issues surrounding statistical analysis in a single location. It became clear in the course of our writing that statistical thinking has invaded the scientific process at several stages other than data analysis, and we preferred to identify and evaluate these influences in every context of their occurrence.

Work on this volume commenced in January 1975. The first draft was completed in the fall of 1976, and a major revision and development was finished in June 1977. A third editing completed the manuscript in 1978. Some decisions were made in the early stages of our writing that warrent comment. First, we have generally not attempted to support our various points with voluminous scholarly references of uncertain pedagogical value. The strategies and tactics described herein may be justified or criticized only in terms of their consequences for a science of behavior—that is, by the reliability and generality of the data and interpretations that result from their application. Therefore, references are used to acknowledge our intellectual debt to earlier writers as well as to direct readers to important basic sources, and we hope we have been thorough in this regard. Second, we have generally relied on hypothetical rather than empirical examples to illustrate both criticized and recommended tactics. This has avoided unnecessary embarrassment for our well-intentioned fellow investigators and has facilitated our careful crafting of each example to the nuances of the point under discussion. At the same time, each example is thoroughly representative of practices or data with which we and many readers are quite familiar, so that the hypothetical nature of these examples should in no way weaken their impact. Their real counterparts can easily be found in the primary literature.Third, throughout these early chapters and, to a lesser extent, throughout the entire volume, occasional reference is made to various methodological practices in the natural sciences and the social sciences. It should be clear that such characterizations are necessarily crude and overgeneralized to some degree, and we apologize for the unavoidable error that results from thematic enthusiasm and literary convenience. The natural and social sciences each encompass a wide range of experimental strategies and tactics, and there is certainly some degree of overlap. We resolutely insist, however, that important methodological commonalities are fewer than often supposed and that the differences we describe are the far more frequent, incriminating, and disappointing observations.

The reader will easily discern our considerable intellectual debt to Claude Bernard, Ivan Pavlov, and B. F. Skinner; their conception of scientific method and the demonstration of its consequences served as the foundation for much of our own thinking. It has been our special fortune to enjoy a close personal and professional relationship with Ogden R. Lindsley who, perhaps more than anyone, clearly grasps the significance of this tradition for the betterment of the human condition. This influence was also greatly crystallized by Murray Sidman's classic, *Tactics of Scientific Research,* and we hope the continuity with our volume is evident.

We are greatly indebted to A. Charles Catania for his thorough reading of and valuable response to an earlier draft of the manuscript, as well as to Ernest A. Vargas for his perspective reaction to an earlier version of Chapter 9. The volume has also been improved by the gracious and expert contributions of Grant Ritter, William M. Hartman, and William B. Noffsinger to the discussion in Chapter 17 and the Appendices. Frances Haemmerlie also provided an important source of advice and encouragement for the first draft efforts. Of course, none of the above should be held in any way responsible for errors of either content of exposition that may remain.

The difficult and important task of preparing the index was masterfully performed by Eleanor Criswell, whose thorough assistance was also manifest in many other areas of preparation as well. We also very much appreciate the skills and patience of Helen Booth and Jay Patel who typed the first draft of the manuscript and especially those of Susan E. Ward who prepared all of the second and third drafts and handled the many tasks required to complete an effort such as this. Ms. Ward was assisted by the diligent proofreading of Patrice Stambaugh.

Finally, we hope the nature of the content of this volume and the concinnity of its exposition certifies the duality of its intellectual creation and verbal execution. In fact, neither of us could have authored this book alone, and our interdependencies in this work have been myriad, symbiotic, and synergistic. Thus, authorship is considered fully equal and is impossible even for us to differentiate with any meaning.

James M. Johnston
H. S. Pennypacker

STRATEGIES and TACTICS of
HUMAN BEHAVIORAL RESEARCH

Those who fall in love with practice without science are like a sailor who enters a ship without a helm or a compass, and who never can be certain whither he is going.

—Leonardo da Vinci

Part I   THE NATURAL SCIENCE OF BEHAVIOR

1 Society and the Science of Behavior

*There is nothing more difficult to take in hand, more perilous to
conduct, or more uncertain in its success, than to take the lead
in the introduction of a new order of things.*
—Niccolo Machiavelli

INTRODUCTION

As the 20th century has unfolded, the importance to the human race of an
accurate understanding of its lawful role and function in the complex order of
nature has become greatly magnified. The history of civilization, from the
earliest primitive recordings to yesterday's news, may be regarded as the
record of our achievement in obtaining enlightened cooperation with the
physical universe. Because of these achievements in discovering and applying
the laws governing a wide range of natural phenomena, we have created the
conditions whereby the survival of our civilization depends on rapid
discovery and application of the laws governing our own behavior.

We need a mature science and technology of behavior. The ultimate
attractiveness of a humane technology of behavior has yet to be seriously
challenged, but the means for achieving such a technology have for some time
been a topic of vigorous debate. It is our intention in this chapter to show that
this debate is but the latest in a long series of confrontations between the

5

probing and disquieting methods of science and the constraining, reassuring, sometimes suppressing forces embodied in the surrounding culture.

THE CONTINUING CONFLICT
BETWEEN SCIENCE AND SOCIETY

History teaches us that most significant technological advances have been preceded by the development of a body of relevant scientific information.[1] History also teaches us that nearly every important discovery has prompted immediate and vigorous social opposition on the part of those lacking understanding of the scientific basis of the technological innovation. The implications of the scientific evidence were often threatening to the conventional wisdom that formed the basis of authority in the social order, causing the guardians of the social order to be particularly energetic in their denunciation of both scientist and practitioner.

Perhaps the classic illustration of this process is found in the ordeals of 16th- and 17th-century astronomers, notably Galileo, whose discoveries were at variance with the traditional view of the Earth's centrality in the heavens. The truth or falsity of Galileo's assertions had no direct implications for maintenance of the social order. The daily lives of medieval Europeans could not be touched by the observations of an astronomer except insofar as these observations contradicted the metaphysical system upon which moral and social authority was predicated. Nevertheless, Galileo was forced by the Church to recant his findings because they partially disputed its doctrines (Dampier, 1942).

The publication of Darwin's *The Origin of Species* in 1859 constituted a much more formidable threat to the sources of moral and social authority because it challenged assumptions concerning man's divine nature and origins. At the meeting of the British Association in June 1860, an admiral of the Royal Navy waved a Bible aloft, reaffirmed the inspirational and literal truth of its contents, and denounced Darwin and all his works. It is said that Samuel Wilberforce, the Bishop of Oxford, characterized Darwin's theory as "hypothesis raised most unphilosophically to the dignity of a causal" and thereupon inquired of Thomas Huxley, a close friend of Darwin's, whether the latter claimed descent from a monkey through his grandfather or grandmother. Huxley's reply was to the effect that he would prefer a monkey

---

[1]The relation between scientific discovery and technological advance is not necessarily immediate and direct. Technological growth may sometimes emerge most directly from existing technology, although it can be argued that the scientific underpinnings of such progress exert a necessary though delayed and indirect influence.

for an ancestor to Wilberforce, who, according to Huxley, "prostituted the gifts of culture and eloquence to the service of prejudice and falsehood." Even in 20th-century America, proponents of evolutionary theory have encountered similar, if occasionally less eloquent, opposition (*Scopes* v. *Board of Education, Nashville, Tennessee, 1925*).

The confrontations between the ideas of Galileo and Darwin and the exponents of moral and political authority of their times are but two examples of an endless dynamic interchange that has characterized the historic relations of science and culture. It is useful to study the records of such confrontations because they highlight a central principle: Under assault, the guardians of tradition appoint themselves to the task of attempting to recertify the assumptions underlying the doctrine from which they derive authority. Darwin's case serves as a good illustration in that *The Origin of Species* called for precise restatement of the biblical documentation supporting the traditional position regarding the nature of life. It may be regarded as axiomatic that the most vigorous opponents of a particular scientific advance are the very individuals or groups whose social influence is most immediately threatened. Consequently, those who come forth to denounce energetically a particular scientific pronouncement concomitantly identify themselves as the representatives of the established order and its supporting doctrine. This observation is especially illuminating later as we attempt to assess the contemporary opposition to the natural science of behavior.

History also reveals that the immediate impact of major scientific advances is often more propaedeutic than practical, but that practical benefits are not long in coming. Galileo and Darwin ignited their respective scientific revolutions as much by proposing major revisions of strategy in attacking the subject matter as by their actual accumulation of new factual knowledge. By proposing new strategies, they gave impetus to the large numbers of immediate successors who carried out the labor of scientific experimentation from whence arose broad factual knowledge and technological application.

Once the practical impact of a new body of evidence became unavoidably obvious, the belief system of the surrounding culture was altered to bring the doctrines underlying political and social authority into conformity with the known facts of science. The scientific revolution launched by Galileo gave rise to the philosophical and political changes of the Renaissance. A major determinant of this process of accommodation was undoubtedly the technological benefits to society that emanated from the science.

With each technological achievement, people reaped the added benefit of increased freedom from devotion to basic, life-sustaining activities, thus multiplying the opportunity for increased pursuit of knowledge through science and still greater benefits of the subsequent technology. Within the last two centuries, society's institutions have evolved in a manner which both recognizes and encourages this spiraling process. Consequently, by the mid-20th century, the natural sciences of matter (physics and chemistry) and their corresponding technologies had become an established part of the social fabric. The agents of moral and political authority were no longer disputatious of the fundamentals of these disciplines, and although broad disagreements still arise from time to time over management of the technological consequences of these sciences, these disagreements are routinely resolved by renewed application of the basic strategies of the science. For example, conventional wisdom dictates that in assessing the alternatives available for technological deployment of our capability to control the release of nuclear energy, we measure such phenomena as radioactive fallout and determine empirically the probable impact of any technological decision on various elements of the civilization.

The time lag separating major scientific advances and their cultural incorporation can be surprisingly long. For example, complete social accommodation to the implications of *The Origin of Species* has not yet been achieved, even after more than 100 years of incredible developments in the life sciences and their enormous humanitarian benefits. The achievements of modern medicine and agriculture are exciting testimony to the burgeoning of 19th- and early 20th-century physiology, botany, biochemistry, and genetics. This flourishing has not occurred without the usual accompaniment of bitter intellectual resistance to the implications of each scientific advance for the origins of traditional social authority. As was the case with the sciences of matter, acceptance of the technology of the life sciences has proceeded more rapidly than acceptance of the basic tenets of the science. There are many people whose lives have been prolonged by modern medicine, permitting them to continue disputing the underlying scientific formulations which are ultimately traceable to Darwin's *The Origin of Species*. Similarly, the vast majority of people whose standard of nutrition depends largely on the technological consequences of 20th-century genetics are unwilling to accept the evidence concerning the origins of life upon which this genetic technology depends. To do so would require as yet unacceptable revisions in doctrines which prevail in matters dealing with the management of life.

As an extension of the conceptual revolution ignited by Darwin, a science devoted to discovering the laws governing the behavior of living creatures has now become a reality. It is upon just such a science that our hope for a humane technology of human behavior depends. Nevertheless, as we would expect, the possibility of specifying and controlling the lawful determinants of behavior, particularly human behavior, has martialed vigorous and sustained opposition similar to that originally directed against the theory of evolution. In order that we may clearly understand the extra-scientific problems inherent in developing an effective technology of behavior, we must carefully examine the historical and contemporary reactions to the proposal that behavior is determined by a set of discoverable natural laws.

THE EVOLUTION OF CONCEPTIONS OF BEHAVIOR

Prescientific Conceptions of Behavior

It may be said that curiosity about the behavior of living creatures, particularly the vertebrates, is older than civilization itself. Fascination with behavior, particularly human behavior, and efforts to isolate its causes can easily be said to be the fountainhead of all great literature. From this tradition of great literature has come not only exquisite descriptions of human behavior but also a detailed reflection of the accepted conceptions of the causes of human behavior from which the moral and social authority of the time was derived. The Greek tragedians, for example, wrote of their players' inevitable misfortunes as being the will of the Olympian Gods—the same Gods whose existence and revelations provided the philosophical basis for the organization and management of Greek society. The characters of Shakespeare's plays behave in ways preordained by the existence of tragic flaws in character, a refinement of the Doctrine of Original Sin characteristic of the rowdy, anti-Papal London that was witnessing the rise of Puritanism in anticipation of the Reformation.

The theme of Freud's reaction against the moral authority of the mid-Victorian era highlights the prevailing conception of the determinants of human conduct. In positing the causes of human behavior to include the baser facts of existence that were repugnant to late 19th-century society, Freud dramatized the extent to which moral authority was derived from theological doctrines concerning the nature of man. These formulations provided explanations of behavior as well as standards of conduct; human beings, as the children of God, were expected to behave as such or suffer consequences too terrible and remote to be the possible target of experimental validation. Still a product of his culture, Freud proposed an equally remote locus for the determinants of behavior in the individual's unconscious.

Contemporary literature perpetuates this process. In the 20th century, the universality of religiously derived accounts of behavior has yielded to the multifariousness of humanism, existentialism, traditionalism, and mysticism. Common to all these explanations, however, is that they are inaccessible to the probing eye of science: the causal agents are defined as unmeasurable and therefore unapproachable by experimental analysis. As we shall see, modern social scientists maintain this tradition by the definition of their subject matter and the methodological practices which necessarily result. It is as though the development of a true natural science of behavior would end a delightful game.

Social Scientific Conceptions of Behavior

The origins of contemporary social scientific approaches to behavior are in the 19th century, particularly in the work of A. Quetelet and Francis Galton. We develop this history extensively in a later chapter when we consider behavioral measurement from a historical perspective. This period is important because it marks the beginning of attempts to measure behavior, although not for its own sake. The latter half of the 19th century witnessed the development of indirect, statistical approaches that incorporated behavioral observations in attempts to define and measure intelligence, various traits and aptitudes, and, more recently, a vast array of hypothetical cognitive and emotional inner states. The development of correlational techniques at the end of the 19th century was a consequence of the need to organize the plethora of hypothetical entities being inferred from measures of the physical attributes and the behavior of large numbers of humans. This development lent the status of quantification to the new social sciences while protecting them from the demand for experimental verification that has always been honored within the natural sciences.

The strategies and tactics of the contemporary social sciences are but elaborate variations of the statistical methods of the late 19th and early 20th centuries. Students of the history of psychology are aware of the infusion between 1900 and 1930 of extensive philosophical advice concerning appropriate methods for conducting the new scientific enterprise. The philosophers of science generally concluded that the subject matter of psychology and the other social sciences was sufficiently different from that of the natural sciences to warrant a general caveat against "aping physics." There followed an empirically fallow period of intense deliberation aimed at methodizing the new science. Consequently, E. G. Boring is said to have remarked that psychology had become a method in search of a subject matter.

Meanwhile, developments in agricultural statistics (Fisher, 1942; Snedecor, 1937) provided quantitative decision-making procedures that gave the appearance of experimental precision to the research being conducted in support of a variety of broad unifying theoretical formulations (Hilgard, 1940; Koch, 1959). Although these expansive efforts at theory construction have largely disappeared, the research methods of the era survive unscathed. Unfortunately, the class of research methods that were thought appropriate to the task of evaluating theoretical hypotheses has proven inadequate to the prior requirement of generating a data base sufficiently reliable and general to support any theoretical superstructure. Coincidentally, a data base that cannot support a theory fares no better in anchoring a technology.

Natural Science Conceptions of Behavior

The history of the natural science of behavior closely parallels that of its nearest living relative, biology. It is difficult to isolate the exact point of emergence of the idea that the causes of behavior might be discoverable through scientific experimentation, but it is clear that René Descartes (1596–1650) had this possibility in mind when, in his *Discourse on Method,* he dispensed with the ancient Greek physiologists' notions of animation by entelechies or souls and substituted a purely mechanistic account of the movement of the complex of structures that defines an organism. This led Descartes to an early formulation of the notion of reflex, although the anatomical and physiological techniques of Descartes' day did not afford him the opportunity to verify that concept experimentally. This work was not accomplished until the latter half of the 19th century, although many 18th-century naturalists had already described the essential phenomenon.

Perhaps it was Darwin who first understood that the behavior of organisms is as much the result of the operation of natural law as is their structure. In *The Origin of Species* (1859), he wrote:

> No one would ever have thought of teaching, or probably could have taught, the tumbler-pigeon to tumble, an action which, as I have witnessed, is performed by young birds, that have never seen a pigeon tumble. We may believe that some one pigeon showed a slight tendency to this strange habit, and that the long continued selection of the best individuals in successive generations made tumblers what they now are; in near Glasgow there are house tumblers, as I hear from Mr. Brent which cannot fly 18 inches high without going head over heels. It may be doubted whether anyone would have thought of training a dog to point, had not some one dog naturally shown a tendency in this line; and this is known occasionally to happen as I once saw, in a pure Terrier; the act of pointing is probably, as many have thought, only the exaggerated pause of an animal preparing to spring on its prey. When the first tendency to point was once discovered, methodological selection and the inherited effects of compulsory training in each successive generation would soon complete the work; an unconscious selection is still in progress, as each man tries to procure, without intending to improve the breed, dogs which stand and hunt best [p. 233].

Here Darwin clearly implies that the behavior of at least certain creatures results from exactly the same processes that differentiate morphological characteristics of species—variation and selection. The full implications of this observation for an experimental science of behavior were not realized until the work of B. F. Skinner in the 1930s.

The importance of method in the study of behavior is nowhere more clearly documented than in the writings of Ivan Pavlov, a physiologist whose conviction it was that through the objective study of behavior one could come to understand the physiology of the nervous system. We shall quote at length from Pavlov as we characterize the essence of a natural science of behavior, for his remarks in the following passages are even more timely today than they were in 1924. Addressing the preemption by psychology of that domain of inquiry focusing on higher nervous activity, Pavlov (1927) wrote:

> What attitude should the physiologist adopt? Perhaps he should first of all study the methods of this science of psychology, and only afterwards hope to study the physiological mechanism of the hemispheres? This involves a serious difficulty. It is logical that in its analysis of the various activities of living matter physiology should base itself on the more advanced and more exact sciences— physics and chemistry. But if we attempt an approach from this science of psychology to the problem confronting us we shall be building our superstructure on a science which has no claim to exactness as compared even with physiology. In fact it is still open to discussion whether it can be regarded as a science at all [p. 3].

After briefly reviewing the contribution of physiologists to the study of reflexes and crediting Sechenov with the possibility that such phenomena could account for higher nervous activities, Pavlov (1927) goes on to say:

> All this, however, was mere conjecture. The time was ripe for a transition to the experimental analysis of the subject—an analysis which must be objective as the analysis in any other branch of natural science. An impetus was given to this transition by the rapidly developing science of comparative physiology, which itself sprang up as a direct result of the Theory of Evolution. In dealing with the lower members of the animal kingdom physiologists were, of necessity, compelled to reject anthropomorphic preconceptions, and to direct all their effort towards the elucidation of the connections between the external stimulus and the resulting response, whether locomotor or other reaction. This led to the development of Loeb's doctrine of Animal Tropisms; to the introduction of a new objective terminology to describe animal reactions (Beer, Bethe and Uexkull); and finally, it led to the investigation by zoologists, using purely objective methods, of the behavior of the lower members of the animal kingdom in response to external stimuli—as for example in the classical researches of Jennings.
>
>   Under the influence of these new tendencies in biology, which appealed to the practical bent of the American mind, the American School of Psychologists— already interested in the comparative study of psychology—evidenced a disposition to subject the highest nervous activities of animals to experimental analysis under various specially devised conditions. We may fairly regard the treatise by Thorndike, *Animal Intelligence* (1898), as the starting point for systematic investigations of this kind. In these investigations the animal was kept in a box, and food was placed outside the box so that it was visible to the animal. In order to get the food the animal had to open a door, which was

fastened by various suitable contrivances in the different experiments. Tables and charts were made showing how quickly and in what manner the animal solved the problems set it. The whole process was understood as being the formation of an association between the visual and tactile stimuli on the one hand and the locomotor apparatus on the other. This method, with its modifications, was subsequently applied by numerous authors to the study of questions relating to the associative ability of various animals.

At about the same time as Thorndike was engaged on this work, I myself (being then quite ignorant of his researches) was also led to the objective study of the hemispheres, by the following circumstance: In the course of a detailed investigation into the activities of the digestive glands, I had to inquire into the so-called psychic secretion of some of the glands, a task which I attempted in conjunction with a collaborator. As a result of this investigation an unqualified conviction of the futility of subjective methods of inquiry was firmly stamped upon my mind. *It became clear that the only satisfactory solution of the problem lay in an experimental investigation by strictly objective methods. For this purpose I started to record all the external stimuli falling on the animal at the time its reflex reaction was manifested (in this particular case the secretion of saliva), at the same time recording all changes in the reaction of the animal* [p. 5; italics ours].

It is clear from Pavlov's writing that his objective was to develop experimental techniques permitting controlled observation of behavior so that he could make inferences concerning the activities of the cerebral hemispheres. The debt owed Pavlov by modern behavioral science is primarily a technical and methodological one. His insistence upon objective measurement and controlled experimental analysis through the careful manipulation of environmental variables paved the way for the later application of these tactics in a scientific enterprise which accepted behavior in its own right as its domain of inquiry. B. F. Skinner, whom we believe should properly be regarded as the founder of the natural science of behavior, acknowledged this debt when he wrote (1970) that it was Pavlov who showed us that if we exert control over the environment, we can expect to see order in the resulting behavior.

The natural science of behavior as an independent discipline formally began with the publication of *The Behavior of Organisms* in 1938. In this volume, Skinner described the emergence of the science as follows:

The investigation of behavior as a scientific datum in its own right came about through a reformation of psychic rather than neurological fictions. Historically, it required three interesting steps, which have often been described and may be briefly summed up in the following way. Darwin, insisting upon the continuity of mind, attributed mental faculties to some subhuman species. Lloyd Morgan, with his law of parsimony, dispensed with them in a reasonably successful attempt to account for characteristic animal behavior without them. Watson used the same technique to account for human behavior and to reestablish Darwin's desired continuity without hypothesizing mind anywhere. Thus was a science of behavior born, but under circumstances which can scarcely be said to have been auspicious. The science appeared in the form of a remodeled psychology with ill-concealed evidence of its earlier frame. It accepted an organization of data based upon ancient concepts which were not an essential part of its own structure. It inherited a language so infused with metaphor and implication that it was frequently impossible merely to talk about behavior without raising the ghosts of dead systems. Worst of all, it carried on the practice of seeking a solution for the problems of behavior elsewhere than in behavior itself. When a science of behavior had once rid itself of psychic fictions, it faced these alternatives: either it might leave their places empty and proceed to deal with its data directly, or it might make replacements. The whole weight of habit and tradition lay on the side of replacement. The altogether too obvious alternative to a mental science was a neural science, and that was the choice made by a non-mentalistic psychology. The possibility of a directly descriptive science of behavior and its peculiar advantages have received little attention [p. 4].

Skinner broke cleanly with the tradition of regarding the study of behavior as a proper subspecialty of physiology or neurology in the following passage (1938) by asserting that an independent science of behavior is prerequisite to an exact science of neurology:

I have already stated my belief that an account which is not a mere translation of behavioral data into hypothetical neural terms must be the fruit of independent neurological techniques, which it is not within the province of a science of behavior to develop. Leaving the material in this form will illustrate the relation between a science of behavior and neurology which should prove most fruitful. In the case of most of the items listed, a number of quantitative properties have been fairly well established. It is this quantification, together with a rigorous formulation, which places a science of behavior in a quite different position from casual observation and analysis.

A quantitative science of behavior may be regarded as a sort of thermo-dynamics of the nervous system. It provides descriptions of the activity of the nervous system of the greatest possible generality. Neurology cannot prove these laws wrong if they are valid at the level of behavior. Not only are laws of behavior independent of neurological support, they actually impose certain limiting conditions upon any science which undertakes to study the internal economy of the organism. The contribution that a science of behavior makes to neurology is a rigorous and quantitative statement of the program before it [p. 431].

Thus, we have in *The Behavior of Organisms* the beginnings of an independent natural science of behavior. Skinner sets forth the scope and program of the science by calling for an objective study of behavior for its own sake, rather than for what it might imply about other phenomena or processes, whether demonstrable or hypothetical.

STRATEGIES OF THE SCIENCE OF BEHAVIOR

What are the distinguishing characteristics of this science that lead us to attach such great importance to its origins and to insist upon its generic separation from psychology and the other social sciences? The answers to these questions constitute the remainder of this volume. However, before discussing the strategies and tactics of the natural science of human behavior in detail, let us preview the general strategies of the science of behavior which establish it as a natural science.

Emphasis Upon Objective Description

The science of behavior seeks to establish lawful relations between the behavior of living organisms and a variety of variables that may be shown to determine it. The objective description of behavior in terms that are readily understood and free of surplus meaning is essential to this activity. The behavioral scientist is concerned with what an organism can actually be observed doing, not with the existence of hypothetical agencies inside the organism that might be thought to cause or give purpose to what the organism is doing. This demand for objective descriptions of behavior as the subject matter of the science is reminiscent of Descartes' early insistence upon objective description of the activities of the muscles and glands without reference to purported control by spirits or souls.

Absolute Unit-Based Measurement

A major characteristic of all the natural sciences, including the science of behavior, is the emphasis placed on quantification of results of observation. Using standard and absolute units of measurement whose meanings are established prior to and apart from the actual measurement operation is central to other methodological tactics, and we shall amplify their role in succeeding chapters. Their importance to the science of behavior can be immediately appreciated if we contemplate the problems of developing a physical science without standard units of mass, distance, and time. As we shall see, the emphasis upon this kind of measurement serves to distinguish vividly the science of behavior from the social sciences in that the latter rely almost exclusively on measurement procedures that lack standard and absolute units.

Experimental Analysis

The major strategy of the science of behavior involves attempting to discover relations between behavior and its determining variables by carefully manipulating and controlling those variables and observing the resulting effects upon behavior. Although specially-equipped laboratories are sometimes used for this purpose, a burgeoning field of applied research demonstrates that they are not an invariant requirement. It is necessary, however, to demonstrate control over relevant determining variables so that observed changes in behavior can be shown to be the result of the operation of those variables. In order to ensure reliability of the demonstrated effects, it is common to make long series of repeated observations of the behavior of one or a small number of organisms. The concern is not with the generality of a particular observation across a large population of organisms but with the reliability and generality of a demonstrated relation between behavior and a determining variable. Failure to demonstrate this relation signals a lack of adequate experimental control, as does failure to replicate the demonstration with other organisms. The highest priority is accorded to establishing the generality of demonstrated behavior–environment relations, rather than with describing the acknowledged variability among organisms. By attaching premature importance to the issue of representativeness or generality, the opposing tradition has perfected a set of methods that preclude detection of determining relations applicable to the individual organism, leaving nothing to assess the generality of.

Statement of Functional Relations

The ultimate product of a natural scientific investigation of the relation between behavior and its determining variables is a statement of the general form: $B = F(X_1, X_2, \ldots)$. Such statements are known as functional relations and state that a certain behavior (or behavior change) is a function of (is determined by) the operation of specific variables X_1, X_2, and so forth. After establishing such statements for the individual under known circumstances, the task of the scientist is to demonstrate the reliability and generality of such statements across individuals and circumstances. This activity often involves specifying the exact conditions under which the functional relation may be expected to apply and those under which its form may be changed. It should be clear that in this activity the behavioral scientist rarely resorts to using statistical hypothesis testing, which, after all, merely permits an actuarial statement about the likihood of a difference or relation existing among groups. The task of the natural scientist is far more exacting—specifying, isolating, and controlling the sources of behavior variability that characterize the interaction of every organism with its environment. To the extent that investigators are successful in this endeavor, extrapolating to groups of organisms becomes an empirical rather than actuarial process.

This brief characterization of the prevailing strategies of the natural science of behavior should be helpful as we discuss in detail converting these strategies into effective tactics for conducting scientific research on the behavior of humans in a variety of settings. These strategies are essential if the science is to have any hope of providing effective technologies. The lay public is painfully aware of the failure of the actuarial strategy to provide a useful technology for dealing with the myriad social problems constituted by the behavior of individuals. It is as yet unaware that the fundamental cause of this failure lies not in the intentions of the social scientists, but in the inappropriateness of their assumptions and, consequently, their tactics.

CONTEMPORARY REACTIONS TO A SCIENCE OF BEHAVIOR

To understand the contemporary reaction to the prospect of a natural science of behavior, it will help to highlight the reaction of the intellectual community to the continuing contributions of B. F. Skinner. Had Skinner not been at Harvard (a center of activity in the philosophy of science) or had he not been in a Psychology Department (his proposals would appear to have been less heretical in a Department of Zoology or Biology), perhaps the initial reaction that his work prompted would have been less intense. However, coming as it did from one of the leading Departments of Psychology in the world, it drew immediate and sustained criticism from the whole spectrum of the social sciences.

At first, sincere efforts were made to incorporate Skinner's work into the prevailing panoply of theoretical undertakings (Boring, 1950; Hilgard, 1940). Skinner not only resisted this distortion of his ideas, he publicly doubted the scientific utility of the entire movement (Skinner, 1950). Koch (1959), in heroically attempting to organize and categorize all psychological activity using criteria imposed by considerations of systematic philosophy, solicited from Skinner a contribution in a manner that would have required the work to conform to a logico-deductive structure. Skinner complied by submitting a charming, off-hand, autobiographical account of his early work that left no doubt concerning the importance he attached to the prescriptions of philosophers of science.

By this time, Skinner had ventured far beyond the confines of animal experimentation. Encouraged by the demonstration that human behavior was no less amenable to investigation by the tactics of natural science than was the behavior of other species (Lindsley, 1956; Lindsley & Lindsley, 1951), Skinner published extensively on matters of cultural and technological significance (e.g., 1953a, 1968, 1973, 1974), even including a major work on the distinctly human phenomenon of verbal behavior (1957).

These and similar efforts from a growing discipline were vigorously attacked by a broad range of social scientists and humanists, and such attacks continue to be centered primarily on two issues—method and philosophy. The methodological differences between a natural science and established practice in the social sciences have already been touched upon. In essence, the decision to study behavior as a phenomenon in its own right is still not accepted by those who insist that behavior is important primarily as an indicator of otherwise inaccessible and often hypothetical processes. However, each demonstration of a functional relation between behavior and an experimentally controlled set of variables makes the inaccessible processes less crucial in explaining behavior. An effective natural science of behavior therefore renders irrelevant the largely hypothetical subject matter of the social sciences. When the inaccessible, hypothetical processes are shown through direct experimental analysis to be merely reifications of variability largely attributable to lack of control and measurement error, the attacks understandably intensify.

Empirically defining the subject matter of the social sciences raises philosophical issues germane to maintaining the social order. Many regard demonstrating functional relations between behavior and the environment as an attempt to promote the philosophical position of determinism regarding the causes of human behavior. Adopting the principle of determinism would, of course, call into question certain assumptions upon which our social institutions are based, primarily the belief that human action results from the exercise of free will, voluntary cognition, or divine instruction.

It is important to understand clearly that the principle of determinism is a metaphysical formulation that has no direct bearing on the conduct of science. The behavioral scientist may assume that all behavior is completely determined, but this is a matter of convenience not ultimately amenable to scientific verification. Furthermore, the issue was not originally raised by the behavioral scientists but by those who saw in the new methods and subject matter a threat to established, but largely undifferentiated, doctrinal origins of moral and political authority. One of civilization's most cherished misconceptions is that human behavior is somehow immune from inclusion in the body of phenomena governed by natural law.

Critical discourse on the methodological and philosophical implications of a science of behavior is only the most recent manifestation of the historically inevitable reaction of a surrounding culture to an important scientific advance. In the previous analysis of the nature and origins of resistance to the discoveries of Galileo and Darwin, we pointed out that the most fervent critics were those entrusted with preserving the intellectual traditions upon which the social order was founded. We suggest that this principle holds today in the case of the critics of the natural science of behavior. The most conspicuous opponents of the science of behavior are the social scientists; their opposition illuminates their function as custodians of the traditional knowledge base with which the society attempts to manage itself.

The experts who advise governments on matters of policy regarding the management of human behavior are drawn from the ranks of political scientists, economists, historians, clerics, sociologists, educators, and psychologists. Moreover, the physicists, chemists, biologists, and physicians who advise on matters of policy pertaining to behavior do so with reference to a body of assumptions and beliefs that are epistemologically divorced from their areas of scientific competence.

Unlike the governmental advisers of the 19th century who were inclined to draw their wisdom directly from the Scriptures, today's authorities anchor their recommendations in a data base which constitutes the subject matter of the social sciences. As we shall see, the methodological dissimilarities between the social and natural sciences suffice to explain the absence of technological remediation of major social problems, notwithstanding the impetus of massive governmental vouchsafement.

The history of science consistently and clearly shows that ultimately the need to know exceeds the need to believe. Furthermore, once having gained knowledge through discovery, people quickly apply it to their own benefit. It is unlikely that knowledge of human behavior will prove the single exception to this supraordinate conclusion of history. We have argued that sweepingly disruptive scientific proposals gain social acceptance only after abundant benefits of the resulting technology. Moreover, such acceptance is often gradual, lagging well behind the dissemination of the technology. We may anticipate that this process will hold in the case of the natural science of behavior. Our task, then, is to hasten the development of a scientific understanding of human behavior and the resulting evolution of a beneficent technology.

2 The Discovery of Knowledge[1]

There are and can be only two ways of searching into and discovering truth. The one flies from the senses and particulars to the most general axioms ... this way is now in fashion. The other derives axioms from the senses and particulars rising by a gradual and unbroken ascent, so that it arrives at the most general axioms of all. This is the true way, but as yet untried.
—Francis Bacon

INTRODUCTION

The condition and practices of any culture at any time reflect a blend of *invented* and *discovered* knowledge. Every member of every culture discovers certain common facts about the physical workings of the surrounding

---

[1]See Chapter 9 of *About Behaviorism* by B. F. Skinner (1974) for an interesting discussion of knowing and knowledge.

environment: fire hurts, things unsupported fall, certain things are good to eat and others are not, etc., but beyond these commonly shared experiences, vast differences among cultures result from the range of experiences available and the shared understanding of the explanations of the phenomena associated with these experiences. Members of advanced Western cultures, for example, now have a very different conception of the nature and composition of the moon than was the case 200 years ago or than is presently the case among the tribes of the Amazon. Because of our technologies of space exploration and communications, we experience the moon in a manner not shared by inhabitants of the Amazon basin. Nonetheless, the moon exists for them too, and in the absence of discovered knowledge, they freely invent knowledge to explain its presence and function in their affairs.

The first chapter suggested that, in the absence of fact, cultures invariably invent knowledge as a basis for formulating rules or codes by which to manage themselves. Cultures may be readily distinguished both historically and contemporaneously with respect to the range and content of the body of invented knowledge which each has incorporated. Of greater importance to cultural survival is the mechanism by which newly discovered knowledge is articulated and allowed to influence the body of invented knowledge. Cultures that discourage the variation in invented knowledge inspired by discovery frequently embody prohibitions or sanctions against the very process of discovery. Historically, this practice can be seen to lead to a lethal ossification that makes the culture unable to withstand competition or conquest. Consequently, it may be argued that from the standpoint of cultural vitality, it is necessary to arrange for the discovery of new knowledge and to provide a mechanism for infusion of such knowledge into the accumulated wisdom of the culture. This chapter is concerned with how discovery of new knowledge, particularly about human behavior, takes place. It begins by briefly discussing empiricism and its role in the rise of science and continues by considering the logical strategies available for organizing and verifying sets of empirically derived statements of fact in an effort to gain explanation and understanding.

EMPIRICISM, OBSERVATION, AND EXPERIMENTATION

The term *empiricism* refers to the doctrine that knowledge can be gained from experience. It is a philosophical position whose full tradition need not be examined here except to point out that it has developed along with science and may be said to be the earliest systematic "philosophy of science." The major premise of empiricism is that knowledge relating to matters of metaphysics, epistemology, and ethics—problems that every philosophical position must address—can be adduced empirically and need not be sought in logical deduction from sets of primitives, traditions of religious revelation, or mystical insight. Crucial to accumulating knowledge empirically are the dual processes of observation and experimentation.

Observation

The point of departure of any empirical inquiry is observation. The process of discovering knowledge begins with the accumulation of data through the human senses, as unconstrained as possible by the operation of other components of the epistomological apparatus. Although this statement may appear obvious, the historical struggle for the primacy of sense data is far from trivial, and the issue has not yet been totally resolved, especially from the standpoint of modern philosophers. Every student is familiar with the emphasis placed on observation as an alternative to the scholastic deliberation that highlighted the passing of the Middle Ages. The suggestion that a solution to the question of how many teeth a horse possesses might be more easily obtained by looking in a horse's mouth than by consulting panels of learned clergy expresses a central tenet of the empiricist attitude. The student is probably less familiar with the fact that even today this attitude enjoys a somewhat fragile acceptance among intellectuals and scientists, although our culture is widely described as fundamentally pragmatic. Certain questions about human behavior are still assumed to be unanswerable due to observational limitations that are assumed *a priori*; if asked about the role of private events in the determination of public behavior (see Chapter 9), many otherwise objective behavioral scientists would reply that private events cannot be studied because they cannot be observed. Should the questioner persist by asking if the knowledge that private events cannot be observed was itself the result of observation, the answer is again likely to be negative on the prior grounds that such observation is known to be impossible and therefore not worthy of attempt. It is interesting to recall that Galileo once invited a professor of philosophy at Padua to view for himself the satellites of Jupiter through Galileo's newly invented telescope; the professor vehemently declined on the grounds that divine law precluded the existence of such phenomena.

Experimentation

The fruits of observation are immeasurably multiplied by experimentation. In the most basic scientific sense, an experiment is a series of acts that culminate in a set of special observations that would not otherwise have been possible. Through the device of an experiment, a scientist arranges the opportunity to make observations under conditions that would not normally occur, conditions deliberately created to allow for the observation. Almost without exception, experimentation is a way of purifying or simplifying the conditions under which observation takes place so that the phenomenon can be more clearly observed. In this sense, the essence of experimentation lies in the process of control, manifested either by the elimination or management of extraneous complexities that make observation difficult in the natural state or by deliberate controlled production of the phenomenon so that observation can proceed at the convenience of the scientist. Thus, the geneticist routinely controls the reproduction of members of the subject population in order to obtain the crosses wanted without having to search them out from among the products of random breeding.

Observation and experimentation combine to permit testing of suspected relations in nature. We often speak of "subjecting that to empirical test," and we mean letting nature (as revealed in the results of controlled observation) be the arbiter of the truth or falsity of the proposal. As Leonardo da Vinci put it around 1510: "And this is the true rule by which those who analyse the effects of nature must proceed; and although nature begins with the cause and ends with the experience, we must follow the opposite course, namely . . . , begin with the experience and by means of it investigate the cause [quoted by W. T. Jones, 1952]."

Scientists quickly learn to state their conjectures in empirically testable form; any proposal that is testable, no matter how absurd it may initially seem, can be evaluated experimentally and the issue decided. This principle is as true of behavioral phenomena as of any other natural phenomena, although many of the traditionally purported causes of behavior are deficient in that they are patently untestable. Nevertheless, they remain the subject of protracted debate and speculation, which is somehow misconstrued as legitimate scientific activity. Early on, a student of the science of behavior must acquire the attitude that the answers to questions will be found in behavioral data, not necessarily in the conjectures of intellectual elders. The requisite skill lies in formulating questions in empirically testable form, a topic that is explored in more detail later in this chapter.

Analysis.   Broadly considered, progress toward understanding complex natural phenomena through experimentation uses the experimental process for purposes of either *analysis* or *synthesis.* Identifying the component parts or relations that comprise a complex whole is the goal of experimental analysis. In conducting an experimental analysis of a complex behavior such as reading, for example, an elemental class such as recognizing words might be selected for initial investigation. The range of variables influencing the frequency and accuracy of that behavior would be explored and would probably include type style, type size, spacing, rate of flash card presentation, word length, familiarity, and so on. Further analysis might concentrate on recognizing syllables, blends, or even letters, and the influence of the same general sorts of variables would be examined. Once the set of determining relations are established for one behavioral subclass, another subclass would be selected and the process begun again. In the course of a series of such investigations, it will become obvious which elements are necessary and constitutive of the whole and which are irrelevant. For example, reported interest in the material being read may or may not contribute to some measurable property of the final performance; the question is empirically testable.

Synthesis.   Attempts at synthesis frequently follow analysis as a check on accuracy and completeness. As Teitelbaum (1977) points out, the acid test of one's understanding of the operation of the constituent parts of a complex event is the ability to synthesize the event *de novo* or, better yet, to create deliberately an entirely new event by recombining and adding new elements. He terms this direct synthesis and distinguishes it from a number of other types, all of which share the function of assessing a program of experimental analysis. Let us examine a simple illustration of the complementary processes of analysis and synthesis. Experimental analysis of the behavior of humans in highly controlled laboratory conditions has produced extensive information on the range of movement capabilities and the functional limitations of the human body. Included in these data are precise statements of the parameters of potential controlling variables (lights, sounds, vibrations, etc). This accumulation of the products of analysis serves as the basis for the design of such novel environments and equipment as space vehicles. Experimental synthesis is demonstrated when the first test pilot succeeds in operating the new craft, in simulator form. This event can only be observed if the original analysis was accurate, since design of the novel environment depended entirely on the results of that analysis. In other words, in this example, synthesis takes the form of arranging for a complex behavioral phenomenon to occur through controlled presentation of the known determinants of the various behavioral elements.

Levels of Experimentation.   In the service of both experimental analysis and synthesis, there are three levels of completeness or elegance that characterize the conduct and results of any experimental investigation: demonstration, correlation, and functional relation. The most basic, *demonstration,* affords an empirical statement of the "if . . . then" variety for single values of the variables in question. Demonstration often reveals the operation of a process or procedure that has not yet been fully defined and quantified, and it occupies an extremely important position in the history of science. Although it involves no series of controlled experimental manipulations and may not fully explain the phenomenon in question, one well-designed demonstration often eliminates a vast array of competing hypotheses. Perhaps no better illustration of this point exists than William Harvey's demonstration in 1628 that blood circulates. He accomplished this by inserting a mercury manometer into an artery of a horse and making pressure measurements over an extended period of time. By knowing the diameter of the artery and the fact that valves exist within the veins that prevent the blood from flowing in both directions at once, Harvey was able to conclude that the only way a sufficient volume of blood could have passed the manometer to provide the obtained data would be if it circulated continuously. This implied that the same blood traveled through both the arteries and the veins, impelling the search for the locus of exchange, later found to be the capillaries. The point is that the demonstration of circulation as the only plausible explanation for the blood volume data eliminated Galen's earlier view that the blood sloshed back and forth, and knowledge was thus correspondingly advanced.

The second level of scientific elegance, *correlation,* requires the identification and measurement of multiple values of the variables in question. From this information, statements of the form "when X_i occurs, Y_i occurs" can be made and tested for accuracy. Repeated observation and confirmation of a particular correlation allows speculation about the probable mechanism relating the two sets of observations. Until very recently, astronomy proceeded almost entirely in this mode, with theoretical advances determined by gathering new correlations contradicting the provisions of previous theory. However, Galileo's ordeal reminds us that regardless of the precision or persuasiveness of new correlations, old theories are not easily abandoned, especially if they embody tenets of social or political significance. The utility of the correlational method is directly proportional to the precision and sensitivity of the measurement involved because that form of experimentation consists solely of measurement. It is obviously not possible to control the movements of the heavenly bodies and thereby perform experiments deliberately manipulating, for example, the period of the earth's rotation in order to determine the impact on the motion of the other planets. Nevertheless, the facts of astronomy are astonishingly accurate, leading to exact predictions of such phenomena as the appearance of comets, eclipses, and the like. Moreover, the improved understanding concerning the probable mechanisms by which astronomical phenomena are interrelated leads to predictions of a different sort—that a certain observation will reveal a hitherto unobserved phenomenon or event. The discovery of the planet Pluto in 1930 by C. W. Tombaugh of the Lowell Observatory was the result of just that process. A confirming observation of that magnitude lends inestimable credence to the theoretical system that demands its occurrence. As we shall see in the following chapter, the correlational strategy has enjoyed widespread use in the social sciences, but its deployment there has not had the benefit of even gross approximations of exact measurement. However, a still more elegant approach is available that involves identifying and verifying functional relations between independent and dependent variables.

The term *functional relation* is a refinement of a "co-relation" in that two classes of variables—independent and dependent—are involved. An independent variable is one that exists independently of the phenomenon to be examined; its presence in no way depends on the dependent variable. For example, in the relation between the amount of rainfall and the size of the wheat crop, rainfall amount is the independent variable, since its occurrence is independent of any property of the wheat crop. In the science of behavior, most independent variables are found in the organism's environment; common examples are lights or sounds, the temporal arrangement of stimuli, and any planned experimental treatments. A dependent variable, on the other hand, depends for its existence on the influence of the independent variable. In the rainfall example, the dependent variable is the size of the wheat crop, since wheat growth is dependent on the amount of rainfall. Behavioral dependent variables are the various measures of behavior which are discussed thoroughly in Chapter 7.

A functional relation is a quantitative statement of the dependent relation between these two types of variables, usually expressed as $y = f(x)$, where x is the independent variable or argument of the function and y is the dependent variable. The relation is ordinarily stated, "y is a function of x," which is taken to mean y is determined, produced, or in a limited sense caused by x. Demonstrating functional relations requires a specific mode of experimentation; the independent variables must be manipulated or controlled and the resulting impact on the dependent variable observed. To the extent that the obtained relation is orderly and reproducible, it may be of the functional variety, although this is not necessarily the case. In order to determine if an observed relation is truly functional, it is necessary to demonstrate the operation of the values of x in isolation and show that they are sufficient for the production of y. By sufficiency, it is meant that y occurs if x occurs—that is, if x, then y. In other words, whenever a given value of x is presented, the corresponding value of y is observed. We have already seen that sufficiency can sometimes be inferred from a correlational statement. However, correlational statements are not necessarily functional relations, since it is not always possible to show that the occurrence of y depends on the occurrence of x. It is often the case that both occur together as the result of the operation of some third variable; the correlation between the heights and weights of people is not a functional relation, since both depend jointly on a variety of independent variables such as genetic composition, nutrition, and climate.

A still more powerful relation exists if, in addition to sufficiency, necessity can also be shown. Necessity means that y occurs *only if x* occurs. A good example of a necessary and sufficient relation in science is the one existing between microorganisms and infection. Infection occurs if and only if microorganisms are present. Not only are microorganisms sufficient to produce infection, they are necessary; infection does not occur unless microorganisms are present. In the natural state, any phenomenon is likely to have a multitude of determinants, and approaching the problem of demonstrating necessity requires experiments in which other potential independent variables are either controlled at a constant level or eliminated. In evaluating the necessity and sufficiency of each, ways must be found to vary them systematically one-by-one while neutralizing all others. Even when this is accomplished, however, necessity can only be inferred. No amount of experimentation can ever *prove* that a given variable is necessary for the production of a given effect, for if the effect were to occur even once in the absence of the suspected variable, necessity is destroyed (though sufficiency may remain). Empirical proof of necessity would require observation of all possible occurrences of the phenomenon, and that is clearly impossible. The alternative is to arrive at a demonstration of necessity through logical or mathematical means, usually in the context of formal theory.

Not all phenomena can be explained in terms of single argument (one independent variable) functional relations. Some events are determined jointly by two or more independent variables and cannot occur unless all are present. In the broadest sense, behavior is such a phenomenon; both an organism and an environment are required if any behavioral event is to occur. The occurrence of either alone is not sufficient to produce a behavioral event. As attempts are made to isolate the determinants of behavior into a class of environmental independent variables, the organismic variables are initially held constant and are later permitted to vary in order to see how the function changes as a result of such variation.

The most powerful and elegant form of empirical inquiry involves applying the experimental method to elucidating functional relations. When successful, such inquiry yields the facts that constitute a form of explanation not contained in the mere statement of a correlation, no matter how precise or nearly perfect the correlation. In other words, tentative answers to the question "Why?" are afforded by functional relations, whereas such a question may not even be properly asked of a correlational finding. Further inquiry into the strategies of explanation in science now requires that we consider the formal role of logical reasoning in the grand process of discovering knowledge.

SCIENTIFIC REASONING[2]

The process of discovering and verifying knowledge scientifically is both empirical and rational. The rational component enters at virtually every stage from posing an experimental question and formulating a plan of empirical attack to interpreting and integrating large collections of experimental findings into coherent explanatory systems. Students of the science of behavior must be as adept at reasoning as they are at observation if they expect to gain any understanding of the lawful workings of the phenomena they have chosen to investigate. Formal reasoning plays a surprisingly large role in the design and conduct of experiments, and it is important to discuss this aspect of the scientific enterprise as directly and candidly as possible lest the student come to the belief, by default, that science consists of mechanically following cookbook formulae, somehow inevitably and magically producing Truth.

It is commonly agreed that there are two basic modes of relational reasoning—induction and deduction. *Induction* involves extending a relation from the particular to the general, whereas *deduction* is described as reasoning from the general to the particular. What is not commonly understood is that both have indispensible roles in scientific reasoning. Many philosophers have attempted to argue that one form should embrace all scientific activity to the exclusion of the other, thus demonstrating only their own naiveté concerning the actual methods of uncovering nature's secrets. Let us first examine the inductive strategy and its role in scientific reasoning.

Induction

The earliest formal proponent of inductive reasoning in science was probably Francis Bacon (1561–1626). Largely as a reaction to the trivia propounded by medieval scholastics relying exclusively on Aristotelian logic as a means of deducing knowledge from Divine generalities, Bacon suggested that one should begin by listing all the facts about an event that can be obtained from observation. Armed with such a list, one then begins classifying the elements of the list according to whether a particular characteristic is present or absent. Finally, the sublists are further classified according to the amount of each characteristic present, whereupon the organizing or underlying principle should finally emerge by induction. This is an important strategy, not only because it dictates that facts be organized with respect to some underlying

---

[2]Chapter 8 of *About Behaviorism* by B. F. Skinner (1974) provides a provocative background discussion of reasoning as a behavioral phenomenon.

property or aspect, but because it forces attention on the collection of facts in the first place. Unassisted induction, however, is probably impossible because it does not provide for the means by which categories were originally selected. Even if pure induction were possible, it would be horribly inefficient because all possible irrelevant categories would have to be explored and evaluated, much as some modern computers play chess. As a unitary strategy, then, induction alone is not practical, but, as noted above, science does not proceed in accordance with a single strategy of reasoning. Aspects of the inductive strategy bear close attention.

We have already alluded to the fact that the inductive strategy forces the accumulation of facts and that this activity is essential to any empirical approach to understanding. Moreover, induction stimulates a relatively thorough search for similarities among facts or phenomena that initially appear very different. The discovery of a unifying principle underlying a set of diverse observations is always a major event in science, for it has the effect of systematizing large amounts of information. Showing that any two events are different (given that one indulges in sufficiently sensitive observation) is relatively easy, but identifying the dimension along which they are similar and illustrative of a common, lawful process is quite another matter. Achievements of that order require demonstrating orderly, repeatable, usually functional relations and a powerful induction, such as Darwin's proposal that the unifying principles of diversity and selection account for the observed morphological disparities among species.

Deduction

Deductive reasoning becomes particularly important when the discipline has matured sufficiently that its basic facts are reliable and formal systematization can begin. Its most rigorous manifestation is the so-called hypothetico–deductive method in which reasoning is from a set of general postulates or axioms to a series of specific theorems that can then be verified by experiment. Each verification not only confirms the empirical relation suggested by the theorem, but substantiates the validity of the postulate set as well. The rules by which relations are deduced from the postulates or established theorems are quite formal (often mathematical) and generate relatively explicit predictions. To the extent that experimental outcomes verify the predictions, confidence in the validity of the postulate set is augmented. If the experimental results fail to support the prediction, and the prediction is a logically valid consequence of the postulates, then one or more of the postulates have been falsified. The logical form of the argument, known as *modus tollens,* is straightforward: If A is true (hypothesis), B is true (deduction). B is not true (experimental disconfirmation). Therefore, A is false. The appropriate strategy under these circumstances is to revise the postulate set until the obtained results could have been predicted, and then to confirm the new prediction by experimental replication. In this manner, the entire enterprise is said to be self-correcting, and, in principle, one could start with virtually any postulate set and eventually refine it until it constituted a parsimonious and valid explanation of the phenomena under study.[3]

One of the problems with a deductive mode of inquiry is that it often leads to a more restricted form of empirical question than when inquiry is approached inductively. The working hypotheses of experiments designed to confirm predictions take the general form, "When x occurs, y will occur." Quite often y fails to occur, and little note is taken of what occurred instead. In contrast, the question form, "What is the relation between x and y?" more often typifies the inductive style, and a well-conducted experimental assault on such a question will yield information of value, regardless of the outcome. In other words, the deductive mode tends to encourage an advocacy style of inquiry wherein experimental results are marshalled in support of propositional statements, whereas the inductive strategy promotes attention to any properly obtained data.

The history of efforts to apply the hypothetico–deductive approach in psychology in the 20th century illustrates a further problem with it. In the 17th century, Newton used the method to arrive at the basic laws of motion in physics, but it is now clear that his success was largely the result of highly precise measurement and a clear correspondence between the formal elements in the theoretical structure and the empirical elements involved in tests or verifications. These conditions had not been met in behavioral science when the first major effort to deploy the hypothetico–deductive method was launched by Clark Hull (1940, 1943). The weakness due to the lack of correspondence between theoretical and empirical elements was immediately apparent (Koch, 1954) and was never overcome. Successful application of the hypothetico–deductive method places a heavy burden on the coordinating definitions which relate abstract concepts in the formal system to experimental operations in the laboratory. To the extent that these definitions are vague or ambiguous, no set of data will constitute an unequivocal test of the formal hypothesis under examination, no matter how rigorous the deductive process. An important lesson emerges from the shortfall of Hull's magnificent enterprise: The rigor and exhaustiveness of a scientific system cannot exceed the degree to which those qualities are present in the data base and, even by 1950, the data base of the science of behavior was woefully inexact and incomplete. Hull will perhaps be best remembered for having inadvertently brought this to light (Spence, 1962).

---

[3]An extensive but readable discussion of these points can be found in Wesley C. Salmon's brief volume, *The Foundation of Scientific Inference* (1966).

Deductive reasoning in science appears in other, less majestic forms than the various major hypothetico–deductive systems. The practice of creating models that emulate the properties and relations suspected in certain natural phenomena and then verifying those relations by experiment is also essentially one of deductive reasoning. The excitement created by the search for the correct model in those disciplines where model building is the dominant form of theorizing is nicely captured in *The Double Helix,* written by James Watson (1968), who, with Francis Crick, won a Nobel Prize in 1962 for discovering the strucure of the DNA molecule. Here again, the utility of the deductive approach is apparently dependent on precisely defining and observing the natural events represented in the model. Most of the efforts at model building in the social sciences, even those relying on highly sophisticated mathematical structures, fail in this regard and therefore lack much in the way of either descriptive or predictive utility. The formal aspects of such systems are not at fault; it is only that the correspondence to reality of defined hypothetical entities is imprecise or unknown, leaving deductions practically untestable.

Fusion of Induction and Deduction

It has already been stated that inductive and deductive reasoning in science are not separable in the sense that one is practiced to the exclusion of the other. The existence of the most formal and elaborate deductive system confirmed by an abundance of empirically verified deductions leaves open the question, "Where did the original postulates or hypotheses come from?" In all instances involving an empirical subject matter, the answer is most probably, "From induction." The source of most original hypotheses or formulations is primarily inductive reasoning; scientists draw on experience with the facts at hand while speculating on the possible nature of other orderly relations. Although the nature of this process is not well understood, most writers on scientific method acknowledge the importance of inductive reasoning in the etiology of hypotheses, theories, and even experimental questions.

A more fundamental, though less widely understood, merging of deductive and inductive reasoning lies at the heart of virtually every experimental inquiry that attempts verification of a relation or prediction. In its simplest form, the dual reasoning is as follows: If the hypothesis (*A*) is true, then a certain result (*B*) will be observed (deduction). Upon investigation, *B* is indeed observed. It is therefore concluded that *A* is true (induction). From the standpoint of formal deductive logic, such reasoning is clearly faulty—so faulty, in fact, that it is referred to by logicians as the *Fallacy of Affirming the Consequent.* From the standpoint of inductive reasoning, however, no fallacy exists, since the (probable) truth of the antecedent, *A,* can be established *only* by observation of the consequent, *B*. In other words, the point of correspondence between any hypothesis (however informal) and empirical test is always inductive in nature. This point is so crucial to a proper understanding of the process by which knowledge is discovered that it merits full development. A simple example serves as a basis for discussion:

1. If the temperature goes below 0°C tonight (*A*), the car will not start tomorrow (*B*).
2. The car does not start the next day (*B* is affirmed).
3. Therefore, the temperature went below 0° (the hypothesis or antecedent is supported).

From the singular fact that the car did not start, the explanation is induced. Notice that the truth of the initial premise is not at issue; there may be extensive data in support of the statement that the car does not start after the temperature has fallen below 0°. In other words, for the car not to start, it is *sufficient* that the temperature falls below 0°C. The logical problem stems from the lack of *necessity* in the initial premise; nowhere does it say that the car will fail to start *only if* the temperature goes below 0°C (e.g., the starter may be defective). To the extent that we are willing to conclude the truth of *A*, we do so inductively. There are clearly other possible explanations for the failure of the car to start, and to the extent that any of these are the case, *A* may or may not be true. Before concluding that the temperature went below 0°C on the basis of the car's failure to start, we would probably seek to affirm other consequents of that antecedent. For example, if it went below 0°C, there should be some frost remaining on the ground or there should be ice in the birdbath. Failure to affirm any of these consequents materially weakens our confidence in *A* because the sufficiency of the original antecedent–consequent statement is presumably beyond dispute. In other words, if it goes below 0°C, water will freeze and the discovery of water in liquid form creates a *prima facie* case that it did not go below 0°C. On the other hand, we can discover frozen water without proving that it went below 0°C, since the water could have been frozen by artificial means and placed where it would be found, however unlikely that may seem.

Affirming the consequent is the predominant form of reasoning in science; Chapter 14 discusses fully the manner in which experimental design supports its practice. In general, the experimental method involves creating the antecedent condition in the form of an independent variable manipulation and then looking for the consequent effect on the phenomenon of interest. If that effect is observed, sufficiency of the relation has been demonstrated. That is, a particular value of *y* is observed when some specific value of *x* is present, and the statement "If *x*, then *y*" is allowed for that instance. Concern then centers on demonstrating the reliability of the relation by repeatedly arranging for *x* to occur and observing that *y* also occurs. Accomplishing this establishes the sufficiency of the relation, but does not address the question of necessity. To be able to assert "y if and only if x," requires demonstrating that no other condition except x is capable of producing y. There is simply no way to accomplish this deductively or by demonstration, since not all possible x's can be empirically tested and eliminated. The proper approach involves arranging for the occurrence of as many plausible alternative x's as possible and showing that none is correlated with the particular y of interest. Confidence in the necessity of x is adduced by eliminating alternatives and by affirming additional consequents. In this process, each confirming experimental outcome is logically weak in isolation, but adds incrementally to certainty of the necessity of the x,y relation. On the other hand, a single negative instance, providing it is reliable, is all but fatal. This is eloquently expressed in a quote from Polya (1954) by Sidman (1960): "If the consequence is clearly refuted, the law cannot be true. If the consequence is clearly verified, there is some indication that the law may be true. Nature may answer Yes or No, but it whispers one answer and thunders the other, its Yes is provisional, its No is definitive [p. 137]."

The process of testing theories by experiment clearly relies on affirmation of the consequent. The reasoning takes the following form: If the theory is correct, a certain relation will be confirmed by experiment. The experiment is performed and yields the expected results. Therefore, the theory is confirmed. Clearly, the experimental result in no way depends on the correctness of the theory, but woven into the fabric of a large number of confirming results, it supports the inductive inference that the theory is correct. Here again, the utility of this reasoning depends on the clarity of the correspondence between the theoretical variables and their empirical counterparts. In order for this strategy of theory construction to be successful, definitional and methodological issues must have long since been settled. The prematurity of the hypothetico–deductive method in behavioral psychology is revealed by the fact that empirical disconfirmations served mainly to spawn methodological arguments, and little or no substantive revision of theory was occasioned by clear experimental contradiction. Because these weaknesses still abound in human behavioral research, a major concern of this volume is with the definition and measurement of behavior in a manner that should help remove empirical ambiguity from at least that aspect of the process, allowing for the possibility of definitive experimental examination of any proposed relations. The process of clearly defining the dependent variable originates in yet an earlier stage of scientific inquiry—formulating the empirical question. Nature will not impart a clear answer to an ambiguous question; thus, a properly framed question is the seminal determinant of all that follows in experimental inquiry.

FORMULATION OF THE EXPERIMENTAL QUESTION

Many writers addressing the topic, "Where do experimental questions come from?" have failed to confront the obvious answer, "From the experimenter's personal and professional history." A useful taxonomy of research questions can be immediately derived from an analysis of the *functions* that the possible answers serve for different investigators. Answers to researchable questions about human behavior can serve a variety of functions. The taxonomy that follows is based only on the distinctiveness of the described functions. No dimension of generality or formal utility is implied, and none should be inferred. The ultimate value of a scientific finding is proportional to its reliability and generality, and the highest standards should always obtain with respect to these criteria. Any empirical question that is properly asked and adequately pursued will yield an informative answer, regardless of the function served by that answer for the investigator.

Curiosity

Although not usually cited, one of the best reasons for undertaking a research project is simple curiosity about behavior and its relation to determining variables. It is unfortunate that people growing up in our society are too often taught to satisfy this curiosity by addressing their elders or consulting authority. Many research training programs perpetuate this tradition by teaching students that the proper source of research questions is the mentor's (or perhaps an antagonist's) theory and that no research of real value could possibly result from their own idle musings. The paucity of technological achievement in the social sciences serves as a persistent reminder of the futility of confining research to the service of prematurely constructed theory. The reader should never lose sight of the fact that some of the greatest scientific achievements have resulted from an individual's unflagging persistence in attempting to satisfy personal curiosity. The simple question, "I wonder what will happen if . . . ?" is the springboard of experimentation, and it is tragic to observe teachers providing "answers" to such questions instead of assisting the asker in arranging an experiment.

Demonstration of a Phenomenon

Addressing an experimental question of the form, "I bet this will happen when . . . " serves another enlightening function. At the least, an experiment performed from this impetus may verify the experimenter's knowledge of a controlling relation required in the production of the phenomenon. In the event the phenomenon is novel or generally unsuspected, as was the case with Harvey's demonstration that blood circulates, a vast new area of inquiry may be tapped. Little is lost if the experiment fails, providing it was done carefully, because other valuable information may emerge, even if the suspected relation is not confirmed. Such speculations often arise when one reads the reports of other investigators or hears such discussions in a public forum. Unanticipated expansion of any body of knowledge may be greatly facilitated by research inspired in this manner.

Exploration of a New Method

New techniques of observation, measurement, or behavioral control are extremely rich sources of research ideas. As an example, using various schedules of positive reinforcement to induce fighting in laboratory pigeons suggests certain parallels for investigating similar behavior in humans. Technical advances, often in unrelated fields, can also occasion exciting speculation concerning their applicability to behavioral research. For this reason, one may see behavioral researchers thumbing through equipment and instrumentation catalogues, looking for new gadgets to deploy in novel ways in the study of behavior. For instance, advances in minaturization and solid state electronic technology are creating possibilities for direct measurement of behavior that were previously undreamed of, rendering obsolete cumbersome procedures requiring platoons of trained observers as well as many indirect methods that rely on verbal report. Valuable information will emerge from carefully exploring the utility of such techniques because a careful analysis of any set of variables (such as are automatically present in a new method or technique) necessarily extends the range of understood determinants of behavior.

Analysis of a "New" Phenomenon

Behavioral researchers may become intrigued with a certain pattern or topography of behavior and realize that no one has undertaken the task of isolating its determinants. For instance, it has long been noted that a small percentage of children exhibit unusual behavioral patterns that include various self-injurious behaviors. Not content with merely labeling such children "autistic" and professing an explanation in psychodynamic terms, Ivar Lovaas and his colleagues undertook to isolate the determinants of these behaviors as part of a program of developing techniques that would effectively alter their frequency (Lovaas & Simmons, 1969). Their work has occasioned an entirely new approach to the therapeutic management of self-abusive behavior as it occurs in a variety of institutional settings and has helped remove it from the murky realm of the bizarre and unexplainable by showing that it results from operation of the same general principles that effectively explain simpler, more "normal" behavioral phenomena.

There are at least three ways in which new phenomena come to light, but only the sensitive researcher is likely to recognize such an event. Researchers concentrating primarily on verifying a theoretical deduction are likely to dismiss the sudden change in behavior occasioned by *equipment failure* as an irritating and costly nuisance. Both Pavlov (1927) and Skinner (1956) attributed major discoveries to equipment malfunction, and just such a happenstance enabled Sidman (1960) to observe a set of conditions controlling avoidance behavior not thought possible within the framework of prevailing theory.

Second, new phenomena are sometimes found in the *literature* in terms of puzzling, unexpected, and yet orderly results. Although it takes a combination of curiosity and experience to uncover such anomalies in a published scientific report, doing so can initiate a rewarding detective story. A report of a mysterious phenomenon triggers a search for clues which will probably occasion an effort to reproduce the phenomenon in a controlled setting. Having done that, the scientific sleuth can then unravel the mystery by assembling the evidence that will indict a previously unsuspected variable.

Finally, there is the ever present source of research ideas implicit in the *social problems* confounding our efforts to create a better civilization. One need spend only a day in a public school, institution for the retarded, correctional facility, or urban ghetto to realize that our current inventory of scientific information about behavior is far from complete. Behavioral events occur in those settings that only the most naively enthusiastic individuals would attempt to explain in terms of empirically established behavioral relations. Of course, theoretical explanations of such phenomena abound, but for reasons described earlier, their predictive utility in matters relating to either change or prevention has been entirely unremarkable. Perhaps a better approach would involve making a fresh start by identifying the phenomena, arranging for precise measurement of them, and then systematically seeking to isolate their determinants.

Extension of the Generality of a Known Phenomenon

Closely related to the foregoing as a function of research undertakings is exploring the generality of certain relations established for one species and/or setting by attempting to reproduce them with other species or in other settings. Some of the applied behavioral literature is valuable to the extent that it accomplishes this objective, for it renders potentially applicable many procedures that determine animal behavior under controlled conditions. Although research of this type usually encounters vigorous *a priori* opposition, the fact remains that none of the *basic* phenomena of behavior that have been carefully delineated with animal subjects have been shown to be nonreplicable with humans. While certain fundamental phenomena may yet be discovered that are unique to humans, that is beside the point. At a time when our society expresses deepening concern with the increase in violence and aggressive behavior occurring in an atmosphere of abundance, it is curious that there have been few efforts to replicate the finding that the manner in which rewards are programmed can transform a pigeon into a fratricidal killer (Azrin, Hutchinson, & Hake, 1966).

Another domain in which research aimed at extending generality can be extraordinarily fruitful includes human behavioral investigations done under highly controlled laboratory conditions. The long experimental tradition of psychophysics has been effectively enlarged by the work of human factors analysts in industry and the military. After the generality of a phenomenon originally demonstrated and studied in the laboratory has been established in a given field setting, further generality may be obtained by extensions to other field settings. Thus, the principles of behavior management first validated in mental hospitals (Ayllon & Azrin, 1968; Ayllon & Michael, 1959) have now been verified in virtually every setting in which behavioral improvement is the focus of professional concern.

Hypothesis Testing

Finally, we come to the function of research activities that many students probably believe (on the basis of their exposure to the literature) to be the only valid one—hypothesis testing from theoretical predictions.[4] In the area of behavioral research, the term hypothesis must be heavily qualified, for there are very few formal theories remaining that dictate singular experiments whose function is to confirm a hypothesis formally deduced from the theoretical corpus. Nonetheless, more modest hypotheses are constantly being subjected to experimental tests, if only to establish greater confidence in the details of the suspected controlling relations. Whenever an experimenter arranges to affirm the consequent of a particular proposition, he or she is testing a hypothesis, although it is rare to encounter the actual use of such language.

Hypothesis testing in this relatively informal sense guides the construction of experiments without blinding the researcher to the importance of

---

[4]The term hypothesis as used here is not to be confused with the statistical null hypothesis, which is really not a serious hypothesis at all, but a logical device that might best be described as a straw man dressed in a tuxedo. We examine the role of statistical hypothesis testing in greater detail in Chapters 4, 5, 11, and 17.

unexpected results. A hypothesis here becomes only a syntactic device for framing a question of nature; it is the degree of honest, unabashed ignorance with which the scientist confronts nature that is directly related to the utility of whatever answer emerges. This is not to say that a hunch concerning the outcome is improper, for such a guess may motivate an important discovery. As Sidman (1960) put it, "A man may have a guess about Nature, and the proof or disproof of his guess may indeed mark an important contribution [p. 4]." But, if the guess and its relation to some preordinate theoretical structure overcontrol the researcher during the course of investigation, the outcome will be only as good as the original guess. Such an orientation to investigation can severely restrict the growth of a discipline, particularly in its early stages. As Skinner observed in 1938, "There are doubtless many men whose curiosity about Nature is less than their curiosity about the accuracy of their guesses, but it may be noted that science does in fact progress without the aid of this kind of explanatory prophecy [p. 44]."

All of the foregoing research functions can generate potentially fertile questions about behavior. However, formulating a research question is only an exercise in verbal behavior, while performing an experiment requires active manipulation of the physical environment. Therefore, the question must be translated into a set of experimental operations that will generate an empirical answer.

TRANSLATION OF THE QUESTION
INTO AN EXPERIMENT

After the question has been carefully conceived, it must be translated into procedures involving at least one independent variable and one dependent variable. Regardless of what the investigator thinks is being asked, nature will reply only in terms of observable changes in the phenomenon measured, and then only with the clarity provided by the measurement system. Measurement actually begins with selecting and defining a class of behavioral events that are to be observed and recorded. Whatever the phenomenon of interest, behavior in some form will be the object of experimental concern. Even those who purport to study such inaccessible processes as ego strength, memory, self-concept, attitudes, traits, and so on, are forced to deal with directly observable behavioral events, and their eventual interpretations are forever bound by the manner in which they measure such behavioral events.

Experimentation almost invariably functions to provide a comparison of the effects of two or more conditions on the phenomenon being measured. Through arrangement of the conditions under which observation occurs, the investigator may also deliberately introduce the independent variable of interest. Again, there may be a distinction between what the experimenter thinks or says is the independent variable and the actual controlling variables in the experiment. Ideally, this discrepancy is minimal because the independent variable has been defined in terms that refer to real events in the environment. In other words, the independent variable must be represented by some environmental event the physical parameters of which are known, specified, and controlled to the extent required. Such a clear description of the independent variable is essential if any factually accurate statement is to issue from the experimental effort. However, no matter how complete and unambiguous the description of the actual independent variable, there remains the question of its relation to its counterpart in the experimental question. The beauty of good behavioral research is that this correspondence is usually quite close; when a study is done on the effect of a reinforcer, for example, there is hardly any doubt as to what element of the experimental environment constitutes the reinforcer. Many of the independent variables of classical interest in the social sciences are not capable of unambiguous translation into experimental operations.[5] A question such as, "What are the effects of cognitive style on problem solving proficiency?" poses a serious challenge for anyone who would try to define and translate "cognitive style" into experimental operations that are objective, unambiguous, quantifiable, and controllable.

Failure to make this translation clear at all levels may result in a serious discrepancy between the generality of the data and the generality of the experimenter's interpretations of the data relating to the experimental question. That is, proper methodological decisions throughout the study may result in reasonably unambiguous and reliable factual outcomes, the generality of which may be quite sound. Such results may be quite valuable, regardless of the question which prompted their production. However, limitations in the proper translation of the question into methodological practices and the prepotent fascination of the experimenter with the original question may guarantee interpretative judgments that are insufficiently constrained by actual experimental operations, thus assuring restrictions on their generality. Discrepancies between generality of data and generality of interpretations will inevitably be discovered when someone tries to apply such interpretations and finds that nature is not convinced.

---

[5]A good number of these variables are not actually independent variables at all, but are in reality dependent variables disguised by their affiliation with some hypothetical construct. It is common practice to obtain a behavioral measure of some sort and classify the subject as high or low with respect to an inferred underlying trait. High and low subjects are then measured on a second task and a relational statement is offered concerning the influence of variation in the trait on performance. At best, a statement of this type is purely correlational at the empirical level, for it relates measures of behavior of one type in one time and place to different measures from another time and place. The inference that the underlying trait is a functional independent variable is wholly gratuitous.

3 Subject Matter of the Science of Behavior

Suit the action to the word, the word to the action; with this special observance, that you o'erstep not the modesty of nature.
—William Shakespeare

THE DEFINITIONAL PROBLEM

Curiosity about the behavior of living organisms predates even the earliest of civilizations. The most primitive art forms are replete with depictions of the actions of a variety of creatures, including humans, and, to the extent that early art is synonymous with early modes of communication, the centrality of behavior to the content of early language systems is evident. The importance of a more or less formal understanding of rudimentary principles of behavior to the development of a civilization becomes apparent when one considers that domestication of animals—no doubt the earliest form of behavioral technology—ranks with the discovery of fire as an antecedent of great importance to the evolution of human culture.

As with other natural phenomena, explanations of the causes of behavior were invented and probably served a valuable organizing function in the transmission of the known facts of behavior from generation to generation. As civilization grew more complex, invented explanations of behavior, especially human behavior, became one of the major forces shaping and defining the characteristics of each culture. In the philosophy, literature, and religion of every society, we confront a common denominator in the form of

41

the set of assumed causes of human behavior upon which was based the authority for social management within the culture.

The ubiquity of these invented causes of behavior has plagued all attempts to bring the machinery of science to bear on the problem of understanding behavior as a natural phenomenon. This has been particularly true with human behavior, although objective descriptions of animal behavior unencumbered by connotations of intent have only become commonplace in the last 50 years. The fundamental problem is one of definition. The inhabitants of cultures whose languages are filled with descriptors of behavior that connote cause have understandably been unable to take the first and most important step toward a science of behavior—defining the phenomenon in a manner that invites objective measurement and allows for implementing tactics that isolate and verify actual causes. To take a familiar example, we are likely to describe the behavior of an individual who is talking loudly in the absence of any audience by saying that the person is hallucinating. This description ignores the actual observable behavior of the individual (sound-generating movements of the vocal apparatus) and imparts instead a well-known set of implied explanations the origins of which may be traced to early demonology. Until recently, there has been no attempt to search for controllable causes of such vocal behavior anywhere but in the individual's "mind" or "personality" or "illness." As a result, the development of a body of scientific fact meeting criteria of verifiability and reproducibility has been thwarted more by linguistic custom than by complexity or inaccessibility of the phenomenon.

Fortunately, the definitional problems pursuant to developing a science of human behavior are not insurmountable. During the past century, the growth of the biological sciences has been both widespread and rapid. This growth has led us to ask questions about behavior with increasing frequency in terms of its implied significance for these disciplines. We shall, therefore, examine the empirical and theoretical origins of the concern for behavior among biological scientists in order to reveal those characteristics of the class of events commonly labeled "behavior" that are of scientific utility. We can then fashion an approach to defining behavior that will be consistent with established knowledge in the natural sciences. Our discussion of the general strategies and tactical nuances of the science of behavior can thereafter proceed securely on the basis that science's subject matter is a properly defined natural phenomenon.

To say that behavior is that which living organisms do is a good place to start, for it excludes from consideration common reference to the behavior of inanimate objects—for example, the behavior of steel under stress, the behavior of the stock market, and so on. It also excludes the behavior of dead organisms, which is the subject matter of the more occult disciplines. If we agree to confine ourselves to consideration of the behavior of living organisms, we are clearly operating within the general domain of biology, the science of life. It follows that a science of behavior will necessarily be included among the biological sciences, and it is to them that we look for clarification of the status of behavior as a natural phenomenon.

BEHAVIOR AS A BASIC BIOLOGICAL PROCESS

What is the biological significance of behavior? Is behavior an epiphenomenon of little interest that occurs as an inevitable consequence of physiological and biochemical processes whose full complexity we are only now beginning to appreciate? Or, is behavior an independent yet conceptually central integrator and shaper of these several processes? Perhaps behavior is the visible product of a set of nonbiological mental processes that operate coextensively but independently of the known mechanisms of living organisms. What light does modern biology throw on these questions?

Role of Behavior in Evolution

The theory of evolution remains the central theme of the biological sciences. Special emphasis in contemporary evolutionary theory centers on the invariance of the DNA molecule and its perpetuation through the processes of morphological variation and natural selection. Often overlooked by this emphasis is the biological maxim that no organism reproduces (transmits genetic material to the next generation) at the instant of its birth; a period of time elapses during which the organism either grows, achieves maturity, and then reproduces, or fails to adapt, dies, and does not reproduce. From the point of view of classical evolutionary theory, the key to a biologically successful outcome is adaptation, which ensures survival until that point in the organism's life when reproduction is a maturational possibility. The process of adaptation must itself be described, and such a description can hardly fail to include an account of the organism's behavior. It is usually true that the manner in which an organism fills this span of time—how it behaves—has something to do with its biological success or failure as defined by the contribution of its genetic material to the gene pool of its species.

From the simplest plant tropisms to the most complex social interactions among humans, the behavior of an organism is a major determinant of its survival. The manner in which it procures nourishment, avoids or escapes predators, selects an appropriate mate, and eventually reproduces are all instances of behavior, variations in which can affect the likelihood of survival. Because adaptation is the key to natural selection and is, in turn, largely dependent on behavior, we may venture the observation that natural selection is in part a behavioral process. Far from being an epiphenomenon, behavior becomes central to the evolution of species and is, therefore, a phenomenon of fundamental importance in the life sciences.

In order to survive and reproduce, an organism must behave adaptively in its environment. That this environment is orderly and lawful has been assured by the fruits of more than three centuries of scientific inquiry. We observe that a multiplicity of organisms continue to survive and reproduce and that there appears to be no differential selection in favor of species with shorter life spans. It would seem clear that the interactions between these organisms and their environments would also be lawful, for were this not the case, those organisms with long time spans between birth and reproduction would more likely fall victim to the cumulative probability of some independent, randomly occurring, fatal event, and their number would decrease. This is demonstrably not the case. The ascendancy of man, a primate whose birth–reproduction span exceeds 10 years (among the longest of the living vertebrates) strongly contradicts any argument against orderly relations between organism and environment. Therefore, the weight of the evidence, of which our own existence is a major part, suggests that the relation between organisms and their environments may be described as lawful.[1] Thus, a science of behavior that seeks to discover and explicate those laws appears not to be a futile undertaking. In fact, over the past quarter of a century, this endeavor has established a substantial body of lawful generalizations that are beyond reasonable dispute and that confirm this fundamental conclusion.

Behavioral Variation and Selection

There is a greater commonality between behavior and natural selection than is implied by the statement that the latter depends on the former. It has been clear since the writings of Wallace and Darwin that the evolution of species depends on two fundamental processes: variation and natural selection. In earlier biological thought, these processes were described as responsible for the manner in which species became extinct and new ones evolved over generations. Although the time frame of this analysis may span hundreds to millions of years, we contend that a more microscopic analysis shows that the grand process is mediated at the level of the behavior of each individual organism through mechanisms akin to variation and natural selection (Skinner, 1966).

---

[1]The emerging discipline of sociobiology has many points of assumption in common with our general position on the role of behavior in the evolutionary process. It is clear from early expositions of this subject matter (e.g., Wilson, 1975, 1978) that the contributions of a mature natural science of behavior are sorely needed if sociobiology is to advance beyond its present conjectural status.

Classical evolutionary theory held that variation characterized the individual members of a species at any given time and that, in interaction with the environment, certain variants possessed greater chances for survival. The same appears to hold for the behavior of an individual organism. Any action of any organism will exhibit variation with respect to one or more measurable properties over repeated occurrences. Even such a simple activity as eating is never repeated exactly; there will always be differences in such characteristics as the time between episodes, bites per episode, episode duration, and the amount and variety of material ingested. Variability is, therefore, as inevitable a characteristic of the behavior of an individual as it is of the morphology of the individuals constituting the species.[2] Also variable and measurable are the environmental conditions that elicit or occasion each occurrence of the action. Through the organism's interaction with the environment, certain forms of the behavior are selected and thereafter occur with greater frequency than other forms. This selection process results from the operation of contingencies of reinforcement (Skinner, 1966), much as the selection by the environment of certain members of species for differential survival was explained by the phrase "survival of the fittest." By "fittest" was apparently meant the individual whose adaptation was successful. Behaviors selected by reinforcement contingencies include those that enhance the organism's survival; indeed, Skinner has argued that natural selection occurs in part with respect to an inherited susceptibility to reinforcement by objects or events that frequently occur in the ecological niche of the species. We are struck by the compelling similarity of the processes of variation and selection operating at the microscopic level of the action forms of an individual organism and at the macroscopic level of the variations in morphology displayed by members of a species through generations over time. Similarities of this sort are not viewed as trivial or accidental by those whose aim it is to extract order and simplicity from the bewildering complex of natural phenomena.

TOWARD A DEFINITION OF BEHAVIOR

A scientifically useful definition of behavior must capture the biological function of the interfacing relation between an organism and its environment. Furthermore, the generality of variation and selection in this relation is

---

[2]This is not to imply that behavioral variability is inherent, invariant, or immutable. The fact that its existence is guaranteed only serves to stimulate the search for its causes, not to certify its permanent immutability. In fact, it is the search for the determinants of behavioral variability that generates the basic strategies of the science. See Chapter 11 for a full discussion of this point.

sufficient to encompass all species; thus, our definition must be equally broad. We would not wish to render a definition that would inadvertently circumscribe our domain of inquiry, particularly if it could be shown that such restrictions led to the accidental exclusion of human behavior. Our definition should also recognize that the relation between an organism and its environment occurs over time. The regularity of this relation through time implies repeatability, and our definition must be worded so as to emphasize its importance.

Traditional Approaches

Earlier attempts to define behavior have usually failed to meet one or more of the above criteria emanating from biological considerations. In most cases, this failure can be traced to the definer's lack of interest in behavior as a phenomenon to be studied in its own right. For example, Pavlov was primarily concerned with analyzing the function of the cerebral hemispheres. He chose as his vehicle for experimental analysis the secretory activity of the salivary glands of dogs, which he conceptualized as an instance of reflex activity. We would certainly wish such activity to be included by any definition of behavior, but not to the exclusion of a larger class of activities whose effects upon the environment are of greater adaptive significance to the organism than is a trail of saliva leading toward or away from a fresh kill. We must again emphasize that Pavlov did not explicitly set out to study behavior and therefore cannot be faulted if his implicit definition fails to do full justice to the biological implications of the term. Difficulties did arise, however, when Watson and others attempted to generalize Pavlov's findings by theoretical extension to a broader range of behavioral phenomena. The salivary response exhibits peculiarities in its controlling relations to environmental variables that make it singularly inappropriate as the representative instance of all behavioral phenomena. Had more care been taken in initially defining the subject matter, perhaps some of the embarrassments of premature generalization could have been avoided.

Naturalists and ethologists have tended to define behavior almost exclusively in terms of a combination of the environmental conditions that elicit it and some hypothetical intraorganismic entity accounting for its elicitation. We read of nesting instincts, courtship patterns, territoriality, and the like, often without reference to the topographical variation in these performances to which the environment is undoubtedly differentially sensitive. Although this custom has become less prominent, descriptive precision in the behavioral taxonomy offered by naturalists and ethologists often still gives way to eloquence of delineation in terms of purpose or intent. What the creature is doing cannot readily be disentangled from why it is purportedly doing it; for example, the salmon are swimming upstream *to* lay their eggs, and the gerbil is musk-marking its territory *to* protect it from intruders. Descriptions of behavior thus laden with implications of autonomous intentionality tend to obscure the necessary role of the environment in defining what is unavoidably a two-way process. Such definitions are reminiscent of an earlier and mistakenly held view of evolution, which proposed that birds' wings evolved in order to enable them to fly or that the purpose of the giraffe's long neck is to permit it to reach food in trees. Such accounts tend to obscure the role of differential selection as a continuous process over many generations, determined at each stage by organisms surviving and reproducing within their environments. There is no descriptive or explanatory value imparted by positing some causal condition existing remotely in the future.

The definitions of behavior implicit in the writings of most psychologists and other social scientists tend to be characterized by either or both of the deficiencies already discussed. Either they confound the definition of the observable phenomena with reference to hypothetical causal or explanatory entities or they exclude reference to the implicit dynamics of the organism–environment interaction that give rise to behavioral variability. The resulting conceptions of behavior hold it to be a static, autonomously inspired phenomenon whose relation to the environment is at most spatial and temporal contiguity, not functional in the biological sense required by adaptation. Behavior, particularly human behavior, often emerges as a kind of property or trait of the organism. The causes of any externally observed variability are conveniently ascribed to hypothetical inner agencies or characteristics, ranging from habit strength through achievement motivation to such constructs as the collective racial unconscious. Skinner (1953a) has even classified the origins of such inner causes as either neurological (e.g., nervous breakdown), psychic (e.g., achievement is the result of a positive self concept), or conceptual (e.g., habits, aptitudes, and traits). Regardless of the origins of such conceptualizations, it is clear they do not refer to behavior as an adaptive biological process dynamically determined by an environment changing through time.

An Empirically Functional Definition

A scientifically useful definition is unlikely to emerge from traditional sources. The definition must delineate a range of phenomena appropriately subsumed within the domain of biology, and it must permit full expression and evaluation of the implications of behavior's importance to the evolution of species. The closest available approximation to such a definition is found in the early writings of B. F. Skinner (1938):

By behavior, then, I mean simply the movement of an organism or of its parts in a frame of reference provided by the organism itself or by various external objects or fields. It is convenient to speak of this as this action of the organism upon the outside world, and it is often desirable to deal with an effect rather than with the movement itself as in the case of the production of sounds [p. 6].

This definition warrants close examination, for it appears to meet most of our requirements. Skinner's definition clearly implies interaction with the environment, even to the extent of providing for defining behavior solely in terms of its effect upon the environment. There is no trace of the teleology common to those earlier definitions, and neither is there reference to causal entities at any level. However, there is no explicit recognition of the continuity through time of the organism–environment interaction. This is the source of the repeatability and variability of behavior necessary not only for adaptation of the organism but for its scientific investigation as well. Let us therefore slightly amend Skinner's definition and offer the following:

The behavior of an organism is that portion of the organism's interaction with its environment that is characterized by detectable displacement in space through time of some part of the organism and that results in a measurable change in at least one aspect of the environment.

Every element of this definition can have a powerful and pervasive impact on the full range of research and technological activity that holds behavior as its domain of interest. We may now examine this definition of behavior in minute detail so as to delineate the subject matter boundaries. Not only may such a thorough examination lay to rest some historical misconceptions concerning the range of appropriate subject matter for this discipline, it may also suggest some of the parameters governing appropriate strategies for measurement, experimental control, and analysis.

We have already alluded to the fact that the phrase *behavior of an organism* circumscribes the domain of behaving things to include only living organisms. Consensual usage of the term "behavior" does not always recognize this limitation. Economists, for example, speak of the behavior of the marketplace or the behavior of the private sector as though the behaving entity were more than or different from a collection of individuals. Actually, they are referring to variability in numerical indicators that unavoidably results from extensive cumulation of the effects of the behavior of individuals. However, the dependence of economic indicators on the behavior of individuals is obscured by reification of such nonorganismic entities as the marketplace, etc. This practice unnecessarily retards recognizing that economics will ultimately be one subdiscipline of the science of human behavior. The same observation applies to political science, sociology, and anthropology, all of which must unavoidably be concerned with the individual behavior that produces phenomena of interest to those disciplines. Given an exact science of human behavior, the generalities of the social sciences will result from aggregations of lawfully determined individual behavior, much as our understanding of the function of a television set depends on application of the laws of physics and electronics governing the operation of its components. Progress in the social sciences would seem to depend on recognition of this fact at the expense of continued investigation into the "behavior" of reified supraorganismic constructs whose existence appears to arise out of convenience rather than nature.

The phrase *portion of the organism's interaction with the environment* may embody the most important concept in the entire definition. Emphasis is placed on the word "interaction" because behavior must be understood as the biological modulus of the *relation* between living tissue and the surrounding environment. Behavior is, therefore, explicitly not a unique province, property, or subattribute of the organism, a misconception easily traced to the influence of the trait psychologies of the 19th and early 20th centuries. The necessary and sufficient conditions for the occurrence of behavior are: (1) the existence of two separate entities, organism and environment; and (2) the existence of a relation between them. Behavior cannot occur in an environmental void, nor can it occur in the absence of living tissue. Furthermore, it happens only when an interactive condition exists as a result of some relational state. Independent states of the organism, whether real or hypothetical, do not constitute behavioral events, because no interactive process is denoted. Being hungry or being anxious are examples of states that are sometimes confused with the behavior they are postulated to explain. Neither of the phrases specifies an environmental agent with which the hungry or anxious organism interacts, hence no behavior is implied. Similarly, independent conditions or changes in the environment do not define behavioral occurrences because no interactive process is specified. An animal walking in the rain gets wet, but "getting wet" is not an instance of behavior. A child may receive tokens for academic performance, but "receiving" does not constitute a behavioral event. However, the academic performance is obviously a behavioral event, as is pocketing the token. What is the difference? To generate an academic performance, the child must act with respect to some portion of the environment, such as a piece of paper, such that the action will change the environment. Receiving a token indicates changes on the part of the environment but no necessary change with respect to the child. The interactive component is clearly missing, hence "receiving a token" does not qualify as a behavioral event. "Placing the token in a pocket" fits our definition, because action by the child results in the environmental change evidenced by the sudden presence of the token in the pocket.

There are many implications of the phrase *characterized by detectable displacement in space through time* that merit elaboration. "Detectable" means perceivable; if it happens, that is ultimately knowable by an observer. Detection of the happening may require instrumentation extending the sensitivity of the unaided human senses, as when we observe the activity of a heart with the aid of a stethoscope or plethysmograph. Advances in instrumentation may even be expected to permit detection of events that augment the present range of behavioral phenomena in ways that we cannot now foresee. The only requirement will be that such phenomena exhibit characteristics consistent with the provisions of this definition.

Displacement in space through time is intended to require movement, however gross or minute. This emphasis on motion is consistent with Skinner's definition and excludes all states of the organism, whether real or hypothetical. Also excluded are the dynamic effects of independent physical forces such as gravity. Falling down stairs is not a behavioral event, although the antecedent stumble would be. Both objects and organisms fall when support is withdrawn solely as a result of gravitational attraction. This is sufficient to explain fully the resulting motion; therefore, no behavioral event is present. Real states of both the organism (e.g., water imbalance) and the environment (e.g., air temperature) are, of course, legitimate independent variables in the science, not to be confused with the phenomenal subject matter.

Displacement in space through time also captures the essence of the common meaning of the term behavior and directs attention toward those characteristics most amenable to direct measurement—distance, time, and number. This element of the definition reaffirms the status of behavior as a continuous process through time, rather than as a discrete, static event or state. Time becomes a universal parameter of behavior and thus figures prominently in the development of suitable units of measurement.

The importance of behavior as a continuous interactive process has been stressed by other writers, notably Skinner (1950), because of the implications for appropriate investigative strategies. It should be clear that repeated observation and measurement across time is a necessary strategy of inquiry if the true and complete account of behavior is to be approached. Only by tracking behavioral phenomena as they change through time can we improve our understanding of the lawful influences of the environment. Shortcut methods that involve single observations on large samples of organisms cannot substitute for repeated observation of a single or a few organisms over extended periods of time. Similarly proscribed is incomplete sampling of the behavior of individual organisms. The standard of observation in the science of behavior is simple but exacting—continuous and complete. Strategies and tactics for approximating this standard in practice are the subject of Chapter 8.

The choice of the phrase *some part of the organism* is intended to emphasize the modern relaxation of the requirement of molarity imposed by some early behaviorists. "Some part" may include the whole organism, but our inquiry need not be constrained by such an obviously quantitative distinction. Taken to its logical limit, this restriction would permit only gross locomotion as the proper domain of inquiry. In fact, no limit beyond those imposed by our present measurement capabilities should be placed on the allowable size of the part of the organism being considered. Furthermore, the word "part" should not be taken in a strict anatomical sense, for it has long since been established (e.g., Lashley, 1929) that the functions of an organism bear no necessary isomorphism to the grossly discriminable components of its structure. It can be argued that 50 years of studying easily dissectable and classifiable pieces of anatomy has not appreciably advanced our understanding of behavior.

The generality of the phrase *some part of the organism* permits deliberate evasion of an old conundrum in psychology, the "appropriate level of analysis" issue. The micro–macroscopic continuum that has often been the basis for creating academic disciplines within the life sciences has not been especially useful in the science of behavior. It has given rise in psychology to subspecialities characterized by competitive theoretical postures, expansive rhetoric in support of those postures, and very few replicable empirical relations. The science of behavior seeks to establish general laws relating past or present environmental events to the behavior of organisms. Such laws are by definition not very general if they apply only to a given species, organisms of a certain age, or a particular level of analysis on the micro–macro continuum. Subdivisions along this continuum arise largely from limitations of observation by the unaided human senses and different rates of measurement innovation in various fields. Any level of scientific analysis requires accuracy and precision in measuring dependent variables and controlling independent variables. We shall see that this requirement does not change when the behavior of humans becomes the object of inquiry.

That results in a measurable change in some aspect of the environment is the most important qualifier for the conduct of a science of behavior. Because the organism cannot be separated from an environment and because behavior refers to relations between the organism and environment, it is impossible for a behavioral event not to influence the environment in some way. This being the case, the environment serves both to anchor one side of the defining relation and to provide the means whereby the relation (behavior) may be detected and measured. In other words, by definition, behavior must be detected and measured by its effects on the environment. This restriction is not as severe as it may first appear. It may be that the only detectable change in the environment is a change in some characteristic of a measuring instrument, such as occurs when the beating heart of an otherwise comatose individual registers changes on an EKG oscilloscope, or when an individual depresses a counter to register an instance of swallowing food. Only that which has been measured is admissible to the body of scientific information, and the facts of behavior are not exempt from this requirement. One way to ensure that we are dealing with behavioral events is to ensure that any defining measurement operation is performed on the environment and that all descriptive and interpretative statements are couched in terms of the organism–environment interaction.

Recognizing that the facts of behavior are statable only in terms of some organism–environment interaction will discomfort many who purport to investigate a subject matter that is only incidentally dependent on these relations for definitional accessibility. For example, the practice of attempting to investigate attitudes using behavior elicited by questionnaires is widespread. Because the behavior is assumed to be primarily determined by the underlying attribute of attitude, such procedures suffer from lack of attention to the details of both immediate and historical environmental contingencies that influence questionnaire responding. Very little effort is directed at examining the effects of changes in the immediate questionnaire environment on subsequent patterns of responding. Completely overlooked are the lawful, dynamic behavioral phenomena that may be lurking just beneath the threshold of discovery, awaiting only an investigator whose conception of the subject matter is coextensive with that which can be measured directly.

Finally, it is necessary to call attention to an additional aspect of the formal definition that has been proposed. The terms "organism" and "environment" appear as primitives, not themselves explicitly defined. Thus, behavior is defined as a portion of an interaction between two primitives. Although these terms will remain undefined in this volume, a few clarifying comments will benefit those readers who might become concerned about the ultimate boundaries of the subject matter allowed by the present definition.

The common meaning of the word "organism"—a complex form carrying on the functions of life by means of separate but interdependent organs or systems—suffices for all present purposes. The problem of distinguishing between organic and inorganic material is a fascinating one in the areas of biochemistry and biophysics which may eventually lead to equally provocative questions concerning the applicability of the laws of behavior to synthetic life forms. However, our science is not yet equipped to address this problem in any but a speculative fashion, and there is little to be gained by tailoring the definition of our subject matter in anticipation of resolving that issue. It may be that future knowledge will modify the scope implied by the present definition; the definition will have served its purpose if it leads to discovering a knowledge base sufficiently general to warrant such an extension.

The other primitive term, "environment," here refers to the conglomerate of real circumstances in which the organism or referenced part of the organism exists. The term may meaningfully include other parts or aspects of the organism distinct from that which is the object of specific inquiry. Thus, the term appropriately denotes a universe of events that differ from instance to instance. A fundamental task of the science is to determine the generality of those relations discovered to hold in specific instances. The ultimate generality of statements concerning environmental determination of behavior will be proportional to the range of environmental circumstances in which the relations can be shown to hold. Therefore, nothing is gained by arbitrarily restricting the term "environment" beyond the extent necessary to differentiate the behaving part of the organism.

In particular, the traditional practice of distinguishing the internal from the external environment on the basis of the gross boundary provided by the skin is explicitly discouraged. The function of the skin in promoting the survival of the organism is hardly coextensive with provision of a demarcation point on either side of which behavioral laws necessarily must take different forms. In fact, from the standpoint of a science of behavior, the skin represents only a barrier to the applicability of certain methods of observation, not to the generality of discoverable fundamental processes.

Our formal language traditions are replete with references to the existence of special determinants of internal behavioral phenomena. These verbal conventions have made it especially difficult to approach internal events with a strategy common to all behavioral phenomena, because differences in causation are uncritically assumed because of the excess meaning developed during our extensive linguistic histories. Nonetheless, the mark of any mature science is the degree of parsimony with which it can render a consistent account of its domain of phenomena. The standard of parsimony must be first and most vigorously applied to those primitive concepts from which a definition of the subject matter is fashioned.

SOME FURTHER IMPLICATIONS

Our definition of the subject matter of the natural science of behavior has profound implications for the resolution of all strategic methodological issues of the science. The implications of selecting different subject matter definitions is fully examined in many of the following chapters; our purpose here is only to urge the reader to be aware of the central role played by the subject matter in determining methodological strategies. As is pointed out in Chapter 4, the nature of the defined subject matter strongly influences the adoption of compatible measurement practices. These then encourage and sometimes force various decisions regarding appropriate control procedures and experimental designs, which in turn facilitate, if not demand, entire interpretative styles. Defining the subject matter of the science of behavior as a directly observable and quantifiable phenomenon intentionally limits the function of the science to describing and explaining measurable variation in specific instances of that phenomenon. The following chapters therefore describe methodological strategies and tactics encouraged by such a subject matter and argue for their proven soundness and superiority for the development of a true science.

The fact that methodological strategy derives directly from the conception of the subject matter leads to a second implication. Within some disciplines, certain methodological disagreements have been improperly allowed to escalate to the level of quasimetaphysical controversies (e.g., humanism vs. behaviorism in education). Overlooked in these disputes is the fact that different definitions of subject matter are involved, each leading to its own methodological practices. If this fact were more generally recognized, much of the heat surrounding such debates would quickly dissipate, or at least be redirected. Meanwhile, the prudent reader should be wary of unnecessary trips to an empty philosophical kitchen.

Finally, an objective and general definition of behavior does more than identify an area of natural scientific inquiry. By allowing for consistent usage of natural science strategies of investigation, it ensures that the body of information developed will satisfy the criteria of reliability and generality that are properly applied to the content of any mature discipline. Sustained application of these strategies will eventually present us with a collection of empirically valid statements about behavior that will be capable of supporting and guiding an attempt at formal theorizing.

That day is not yet at hand, although it may not be as far in the future as many think. Theorizing in the absence of a body of reliable functional relations is, as we pointed out in Chapter 2, largely a waste of time because the odds are overwhelmingly against making an accurate prior guess as to what the facts will be. Some facts of behavior are now being established, however, and modest efforts at theory development have already started (e.g., Honig & Staddon, 1977). For the time being, it is appropriate that such efforts are primarily inductive with no sweeping general conclusions occupying the position of postulates in a complete formal system. By adhering rigorously to a clear conception of the subject matter and the strategies it enables, we can be confident that when such a theory is finally attempted, there will be facts available to support it.

4. Traditions of Behavioral Measurement

Great blunders are often made, like large ropes, of a multitude of fibers.

—Victor Hugo

INTRODUCTION

Measurement is the cornerstone of all scientific activity. The history of science is coextensive with the history of measurement of natural phenomena, for, without measurement, science is indistinguishable from naturalistic philosophy. To the extent that natural phenomena yield to measurement, they become removed from the domain of philosophical discourse and emerge as the subject matter of scientific inquiry.

Scientific measurement of natural phenomena is a process involving quantification of observations with respect to a reference scale composed of and defined by units that are both absolute and standard. As we shall see, the absolute and standard character of the units of scientific measurement is of

55

the utmost importance in assessing contemporary strategies for discovering facts about human behavior.

One can readily trace the history of science solely in terms of the history of the invention and application of units of measurement. Closely related to this history is the history of mathematics, which, from the scientific standpoint, may be viewed as a system of rules for combining and manipulating the results of quantified observations. Science and mathematics have, therefore, developed in a more or less symbiotic and harmonious fashion. This chapter begins by tracing the development of measurement in science to the end of the 19th century. Our purpose is to convey to the reader the richness and continuity of the measurement tradition that has since been adapted to the needs of a natural science of behavior. This preparation also enables us to contrast these traditions with the measurement traditions common in the social sciences. As a result, we hope to leave the reader with a thorough understanding of two fundamentally different approaches to the problem of behavioral measurement and their distinct and pervasive implications for further methodological strategies.

EARLY HISTORY OF SCIENTIFIC MEASUREMENT

Measurement Prior to the 17th Century

The earliest records of scientific measurement date from around 3000 B.C. and are found in the remains of the Sumerian civilization of the Tigres–Euphrates Valley (Mason, 1953). This culture left cuneiform records indicating the development of a number system and a modest algebra, which permitted them to perform the physical calculations necessary for surveying and building. The Sumerians had apparently both developed the concept of number and applied it to the dimensional quantification of length.

From the Egyptian and Babylonian civilizations, we observe the beginnings of the measurement of time, which is coincident with the origins of the science of astronomy. The Egyptians, for example, developed the calendar and decimal number system, and around 2000 B.C., the Babylonians developed the seven day week, as well as our present system of days, hours, and seconds as units of time.

Refinements in measuring space and time were the principal contributions to measurement made by the ancient Greeks. Their major scientific contribution appears to have been in the collateral areas of astronomy and geometry. Hipparchus (ca. 130 B.C.) combined Babylonian observation procedures with Greek geometry to produce the basic system of astronomy, which, as later codified by Ptolemy, survived until the 16th century. Hipparchus also invented the practice of representing points on the Earth's surface by geometric coordinates, the foundation of Descartes' analytic geometry. Both Archimedes and Euclid are known to have used the degree as the unit for measuring angles, and Euclid's geometry remains as an elegant example of a formal mathematical system that is valid both logically and empirically.

The Middle Ages are not generally regarded as a period of great advancement in either science or mathematics. Nevertheless, further refinement in the techniques of measuring physical distance gave rise to major advances in the technology of navigation, which in turn spawned the Age of Exploration. The essential phenomena of magnetism had been discovered by the 13th century so that such voyagers as Columbus and Magellan were able to navigate with the aid of a magnetic compass.

The Medieval period is best remembered for the contributions of a handful of natural philosophers, notably Roger Bacon, Robert Grosseteste, and Nicolaus Copernicus. The latter's questioning of certain fundamental assumptions concerning the arrangement of the heavens paved the way for the explosion of scientific inquiry that began in the late 16th and early 17th centuries with Galileo. It is important to note that Bacon and Grosseteste began inquiry into the nature of light and, in the process, pioneered the earliest technology of optics (Crombie, 1961). Bacon, moreover, was among the first to speak of "laws of nature" and to suggest the possibility of describing such laws mathematically. It had previously been customary, in the wake of Aristotelian philosophy, to regard both the physical world and mathematical systems as logical ideals to be contemplated. Roger Bacon's work in optics in the 13th century was probably the first instance of an effort to employ mathematics to elucidate principals of nature induced from observation.

Measurement in the 17th Century

Advances in scientific measurement in the 17th century are clearly too numerous to catalog here, and we shall mention only a few of the major developments that bear directly on the emergence of an overall strategy of scientific measurement. In addition to the contributions of Galileo and Descartes already touched upon in Chapter 1, the 17th century witnessed the beginnings of the science of chemistry with the work of Boyle (1627–1691) and Cook (1635–1703). In 1628, William Harvey revealed his discovery of the circulation of the blood with what remains one of the classic demonstration experiments in the history of experimental science (see p. 26). Harvey's work marks the beginning of experimental biology, building on the earlier work of Hippocrates and Galen and the careful anatomical studies of Leonardo da Vinci.

Early in the 17th century, Napier (1550–1617) introduced the idea of continuous measurement of proportion and, in so doing, invented the logarithm. A number of people then developed logarithmic tables, which greatly reduce the computational labor involved in physics and astronomy. The slide rule was developed in 1622 and still consists of two logarithmic scales sliding over one another. Pascal and Leibnitz later developed the first calculating machines, which were essentially mechanical abacuses.

The 17th century also witnessed the development of instrumentation, both as an extension of the senses and as an aid to measurement. Of course, Galileo's perfection of the telescope was the critical event in the development of astronomy, but this technology for manufacturing lenses immediately spawned the microscope, which was probably invented in Holland. In any case, it was the Dutch scientist Leeuwenhoek (1632–1723) who first observed bacteria and spermatozoa with the aid of magnifying lenses.

Other basic instruments were developed or improved during this period, notably the barometer and thermometer. It was with such instruments that new types of measurement units (e.g., the Fahrenheit degree) were defined in terms of calibrated operation of standardized instruments. In other words, the 17th century marked the beginning of scientific measurement of phenomena that cannot be detected without the aid of instruments and whose units are, therefore, at least partly defined by known properties of the instrument. It should be clear that the existence of such phenomena was not a consequence of the invention of the instruments, only that the units in terms of which they were measured were sometimes reflective of characteristics of the instrument. By the 18th century, such measurement became commonplace, especially as experimentation began with electricity. Such units as the ohm, watt, volt, and ampere carry the names of the men who invented the devices with which to measure those phenomena that could be detected only by application of such instruments.

Another major occurrence of the 17th century was the development of nonfinite mathematics, notably the calculus invented independently by Newton in England (1666) and Leibnitz in Germany (1675). This development, when coupled with Descartes' earlier refinement of Hipparchus' invention of physical coordinates into analytic algebraic geometry, provided the language for theoretical description and measurement of continuous phenomena such as motion, acceleration, and various limiting processes. With this tool, Newton was able to synthesize the known facts of physics and astronomy into a theory of mechanics that survived intact until the early 20th century. Moreover, the calculus provided a mathematical system in which formal deductions could be restated in the form of scientific predictions to be verified by measurement.

An important by-product of the invention of the calculus was not realized until the 18th century, although the problems were well formulated by 17th-century mathematicians such as De Moivre, Fermat, and Pascal. The impetus provided by economists, administrators, and gamblers concerned with such uncertain matters as annuities, insurance, and the outcomes of games of chance led to the development of the calculus of probabilities and, eventually, to modern statistics. We see later that this development constitutes the origin of social science measurement, which blended the calculus of probabilities with the social philosophy prevalent in the 18th and 19th centuries.

Summary and Implications

Let us pause to summarize and elaborate on the implications of early scientific measurement that emerged between the time of the early Egyptians and the later 17th century. Three more or less distinct stages are discernible in the history of scientific measurement. The most primitive stage involved the development of number systems, conventions for enumeration (counting), and standard units of the physical dimensions of time and space. These developments were necessary as science moved from the act of mere classification of sense data to the level of quantitative description implied by measurement. In other words, precise measurement systems permitted objective classification of shared perceptions and provided the basis for meaningful discourse concerning those perceptions.

The second major feature to emerge from the history of scientific measurement is the parallel development of mathematical systems and models. Throughout the history of the natural sciences, applying the tools of mathematics was usually preceded by collecting and accumulating extraordinary amounts of factual data. The nonfinite calculus developed by Newton and Leibnitz was not developed in the abstract. Rather, the calculus and Newton's consequent Laws of Motion may be regarded as the final chapter in the story of direct physical measurement, which took over 5000 years to unfold.

There has been an unsettling tendency in the 20th century to ignore this fact. Because formal mathematics has now developed into a separate discipline and is no longer exclusively the consequence of a need to organize vast accumulations of scientific data, it has become fashionable to attempt to reverse the traditional process by first borrowing or creating a mathematical system and then initiating a search for data that it will organize. Although it is true that Newton's calculus permitted systematic formal deductions that could be translated into scientific predictions, it is not true that every mathematical system necessarily displays this degree of correspondence to the workings of the universe. The mathematical model building enterprises of today often lack the extensive naturalistic data base that gave Newton's calculus its enormous descriptive and predictive power. For example, predicting the exact time and location of a comet's appearance is not a triumph of the calculus alone, but requires a vast body of data describing the relative positions of the numerous entities in our galaxy. Elaborating the mathematical model will not, unfortunately, compensate for the absence of an objective, independently verifiable data base. The discipline of macroeconomics enjoys access to the most sophisticated mathematical models in history, yet remains unable to forecast precisely significant oscillations in the major elements of our national economy.

The third significant facet of the history of scientific measurement is the emergence of measurement through instrumentation. Although the development of instrument technology was well under way by the end of the 17th century, it fairly exploded in the late 18th and 19th centuries during the Industrial Revolution. The development of scientific instrumentation, particularly in the life sciences, has made a valuable set of measuring devices available to the behavioral scientist. The urge to advance and refine measurement devices remains properly vigorous; however, an important cautionary note must be sounded. The development of measuring instruments almost always followed the isolation and identification of the phenomenon that the instruments were designed to measure. Although new phenomena have been discovered with instruments designed for another purpose, this remains the exception rather than the rule. Nevertheless, fascination with instrumentation has often led scientists to define phenomena *solely* on the basis of the behavior of instruments. This extreme form of operationalism[1] is typified by the practice of attempting to study human cognition by computer simulation. Programming a computer to "solve problems" in ways that seem to mimic human efforts inextricably involves the computer circuitry in both the model and the process. Such metaphors of computer technology as input, output, storage, coding, retrieval, and so on, appear to have acquired the status of biological reality and have become the subject matter of a highly specialized "science." Actually, these terms have no necessary biological referents, and the "behavior" of a computer resembles that of a human in only a limited sense. Originally, it was hoped that such activity would have heuristic value in guiding research into nervous system functioning, but the supremacy of fascination with the computer, as evidenced by the distinctive emerging language, has rendered this ideal all but unattainable.

It can be argued that a similar fascination with biomedical instrumentation has occasionally misdirected the efforts of many whose announced intention it is to study behavior. Again, naive operationalism gives rise to a synthetic reification of ancient constructs that Descartes discarded in the Middle Ages for their lack of explanatory utility. For example, modern electronic technology has given us the capability of monitoring with astonishing precision the minute electrical phenomena that are attendant to all living

---

[1]Briefly, operationalism is the doctrine that scientific constructs are defined by the operations through which they are measured (Bridgeman, 1927).

tissue. Investigators therefore confidently attach electrodes to various surfaces on the human body and observe the correlation between potential or resistance changes and various events in the surrounding environment. In attempting to explain those correlations, however, some researchers invent names for the systematic and orderly fluctuations in the data, then ascribe process or explanatory status to their inventions. As an illustration, a drop in skin resistance coupled with an acceleration in cardiac and respiratory activity defines "arousal," which is also used to explain the drop in skin resistance, etc. Unfortunately, fluctuations of a solid state polygraph bestow upon the concept of "arousal" no greater scientific utility for the explanation of behavior than Hippocrates' concept of humors contributed to the science of physiology.

The implications of these historical points for the development of a natural science of behavior must be well understood. The evolution of the natural sciences of matter was largely coextensive with the development of instrumentation and language systems for measuring and describing their independently defined subject matter. The development of instrumentation within each discipline was and still is dictated primarily by the nature of the phenomena studied by that discipline, and the science of behavior must follow the same strategy.

As we see later in this chapter, the tradition established by the measurement strategies of early natural science continues uninterrupted to the present day in the fledgling natural science of behavior. During the late 18th and early 19th centuries, however, a number of intellectual developments coalesced to ignite a major departure from the tradition of natural scientific measurement. This deviation has its origins in a disadvantageous philosophical conception of the nature and the causes of variability, and it has evolved into a set of measurement strategies that constitute the animus of the modern social sciences.

THE ORIGINS OF VAGANOTIC STRATEGIES

We noted earlier that late in the 17th century, mathematicians began using the principles of Newton's calculus to formulate the theory of probability. Support for this work came in part from the wealthy patrons of the mathematician–scientists of the time. These benefactors often sought a return on their academic investment in the form of increased revenue at the gambling tables. During this same period, concern with the reliability of measurement began to emerge; the study of error appears to have its origins in 1806 in the work of Legendre, who, along with Euler and Gauss, developed the least squares method for extracting the best measure of a physical event from a set of measures that displays variability. In 1778, Laplace produced the continuous equation of the law of error, and the connection with the calculus was made. The mathematics of probability had become as formally rigorous as the mathematics of motion.

The importance of Laplace's provision of a nonfinite calculus of probability can hardly be overemphasized in the consideration of the subsequent application of this mathematical system. Nonfinite mathematics embodied the notion of *limits* from which it is but a short step to the notion of approximation of an ideal. Thus, the mathematics of probability provides a way of estimating a "true" value from quantitative assessment of the dispersion among empirically measured estimates of that value. A rather elementary theorem in probability theory holds that as the sample size upon which such estimates are based becomes larger, the error of estimate of the "true" moment of the distribution becomes smaller. The consequence of this theorem for measurement practices was profound: The possibility of discovering and even defining "true" values out of apparently uncontrollable variation rendered quantifiable a vast range of phenomena that had previously been discussed only in qualitative or metaphorical terms.

Descriptive Use of the Normal Law of Error

The use of the mathematics of probability to estimate "true" values fascinated the Belgian statistician Adolphe Quetelet (1796–1874), who is regarded by many as the founder of the social sciences.[2] While still in his 20's, Quetelet ran across the earlier efforts of Laplace and Fourier to apply statistical techniques to the description of census data. Although trained as an astronomer, Quetelet had a profound interest in human affairs and quickly grasped the possibility of using the calculus of probability to estimate the ideals of measurable human characteristics, much as calculus provided defined quantitative descriptions of the motions of the planets. It was Quetelet's notion that every individual represented an attempt by nature to achieve perfection, but that, like a person shooting at a target, nature's aim was never exact. For example, by collecting a large number of measures of people's heights and observing that the distribution closely resembled the curve of the Normal Law of Error, Quetelet could easily calculate the "ideal" height. He went on to suggest (quoted by Lazarsfeld, 1961) the use of this technique to "measure the qualities of people which can only be assessed by their effect [p. 170]." Quetelet suggested, for instance, that we might measure the attribute of drunkenness by observing the frequency with which a given individual gets drunk. Again, large numbers of such observations would yield a distribution

---

[2]The contributions of Quetelet are beautifully summarized by Paul Lazarsfeld in H. Woolf (1961).

from which it would be possible to estimate the natural idea or at least provide a stable description of the prevalence of the tendency in the society.

It is important to note the teleological assumptions underlying Quetelet's work. The existence of natural norms or ideals was assumed, not demonstrated, and the results of the statistical manipulations upon the variability of direct observation only served to affirm the consequent. In doing so, Quetelet was merely reflecting the philosophical temper of his day. His first major work, *Sur l'homme et le développement de ses facultés,* was published in 1835—nearly 25 years before the appearance of *The Origin of Species.* No sacred oxen were gored by Quetelet's assumption of natural ideals being imperfectly achieved in the individual case. To the contrary, the existence of error in the moral sense justified the religious and social authority of the day. No doubt great comfort was drawn from the use of error of a different sort to describe social phenomena. Of more concern to us is Quetelet's willingness to use manifest variability as the basis for defining latent entities or characteristics. Although Quetelet was apparently careful to avoid attaching causal significance to such characteristics, his successors have not been. It is easy to see how Quetelet's work gives the prestige of quantification to such supposed determinants of human behavior as traits, personality attributes, and so on, which were already prominent in the language of the culture. Quetelet thus accidentally arranged the conditions for reintroducing into science, albeit by different names, a whole class of explanatory variables whose origins are philosophical or religious rather than empirical.

Psychophysics

Quetelet's use of observed variability was primarily for the purpose of estimating ideals or norms as well as propensities and dispositions. It was Gustav Fechner (1801–1887) who, working in an entirely different tradition, developed the idea of combining observed variability with the mathematics of probability to create units and scales of measurement. Fechner was interested in establishing a correspondence between changes in the physical energy directed at a human observer and the private experience of that observer. Earlier, Ernst Weber had shown that the ability of the observer to detect a change in physical stimulation was a constant function of the proportion by which the stimulating energy was increased or decreased. Thus, the amount by which one light must vary in intensity in comparison to a reference light before a subject will report seeing two lights of differing intensities depends on the intensity of the reference light. In making such determinations, the intensity of the comparison light is adjusted until the subject reports a difference. Fechner proceeded to make a larger number of such adjustments until he found a difference value for which the subject reported noticing a difference on 50% of the occasions it was presented. The corresponding physical difference between the two lights then defined one sensory scale unit or JND (Just Noticeable Difference). S. S. Stevens (1957) referred to this procedure as "measurement by confusion," because variability in the subject's behavior is clearly the substrate from which the measurement units are defined.

Let us pause briefly in order to underscore the importance of this development. The contributions of Quetelet and Fechner constitute the basic point of departure of entirely new definitional measurement strategies in science. Observed variability in measured natural phenomena is described with the aid of the calculus of probability and, from these descriptions, not only are new phenomena defined, but units for scaling them are created. Two separate procedures (that do not necessarily occur together) are involved here, and both may be described by the adjective *vaganotic*.[3] Vaganotic definition denotes the practice of defining phenomena into existence on the basis of variation in a set of underlying observations. Similarly, vaganotic measurement refers to the creation of scales and units of measurement on the basis of variation in a set of underlying observations.

We can find no precedent in the natural sciences for this method of defining phenomena and their units of measurement.[4] The use of procedures wherein the phenomena being measured and/or the units of measurement are defined

---

[3]*Vaganotic* is derived from the Latin *vagare* (to wander) compounded with the Latin *notare* (to designate with brand or mark) and hence conveys the characteristic of instability in the meaning of the entity thus described. Although we generally eschew the practice of introducing new terms into the scientific vernacular, precision and economy of exposition, together with the overriding importance of differentiating among scientific measurement strategies, justifies it in this case. Furthermore, the distinction we draw has been anticipated by other writers, notably Boring (1920), but has not previously been reduced to categorical description. Such dimensions as ideographic-nomothetic and ipsitive-normative have been offered to furnish a basis for discussing the general issue of individual versus group sources of data, but do not embrace the underlying question of units of measurement.

[4]However, we can invent one to highlight the absurdity of such a practice were this to be applied in the natural sciences. Let us imagine a scientist who needs to determine the length of a certain object. No scale unit such as the centimeter exists, and, thus, there is no calibrated ruler with which to perform the measurement task. The resourceful scientist has a large ball of string, however, and proceeds to cut lengths of string that match all of the objects in the laboratory and surrounding buildings, thus ensuring a large representative sample of string bits. The scientist collects the string segments and presents all possible pairs of them to a panel of trained judges with the instruction, "Tell me which one is longer." Using the method of paired comparison analysis, the scientist can extract from these judgments a scale of subjectively judged lengths and can then assign to the object the scale value obtained for the matching piece of string. If the scientist wished, he or she could even assign a unit name to the string length that matches the object and proceed to measure other objects in terms of this unit. No problem exists until another scientist in another laboratory wishes to investigate the same phenomena and faces the task of measuring the lengths of other examples of the same kind of object. The same process used to arrive at scale values and a unit in the second case will obviously yield different values and a different unit, with fatal effects on the discovery of facts about the class of objects under study.

in terms of variability characterizing a set of otherwise direct observations seems peculiar to psychology and the other social sciences. This difference is perhaps the most fundamental one between the natural and social sciences. Not only does it dictate a vastly different approach to defining and quantifying subject matter, it also has profound implications for the tactics of experimental design, control, and interpretation.

Fechner's work launched the discipline of psychophysics, the history of which has been well documented by Boring (1942, 1950, 1961). Boring (1961) points out that Fechner's dubious assumption that the JND provided a unit of subjective magnitude impeded progress in psychophysics until the development of direct scaling methods by Stevens in the 1950s.

Mental Measurement

An even greater impact of Fechner's thought on the contemporary scene is traceable through the work of Francis Galton. Galton (1822–1911), who happened to be a cousin of Charles Darwin, synthesized the ideas of Quetelet with those of Fechner and launched the mental measurement movement. Galton was evidently impressed by Quetelet's vast accumulation of instances in which the Normal Law of Error also described the distribution of various characteristics in the human population. He assumed, as Quetelet probably had, that mental ability was similarly distributed. Following Fechner's innovation, Galton mapped the theoretical normal distribution onto a 14 step, equal interval scale and, in one grand gesture, invented not only the concept of intelligence, but a means of measuring it as well. This idea was put to immediate practical use by Binet (1857–1911) in France and Cattell (1860–1944) in the United States. These men created tests composed of items selected for their ability to elicit samples of performance that would display variability across a number of individuals. Because this variability was distributed in accordance with the Normal Law of Error and because Galton has defined mental ability in those terms, it was natural to assert that these were tests of mental ability. The sustained impact of this activity upon American psychology is due in no small measure to the entrepreneurial abilities of Cattell, who founded or edited a number of prestigious journals in addition to forming the Psychological Corporation for manufacturing and selling mental tests. Mention of Cattell's early leadership in the American Psychological Association completes our account of the forces that forged virtually unified adoption of the stratgies of vaganotic definition and measurement early in the history of psychology.

Statistical Scaling

The story of the Normal Law of Error as a basis for description has one final catholicizing installment—the use of the techniques of statistical inference for purposes of scaling. In 1889, Galton published *Natural Inheritance* in which he observed the existence of what he called "co-relation" between certain variables measured in the population (e.g., the heights of fathers and sons). He also noticed the phenomenon of regression toward the mean, and according to Boring (1961), gave the problem to F. Y. Edgeworth for mathematical solution. Edgeworth developed the index of a correlation from which Karl Pearson worked out the product moment method of linear correlation in 1896. In hindsight, it is clear that Pearson's development of the mathematics of correlation was a crucial step in the history of vaganotic practices. Correlational procedures enable the investigator to separate variability that is shared from that which is unique among variables. From the implicit assumption that variability may be used to define and measure phenomena, the investigator is then encouraged to invent names for these components of variability, investigate their relation with other similarly defined entities, and so on, *ad infinitum*. Current practices in factor analysis and multidimensional scaling illustrate this strategy. Not surprisingly, a proliferation of jargon results from the problem of finding names for all the little particles of variability that are created by these methods.

Vaganotic measurement of differences, which has become the standard device for evaluating experimental effects in American psychology and education, emerged from the work of Ronald Fisher and his student, W. S. Gosset. Gosset elegantly demonstrated in 1908 that the error in using a sample mean as an estimate of a population mean could be inferred probabilistically from the variability of the sample observations. This made possible the actuarial assessment of differences among sample means, again with reference to the Normal Law of Error. The logical rationale underlying this practice derives from the device of proof by contradiction. It is assumed that the variability observed in a set of experimental observations is not due to the operation of a specified experimental treatment. One then calculates the probability of obtaining the observed differences among means under these conditions. If that probability is sufficiently small, one concludes that the observed differences are the result of something other than natural variability, thus contradicting the original assumption. The experimental treatment is then selected as the most likely explanation.

The fact that this procedure constitutes vaganotic measurement in exactly the same sense as does Galton's 14-point scale of mental ability may not be immediately obvious. To understand why this practice, usually referred to as hypothesis testing, extends the measurement practices of Galton, one need only carefully examine the conventional use of formulae for calculating the t-ratio.[5] The standard formula for calculating t is given by:

---

[5]An identical argument can be made in the case of the F-ratio as used in the analysis of variance.

$$t = \frac{(\bar{x}_1 - \bar{x}_2) - (\mu_1 - \mu_2)}{S\bar{x}_1 - \bar{x}_2}$$

where $\bar{x}_1$ is the mean of the first sample, $\bar{x}_2$ is the mean of the other sample, $(\mu_1 - \mu_2)$ is the hypothesized difference in population means (usually 0), and $S\bar{x}_1 - \bar{x}_2$ is the standard error of the difference in means.

Critical to our discussion is the quantity $S\bar{x}_1 - \bar{x}_2$. Known as the estimated *standard error of the difference,* it is calculated as follows:

$$S\bar{x}_1 - \bar{x}_2 = \sqrt{\frac{S_1^2}{n_1 - 1} + \frac{S_2^2}{n_2 - 1}}$$

where S_1^2 is the sample variance of the first sample, S_2^2 is the sample variance of the other sample, and n_1 and n_2 are the respective sample sizes.

The quantities S_1^2 and S_2^2 are measures of the variability observed in the two samples and are completely determined by the measures that comprise the samples. Calling the quantity $S\bar{x}_1 - \bar{x}_2$ a standard error does not make it standard in any but the most local and temporary sense. It is "standard" only with respect to the samples of observations obtained and thus owes its fleeting existence entirely to whatever variability characterizes the samples. As a reference value against which the magnitude of the numerator is compared, this "standard error" is determined by the same set of measurements that define the quantitative differences it is proposed to assess. The actual assessment process is removed one step from computation of t. The decision whether the obtained difference in means is large enough to warrant rejection of the null hypothesis is made by consulting a table of probabilities associated with various values of t under conditions where the true difference is 0. The tabled values relate variation in t to probability values in a perfectly legitimate mathematical manner. However, the *use* of these values tends to be binary and categorical; a result is *significant* if the associated p value does not exceed a certain amount, usually .05.

In summary, obtained variability is again used to devise a scale whose units are mappings of discrete densities under the curve describing the Normal Law of Error, exactly after the fashion of Galton and Fechner. The resulting scale is composed of only two categories—significant and nonsignificant—and assignment to one or the other bears no fixed relation to the absolute size of the difference under examination. Fisher, Gosset, and their numerous followers in the discipline of mathematical statistics should not be held responsible for the fact that their mathematically valid procedures for assessing deviations of a random variable have been subverted for use as measuring devices in the social sciences. Fisher could hardly have anticipated that in his discussion of fiducial limits, his arbitrary example of .05 would become the index point of a rigid binary scale for measuring the quality of scientific research. This unfortunate degradation has, nevertheless, become the ultimate consequence of the 19-century insight that variability could be used not only to define otherwise nonextensive phenomena, but simultaneously to create units and scales for their measurement.

THE ORIGINS OF IDEMNOTIC STRATEGIES

The tradition of scientific measurement that insists upon enumeration in terms of exact, standard, and absolute quantities or units was by no means stifled by the activities of Quetelet, Fechner, and Galton in the 19th century. As a matter of fact, with the exception of the undue attention paid their work by philosophers of science in the early 20th century, we may conclude that the vaganotic tradition inspired by these men has been largely ignored in natural scientific circles.

It would be beyond both the scope and purpose of this volume to attempt to summarize the vast array of innovations that occurred in scientific measurement during the 19th and early 20th centuries. Instead, we pick up the thread of innovation that begins with Legendre's attempt to smooth measurement error as it winds its way through the scientific and technological revolution of the 19th century, eventually presenting us with the rudiments of a technology for direct measurement of behavior.

As an astronomer, Legendre was concerned with the fact that simultaneous observations by different observers displayed variability. As we have seen, he approached the problem by using the calculus of probability to compute a value about which the variation was minimized. Although probably improving the accuracy of estimated measurement, this solution did nothing to control or eliminate the variability among observers. Of course, at no time did Legendre rely on observer variability to define the subject matter of his inquiry. His legitimate use of descriptive statistics to quantify measurement error should not be misconstrued as an early precursor of vaganotic definition, because the phenomena to be studied existed prior to any measurement whatsoever.

A subsequent 19th-century astronomer, F. W. Bessel, noticed that different observers reacted with different latencies to the appearance of a star in their telescopic field of view. By carefully equating the aiming point of each observer's telescope, Bessel found that part of the variability in the observer's latencies was constant for each individual. The notion of reaction time thus came into being and with it the impetus for technical refinement of timing devices capable of measuring very short intervals. Better experimental estimates of personal reaction times were made by having people observe a swinging pendulum, an innovation also attributed to Bessel. Bessel may have been among the first to measure directly a universal dimension of behavior, its latency.

Measurement of reaction time also played a critical role in the experimental psychology of Wilhelm Wundt (1832–1920). Wundt trained in medicine and physiology, and his pioneering work in perception clearly extended these disciplines. As a disciple of Helmholtz, Wundt knew the value of proper experimental control, and there is reason to doubt that he was overwhelmed by Fechner's indirect psychophysical scaling techniques (although he did use Fechner's methods in his studies of perception). From our point of view, Wundt's principal contribution lies in his attempt to develop a "mental chronometry." He evolved an elaborate scheme for timing (and, hence, presumably measuring) what he thought to be conscious processes. He gradually complicated the stimulus array and response requirements for a particular subject, and reasoned that by subtraction of the successively longer reaction times, he could get a measure of the time required for such processes as apperception, cognition, association, and judgment. Regardless of what Wundt thought he was measuring with these methods, his units of measurement remained standard and absolute; he was unquestionably measuring a characteristic of overt human behavior that changed in orderly ways as a result of controlled changes in the environment. In addition, from Wundt's laboratory came further advances in the instrumentation for behavioral timing.

The use of simple counting to measure behavior, an idea also suggested by Quetelet, developed further in the late 19th century. Both Galton and Binet were prodigious counters and were obliged to count the occurrences of certain behaviors in order to obtain a measure of test behavior in response to test items, although the variability obtained in their data was not subject to further experimental analysis. Perhaps the first investigator to attempt experimental isolation of the sources of variability in counts of behavior was Hermann Ebbinghaus (1850–1901). In 1885, Ebbinghaus began using numerical frequency of verbal recall as a measure of strength of association or memory. Ebbinghaus was influenced by Fechner to the extent that Fechner suggested the possibility of measuring psychological events, but he did not incorporate Fechner's notion of scaling. Instead, he invented a novel experimental independent variable, the nonsense syllable, and defined and investigated the phenomena of learning and memory in terms of simple, direct counting procedures (number of trials to completely learn a list, number of items recalled as a function of the passage of time, etc.).

The extension of the natural science approach to measurement to animal behavior has its origins in the work of E. L. Thorndike (1898) who, in pursuing an understanding of animal intelligence, arranged puzzles for animals to solve and recorded both the time for solution and the number and nature of unsuccessful attempts. Although the object of Thorndike's inquiry was not directly accessible to measurement, it is important to note his reliance on environmental control and his use of absolute units to describe behavior.

Probably the earliest and still among the most elegant uses of instrumentation in the measurement of animal behavior is in the work of Pavlov. In describing his measurement procedures, Pavlov (1927) wrote:

> The secretory reflex presents many important advantages for our purposes. It allows an extremely accurate measurement of the intensity of reflex activity, since here the number of drops in a given time may be counted or else the saliva may be used to displace a colored fluid in a horizontally placed graduated glass tube [p. 17].

One of the first reports of automatic behavioral recording may also be found in Pavlov's (1927) writings:

> As the saliva flows into the hemispherical bulb the colored fluid is displaced along the graduated tube where the amount of secretion can be read off accurately. Further it is not difficult to fix up an automatic electrical recording device which will split up the displaced fluid into drops of exactly equal volume and reduce any lag in the movement of the fluid to a minimum [pp. 18–19].

Three important features characterize the work of Wundt, Thorndike, Ebbinghaus, and Pavlov and place it squarely in the natural scientific tradition. First, their units of measurement were standard and absolute. None went the route of Fechner and Galton and developed vaganotic scales of measurement. Second, all apparently viewed variability as the scientific window through which to observe the workings of basic controlling relationships. All four of these investigators were admittedly concerned with phenomena other than behavior for its own sake, but none succumbed to the temptation to mix behavioral variability with the theory of probability and produce a substance from which to fashion tools of measurement. The third feature that characterizes the work of these four investigators is their shared tactic of collecting a large number of observations from each of a relatively small number of subjects. Ebbinghaus is known to have used only one subject, himself. Surprising as it may seem to some readers, the quality of their science did not suffer as a result of such paucity of sample size. These investigators were concerned with establishing the relations between controlled aspects of the experimental environment and the behavior of their subjects, not with describing the variability of static characteristics in a population.

From the standpoint of the development of a science of behavior, the works of Wundt, Ebbinghaus, Thorndike, and Pavlov established the feasibility of applying traditional scientific measurement strategies to behavioral phenomena. Inasmuch as these measurement practices differ so dramatically from the vaganotic strategies common in the social sciences and because both enjoy widespread contemporary usage, it becomes important to have a single descriptor for the type of measurement we are now considering. We have chosen the term *idemnotic*[6] to denote the type of measurement that incorporates absolute and standard units whose existence is established independently of variability in the phenomena being measured. As we see in subsequent chapters, the implications of this measurement strategy for the scientific study of behavior are pervasive. We argue that, generally, tactics of subject matter definition, experimental design, reduction and analysis of data, and interpretation are encouraged by the measurement strategy adopted.

Logical symmetry suggests that, as in the case of vaganotic practices, the term idemnotic could refer to the manner in which phenomena are defined as well as to the nature of measurement units. Thus, an idemnotic definition would be made without reference to variability in a set of observations made along some underlying dimension. Certainly this usage would not be inappropriate in that attention would be called to the separate functions in scientific analysis of named properties of events and their variability; however, except for the historical digression occasioned by the emergence of the vaganotic tradition, such clarification seems largely unnecessary and hence redundant. That virtually all natural scientific definitions are idemnotic has implications for other methodological issues that are of at least equal importance to the consequences of idemnotic measurement.

SIGNIFICANCE OF MEASUREMENT STRATEGY

We now consider a few of the more general consequences of adoption of a vaganotic as opposed to an idemnotic strategy for the enterprise of knowledge production. Although these comments are of particular relevance to the generation of scientific knowledge about behavior, we believe their applicability extends to all domains of natural phenomena.

Further Idemnotic Characteristics

The idemnotic–vaganotic distinction is a simple bifurcation of a highly complex historical dimension. We can better appreciate the significance of the schism if we briefly explore two additional facets of the idemnotic strategy—standardization and anchoring to arbitrary constants. The earliest

---

[6]Idemnotic is derived from the Latin *idem* (the same) compounded with the Latin *notare* (to designate with brand or mark) and thus communicates the stability of meaning of a unit of measurement that is standard and absolute.

forms of idemnotic measurement involved invention of standard units for the description of the three physical parameters—distance, mass, and time. Very shortly thereafter, new phenomena were described and investigated in terms of compound units resulting from algebraic combinations of the basic three. For example, the Greeks worked with velocity (distance/time) and density (mass/distance³).

Beginning in the 16th century, new units of measurement, often associated with special instruments, were described. An attempt was made to standardize such units by defining them with respect to common elements. For example, we define the Newton (N), a unit of force, as the force required to give a mass of 1 kg an acceleration of 1 m/sec^2. Pressure units are force units divided by area units, for example, N/m^2; a convenient reference is the force of atmosphere pressing on the earth. Thus, a unit called the atmosphere (atm) is advanced, its value being 10.3×10^5 N/m^2. Measurement of atmospheric pressure is often in terms of millimeters of mercury (mm Hg), one of which is the pressure exerted by a column of mercury 1 mm high. It is also equivalent to 1/760 atm and came into being through the invention of the mercury barometer in 1643 by Torricelli. Clearly, this unit can be reduced to a combination of the three basic dimensions—distance, mass, and time.

During the Age of Reason, the French attempted to anchor all physical measurement in natural phenomena, thinking that by doing so they would achieve an invariance dictated by the constants of nature. For example, in adopting the metric system in 1791, they defined the meter as the distance from the equator to either pole $\times$ 10^{-6}. Nowadays, length and time can be anchored to atomic phenomena by reference to certain wavelengths of light and atomic vibrational phenomena, but no such natural standard exists for measuring mass. This poses no problem, however, because standards for the meter, kilogram, and second exist independently of natural referents.

The desire to anchor units of measurement in natural phenomena may have been partly responsible for Quetelet's efforts to divine the existence of social phenomena out of observed variation. Had it been possible to establish the existence of such phenomena independently of such variation, a constant value could have been selected as an anchor for an idemnotic scale. This, of course, was not the case. The existence of sensation was established by observing behavioral variability (from which Fechner defined the JND), but the existence of the atmosphere was not similarly established by observing pressure variations. Because the atmosphere was defined and known to exist prior to measurement of pressure variations, an arbitrary but absolute value of pressure could be selected as a reference value for a standard scale. Fortunately, behavior, like the atmosphere, is an objective phenomenon whose existence does not depend on inference from a more basic substrate.

Contemporary Behavioral Usage

This idemnotic measurement tradition finds full expression in the contemporary natural science of behavior. As we shall see, behavior possesses many of the characteristics of matter in motion, and the same principles of measurement are applicable. Units have been developed for describing frequency and acceleration, as well as the more primitive dimensional quantities of speed and latency. Unfortunately, a large segment of the scientific community that considers behavior as its subject matter has its origins in the vaganotic tradition of the social sciences and, accordingly, has been unable to reap the benefits of standard and absolute unit-based measurement.

Contemporary vaganotic measurement practices may be located in a crude two-dimensional space defined by the presence or absence of a formal, labeled unit and the extent to which variation is either implicit or explicit in the construction of the scale. For example, the Thurstone Case V method of paired comparisons for scaling preference makes explicit use of the variability in the preferences of observers making pairwise comparisons among a set of objects, but does not attach an independent unit label to the numerical outcome. Perhaps a more widely known illustration is found in such aptitude tests as the Graduate Record Examinations, the Scholastic Aptitude Test, etc. On the other hand, statistically averaged performance on achievement tests is used to define performance expectation for various grade levels and these quantities are invested with a time label—for example, 5.2 years. Determination of mental age norms for certain intelligence tests follows the same practice.

Often, the underlying variability is only assumed and does not enter into the calculation of scale values. Technically, such measurement is not even vaganotic as we have defined it, although most of the criticisms obviously apply. "On a scale from 1 to 5, how do you like this dessert?" typifies this practice. Because there is no answer to the question, "One to 5 what?", it is obvious that no unit label is imparted to such numbers. Variability is nonetheless assumed and enters the measurement process when the allowable range is decided. For example, "3" on a scale from 1 to 10 presumably means something different from "3" on a scale of 1 to 5. In order to evaluate the response, "3," it is necessary to know the limits of possible variation.

It is difficult to find cases in which the underlying variability is only assumed, but a formal unit label is nevertheless present. Informally, "points" on various scales serve the linguistic function of a unit and this practice is widespread. Classroom achievement tests, developmental rating scales ("Score 1 if the student does it, 0 if the student does not"), and various trait inventories are but a few examples of measuring devices that are not derived from explicit variability but nevertheless yield results that connote a unitary dimension.

Variability

The fundamental task of all science is to account for variability within and among natural phenomena. A necessary first step in the accounting process has always been quantifying observations to obtain an accurate description of the variation that occurs. Unfortunately, the use of variability as the sole determinant of scales of measurement almost forces, for the sake of consistency, the assumption that such variability is both inherent and invariant in the phenomenon under consideration. Either of these assumptions is practically fatal to the development of an exact science, although, in combination, they are comforting to the proponents of the view that such an exact science of behavior is an *a priori* impossibility. The assumption that variability is inherent, as Sidman (1960) has capably pointed out, discourages the search for its causes. The strategic essence of the experimental method in science involves treating variability as the subject matter to be understood and explained. But understanding and explaining must be preceded by measurement, and this measurement must be in terms of units that are not themselves possessed of the same variability as the phenomenon they are designed to quantify.

The widespread use of vaganotic measurement procedures, particularly in the social sciences, has lent tacit support to the implicit contention that human behavior is inherently variable and thus qualitatively different from other natural phenomena. We must recognize that as a consequence of vaganotic measurement, this assertion has come to be accepted by definition rather than by demonstration. The assumption of inherent variability has become tantamount to the proclamation of a scientific sanctuary for the philosophical doctrine of indeterminism, a critical proposition of the body of invented knowledge from which many prevailing conceptions of the causes of human behavior are drawn.

The alleged uniqueness of human behavior among natural phenomena has long been proffered as justifying the development of methods of investigation different from those of the natural sciences. The results of applying these methods further encourages the assertion of inherent variability, because they are inevitably characterized by the presence of unexplained residual variance that is often measurement induced. Because the phenomena under study are constantly changing, vaganotically obtained units of measurement are changing as well, and the discovery and communication of lawful relations becomes virtually impossible. For example, vaganotic definition and measurement of intelligence ensures that whatever is represented by any proposed unit (such as an I.Q. point) varies with each restandardization of the test. As a result, such questions as the role of genetics in the determination of intelligence will never be answered at the population level because, as the independent variable (genetic composition) changes, so does the measure of the dependent variable. In addition, any discourse concerning vaganotically defined phenomena is confusing at best; at its worst, it is meaningless, an assessment of such terminology being rendered with increasing frequency by the lay and professional public. Many people who have become accustomed to measuring their own weight in pounds and their consumption of electricity in kilowatt hours have difficulty comprehending a measure of their child's academic achievement given in terms of other children's academic achievement expressed as a unit of time.

Perhaps the best illustration of the strategic differences emanating from vaganotic versus idemnotic measurement is in the resulting methods of handling the variability among individual characteristics within a population, which so fascinated Quetelet and Galton. As we have seen, both Quetelet and Galton took this variability as given. The former measured and described it; the latter used it as a means of scaling the entity to which he attributed its existence. In contrast, Gregor Mendel (1822–1884) viewed the obvious morphological variability among members of a species as something to be explained and, along with Galton, suspected that heredity might be partly responsible. In his classic experiments with garden peas, Mendel showed that by controlling the principal factor responsible for heredity, one could produce populations of garden peas whose mathematical distributions of characteristics were not only predictable but changeable at will. As a result, research in the physiology and chemistry of reproduction was greatly stimulated, and we now have a rather exact science of genetics. It is doubtful that the subsequent benefits to humanity would have resulted had Mendel been disposed to regard the variability in color and conformity of garden peas as the basis for the creation of a scale for measuring "peaness."

Other Methodological Decisions

Another source of significance concerns the extent to which the accepting of either vaganotic or idemnotic measurement strategies influences other basic methodological decisions. This influence is pervasive, usually unrecognized, and often quite powerful in its ultimate effects on the characteristics of the data that are generated and on our interpretations of their meaning. The following chapters explore the interrelatedness of the methodological decisions that the researcher must make, but it should be clear that the general measurement strategy serves as origin for other decisions by limiting, permitting, encouraging, and sometimes requiring the selection of various tactics.

For example, a vaganotic approach encourages measuring the behavior of a relatively large number of subjects, which in turn necessitates defining responses that can be observed in a manner compatible with large groups. These tactics come close to requiring group comparison experimental designs that usually force the use of inferential statistics to assess variability and determine interpretative conclusions. This topic is discussed more fully in the next chapter.

By comparison, idemnotic measurement is somewhat less forceful in its influence, not so much encouraging or requiring subsequent decisions as permitting the possibility of measurement, design, and interpretative tactics that can lead to markedly superior data characteristics. The use of standard and absolute units allows the definition of responses in a form that facilitates direct and continuous observation of a small number of subjects individually, thus permitting the use of more powerful experimental designs that approach variability in a vastly different and more productive manner. As we see in later chapters, these tactics lead to data that actually constitute a different subject matter with characteristics allowing a strikingly dissimilar interpretative process.

Subject Matter

One sphere of influence of measurement strategies is of such seminal import as to merit special attention. A subtle but significant reciprocity distinguishes the relation between the conception of the subject matter under investigation and the measurement strategy chosen to approach the investigation. Answering the "chicken or the egg" question raised by the mutual causation between subject matter definition and measurement strategy is less important than understanding the relations and their implications. Whichever comes first or exerts more control, it is clear that the conception of the nature of the subject matter to be investigated is a major consideration in selecting a measurement strategy. Defining behavioral events that are hypothetical, inferred, or otherwise beyond direct observation encourages the choice of indirect measurement practices that are usually vaganotic in style. Interest in overt behavioral events prompts describing them with standard and absolute units of measurement. Further, establishing criteria for observational and measurement reliability becomes far less difficult when the units of measurement are stable.

The correlation between subject matter definition and measurement strategy is less than perfect, and conflicting examples are not difficult to find.

However, the assumptions with which we approach a subject matter are potent sources of control over many experimental decisions, the first and most important of which is selecting a guiding measurement strategy.

On the other hand, the impact on subject matter of the measurement strategy to which a research program has been committed is probably less obvious and well understood. The vaganotic strategy guarantees that the data upon which interpretations are based will be minimally composed of both the variability that is imposed by the treatment and the variability that results from the repeated measures required to define the scale and units. Such data actually constitute a qualitatively different subject matter from those generated by idemnotic measurement, which, under ideal application, exhibit only treatment-imposed variability. This discussion of the "pure" case does not acknowledge the influences on the data of other methodological practices encouraged by these two strategies. For example, vaganotic measurement usually predisposes the researcher toward using a relatively large number of subjects across whom the repeated measures are made. The resulting data are then collapsed statistically so that an estimate of the treatment effect is furnished by a group or cell mean. Of course, an extraneous source of variability—that attributable to differences between subjects—has been allowed to enter into determining the treatment effect, even if only as an error term against which to scale differences. The necessity of evaluating mean differences against an error term also highlights the major weakness of vaganotic measurement: No absolute unit exists in terms of which to describe any difference that exists. The use of a small number of subjects, each serving as its own control, not only avoids these problems, but encourages attempts to describe, identify, and control extraneous sources of variability so as to clarify the environment–behavior relation as it applies to a single individual.

Finally, differences in the process of interpretation highlight the differences in what have become two fundamentally different subject matters. In both cases, conclusions are drawn about the effects of manipulated variables that are intended to apply to the individual case; however, only with the tactics encouraged by idemnotic strategies has the subject matter been preserved in an undiluted form that facilitates interpretations legitimately generalizable to the individual. The practices often associated with vaganotic measurement require that interpretations be controlled by the end result of a statistical digestive process that completes the transformation of what were once individual data into a homogenized subject matter no longer entirely a natural phenomenon. Many writers (e.g., Krantz, 1972) have lamented the apparent chauvinism and lack of integration of the disparate literatures that have arisen to accommodate these two distinct subject matters. The underlying differences, however, are largely irreconcilable because the differences in the basic strategies of measurement are unresolvable.

Technology

The hope for an effective technology of behavior is predicated on developing an exact science of behavior. Such a technology must have the same applicability to the individual case as does its parent science. It is only by discovering and describing in general form the behavioral relations governing the interaction between single organisms and the environment that specific technological applications of these relations can be created.

It is plausible to assert that the abundance of technology that has emanated from the natural sciences in part results from their reliance on idemnotic measurement. The availability of standard, absolute units has facilitated accumulating and refining knowledge in a fashion that is simply foreclosed by reliance on varying measurement scales. Only when relations have been demonstrated to be stable and general can they be extended and relied upon for technological innovation. We argue that such demonstration is virtually impossible in the absence of stable measurement, and therein lies a partial explanation of the failure of any vaganotically based approach to the study of behavior to bestow upon the culture any but the coarsest of screening and labeling technologies.

The final chapter of this book discusses different continua of behavioral investigations, investigations that range from the animal laboratory to the daily environment of people. We contend that there are no justifications for measurement *strategies* being different in any setting or for any behavioral question. Furthermore, this argument can be extended beyond technological development to technological application, in which the only questions raised are those involving maintenance. A common measurement strategy that is as applicable to the single instance as to the general case is a prerequisite for an effective technology at both levels. Once the tactics of idemnotic measurement become commonplace in the realm of technological development and application, a mutually productive interplay with the parent science is enhanced. Discoveries and innovations applicable to the single case may be described in a manner conducive to analysis and eventual generalization, the province of the basic scientist. As such generalizations are firmly established, we can anticipate a profound revolution in our understanding and management of behavioral phenomena.

5 Traditions of Experimental Design

A real experimenter, in fact, so far from being willing to introduce an element of chance into the formation of his scientific conclusions, has been steadily exerting himself, in the planning of his experiments, and in their execution, to decrease or eliminate all the causes of fortuitous variation which might obscure the evidence.

—Ronald Fisher

INTRODUCTION

As discussed in Chapter 2, the purpose of experimentation is to provide empirical comparisons when naturalistic observation alone is insufficient. By creating special conditions of observation (known as an experiment), a scientist may gain access to facts that will support certain kinds of reasoning that are not valid in the absence of such conditions. Within the last century, however, the nuances and complexities of the methods of experimentation have become the focus of a broad, generic subdiscipline known as *experimental design* or the *design of experiments*. The subject matter of this field has come to depend heavily on statistics and cuts across many areas of scientific endeavor. It is now accepted that by properly applying the principles of experimental design, anyone can force nature to provide useful information about almost any subject. Concern about the relevance or importance of the experimental question has given way to emphasis on the quality of the formal design through which an experimental attack on the problem is to be mounted. The interdependence of experimental design and methods of statistical data analysis has created a situation in which legions of experts in "research method" with little knowledge of the relevant subject matter are regularly advising both scientists and policy makers on the propriety of proposed empirical inquiries. Our aim in the present chapter is twofold: We first take a brief historical glance at the evolution of experimental method in the natural sciences and then focus more closely on the origins and practices of contemporary "experimental design," evaluating their applicability to the natural science of behavior.

EARLY HISTORY OF
NATURAL SCIENCE EXPERIMENTATION

Formal experimentation is usually traced to the writings of Roger Bacon (1210–1292) and William of Occam (d. 1347), although it is now clear that the Arabians of the Middle Ages performed important experiments sometime earlier. According to Dampier (1942), the Muslim physicist Ibn-al-Haitham (965–1020) accomplished major feats in experimental optics using spherical and parabolic mirrors and even understood atmospheric refraction. The translation of his work into Latin must surely have been a major impetus to Bacon and his contemporary Robert Grosseteste. Nevertheless, intellectual life in the Western World was heavily dominated by scholastic theology until the 13th and 14th centuries, and there was little demand or tolerance for natural experimentation under those circumstances.

Probably the single figure most responsible for breaking with theological tradition in the study of nature was Leonardo da Vinci (1452–1519). Unlike his predecessors, Leonardo approached inquiry from a purely practical perspective, investigating and experimenting as necessary to develop solutions to problems in the vast range of topics that interested him—art, biology, engineering, military tactics, physics, physiology, and zoology. Unfortunately, Leonardo published very little, although he was widely known in Renaissance Italy. His notebooks have only been recovered and published in the 20th century; much of the fundamental science of the 16th and 17th centuries was anticipated by Leonardo, but his work was as unavailable to Galileo and Kepler as that of Archimedes had been to him.

Throughout the 16th, 17th, 18th, and most of the 19th centuries, scientific experimentation consisted of reasoned demonstration assisted by precise measurement. An interesting illustration of such activity is the work of van Helmont (b. 1577) who according to Dampier (1942):

> planted a willow in a weighted quantity of dry earth, supplied it with water only, and at the end of five years found that it had gained 164 pounds in weight, while the earth had lost only two ounces. This was a very ingenious proof that practically all the new substance of the willow was made of water, indeed quite a convincing proof, until Ingenhousz and Priestly, more than 100 years later, showed that green plants absorb carbon and carbon dioxide from the air [p. 127].

William Harvey's demonstration of the circulation of the blood (1628) similarly illuminates the type of experimental reasoning on which it depended.

It is useful to examine the growth of a single field of inquiry from the standpoint of the critical advances made by experimentation. A convenient example is the study of electromagnetic phenomena, partly because such phenomena were puzzling and given to easy misinterpretation by early thinkers. Progress in correcting such misinformation came slowly and only by carefully reasoned experimental analysis. Elegant experimental reasoning was furnished early by William Gilbert of Colchester (1540–1603) whose work with magnets led him to conclude that the earth was a giant magnet whose poles did not quite coincide with the geographic poles. Gilbert also coined the term electricity to describe the forces that resulted when various materials, especially amber, were rubbed together.

Oddly enough, it was not until the work of Farraday in 1831 that the connection between electrical and magnetic phenomena was made, although it was probably suspected by Franklin and others. The problem was that a controlled source of electricity was not available before the early 1800's; the history of experimental science makes it clear that rapid progress in a field usually awaits discovery of methods of producing the essential phenomena at will. Whereas in 1752 Franklin was able to charge a key with a series of Leyden jars and conduct his famous kite experiment, which demonstrated the electrical nature of lightning, it was an observation in 1786 by Luigi Galvani that paved the way for storage batteries. Galvani noticed that if the nerve and muscle of a frog's leg were simultaneously touched by two dissimilar metals and then the metals brought into contact, the leg would twitch. He thought the phenomenon was the result of "animal electricity," but, in 1800, Alessandro Volta (1745–1827) showed that no animal was necessary—the electrical charge was the result of chemical action. Volta arranged strips of zinc and copper separated by paper in a salt solution and was able to produce electrical energy from this "pile," as it came to be called. Farraday invented the first electric motor in 1821 and, following Oersted's 1820 observation that a wire leading away from a Volta pile will produce deviations in a compass, verified the existence of electromagnetic phenomena as described above. Over 200 years of effort were required to move from the discovery of magnetism to its understanding as a basic electrical phenomenon. We could easily trace the history of similar scientific odysseys, such as the discovery and classification of gasses, from the efforts of the early Greeks through the work of van Helmont, Priestley (1733–1804), Cavendish (1731–1794), and Lavoisier (1743–1794), or, as we briefly attempted in Chapter 2, the evolution of mechanics from Galileo through Newton and Einstein. Through any such historical travel one fact clearly emerges, regardless of the discipline in question. Experimentation was arranged to permit a single observation at a time, usually under known or at least controlled conditions. Observations were then repeated a second and a third time to ensure the repeatibility of the first. To be sure, the results of any series of observations were not identical; concern with measurement error can be seen in the work of Leonardo and Galileo as well as the later, more sophisticated, treatment afforded by Legendre (see Chapter 4). Nowhere, however, do we see experimental method dictated by a concept of chance or random variation in the phenomena under study. The origins of that mode of experimental inquiry, which we shall call groups comparisons, are altogether different.

EARLY HISTORY OF GROUPS COMPARISONS

The origins of the distinctly modern practice of using composite group measures as a basis of experimental comparisons are quite complex and difficult to trace. In an excellent book on the history of statistics, Helen Walker (1929) cites three major and diverse traditions as fusing to create the discipline of statistics. To these, we later add a fourth tradition—agricultural experimentation—that joins Walker's three as the essential elements that combine to give the rationale underlying scientific inference on the basis of groups comparisons. Let us first briefly recount the three traditions Walker identifies.

Social Enumeration

The oldest of the three traditions can be traced to biblical times when King David is said to have counted his people, sheep, etc. The various early civilizations, including those of Babylon, Greece, and Rome apparently made periodic tabulations of people and property, perhaps for tax purposes. In the Middle Ages, Pepin the Short and Charlemagne forced the Church to account not only for the land it held but also for the serfs who lived on it. In England in 1086, there existed the Doomsday Book, which listed the names of landowners and an inventory of their serfs and property.

By the early 14th century, descriptive economic statistics had appeared in the form of records of tariffs and customs duties in Paris markets. Also begun at that time was the practice of registering marriages and deaths; baptisms were added in the 15th century, and all such registrations were the responsibility of the Church. In 16th- and 17th-century England, outbreaks of plague inspired maintaining the Bills of Mortality (a death registry), which was gradually refined to include not only the sex of the deceased, but the occurrence of any baptisms as well.

These and similar events are seen by Walker as contributing to a tradition of political enumeration, whose full realization occurs in the modern decennial census. Actually, census taking appears to have originated in Canada in 1605, with the Scandanavian countries following soon thereafter. England did not initiate a formal census until 1801, although the practice of keeping birth and mortality data apparently persisted from the time of the plague. The close of the 18th century witnessed many political upheavals, among them the American and French Revolutions; with these came elected forms of government that required political census taking for purposes of apportionment. Thus, the first American census was conducted in 1790, as required by the Constitution; previous apportionment to the Continental Congress was evidently on the basis of state boundaries alone. At that time, census taking had already been going on in Norway, Sweden, and Denmark for at least 50 years; it became a regular function of the Swedish government in 1756.

Economic Quantification

The second major tradition from which modern statistical practice derives accompanies the rise of the mercantile economies following the Age of Exploration. As the foregoing discussion indicates, this tradition is at first indistinguishable from that of social or political enumeration; many of the early monarchs required periodic tabulations not only of their subjects, but of their resources so that decisions of military strategy could be made on the basis of something other than pure guesswork. We have already mentioned that economic tabulations were made in 14th-century France in terms of transactions, not just holdings. In the late 16th century, there appeared a document entitled *Secret of French Finances*, which Walker believes may represent the first effort to use such data in formulating state policy.

At about this time, people began using such enumerative data for predictive purposes. Walker argues that the first effort to use enumerative data to examine the regularity of social phenomena was Captain John Graunt's *Observations on the London Bills of Mortality* (1662). In 1693, the astronomer Halley published *An Estimate of the Degrees of Mortality of Mankind, drawn from Curious Tables of the Births and Funerals at the city of*

Breslaw; with an attempt to ascertain the Price of Annuities upon Lives, which marks the first attempt to base annuities upon actuarial data. Thus was the insurance business born in the modern actuarial sense. We agree with Walker that it is beyond mere coincidence that astronomers such as Halley and Legendre, as well as Quetelet over 100 years later, played a role not only in developing statistical procedures for refining observational data in their laboratories, but in the inductive use of demographic measures as well. This leads us to the third major tradition, probability theory.

Mathematical Statistics

We have already recounted the development of this discipline in some detail in Chapter 4. For the present, we remind the reader that by the end of the 18th century, the mathematics of probability had progressed from its origins in the letters of Pascal and Fermat around 1650 concerning gambling problems to the formal statements of the Normal Law of Error furnished by Laplace (1778) and Gauss (1809). With the advent of the formal calculus of probabilities late in the 18th century, the stage was set for using collections of quantitative characteristics of individuals within groups as a basis for inductive generalizations concerning social phenomena. Prior to this time, the practical significance of the theory of probability had not been appreciated beyond its applicability to games of chance. Much earlier, Abraham De Moivre (1667–1754) had developed a close approximation to the normal curve (1738) on purely mathematical grounds, reasoning from the distribution of coefficients in the binomial expansion $(a + b)^n$. He saw the significance of this as largely theological, supporting a concept of Great First Cause (Walker, 1929): "And thus in all cases it will be found, that although Chance produces irregularities, still the Odds will be infinitely great, that in the process of Time, those Irregularities will bear no proportion to the recurrency of Order that naturally results from Original Design [p. 17]." Similar thinking is evident in the work of Jacques Bernoulli (1654–1705) and other moral philosophers of the period.

The developments in formal probability theory that occurred at the turn of the 19th century furnished powerful mathematical tools with which to provide quantitative descriptions of various phenomena that seemed to obey the normal distribution, as well as to estimate with astonishing accuracy the likelihood of occurrence of particular instances. As we have seen, the 19th century witnessed vigorous development of this potential in a number of areas, including the invention of measurement practices that seemed to bypass the need for absolute units. Two early 19th-century figures, Augustus De Morgan and Adolphe Quetelet, are at the apex of these developments; it will be useful to sketch briefly their contributions apart from the origins of vaganotic measurement.

FORMAL DEVELOPMENT OF GROUPS COMPARISONS

Augustus De Morgan

Augustus De Morgan (1806–1871) was among the first to grasp the enormous potential of mathematical statistics for addressing complex practical problems in human affairs. In 1838, he published *An Essay on Probabilities and on Their Application to Life Contingencies and Insurance Offices* in which he presented simplified rules for the mathematically uninitiated that would (as quoted by Walker, 1929): "enable them to obtain at least the results of complicated problems, and which will therefore, permit them to extend their inquiries further than a few simple cases connected with gambling [p. 26]." Also, around 1838, De Morgan wrote a speculative article on probability theory in which he suggested its applicability to evaluating the truth of testimony, the correctness of jury decisions, and the occurrence of miracles. He even suggests comparing 500 trials for which a jury renders an immediate verdict to 500 in which it deliberates two or more hours to see which set of verdicts displays the smaller percentage of error. This may very well be the first suggestion of an intergroup experimental comparison and clearly forecasts the reasoning which statistical theory would later serve. Its importance at the time, however, lay in the promise offered for coping with established problems dominated by the ingredient of uncertainty. Of course, the guilt or innocence of a defendant was and continues to be an uncertain matter, which must often be determined by methods of approximation, even though the penalty might be excruciatingly exact.

Adolphe Quetelet

It is clear that the dominant figure of this tradition was Adolphe Quetelet. It was Quetelet more than anyone else who melded the actuarial properties of large collections of data with the mathematics of expectation furnished by the Normal Law of Error. Quetelet clearly saw the value of gathering detailed demographic data on an orderly and regular basis and was quite naturally convinced of the connection between all manner of social phenomena and the laws of probability by the fact that the bell-shaped distribution kept reappearing. He founded the London Statistical Society in 1834, and the *Commission centrale de statistique* in 1841, and he organized the first International Statistical Congress in 1853. A man of prodigious energy, Quetelet was apparently determined to ensure the availability of an adequate data base for further development and application of statistical techniques.

We mentioned earlier that Quetelet was a wide ranging intellect. He regarded the new statistical method as equally applicable in all fields from agriculture and anthropology to zoology, depending only on the existence of an observational data base. Like his predecessors, he apparently regarded the persistence of the normal curve as evidence of some supraordinate Regularity. His concept of the "average man" as a natural ideal was discussed in Chapter 4 and came to have a profound effect on anthropologists, physicians, and educators for the next 100 years. From our point of view in the present chapter, however, it was in the area of moral measurement that Quetelet established the most important precedents.

Quetelet delivered a paper entitled "*Recherches sur la penchant au crime aux differents ages*" in 1831 in which he related such factors as age, sex, education, climate, and seasons to the incidence of crime. He observed (as quoted by Walker, 1929) that these relations were highly stable *from year to year*:

> Thus we pass from one year to another with the sad perspective of seeing the same crimes reproduced in the same order and calling down the same punishments in the same proportions. Sad condition of humanity! We might enumerate in advance how many individuals will stain their hands with the blood of their fellows, how many will be forgers, how many will be poisoners, almost we can enumerate in advance the births and deaths that should occur. There is a budget which we pay with frightful regularity; it is that of prisons, chains, and the scaffold [pp. 40–41].

Aside from the charming manner in which Quetelet states a problem that still persists after 150 years, it is important to note his use of characteristics obtained from successive samples of different individuals to induce a general process presumably characteristic of a single individual. Walker (1929) identifies the fatal flaw succinctly: "He suggested that instead of making numerous observations on an individual as he progressed through life, the changes from one age level to another might be studied by making observations on large numbers of people at different ages [p. 41]." This suggestion, and the enormous volume of applications made of it by Quetelet, clearly establishes the precedent for drawing inferences concerning the nature of dynamic individual phenomena on the basis of statistical comparisons made between large groups of individuals. The full development of an experimental method based on this practice did not occur until the late 19th and early 20th centuries; it is to the major figures of this period that we now turn our attention.

Francis Galton

The evolution of the statistical method into a foundation for designing experiments was greatly assisted by the work of Francis Galton (1822–1911) whom we encountered in Chapter 4. Galton's impact on the modern social sciences is probably largely due to his expansion of the new discipline into the area of education, thereby not only touching the lives of virtually every Englishman until the present day but also defining a subject matter area that remains a mainstay in psychology—mental measurement. As we indicated earlier, Galton was convinced that mental abilities must obey the Normal Law of Error in much the same fashion as physical characteristics demonstrated by Quetelet. His adoration of the normal curve is nicely captured in the following excerpt from *Natural Inheritance* (1889):

> I know of scarcely anything so apt to impress the imagination as the wonderful form of cosmic order expressed by the "Law of Frequency of Error." The law would have been personified by the Greeks and deified, if they had known of it. It reigns with serenity and complete self-effacement amidst the wildest confusion. The huger the mob and the greater the apparent anarchy, the more perfect is its sway. It is the supreme law of Unreason. Whenever a large sample of chaotic elements are taken in hand and marshalled in the order of their magnitude, an unsuspected and most beautiful form of regularity proves to have been latent all along [p. 86].

Earlier in the volume, he stated:

> I need hardly remind the reader that the Law of Error upon which these Normal Values are based, was excogitated for the use of astronomers and others who are concerned with extreme accuracy of measurement, and without the slightest idea until the time of Quetelet that they might be applicable to human measures. But Errors, Differences, Deviations, Divergencies, Dispersions, and Individual Variations, all spring from the same kind of causes . . . . All persons conversant with statistics are aware that this supposition brings Variability within the grasp of the laws of Chance, with the result that the relative frequency of Deviations of different amounts admits of being calculated, when these amounts are *measured in terms of any self-contained unit of variability* [pp. 54–55; italics ours].

Here is a clear statement from Galton concerning the utility of what we have called vaganotic measurement, the use of units derived from variability in the phenomenon itself.

It was Galton's fascination with variation within and between wide arrays of measures that led him to attempt something not previously undertaken, which was to have a profound effect on experimental reasoning in the future. His observation of "co-relation" between characteristics (measured in terms of variability) across generations led him to develop the first mathematical expression of correlation. We have already discussed the impact of this invention on the field of mental measurement; however, one point must be emphasized. A general mathematical method of obtaining correlations, regardless of the underlying dimensions of measurement, added to the arsenal of statistics a means of determining *association* which is, of course, of great utility in experimentation. In order to make statements about relations that might exist between variables, it is first necessary to be able to document the existence of such relations. The mathematics of correlation permitted this to be done in the case of the masses of uncontrolled actuarial data that Quetelet, Galton, and others caused to be collected. However, it was not until the genius of Karl Pearson was directed at the problem that the full mathematical and theoretical generality of Galton's invention was realized.

Karl Pearson

Karl Pearson (1857–1936) was probably first attracted to the field of mathematical statistics by the work of Galton and its implications for the scientific study of heredity. He took the problem of correlation from the level of the simple statement that Galton had proposed and the development of the first correlation coefficient by Edgeworth in 1892 and subjected them to full mathematical development. In a series of papers entitled "Mathematical Contributions to the Theory of Evolution," Pearson introduced not only the mathematics of correlation but also the idea of moments of any distribution, the term "standard deviation," and the general mathematics of sampling distributions. In 1898, he developed a general method for determining the sampling error of any moment of a distribution. When it was observed that many sampling distributions were themselves normal, the foundation for experimental inference on the basis of theoretical probability distributions was solidly laid.

Ronald Fisher

The towering edifice that has come to be known as modern experimental design was not constructed by Pearson, but by Ronald Fisher and his students and followers. Fisher was trained as a mathematician and biologist and, like many of his contemporaries, was fascinated by the mathematical issues underlying evolution and heredity. Unlike some contemporaries, however, he turned his attention early to a broad new domain of field research—agriculture. Fisher and his followers developed statistical methods for evaluating agricultural data collected under carefully controlled growing conditions and elaborated the procedures whereby experiments should be conducted to permit proper comparisons and reasoning from large sets of data. This is the formal origin of the phrase "experimental design" and, as we indicated earlier, it clearly implicates agriculture as the fourth tradition from which modern groups comparison practices emanate.

The pivotal event was the articulation of the test for the significance of hypotheses, a process begun with the publication in 1908 of W. S. Gossett's classic paper, "The probable error of a mean" and effectively concluded by the publication in 1935 of Fisher's *The Design of Experiments*. The great importance of Gossett's work has already been touched on; he showed that the variance of a sampling distribution of a mean could be estimated from the data in the sample and provided a mathematical basis for accommodating the loss of precision that occurs in inverse relation to the size of the sample. Thus, from observed variability in a series of measures, it became possible to establish limits on the probable error of the estimate of the mean of the parent population and, even in the case of small samples, to calculate the likelihood that a particular value could be the true mean of the population from which the given sample was drawn. The actual form of the sampling distibution of a sample mean varies with the size of the sample, yielding a family of such distributions that approach normality as the sample size increases. Gossett's t-distribution provides the likelihood of a sample mean deviation of any magnitude for any size sample and thus extends the reasoning associated with the normal curve. This procedure was quickly extended to differences between sample means, and the well-known test of the null hypothesis that the means of the parent populations are equivalent was then available to researchers. Fisher extended the reasoning to groups of means when he introduced the analysis of variance (Fisher, 1925), and the techniques were greatly elaborated, both practically (Cochran & Cox, 1950; Snedecor, 1934) and theoretically (Mann, 1949; Mood, 1950; and many others) over the next three decades.

In the time since Fisher's original work, there have been both disputes and refinements of the basic techniques of statistical inference and hypothesis testing. In particular, J. Neyman and E. S. Pearson introduced the "likelihood ratio test," which is a mathematical technique for deciding which statistic will give the most powerful test of a particular hypothesis (i.e., correctly allow rejection of a false null hypothesis). From this point of departure (with which Fisher essentially disagreed on the grounds that it is experimentally illogical) have come a large number of statistical procedures, including the so-called nonparametric methods that require fewer assumptions concerning the nature of the hypothesized parent population. No purpose is served by recounting these developments, for the reader will soon discover what may already have been suspected—we find the reasoning underlying all such procedures alien to both the subject matter and goals of a natural science of behavior and regard the utility of group comparisons as extremely limited, no matter how elegant the mathematical treatment of data they afford. We should note, however, that these methods have enjoyed almost unchallenged acceptance in psychology, education, and other disciplines that purport to be concerned, at least on occasion, with behavior. The origins of this acceptance are clearly coincident with the influence of Quetelet and Galton on the social sciences and the apparent utility of their methods for mental testing and educational classification.

More recently, the work of Fisher and his followers has been adapted to virtually all efforts at experimentation in these disciplines. Among the first to use the model of the analysis of variance as a basis for experimental design and subsequent reasoning in experimental psychology was David A. Grant in 1945, and soon after, standard textbooks (e.g., Lindquist, 1953; McNemar, 1949) presented these models along with simplified computational procedures as the basis for controlled experimentation in psychology and education. Today, students in these disciplines have available a wide array of "cookbooks" that present the problems of experimental design almost exclusively in terms of the statistical models by which the data may be analyzed rather than from the perspective of arranging opportunities to make comparative observations under conditions not readily found in natural contexts. As a result, students learn a process of scientific inquiry that is almost totally inverted; instead of using questions about natural phenomena to guide decisions about experimental design, models of design are allowed to dictate both the form and content of the questions asked. Not only is this antithetical to the established role of experimentation in science, the types of questions allowed by groups comparisons designs are largely inappropriate or irrelevant to gaining an understanding of the determinants of behavior.

EXPERIMENTAL DESIGN IN THE SCIENCE OF BEHAVIOR

The tradition of designing experiments in accordance with the requirements of tests of statistical hypotheses has ossified into the methodological backbone of the social sciences in this century. With the exception of certain applications in the applied life sciences, however, the natural sciences have largely ignored these prescriptions, much as they have ignored the parallel development of vaganotic measurement discussed in Chapter 4. In particular, those major contributors to a natural science of behavior who could have adapted groups comparison methods of experimentation have been conspicuous by their failure to do so. Pavlov reports not a single correlation coefficient or t-ratio in the entirety of *Conditioned Reflexes*, although that research was contemporaneous with Pearson's and Gossett's work and Pavlov was almost certainly aware of their activities.

More recently, the writings of B. F. Skinner, Murray Sidman, and others have attempted to clarify the many reasons for their steadfast adherence to the strategies of natural scientific experimentation in the study of behavior. We quote from these authors extensively throughout this volume and present the alternative to groups comparison designs at length in Part III. For the present, however, it is important to examine the two most fundamental reasons for our concurrence with the views of Pavlov and Skinner concerning the inappropriateness of groups comparison design tactics in the study of behavior.

Behavior as an Individual Phenomenon

Behavior is defined as a part of the interaction between organism and environment. As such, its occurrence is always peculiar to individual organisms, and it is only those peculiarities that are of scientific interest if our subject matter is behavior. Our extended discussion of the history of group statistical techniques should have made it clear that these methods were inspired by an entirely different set of problems, ranging from census enumeration to predicting the relative frequency of occurrence of events in large populations. For such purposes, these methods are beautifully suited and highly effective. The methods of experimental design and analysis introduced by Fisher are equally suited to the purposes for which they were developed—population genetics, agricultural research, and industrial quality control. In these areas, the individual case, be it fruit fly, ear of corn, or light bulb, is of little concern, and descriptions of population characteristics in terms of means and standard deviations are more than adequate for the inferences that group experimentation permits. Fisher himself clearly and carefully explained that the types of valid inductive inference were from samples to populations, not from samples to the single case (Fisher, 1956). To be sure, there are also valid applications of these procedures to certain problems in psychology and education. Large-scale educational evaluation, for example, is not concerned with whether and why a particular procedure is effective with a particular child, only with its effects on a population of children taken as a whole. The former is a behavioral question, whereas the latter is an actuarial one; it should not be expected that methods appropriate for one class of questions would apply to the other. The popular volume by Campbell and Stanley (1966) is an excellent reference for workers in the area of evaluation research. Its applicability to the study of behavior, however, is another matter.

The problem lies in the generality of groups comparisons to the individual case. Because behavior is a phenomenon that occurs only at the individual level, the science of behavior must have as its goal the understanding of the individual organism's interaction with its environment. Once that is accomplished, the question of generalizing the results from one or a few individuals to a larger number can be properly addressed. However, as we detail throughout this volume, beginning at the group level and attempting to generalize to the individual case is virtually impossible, in spite of Quetelet's contrary conviction. Even if it were possible, it is surely not the *best* approach because error is introduced to whatever extent a given individual deviates from the group norm. As Dunlap pointed out in 1932 (Herson & Barlow, 1976), there is no such thing as an average rat. In making this observation, he was echoing the assessment of the futility of statistical procedures in the study of physiology made by Bernard in 1865 (1957). Methods for studying behavior must isolate and identify the determinants of the individual's behavior, and experimental comparisons based on groups are inappropriate by definition. If valid generalizations to the individual case could be made on the basis of group data, scientists concerned with behavior would probably have adopted the methods with enthusiasm, particularly because they are very often experimentally economical. Unfortunately, our need for a scientific understanding of the determinants of human behavior has been almost totally unfilled during the last 150 years in which groups have served as the basis for experimental comparisons.

Behavior as a Continuous Phenomenon

The second problem with the use of groups comparison techniques in the experimental study of behavior is a variation on the problem of representative sampling. Behavior is a continuous process, changing through time as a function of the influence of its determining variables. Mathematical methods for *describing* such processes have been developed and are briefly described in Chapter 17. Quantitative description of behavior, which must precede experimental analysis as measurement always precedes experimentation, must be sensitive to this dynamic property and must be essentially continuous. Further, a crucial facet of the subject matter of the science of behavior concerns the nature of this change over time, and that nature cannot be understood unless the phenomenon is tracked through time. Unfortunately, the bulk of the design models that have evolved from the groups comparison tradition become awkward and unmanageable in the face of continuous measurement, as well they should. The validity of these models for groups comparisons partly rests on the extent to which the underlying data conform to certain assumptions of independence, so that the collections of discrete measures necessary for performing the analytical techniques must be corrected for any correlation. But, collecting discrete measures of a continuous process necessarily presupposes a sampling procedure, and this requires assumptions about the representativeness of the sampling. In order to satisfy those assumptions, one must know the nature of the universe from which the sampling is done, and that is precisely the question the science is seeking to address. In other words, using groups comparison methods of experimentation forces one to second guess by assumption the very phenomenon under investigation. This strategic defect has evidently been overlooked by a number of well-intentioned individuals who are laboring mightily to reconcile the requirements of a science of individual behavior with the tactics of data analysis and experimental inference provided by the tradition of groups comparison. Meanwhile, we offer the following exposition of those methods of science that foster comparison based on observation, not assumption, and inference based on replication, not speculation.

Part II MEASUREMENT

6 Definition of Response Classes

The analysis of behavior is not an arbitrary act of subdividing, and we cannot define the concepts of stimulus and response quite as simply as "parts of the behavior and environment" without taking account of the natural lines of fracture along which behavior and environment actually break.

—Skinner

INTRODUCTION

The definition of behavior offered and explored in Chapter 3 primarily delimits the domain of phenomena of interest for the behavioral scientist. It is of very little practical assistance in the problem of approaching the subject matter experimentally. What is needed is a strategy for decomposing the broadly encountered phenomena of behavior into units suitable for experimental analysis.

SOME GENERAL ISSUES

Following conventional usage, the term *response* in this volume designates the single instance of any class of behavioral events under consideration. Thus, the class of behavioral events called "opening doors" is composed of a number of unique door opening responses. Our concern will be to develop tactics for defining and classifying responses in a way that preserves the generic implications of the definition of behavior while permitting unambiguous designation, observation, and measurement for purposes of controlled experimentation. As these tactics are discussed, the reader should bear in mind that the defining characteristic of behavior—a portion of the interaction between organism and environment—applies fully and equally to the term "response." Certain usages may convey the impression that responses (instead of the organism) interact with the environment, but such an interpretation is not intended and would be improper in light of the discussion in Chapter 3.[1]

The term "response" has certain unfortunate connotations that merit brief acknowledgment. Popular and conventional scientific usage strongly implies reaction to some stimulus or goad, which subtly connotes a form of explanation that may or may not be empirically justified. The reader should resist this connotation in the absence of empirical demonstration and should use the term only as a designator of the unit of analysis for which causes remain to be verified.

Units of Analysis Versus Units of Measurement

Definition of a response as the unit of analysis in a particular experiment is not equivalent to specifying a unit of measurement. Idemnotic measurement requires separate, standard units of measurement, whose nature and assignment are discussed in the next chapter. There has been widespread confusion on this point, owing in no small part to the absence of explicit units of measurement in most psychological data and the tendency of some to compensate for this omission by having the unit of analysis serve a double function. This confusion has retarded recognizing the importance of idemnotic measurement to a science of behavior and has also given impetus to disputes about appropriate techniques of measurement that were primarily the result of variation from laboratory to laboratory in the manner in which the response of interest was defined. Disharmonies of this type may be expected in a young science, but their longevity should not exceed the period required for identifying and clarifying the underlying issues.

---

[1]Equally inappropriate is using behavioral descriptions (hyperactive, aggressive, etc.) to label organisms, because to do so ignores the environmental component of the behavioral term.

It should also be understood that selecting a unit of analysis, or response, is a matter of experimental necessity, not philosophical approbation. Defining a class of responses for purposes of a particular experimental analysis is never tantamount to asserting the validity of the selection as the ultimate, irreducible unit of behavior analogous to the molecule or atom of the earlier sciences of matter. Nor should the selection be castigated for appearing to fail to satisfy this epistemological criterion. The standard by which a response class definition is judged is strictly empirical and relates directly to the ease with which discerning orderly relations is permitted by its use. The appropriate unit of analysis in one experiment may properly be further reducible in another context. For instance, dismantling a carburetor may be the proper unit of analysis in one situation whereas loosening nuts might be the subject of a more refined analysis in other circumstances. The generality of the relations observed across experiments is a matter of empirical rather than definitional concern, and it is specifically through such empirical inquiry that the most powerful generalities of science are apprehended. Premature arbitration on the matter of the ultimate, irreducible unit can only forestall or preclude discovery of such generalities. Therefore, the existence and nature of the "behavioral atom" is a theoretical, even philosophical, issue of no immediate concern to the practicing investigator.

Importance of Response Definitions

The attention devoted to specifying the unit of analysis has often been disproportionately small relative to its subsequent tactical importance. The nature of the response definition and the details of its ensuing implementation will have a continuingly powerful and pervasive effect on numerous aspects of measurement, as well as on experimental design and interpretation. Inadequately specifying the response to be investigated is likely to effect observed variability substantially and irreparably at all stages of collecting and analyzing data. For example, one form of improper description occurs when the specified class is actually composed of two or more functionally different response classes, each of which may have its own sources of influence that can mask the control of the independent variable over the real response of interest because of a contrasting effect on the collateral response being measured. In other words, the treatment being manipulated may exert an accelerative effect on one of the response classes and either no effect or a decelerative effect on the other response class. However, because individual responses from both classes are subsumed by the definition, the net effect observed will probably seriously misrepresent the true effects on the response class of actual interest. The nature of such misrepresentations originating from this single definitional error are obviously unpredictable in the specific case and may range from obscuring successful control to encouraging inappropriate conclusions about "apparently" successful regulation of the response classes intended for investigation.

Difficulties such as this are less frequent in relatively restricted laboratory settings, where the criteria tend to be dictated solely by the ideal demands of the research program. The laboratory investigator is usually concerned with defining a single, relatively molecular response that is easy for the subject to emit repeatedly with a consistent topography, sensitive to the variables under examination, and automatically observable.

The investigator working in field settings and faced with the characteristic demands of extralaboratory environments has a far more difficult task. Specifying a response may be restricted by the importance of the response to others, rather than by its suitability for scientific investigation. The behavior of interest may occur infrequently, with inconsistent topography, or with varying functional effects. Observing and recording may be handicapped by a variety of complications. Moreover, it is usually the investigator's job to identify those variables to which the response is sensitive or to impose variability upon the response, rather than to select a response already known to be sensitive to variables and procedures of interest. In spite of these complications, the definitional considerations of the restricted laboratory setting are important to field investigators for exactly the reasons that their white-coated colleagues adhere to them. Because both groups are ultimately concerned with specifying and controlling the variables determining the behavior of interest, adhering to strict criteria for response definition is equally important to investigations in all settings. It can even be argued that because of the added complexities characteristic of applied settings, such concerns acquire even greater importance there than in the laboratory. Because field settings are replete with sources of variability beyond the ability of the investigator to control or sometimes even identify, it is tactically imperative that every effort be made to eliminate those sources of variability that can be easily anticipated and controlled.

STRATEGIES OF RESPONSE CLASS DEFINITION

Learning to Label Behavior

When we describe, label, or refer to our own behavior or to the activities of others, we do so with surprisingly consistent accuracy. Although some misunderstandings and confusions may be persistently recalled because of the inconvenience or embarrassment they caused, the success of our communication with others concerning human activity is the more startling observation, considering the complexity of human behavior and its stimulus environment. We learn and constantly improve upon this skill by continually refining our references to the stimulus conditions surrounding the actions being described. We do not usually define behavior independently of ongoing stimulus events; instead, our history of experiences with behavior is constantly providing us with improved estimates of the correspondence between different actions and their defining stimulus relations.

This is especially easy to observe in a young child who is learning to discriminate and label objects in the environment. Although all four-legged, hairy creatures may at first be called "doggie," stimulus characteristics distinguishing dogs and cats gradually gain control of the use of the appropriate labels. This process depends heavily on the contribution of family members who gently assist the acquisition of verbal behavior by promoting and praising approximations to acceptable utterances in the language. A young child's skills in labeling behavior are the results of a similar process, except that action replaces object as the subject of the labeling. The behavioral event being labeled together with its specific environmental context occasion the labeling response in the child, and these responses are then followed by appropriate social consequences.

It is important to understand the manner in which this proficiency in labeling is achieved, because such an analysis highlights the controlling relations between antecedent and consequent stimuli and behavioral events. A diagram facilitates our explanation.

Figure 6.1 shows schematically the relation among action events and surrounding environmental events that differentiate one response class from another. In Panel A, a relation between certain antecedent environmental events and a certain set of action events is indicated by a lined enclosure. Some of the same and some different action events are also related to specific consequent environmental events by another lined enclosure. The

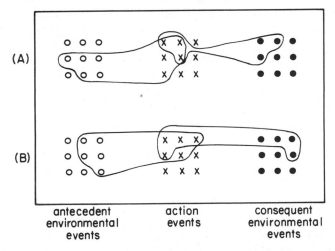

FIG. 6.1. Schematic representation of relations among environmental and action events determining behavioral labeling.

intersection of these two sets thus defines a class of response instances. In Panel B, the addition and removal of some antecedent and consequent events defines two new relations that include the addition and deletion of some action events. The resulting intersection thereby defines a new response class. The process depicted in Fig. 6.1 can be repeated an indefinite number of times to create an infinite collection of response classes.

Let us illustrate this important process of identifying collections of distinct responses in terms of their common relations to environmental events. Consider the activity of a batter in a baseball game. With reference to Fig. 6.1, swings of the bat are clearly the action events whereas pitched balls constitute (for our purposes) the class of antecedent environmental events. The class of consequent environmental events is defined by the results of bat swings: misses, balls landing in foul territory, balls landing in fair territory, etc. How would we differentiate between the response classes of hitting fouls and hitting home runs? Obviously, both responses require that a ball has been pitched. In order for the batter's swing to be called "hitting a foul," the ball must be struck and then land beyond the baselines. On the other hand, for the effort to be classed as a home run, the ball must be struck in a manner that propels it in fair territory beyond the reach of all fielders' prompt retrieval. Thus, both responses are defined by specific sets of relations among antecedents, actions, and consequences.

It should be clear that the environmental events surrounding the actions to be labeled are at least as important in determining the verbal labels as is the form or topography of the action itself. The constant distillation of stimulus events and related action events of interest is conducted with reference to the orderliness of the correspondence that results as stimulus events are added and subtracted.[2] Everyday communication about behavioral events results from effective modulation of exhaustively specifying stimulus and action elements in the interest of ease and efficiency and is made possible by the linguistic provision for less than absolute constancy between response labels and their defining conditions. By virtue of an implied interchangeability among certain elements within these sets, it is possible to speak meaningfully of generic response classes whose members are functionally equivalent, though possibly elementally different. (Hitting a base hit is a large generic class when we consider all the places safely hit balls can land, but all members of this class are functionally equivalent—the batter gets to a base.) The permissible variation is determined by the consistency of social reaction evoked by using a certain label under varying circumstances. As long as a

---

[2]A provocative and comprehensive discussion of the orderliness of the correspondence between action events and environmental events and the utility of this correspondence in classifying behavior is found in Skinner (1935). Here, perhaps for the first time, is an identification of the confusion that arises when stimulus–response relations are used both for definitional and explanatory purposes. We follow Skinner in allowing such relations to serve only their primary definitional function.

listener behaves appropriately, the label is functional in communication, and the particular combination of controlling environmental and action events will remain an instance of the labeled class.

Identifying Functional Response Classes

The above discussion of how we label behavior should make it clear that although each individual response is unique, collections of responses can be meaningfully related by attending to common functional relations with groups of distinct antecedent and/or consequent stimulus events. For example, a variety of different door opening responses can be classified together because they have in common a high correspondence with the antecedent stimulus class of doors and the consequent class of open doors. Generic classes of stimuli and responses can thus be inductively defined by delimiting the range of elements in correspondence to whatever level of specificity is desirable and practical. The response class of opening doors can be made larger or smaller by expanding or narrowing antecedent and/or consequent stimulus classes while attending to the changing correlations. An arbitrary criterion for response class membership may be avoided by referring to the optimum orderliness of changes in the correlations as stimuli and responses are added or subtracted from the classes. Individual responses sharing classes of defining stimulus properties constitute generic response classes.[3]

Figure 6.1 shows that three possibilities exist for doing this in the most abstract sense: One discrete class is formed by considering only correspondences between environmental antecedents and action events; a second class is produced by all correspondences between action events and subsequent environmental events or effects; and the third is a combination of these wherein both antecedent and subsequent environmental events are required to specify the response class. The generality of these three sets of relations has long been recognized, and specific terms denoting them are widely accepted.

The term *respondent* refers to the largest generic response class defined by a high, stable correspondence between environmental antecedent and action events. Examples of respondents include startling at the sound of a gun, salivating at the sight of food, and wincing when one's toes are stepped upon.

An *operant* refers to the fact that a collection of unique responses produce (are correlated with) the same effect in the environment. For example, the operant "getting out of a seat" by a school child includes a wide variety of response topographies that together constitute a generic class because each of the individual responses has the equivalent functional effect of removing the child from contact with a school desk.

---

[3]In the remainder of this volume, the term "response" is used alone in all cases where the context clearly implies either "class" or "instance" or where the distinction is unimportant.

The third generic response class, requiring specific correspondence between the action event and both antecedent and subsequent environmental events, has been termed a *discriminated operant*. An example is the behavior of someone cooperating with a partner on a task. A variety of different responses are available for inclusion into a generic class, but a functional definition includes only those actions of the individual that *both* followed actions of the partner and facilitated progress in the task.

Labeling Response Classes

Labels are eventually attached to generic response classes at all levels of universality from a single discrete instance to classes as inclusive as "operants." This process is essentially one of experiential induction and refinement. Thus, labels are bestowed and refined through use, and the constancy of a label is dependent on the constancy of the behavioral phenomena to which it refers. A class like "respondent" retains its utility because of the constancy of the correspondence between environmental antecedents and responses that together serve to define it. The practice of allowing such classes to emerge at every level, rather than being determined in advance by rational definition, has great scientific value. Elements among the class may differ widely with respect to certain obvious characteristics such as topography; yet, because of the communality of effect, they are functionally equivalent. Events that are functionally equivalent are likely to share common determinants. Discovering these determinants will prove less difficult in the long run than will isolating the determinants of phenomena that resemble each other in a superficial or irrelevant aspect. As Skinner pointed out on several occasions, chemistry made its major advances only after it was discovered that weight, not color or shape, was the appropriate unifying dimension for classification.

It is unlikely that similar advances will occur in the science of behavior until the practice of decomposing and labeling classes of behavior in accordance with nonfunctional coding categories is discontinued. Imposing such irrelevant dimensions as limitations in observer skills, popularity of a particular published coding form, logistical convenience in certain institutional settings, and consistency with prevalent theoretical postures upon an otherwise unrestricted universe of behavioral events only impedes discovery of the natural, functional classificatory system. The possibility of developing a universal classification system solely on the basis of *functional* standards is all but guaranteed by the role (function) of behavior in adaptation and survival (see Chapter 3). Although results obtained in the context of definitional structures imposed with the above motivations may be quite orderly and agree nicely with the investigator's predictions, their generality to other situations is almost invariably negligible.

In contrast, the science of behavior requires that all definitional and measurement tactics adhere to a criteria of strict functionality, stripped of all possible surplus meaning and interpretation imparted by ill-considered use of terms from the natural language. For example, an investigator in a nursery school setting may wish to study "play behavior." How is play behavior to be functionally defined and measured? The term "play" has a legitimate behavioral referent—a subset of all responses that a child emits. What environmental contexts define the response classes into which these responses can be sorted? If no such classes can be isolated and recorded, we are forced to conclude that the term "play" is only functionally valid to the extent that it evokes a consistent response in some observer. As a discipline moves from naturalistic observation and taxonomy to precise measurement and analysis, categories that were functionally valid in the linguistic sense (everybody agreed on the assignment of instances) may fail to reflect orderly correspondences at the level of refinement afforded by sensitive descriptive measurement of the defining attributes. A science whose basic constructs depend solely on the natural language habits of the observer has little chance of systematic growth and success, as attested to by the fate of phrenology in 20th-century psychology.

Rather than clinging to the category "play," the investigator might better elect to specify the broadest possible range of behaviors of the target child and then begin classifying them in terms of communality of environmental effects. For instance, one classification might delineate those movements resulting in physical contact with another child, another might be defined by their effect on objects (toys, etc). in the environment, and so forth. Once such a classificatory scheme emerges, measurement of the several classes can be undertaken in an objective and reliable manner. After measurement has been achieved, experimental analysis may be attempted; independent variables may be selected and controlled and the effects observed in terms of changes within and across the classes of behavior. If, as is likely to happen, the effect of introducing controlled indepedent variables is to introduce noise into the data so that the measured properties of some members of the class change while others do not, the investigator should not yield to the temptation to use statistical averaging techniques to dampen the noise. Rather, functional classes may be further defined according to the communalities of an additional set of environmental factors. By repeating this process with several independent variables and occasionally replicating to ensure stability (definitional reliability), the investigator will inevitably accumulate a body of objective *facts* about the behavior of the individual under investigation. The meaning of these facts will be independent of their interpretation, because their orderliness derives from a property of nature under specific experimental control, not from an idiosyncratic observational bias imposed by the investigator.

The investigator may eventually attach verbal labels to the functional classes emerging from the process of measurement and control. Selecting these labels is a crucial activity that must be guided by a thorough understanding of the role played by linguistic factors in scientific communication. Any verbal label exerts a certain stimulus function on both the user and the audience. The impact on the user, in this case the investigator, is determined primarily by his or her idiosyncratic history through which the label acquired whatever linguistic function it serves. The investigator may insist that, "I know what I mean by play behavior" and, therefore, apprehend no need for the sort of functional definitional process we have suggested. This attitude usually disposes the holder to substitute a personal verbal history for an experimental analysis as the definitional mechanism with which to classify the subject matter of concern. This kind of substitution eventually produces a body of inspirational prose instead of a quantitative data base as the foundation for the induction of scientific laws. Although quantified measurement may be attempted later, the results must necessarily be spurious to the extent that a stable, empirical definition of the phenomenon is lacking.

Selecting a verbal label for a response class should anticipate the ultimate effects of the label as a verbal stimulus for members of the eventual audience. Psychology is replete with terms borrowed from the natural language and given technical meanings that compete, often successfully, with the more frequently used natural meanings. Terms such as stimulus, response, habit, drive, reward, and so on, are laden with surplus meaning that makes learning to use them in their correct technical sense a difficult task. Furthermore, response class labels such as avoidance, aggression, self-stimulation, preference, and attention are rarely anchored to discrete sets of environment–action correspondences and carry strong implications of cause or explanation that contaminate their utility as descriptors. For example, attempts to delineate the referents to a child's aggressive behavior in a discussion with teachers or parents become quickly and hopelessly befouled with hypothetical causes: "Your child is only aggressive when frustrated," or "my child bites people to get attention."

The clarity of communication about behavior with the aid of verbal labels for response classes is probably inversely proportional to the range of response topographies in the class being described. Thus, "door opening" is relatively unambiguous because there are a limited number of response topographies and environmental changes to which this term consistently applies. On the other hand, a term such as "playing" may subsume an almost limitless set of behavioral events, and empirical generalities applicable to the entire set may not be available for some time. Meanwhile, there is no assurance that results obtained by one investigator, who uses the term "play" to refer to a specific restricted set of properly defined responses, will apply to a different set used by a member of the scientific audience to whom the results are addressed. Many disputes over replicability and generality originated in this definitional slippage, but this source of disparity is typically overlooked in favor of efforts to delimit the population of organisms for which generality might hold. Thus, loose definitions of behavior force inappropriate restrictions on intersubject generality. This process results in reasserting the impossibility of discovering general laws of behavior in the face of the overwhelming complex of individual differences, and another scientific misfire thereby occurs from not clearly specifying the phenomenon of interest.

There is no immediate solution to the problems posed by the necessity of using language in scientific communication. The movement known as operationalism, which sought to restrict scientific definitions to the operations by which phenomena were observed or measured, was a step in the right direction, but was generally found too limiting in the natural sciences. Operationalism in psychology was widely discussed, but rarely practiced except for numerous premature attempts to lend rigor to such hopelessly vague notions as anxiety and intelligence.

Using the strategy of operationalism in defining response classes has rarely been attempted, in spite of its resounding success in early operant conditioning research (Skinner, 1953b). The operations for defining a pigeon's key peck, for example, are among the most unambiguous ever to emerge in any field, and the wealth of consistent, coherent, and replicable data that have been collected on that response class attests to the utility of a good operational definition as a starting point. Even in this relatively pure instance, however, occasional concern is expressed that the range of topographical variations allowed does not fully reflect the meaning of the word "peck," and some question whether "that behavior is really pecking."

Nonetheless, the key-pecking example clearly elucidates the necessary strategy. Specifying exactly the environmental events (switch closures) that result from movements by the pigeon delineate a fully functional response class. Though some subjectivity may still be associated with the word "peck," its contribution to scientific confusion is overwhelmed by the clarity and precision of the resulting data. This strategy easily generalizes to other classes of behavior, provided that attention is shifted from the implications of the verbal label to a clear specification of the environmental antecedents and/or consequents that consistently accompany instances.

TACTICS OF RESPONSE CLASS DEFINITION

Functional Response Class Definitions

The preceding discussion of strategic considerations in decomposing behavior into observable responses contended that the relations between the action of interest and the surrounding environmental stimuli are of paramount importance. Descriptions of response classes are accomplilshed by delineating a portion of the organism's repertoire by specifying functional relations between the action and environmental events and are thus termed functional response class definitions. Their explanation and rationale having already been thoroughly expounded, some tactical implications can now be addressed.

Specifying response classes in terms of antecedent and/or consequent stimuli with which there are functional relations has the obvious benefit of clarifying sources of environmental influence that must eventually be identified and understood. This definitional process is, therefore, the first step in the analysis of behavior. A subsequent effect of this process is the composition of a generic response class whose individual responses will necessarily have a common susceptibility to influence by specific classes of antecedent and/or consequent stimuli. This outcome diminishes the likelihood that the effects of the experimenter's manipulation of independent variables will be confounded with the effects of different ambient sources of influence. Interpretations of greater reliability and generality are made possible by constructing response classes having homogeneous relations with uncontrolled influences in the experimental setting.

As an example of some of these considerations, let us assume that we are investigating children who are described as being afraid of their parents and who apparently go out of their way to avoid them. Suppose, for example, that a particular child often hides from that child's father when the father approaches the area where the child is for any reason. In light of our earlier discussion, we would approach this problem by first noting all movements that result in the child's occupying a different location. We would then attempt to specify the range of antecedent events that immediately precede such movements. We would also consider in some detail the environmental consequents of each movement, taking care to note the proportion of times the class of movements was followed by spatial separation from the parent. If, as might be expected, a high correspondence emerges between instances of the father approaching and the initiation of such movements, and if a large portion of the movements preclude immediate interaction with the father, we will have begun to isolate the response class, "hiding from father." Definitions of the hiding response class incorporating individual responses having correlations with different antecedent and consequent stimulus classes than these may provide increased sources of variability. This result is particularly likely with experimental treatments that change the occurrence of some but not all of the smaller response classes that might be included in the larger defined class. For instance, if the definition of hiding responses did not include the approach of the father, then crawling under the porch upon the appearance of the neighbor's dog would be incorrectly designated as part of the response class, and an untimely demise of the dog would incorrectly appear to reduce hiding from father. The hypothetical data in Panel A of Fig. 6.2 shows how such a misinterpretation would arise.

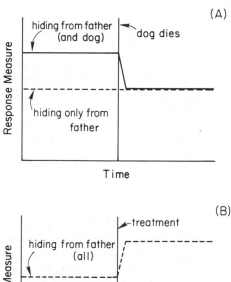

FIG. 6.2.   Schematic display of data from different response class definitions.

Another kind of distortion arises if the definition incorporates only a portion of the class of responses dictated by common stimulus relations. In this case, it is possible for treatment-induced changes to occur in the defined response class while additional response instances actually in the class of interest but not formally included do not change or change in an opposite manner. This would be the case if "hiding behind couch" responses were the only class specified; the occurrence of all other responses that successfully avoided the father might increase while "hiding behind couch" responses were actually decreasing. Once again, as Panel B of Fig. 6.2 illustrates, tactical errors at the definitional level would encourage interpretative decisions at variance with the facts of nature. Unfortunately, the instance of such errors can only be suspected (and hardly ever verified) when attempts to establish generality through replication do not succeed.

One final point is that in a somewhat trivial sense, any response that has been recorded has been functionally defined, if only with reference to its effects on the detection device, be it human observer or automatic transducer. In other words, the process of detection constitutes a change in a class of consequent environmental events that would presumably not have occurred in the absence of a response and that exhibits a virtually perfect correspondence with the movement itself. Whereas this consideration provides a vital criterion by which observing and recording procedures may be assessed (see Chapter 8), it should not constitute sole justification for the claim that a functional definition exists. The functional significance of behavior for the organism's adaptation and survival can only be examined with the aid of proper functional definitions relating movements to real environmental changes, not just to changes in transient and incidental recording devices.

It is not always possible outside of the laboratory to follow the considerations urged by functional response definitions. The correlations of movement classes with stimulus classes may be multiple or too subtle for realistic detection. Observing and recording certain response classes may present insurmountable ethical or financial difficulties, leading the investigator to substitute another response class or reluctantly deal with multiple response classes. Nonetheless, although these complications may preclude adherence to the ideals of functional definition, the influences that give rise to its importance will remain pervasive forces in the data and will ultimately determine the character of the science.

Topographical Response Class Definitions

Our earlier definition of behavior forecast the possibility of a second set of definitional practices. Whereas purely functional response class definitions ignore variation in the form or topography of each response in the class, it is obviously possible to ignore such functional relations by using form alone as the desired dimension of homogeneity for describing response classes. Specification of a response class solely in terms of the form in three-dimensional space of all instances constitutes a topographical definition. In one sense, this is an easy means of specifying the limits of response classes because the form of a response is often its most obvious characteristic. It is only necessary to describe some limits to the form, and observation is relatively straightforward.

Complictions may appear at later stages of the investigation, however, because topographical definitions may engender all of the difficulties imposed by subsuming different functional response classes under a single topographically defined class. Moreover, disregarding environmental determinants of topographical variation will plague the research in the guise of persistent variability, precluding the establishment of stable baselines and contributing to unreliable experimental effects.

These admonishments notwithstanding, there are indeed circumstances in which the topography of a portion of a repertoire is the dimension of compelling interest. It may be that the form of the response is the primary feature of interest, independent of the stimulus conditions prompting occurrences of the behavior and the consequences that affect future occurrences. For example, the topography of behavior is of central importance in early instruction in handwriting. The effects of writing topography (the exact shape of the letters) are not crucial as long as the letters can be read, but when the skill is first taught, it is considered helpful to emphasize a narrow topographical standard. The teacher may actually be able to read a child's crude approximation with perfect fluency, but the topography of the child's response is still improved to meet the requirements of the criterion.

Another example of the utility of a topographical response definition might be the case of obscene language in a 10-year-old child. It is the form of the response that is of primary importance, independent of both the social legitimacy of the prompting conditions and the effects of the obscenities on others. In addition, it would be virtually impossible to specify the consequent stimulus conditions defining a meaningful functional response class because reactions would vary within and between listeners.[4]

Variations and Refinements

The two preceding subsections have identified the characteristics of functional and topographical response class definitions. A number of possible variations on and refinements of these definitional tactics exist that can sometimes serve necessary and useful research goals. However, it must not escape notice that the following extensions do not involve any considerations that are new to this chapter. The conceptualization of behavior as "a portion of the organism–environment interaction" permits only two basic tactics of response class composition—functional and topographical—and all constructional practices necessarily elaborate one of these two fundamental themes.

Added Temporal Dimensions.   It is sometimes of interest to append the consideration of some temporal dimension of a behavior to the functional or topographical requirements for composing a response class. (It is impossible to define a response class solely in terms of a temporal dimension.) A special case of this variation involves the time between occurrences of discrete response instances. This is tantamount to requiring that all responses in a class meet the further qualification that no more (or no less) than a certain amount of time elapses following the preceding response. This response class

---

[4]This is the essence of the difficulty our legal system encounters in attempting to define obscenity.

refinement might be imposed when the frequency or pacing of responses is of such interest that individual responses otherwise sharing the same functional or topographical features can be excluded. An example is crew racing, in which the response time between the pulling of the oars, regulated by the rhythmic chanting of the coxswain, is a major determinant of the outcome of the race.

Another temporal refinement adds the dimension of stimulus–response latency to the basic functional or topographical requirements for a response class. In this case, a particular response is included only if there is a certain minimum or maximum latency between some stimulus event and the onset of the response. This option might be exercised when a safety engineer is interested in how quickly an employee initiates corrective action following the signaling of an unsafe condition.

Finally, the added temporal dimension may concern the time required for completing the individual movement. That is, in addition to either functional or topographical features, the duration of each response from beginning to completion may be the characteristic of major importance, as is the case in surgery in which the concern is the rapidity with which a bleeding artery can be tied off.

Response Products. It is not uncommon for the most obvious environmental effects of responses in a class to be some physical product that they produce. Examples include an English composition that results from writing behavior, completed subassemblies in a factory as a consequence of assembling behavior, or the litter in a city park as an effect of use by the citizenry. Using such products to define response classes is a useful tactical variation of the strategy of functionally defining response classes.

Sometimes measuring the product or result of a response class is the only feasible means of observing and recording (see Chapter 8). This is usually the case when it is necessary to record infrequent instances of behavior over extended periods of time without the benefit of mechanical or electrical devices. The National Park Service employs this tactic when it estimates the density of use of a remote mountain hiking trail with a log book that hikers are asked to sign when they start out. A variation of this practice is the use of *behavior seals*, exemplified by the classic spy tactic of placing a hair across a closet door before leaving a hotel room so that, upon returning, one can tell if the closet has been searched by seeing if the hair has been disturbed.

Response products can be a highly practical and perfectly valid basis upon which to designate a response class. There are, however, two special considerations that can complicate interpreting data gathered with this kind of definition. For example, the owner of two young puppies who comes home to find a single pile of excrement on the living room rug will recognize the problem of attributing authorship of the defecation response that resulted in the odiferous product. This is the same problem that faces the teacher who observes that the English composition turned in by nearly illiterate Johnny is striking in its resemblance to the literary style of his erudite girlfriend. A park ranger may, likewise, question the existence of a group of hikers that included George Washington, John the Baptist, and Lenny Bruce.

In addition to determining the authorship of responses, a further caveat peculiar to response product designations is illustrated by attempting to determine the number of people using a city park by counting pieces of litter. It is sometimes impossible to assure a one-to-one correspondence between response products and actual movements. For the investigator trying to influence the frequency of a response, this kind of definitional tactic may reveal that the response either did not occur or occurred at least once; however, there may be no means of determining the exact number of occurrences. This possible insensitivity is often intolerable for any but the coarsest descriptions.

Another possible limitation of this definitional tactic (and of all functional definitions) arises from the inherent lack of contact with the topographical variations that characterize the movement class. Simply viewing a response product usually conveys very little of the topographical detail of the movement that produced it. It is, of course, possible that by tightly specifying the antecedent and subsequent environmental conditions that surround the movement, very little topographical variation will be allowed and can be safely disregarded. Filling in the blanks on a machine-scored multiple choice test furnishes a convenient example; if the "wrong" blank is filled in for a particular item, that fact provides little or no behavioral clue as to the reason for the error. Those concerned with improving the topographical or temporal details of a particular class of responses usually find that sole reliance on products for definitional purposes is intolerably limiting. On the other hand, designation of responses by products alone may encourage detecting useful topographical variations that would otherwise be precluded or neglected.

These potential limitations demand the extreme caution of the researcher who is considering defining a response class solely in terms of products. However, if response authorship and a one-to-one correspondence between movements and products can be assured and if topographical variation is not of concern, this tactic may be extremely useful. The response product itself may be the focus of social or research interest, as is frequently the case in industrial, educational, and training settings. In industry, the predominant concern lies with assembling marketable products, and the response topographies required for their construction are often adequately constrained by the equipment the worker uses. Similarly, in educational and training enterprises, evaluation functions are most easily served by attending to the final products of various academic responses (although instructional goals probably necessitate interest in exactly how academic products are created).

Whatever the setting, a notable convenience of this definitional practice is the fact that the observational chores are often reduced to the relatively simple task of enumerating tangible products.

Individuals in Groups. Thus far, we have considered various means of composing response classes for an individual subject. This is appropriate, because interest usually centers on the description, analysis, and prediction of the behavior of an individual. However, there are times when primary interest lies in individuals only as contributing members of a group, and it is the aggregated behavior of such individuals that we might call the "behavior" of the group. It is imperative to remember that this is an arbitrary designation. *The group is not an organism and therefore cannot behave*; the individuals in it behave. Hence, there exists no such natural phenomenon as "group behavior." Nevertheless, the collected behavior of the individuals in a group may, on occasion, be the focus of investigation. In such cases, the definitional tactics already described may be modified to apply to this behavior.

There exist three basic ways in which the behavior of individuals can combine to constitute aggregate actions. The first is exemplified by studying the noise made by a class of second graders. If a recording device is used to make a continuous record of sound levels in the classroom, the collective and equivalent response effects of some or all individuals are being measured simultaneously. In this case, a functional definition of the group's responding takes into account the prompting stimulus properties of the group's other individuals on the response of each person in the group.

In a slightly different light, interest may center on an arbitrarily defined collection of individuals who do not interact among themselves in the traditional sense of a group, but who may all respond in the same way in the same setting at least once. This is illustrated by the purchasing behavior of customers in a commercial establishment. We might arrange to identify (by means of sales receipts) purchasing responses emitted by a collection of different people who each make at least one response while in the store.

Finally, consider the case in which each individual makes a distinctly different behavioral contribution to a group effort. For instance, a manufacturer is interested in the single product resulting from different responses of different workers.

The unique implications that must be acknowledged in defining group response classes are inexorably related to the fact that the behaver is not a single organism, but is instead a number of different behaving organisms. It is imperative that this condition restrict experimental interpretations, and the extensions of this restriction are pervasive. For instance, it is virtually impossible to isolate the causes of variation in some measure of the group "response." A decrease in the sound level of the second grade class could be produced by many variations in the noise-producing activities of the different students. The data would not reveal whether absenteeism was high or whether only some of the students were quiet while others were just as noisy as previously. Alternatively, if half the class had gotten quieter while half had gotten louder, data showing no change in class noise levels would not indicate this.

A related difficulty is that whether or not experimental manipulations designed to change the group's "behavior" are successful, the effects of such interventions are always on the behavior of the group's different individuals, although only a collective response is measured. It is unlikely that a single intervention will identically affect all individuals with their unique histories and determining environments. Because only an aggregate response is measured, an understanding of how the effect on the group response was produced through the individuals will be unavoidably obscured.

Legitimate deployment of group response definitional tactics is a rare though not impossible occurrence in the science of behavior. Certain phenomena peculiar to crowds and mobs are undoubtedly best described in this manner, although the search for the determinants of these phenomena in the behavioral histories of the members of the throng requires appropriate behavioral definition at the individual level. However, researchers professing a general interest in behavioral phenomena all too often justify group definitional practices on the grounds of economy or convenience, thereby unwittingly exposing themselves to the interpretative hazards discussed above. This is especially true in educational contexts, in which the interest may be in changing the collective performance of all the pupils in a district, or in whether or not a particular procedure applied uniformly to all trainees reduces the total training time for the group as a whole. Regardless of such interests, behavior is a process characteristic of individual organisms, and its determinants can only be discovered at that level. Blurring the effects of these determinants by studying aggregate phenomena only loosely related to them severely retards the discovery process while perpetuating the dissemination of misinformation.

Response Opportunities.   The final definitional tactic to be discussed is neither a variation nor a refinement of any of the foregoing, but might be more accurately described as a definitional observation. Because behavior is one of the characteristics of living as opposed to dead organisms, it may be correctly argued that a living person cannot *not* do anything. A person can, however, not do a particular thing at a certain time, and when it is that particular response class that is of interest, it is occasionally tempting to talk about "not doing something." It must be realized, of course, that when someone is not engaging in the behavior of interest, that person is doing some other things, because no one can be in a behavioral void. Nevertheless, it is possible to describe "not doing something" if the beginning and end of those an inductive leap of no slight risk. Before exploring the difficulties that plague this practice, it is important to realize that when interest seems to focus on a corresponding behavioral opportunities can be clearly specified. This is frequently arranged with reference to some antecedent stimulus event that might normally participate in defining the generic response class. For example, a child's "response" of not hitting other children would probably be defined with reference to a more specific list of antecedent events such as having a toy taken away, or being hit by another child.

Clearly, however, extrapolating conditions defining an observable response class to the case of a class that is nonobservable by definition involves nonresponse, the concern, in fact, lies with a particular response that occurs infrequently. It is more accurate to insist that there is no such phenomenon as a nonresponse; rather, there is a response class for which particular instances can occur or not occur, and it is this class that is the object of inquiry.

A practical complication with response opportunity definitional tactics lies in the functional designation of the prompting stimulus event used to specify an opportunity for the response to occur or not occur. The antecedent stimulus may, in fact, also be a signal prompting the occurrence of a number of other responses that are incompatible with the response of interest (e.g., running away instead of hitting). In other words, the response may not occur because it cannot, even if the experimenter is unaware of this conflict. In addition, the defining stimulus event may lose its functional effect on the response and thus its meaning as a defining stimulus property (e.g., the toy taken away is no longer a reinforcer). Also, other stimuli in the environment (e.g., being teased) may enter into such functional relations even though they may not have originally provided opportunities for the occurrence or nonoccurrence of the response. In other words, specifying the functional antecedents of a nonresponse entails special imperilments.

Another kind of difficulty concerns the class of consequent stimuli to which the response opportunity is related. Whereas it may seem reasonable to talk about the effect on the environment of "not doing something," other responses were necessarily emitted when the response of interest was not, and each had its environmental effects. In addition, manipulating the consequences of the nonoccurrence of a response in order to influence its probability of occurrence means arranging consequences that are actually contingent on whatever responses are occurring instead. The contiguous relation between the nonresponse and some environmental consequence does not guarantee that a functional relation will result. More probably, the functional relation will involve some other, unidentified responses. For example, the nonhitter might discover that biting is a more effective way of inducing compliance on the part of adversaries, and the parent who praised nonhitting might actually increase the frequency of biting. All of these considerations underscore the importance of defining, observing, and recording the *occurrence* of a response selected from the existing and observable repertoire of the organism.

ADDITIONAL CONSIDERATIONS

Response Sensitivity

It should be obvious that any investigator would wish for a response definition to specify responses that are sensitive to those independent variables intended for experimental manipulation. Too often, however, special considerations in applied settings (such as the social or clinical significance of the behavior) dominate definitional decisions, and sensitivity to experimental variables can become a luxury. Unfortunately, the consequences can be experimentally fatal.

Experimental analysis requires that response parameters exhibit wide variability so that the effects of independent variables may be easily detected. This creates the necessity for response sensitivity. Some sensitivity is usually sacrificed when the response occurs at the extremes of frequency. If any kind of upper or lower limit on the frequency of a behavior is operative, the measured responses may not reveal the effects of a variable that would otherwise exert an influence. For instance, in an assertiveness training program, the response of initiating conversations is clearly limited by the number of possible daily contacts. If a certain client is already initiating conversations at all opportunities, it would be impossible for a change in a powerful contingency to increase the response frequency further. In addition, if a response occurs only rarely, it may receive too little exposure to an experimental variable and as a result not manifest a functional relation that might be readily observed if the exposure frequency were greater. In other words, selecting a response class whose members occur as infrequently as once a month entails the risk of not revealing the effect of an independent variable that would be powerful if the frequency of occurrence were higher.

Even when a measurable parameter varies over a wide range, another danger may be that it is almost entirely dependent on a single variable not under the control of the experimenter, causing insensitivity to manipulated variables. For example, it is commonly observed in educational settings that academic responses are so heavily influenced by social variables that potentially potent curriculum innovations are interpreted to be ineffective. Even if this were not the case, the defined response must still be subject to the effects of the variable under investigation. This is expecially true in field settings in which the goal is often to isolate variables to which the response of interest is sensitive, instead of investigating the effects of preselected variables.

Finally, the consideration of response sensitivity must include cases in which the defined response is sensitive to too many variables, especially those not known to or under the control of the experimenter. The result will be a high level of noise that cannot be dampened enough for the influence of a single variable to be observed. There is probably no better illustration than verbal behavior; psychotherapists' influences on self-deprecating statements may be difficult to detect because of a vast array of other determinants of such responses.

If it seems from this discussion that response sensitivity added to the other concerns may be the straw that breaks the camel's back, it sometimes is. The inability to define (and observe) a response appropriately sensitive to variables under investigation can preclude experimentation (or at least make it futile) and will always be eligible as an explanation of why a behavior was not influenced by some treatment. In the long run, it is easiest and most efficient to satisfy empirically the requirement of response sensitivity prior to formal experimentation, thus minimizing the chances for fruitless and costly manipulation of experimental variables.

Unit of Analysis

In discussing strategies of response class definition at the beginning of this chapter, we called attention to the fact that there is no single point on the molar–molecular dimension that specifies a uniquely and universally appropriate unit of analysis. The partitioning of one response class out of the repertoire of an active organism is always arbitrary to some degree. Deciding the power to which the microscope of measurement should be adjusted (especially in field settings) partially depends on the question prompting the research, data already available, and the degree of experimental control that is attainable. The salient issue is the breadth or specificity of the defined response class. Even with good functional definitions, numerous subclasses of responses may be extracted from the relatively molar slice of behavior originally described. For example, in examining the behavior of an assembly line worker installing wheels on each car moving past the work station, the response class of installing wheels can be defined as the entire chain of responses from picking up the wheel to tightening the last nut, and the whole chain will constitute a single unit of analysis. This unit, however, can also be decomposed into any number of functionally and/or topographically different response classes still comprising the larger unit. Each of the subclasses can be further decomposed for unitary analysis, or subclasses can be recombined at any level to produce different functional response classes. The number of possibilities is virtually limitless.

The "size" of the selected unit of analysis can be most important. Too small a slice of behavior may display variability whose determinants have no direct relevance for the question under investigation, whereas too large a slice may mask potentially important sources of variability. The convenience of the latter case ensures that it is the more frequent cause of difficulties. For instance, simply recording the frequency of the entire assembly task will not show whether a low response rate results from an improper sequence of certain response subclasses, the topography of a particular response subclass, or the occasional intrusion of other response classes that interrupt the chain.

There are two special cases of this aspect of response definition that require further discussion. Specifying the unit of analysis can be a particularly difficult problem when the behavior of interest occurs at the extremes of frequency. Let us first consider the example of a delinquent youth in a training school who repeatedly strikes peers and often gets in fights with them. The response of hitting someone may occur with moderate frequency throughout the day, but sometimes a number of responses may occur closely in succession, especially when the victim retaliates. It may be difficult to observe discrete hitting responses accurately under these conditions. One solution (which need not violate functional strategies) is to combine each collection of such instances into an *episode* of responding that constitutes a single response class of lesser frequency. This tactic is not without pitfalls, however. For example, it may be that the youth decreases the number of episodes per unit time, but increases the number of responses in each episode, or it might be more likely that the converse would occur. In both instances, the result of shifting to a more molar unit of analysis is the possibility of obscuring important changes in responding.

The second special case arises when the response of interest occurs very infrequently. One such instance might be customers who make purchases in the stores in a large shopping mall. An individual customer may actually purchase items only occasionally (two or three times a month), providing a baseline whose variability is truncated by proximity to its lower limit. A tactic that can ameliorate this handicap involves carefully examining the different responses that compose the larger unit in an effort to discover a response class that is invariably part of the larger unit but that may occur independently and hence more frequently. In the example, it may be observed that purchasing is always preceded by walking around to different stores, looking at merchandise, or asking questions of salespersons. These behaviors may occur much more frequently than actual purchasing and may thus provide the investigator with meaningful response classes more suited to analysis but equally relevant to the original question.

Defining response classes involves delicate interplay of demands and limitations from different sources. Most importantly, the nature of behavior as a natural phenomenon requires taking account of the role of environmental factors in the basic definitional process. The experimental question, the investigator, the research design, the social significance and the characteristics of the subject's behavior, and the features of the research setting may exert conflicting influences. This necessitates a balanced compromise among the different interests that must be guided by the issue of how much precision is needed in each case. For instance, a certain degree of inaccuracy in response definition may be acceptable if other aspects of measurement and design are sufficiently stringent in their demands on the data that the final results are valid and generalizable. Of course, if there are unavoidable sources of error elsewhere in the experiment, there may be only very close tolerances permissible for the response class definition. However, because the barriers to accurate measurement and convincing experimentation are still unknown at this early stage, it is incumbent on the researcher to spare no tactical effort to minimize definitional sources of error that are within his or her control.

7 Dimensional Quantities and Units of Behavioral Measurement

Time is nature's way of keeping everything from happening at once.

—Anon.

INTRODUCTION

Measurement has already been defined as the process of assigning numbers and units to objects or events. For this definition to be of any value, a clear understanding of the meaning of the word *unit* is imperative. According to Webster, a unit is "a determinate quantity adopted as a standard of measurement." Used in science, the phrase "of some dimension of a property of a natural phenomenon" is inserted in the definition after "quantity" to

119

underscore the anchoring of the measurement process in the real world. Thus, using the phrase "unit of measurement" scientifically implies that measurement is accomplished in terms of standard quantities or amounts of some dimension of the unit of analysis. Clearly then, the unit of analysis and the unit of measurement are related to the extent that the existence of one permits designation of the other, but they are in no sense equivalent. Variation in the unit of analysis requires a fixed unit of measurement for its description (an epistemological precept ignored by the progenitors of vaganotic measurement), and thus they cannot be identical (see Chapter 6).

In our earlier discussion of the history of measurement in science, we noted that the natural sciences have uniformly relied upon absolute units of measurement and that the history of science is in many ways coextensive with the development of such units. Absolute units are those whose definition is independent of the measurement operation (though not necessarily of the measuring device) and that are not defined inductively from variability in the phenomenon under consideration. Chapter 4 described this as the essence of idemnotic measurement. In extending idemnotic measurement to the natural science of behavior, it might be presumed that a search should be conducted for absolute units of behavioral measurement, if only to justify using the term "natural." Such a search, however, can advance with greater certainty if we first consider the purposes served by measurement, not only in science but in all human affairs.

THE IMPORTANCE OF UNITS

Simple quantification is a necessary component of the three basic functions of measurement—description, comparison, and prediction. The most fundamental use of quantification is for simple *description*—the act of attaching a number to a phenomenon or event to distinguish it from others that might otherwise be considered equivalent. If quantification has occurred, any two objects or events may be *compared* with respect to the results of that process. Comparison is almost always made in terms of a measurable dimension of a common property shared by the objects or events. Simple descriptive quantification does not require a dimension. *Prediction* may be defined as the anticipated outcome of a presently unknown or future measurement. It is the most elegant use of quantification upon which validation of all scientific and technological activity rests. Accuracy and confirmation of prediction establish the generality and continuity of scientific laws and occasion the confident application of such laws in developing technology.

In addition, measurement involves attaching some unit to the numerical result of the quantifying operation. As stated above, the unit explicitly refers to the dimension of the object or event being measured. When asked to report

THE IMPORTANCE OF UNITS   121

one's height, one might say, "182 centimeters"; the number 182 is an incomplete response to the query, because a dimension has not been specified. Addition of the unit "centimeters" specifies a standard, referent instance of length, the dimension in question. Because the centimeter is an absolute and invariant referent, the descriptive phrase "182 centimeters" has only a single meaning, and its application to the single case is therefore unambiguous. If, however, the centimeter were defined vaganotically as, for example, the standard deviation of the length in inches of 100 randomly drawn pieces of string, the constancy of the unit would be destroyed, although reference to the dimension of length would remain. The meaning of the unit so defined would vary with each sample of 100 pieces of string and would, consequently, be useless as a descriptor of the length of a single object without reference to the population from which the calibration sample was drawn. Thus, even at the level of description, measurement in terms of absolute units possesses distinct advantages.

In performing the function of comparison, using absolute units is requisite to meaningfully applying the laws of arithmetic, not to mention higher mathematics, to the results of measurement. One can compare 6 to 2 by saying that 6 is 4 greater than 2, or 3 times 2. Specifying an absolute unit such as grams makes these statements true with regard to the dimensions of weight. These mathematical statements are not necessarily true, however, in the case of a relative unit such as "years" of mental age, because the relation of the unit to the assumed underlying dimension of intelligence is not invariant and cannot be combined by either addition or multiplication. Because such units are subject to redefinition as often as measurement takes place, 5 today may become 7 tomorrow. It is difficult to build a body of quantitative fact over time with such mercurial properties inherent in the measurement.

A brief example will highlight the need for absolute units in comparisons. Suppose we wish to go out for an evening on the town and enjoy a steak dinner, but are operating on a limited budget. In order to avoid embarrassment, we decide to comparison shop by calling two restaurants. One says the cheapest steak on the menu is $4.95; the other says that steak begins at 1.5 standard deviations (90¢) above the mean price of all entrees. Which restaurant has the cheaper steak? How much cheaper? These questions cannot be answered, because the unit (S.D.) given by the second restaurant has no relation to that used by the first. Indeed, the present value of 1.5 S.D. above the mean would change with each addition of a new entree (assuming the actual price of the cheapest steak remained constant), or, if the 1.5 remained constant, the actual price of the steak could vary with any change in the menu. Of course, if the second restaurant were to provide the dollar value of the mean and standard deviation, we could compute the price of the steak and make a comparison in terms of the idemnotic unit, dollars. The point is, we cannot make a useful comparison from the information given, although it is customary in educational settings to support comparative decisions involving children with exactly the type of measurement offered by the second restaurant.

Prediction differs from the two simpler uses of measurement by almost always requiring repeated measurements taken over time. As changes in the results of successive measurement operations are noted, a statement describing these changes as a function of time may be generated and used to predict the outcome of a measurement made at a specified future time. Suppose, for example, a pipe bursts and begins discharging water into our basement. If we measure the depth of the water at a certain time and repeat the measurement five minutes later, we can accurately predict how deep the water will be at the end of an hour, assuming the rate of flow remains constant and we know the shape of the basement in three dimensions. We can also determine the exact time at which the furnace will disappear under water. It would be of little value, as we place a frantic call to the plumber, to know that the volume of our basement is 1.3 standard deviations above the mean for the neighborhood or that there was 100% agreement among three independent judges that the size of the hole in the pipe was less than 2 on a 5-point scale.

Incorporating absolute units in the measurement process obviously affords indispensible benefits in description, comparison, and prediction. Inasmuch as these operations constitute a major portion of the quantitative activity within any science, it is imperative that absolute units of behavioral measurement become standardized and universally applied if the science of behavior is to reach its potential as a coherent and fully integrated discipline.

THE NATURAL BASIS FOR UNITS

In our earlier discussion of behavior as a biological phenomenon, we stressed the fact that behavior is an important and continuous interface between an organism and its environment and that, for convenience, this interface can be viewed as a series of discrete interactive events (responses) that take place through time. At issue in selecting a measurement unit is the necessity of ensuring sensitivity to the details and nuances of change in this interactive process. In other words, whatever unit is chosen must have immediate and obvious validity for description of the organism-environment interaction and must be capable of reflecting changes resulting from deliberately imposed changes in the environmental component. One would hardly use a ruler to measure temperature, not because units of length are not absolute or sensitive, but because they do not apply to the dimension or property being measured. If natural phenomena are to be measured scientifically, properties of interest must be expressed in terms of their quantifiable aspects, called *dimensional quantities,* for which units may be identified. Thus, the property of motion gives rise to the dimensional quantities of speed and acceleration; the property of physical extent yields the dimensional quantities of mass and distance. A property cannot be described quantitatively until an appropriate dimensional quantity has been specified, whereupon a unit specifying some standard amount can be selected.

Single Response Dimensional Quantities

What are the properties of behavior from which suitable dimensional quantities (and subsequent units) may be extracted? Such properties must be universal—that is, common to all behavioral events in the same sense that linear extent is common to all real objects. Furthermore, they must not be trivial, but must relate to or derive from the functional significance of behavior to the survival of the organism.

Not surprisingly, the considerations that led to our general definition of behavior also imply the universal properties underlying dimensional quantities from which measurement units may be derived. Instances of behavioral transactions between organism and environment occur in time and take time for their occurrence. Thus, one property of any instance of a behavior is its *temporal locus,* whereas another is its *temporal extent.* The importance of time as a parameter describing the flow of events that determine the survival of an organism can scarcely be gainsaid; hence, we may be assured that a temporal basis for dimensional quantities will not purchase triviality for the sake of universality. Time is a fundamental parameter of behavior. The properties of temporal locus and temporal extent share time as a common parameter and are represented by the dimensional quantities of *latency* and *duration,* respectively. Whatever else one may wish to say about any instance of behavior, it will always possess these dimensional quantities that represent nontrivial characteristics of behavior as a mechanism of adaptation.

Instances of behavioral transactions between organism and environment also possess the third universal property of *repeatability* through time. The characteristic of repeatability is likewise critically related to the functional value of behavior in survival. If an organism is to survive to reproduction, it must react in a consistent manner to each recurrence of specific environmental demands. An organism that required 20 years to mature, but could eat only once would either contradict all known principles of metabolic homeostasis or would not survive to reproduction. Repeatability of behavior is, therefore, requisite to adaptation and survival and dictates the dimensional quantity known as *denumerability* or *countability.*

Thus, there exist three fundamental dimensional quantities of behavior that may form the basis for creation of units of measurement: countability, latency, and duration. Every instance of a behavior may be characterized by the temporal location of its occurrence relative to other environmental and/or behavioral events, and the time required for its occurrence. Any series of such instances possesses denumerability, and the instances are, therefore, countable. These dimensional quantities of behavior are universal in that they exist in every case.

Response Class Dimensional Quantities

These three fundamental dimensional quantities are universally characteristic of the single instance of behavior (with the countability dimension having 1 as its only value). Expanding the domain to a class of instances reveals additional dimensional quantities that universally describe series of occurrences of single instances of the response class. That is, when a collection of responses are considered in toto, certain dimensional quantities not applicable to the single case emerge. Of greatest scientific impact is the dimensional quantity of *frequency,* which reflects the properties of both temporal locus and repeatability and is universally descriptive of any collection of responses that occur in real time. Skinner (1938) regarded a measure of this dimensional quantity as the fundamental datum in the scientific study of operant behavior and devised ingenious methods for its measurement in the laboratory.[1]

Closely related to the dimensional quantity of frequency is the capability of behavior to exhibit change over time. Just as matter in motion possesses the dimensional quantities of velocity and acceleration, behavior recurring in time reveals momentary frequencies that change over time. Differentiating frequency with respect to time yields a dimensional quantity known as *celeration* (Lindsley, 1969), which is a universal quantifier of the dynamic, changeable character of behavior. Measures of this dimensional quantity (e.g., responses per minute per day) resemble measures of physical acceleration in that the basic parameter of time appears twice in the descriptor. Thus, two fundamental properties of behavior—temporal locus

---

[1]Skinner actually used the term *rate* rather than freqency to describe this dimensional quantity, although the two are often used interchangeably. We prefer the term frequency because of the closer kinship to its standard scientific usage denoting the number of repetitions of a periodic process per unit of time and because of the confusion induced by the myriad other meanings of the word rate (i.e., price, "what is the going rate for a single room?"; subjective quality, "How does this contestant rate?", etc.). Unfortunately, there is another generic scientific meaning of the term frequency that refers to the number of a specific set of events per unitary value of an independent variable (e.g., number of responses per reinforcement, number of children per household, etc.). However, there is little danger of confusion, because the unit associated with the behavioral dimensional quantity of frequency will always include a time factor (e.g., responses per minute).

and repeatability—combine to define the dimensional quantity descriptive of change.

A third dimensional quality characteristic of a set of repeated instances of a class of responses is known as *interresponse time (IRT)*. Technically, the IRT of a given response is defined as the time interval separating the onset of that response instance from the cessation of the previous response instance.[2] The temporal locus properties of two responses therefore combine to define this dimensional quantity of the single case; the property of repeatability is thus invoked in specifying an IRT. Any single response has a temporal locus, but the IRT can only be designated with reference to the temporal locus of the preceding response, so two responses are required.

There are a number of other dimensional quantities that may be applied to a class of responses occurring serially in time. Such quantities as *quarter-life* (a measure of the time required to emit 25% of the responses that are eventually emitted between occurrences of a reinforcing event that is delivered in accordance with a fixed-interval schedule) and *IRT's per opportunity* (a measure of the likelihood of occurrence of specific IRT values that accounts for the mutual exclusivity of all shorter IRT's in each instance of a given IRT range) have been defined to provide technically useful descriptions of patterns of response occurrence that are also derived from the basic properties of temporal locus and repeatability. In principle, many such dimensional quantities can be specified, but their descriptive utility and generality must be established in the course of scientific practice.

Multiclass Dimensional Quantities

The repertoire of any behaving organism is composed of a vast multitude of response classes, more than one of which is likely to be observed in even short periods of time. Dimensional quantities applicable to the separate response classes are also applicable to aggregate classes. Thus, if each response class has a frequency, so does any combination of classes. Classes do exhibit countability, just as countability is a dimensional quantity of a single class or collection, but it is probably meaningless to speak of a frequency of the repertoire, because classes do not exhibit the property of recurrence as single instances do. Behavior, from the single response to the response class to the multiclass repertoire, is possessed of no shortage of measurable dimensional quantities, but this fact alone does not guarantee utilitarian measurement in the scientific sense. Among other considerations, meaningful units of

---

[2]IRT is also occasionally defined as the interval separating the onsets of two successive responses. This is done in cases in which the duration of responses is extremely small and the error resulting from their inclusion is negligible.

measurement and operations of combination must be specified. It is to this problem that we now turn.

SPECIFYING UNITS AND MEASURES

Units of measurement depend on dimensional quantities for their existence and definition. A unit is a fixed, standard amount, usually arbitrarily selected, of a dimensional quantity. Once selected, a unit provides a stable referent for any quantitative statement made with respect to the dimensional quantity, and measurement becomes not only possible, but meaningful. Thus, statements about amounts of the dimensional quantity of linear extent can be made in terms of units such as the meter (defined as 1,650,763.73 wavelengths of a certain orange line in the spectrum of the Krypton isotope of atomic mass number 86). All other units of length can be exhibited as multiples or submultiples of this quantity. Units of the various dimensional quantities of motion (velocity, momentum, acceleration, etc.) are formed as compounds of the unitary quantities of the basic dimensional quantities of distance, mass, and time. For instance, velocity is measured in terms of meters per second, momentum in terms of kilogram meters per second, and acceleration in terms of meters per second per second.

Basic and Compound Units

The dimensional quantities descriptive of a single instance of a behavioral class are latency, duration, and countability. Latency and duration measures have time as a common, parameter, and *units of time* are used to specify precisely unitary amounts of these dimensional quantities. Time units are absolute and standard across all applications, based as they are on atomic phenomena that do not vary from one instance to the next; the second as the basic unit is defined with reference to the vibration frequency of the cesium atom of atomic mass number 133. Against this standard, all timing devices can be calibrated and checked for accuracy. This would be impossible if the second as a unit of time measurement were defined vaganotically by the variability in rate of motion of a random sample of clocks. Time units are, therefore, absolute and universal descriptors of two of the three dimensional quantities of behavior and are, thus, basic units of behavioral measurement.

The dimensional quantity of denumerability or countability requires that a universal property of all instances be designated as the unit descriptor. The very fact of recurrence impels applying the concept of *cycle* as the unit designator of the single instance, because it is used in the natural sciences as the generic descriptor of the unitary instance of any naturally recurrent phenomenon. The cycle as the basic unit of measurement of the dimensional quantity of countability reflects the universal property of repeatability as characteristic of any behavioral unit of analysis. Thus, regardless of the characteristics defining a response class of interest, all responses in that class are single cycles of a recurrent or repeatable process. Measuring any unit of behavioral analysis, then, can be achieved by specifying the quantitative extent, or countability, of its cycles. This is accomplished by counting.

Enumerating cycles plays a substantial role in specifying units for measurement of the dimensional quantities of a class of recurring instances. The dimensional quantity of frequency is described by the compound unit of the generic form *cycles per unit time.* The defining dimensional quantities of latency and countability are thus combined in this compound unit, assuring descriptive measurement in terms exactly isomorphic to the dimensional quantity of interest. Describing recurring behavioral events in terms of cycles per unit time uses the dimensional quantity of frequency in exactly the manner that it is used in describing similar properties of sound or electromagnetic phenomena. The characteristic common to all is repeatable motion, for which frequency is an invariant dimensional quantity.

The universal dimensional quantity descriptive of behavior change is celeration, a measure of frequency change with respect to time. The natural generic unit for quantification of this dimensional quantity is the compound *cycles per unit time per unit time,* just as feet/sec^2 is a conventional unit for measuring velocity changes of a moving object.

Other dimensional quantities associated with response classes include interresponse time, quarter-life, and IRT per opportunity. These quantities all reflect the behavioral properties of repeatability and temporal locus and are measured with appropriate time and cycle units. The unit of measure for IRT is *time per cycle,* which, in the case of a specific single response instance, reduces to a time unit. In describing quarter-life, cycles and time units combine in the form of cycles × time per cycle, the cycles cancel, and a time unit is left as the descriptor. In measuring IRT per opportunity, cycles having specified IRT characteristics are collected and counted, and these cycle counts then serve as measures of the specific categories. Pattern characteristics are described by an ordered sequence of such cycle counts.

The foregoing extensive discussion of behavioral properties, dimensional quantities, and units of measurement is undoubtedly new to many readers. As an aid to organizing and working with this material, Table 7.1 is a summary of the relations of properties to dimensional quantities and dimensional quantities to units.

Moving from the multi-instance class of equivalent responses to the multiclass repertoire does not appear to occasion the emergence of any additional properties of behavior, hence no new dimensional quantities exist for which units must be specified. Repeatability, temporal locus, and temporal extent are sufficient to describe all classes and responses within classes, and

TABLE 7.1
Properties, Dimensional Quantities, and Units of Behavioral Measurement

Property	Dimensional Quantity	Unit
Temporal Locus	Latency	Time Units
Temporal Extent	Duration	Time Units
Repeatability	Countability	Cycle
Temporal Locus and Repeatability	Frequency	Cycles/Unit Time
Temporal Locus and Repeatability	Celeration	Cycles/Unit Time/Unit Time
Temporal Locus and Repeatability	IRT	Time/Cycle

the concept of a repertoire of multiple classes exists more for the purpose of simplification and organization than for exhaustive description.

The dimensional quantity of countability exists trivially with respect to classes; if distinct classes can be identified and defined, they can be counted, the count measure serving to summarize this property of the repertoire. Class countability is not a basic property of behavior but a consequence of our classificatory practices. Classes are not possessed of repeatability apart from the extent to which that property characterizes responses within them; hence, the dimensional quantity of class countability does not derive from a fundamental property of behavior.

The existence of multiple classes does permit the logical identification of behavioral events that are contained in the union, intersection, or ordered sequence of two or more classes (see Chapter 6). Such composite elements necessarily exhibit the temporal and repeatability properties of any other behavioral events, so that frequency and celeration, for example, can be measured with the aid of the appropriate units.

To illustrate, consider two response classes, R and S composed of instances r_i and s_i, respectively. We can specify an event as defined by the occurrence of r_i, or s_i, r_i and s_i together in either order, r_i followed by s_i or s_i followed by r_i. The set of all instances defined by any one of these four conditions would constitute a legitimate composite response class. Consequently, units of the form cycles per unit time, time per cycle, etc., are applicable, and quantification can occur as with the multi-instance class with the relevant dimensional quantity preserved.

Measures

Descriptive measurement requires more than specifying a unit. Measurement also involves assigning a number symbolizing the quantitative extent of the dimensional quantity represented by the specific case. Together with the appropriate unit, this quantity constitutes the unique *measure* of the observed object or event. This process is straightforward in the measurement of dimensional quantities of a single instance, because the quantity of cycles is always 1.0 and temporal quantities can be determined with the aid of calibrated timing devices. However, when a class of responses is involved and each response has a different time measure associated with it, the problem of obtaining a composite measure of the class dimensional quantity is more complex. For example, determining the number to combine with cycles per unit time in specifying a particular frequency involves additional operations of combination not immediately implied by either the dimensional quantities or their units. Measures of individual responses can, as mathematical quantities, be combined algebraically in a variety of ways to produce measures of response classes. The question is, which operations are meaningful in that they leave the dimensional quantity intact?

Because response instances occur serially in time, it is convenient to represent the members of a response class as an ordered series, $r_1, r_2, \ldots r_n$. Each response, for example r_i, has a cycle count (1) and a temporal locus, t_i, which is either its IRT with respect to r_{i-1} or its latency with respect to some antecedent environmental event. In either case, t_i is a number and a time unit (e.g., 15 seconds). The measure of each such response can be defined as $1/t_i$. In the case of the t_i's, addition is permissible, but multiplication is not, because a new dimensional quantity would be defined by any higher power of t. Summing the time measures of the n responses in the series produces $t_1 + t_2 + t_3 + \ldots + t_n = \Sigma t_i$. Similarly, the individual cycle measures (trivially 1 for each cycle) can be summed $(1 + 1 + \ldots + 1)$ and the total will be N, the number of cycles in the series. Just as the count measure is divided by the time measure to produce the compound measure $(1/t_i)$ of the single response, so can the composite measures be combined to produce a single measure for the class. Creating the same ratio yields $N/\Sigma t_i$, or total count divided by latency. This quantity is recognizable as the measure of the countability of the series divided by the aggregate of the temporal loci of all responses in the series. The fraction $N/\Sigma t_i$ can be reduced to produce a unitary value of time in the denominator, leaving as the final measure a quantity of the form n cycles/unit time. This result, n cycles per unit time, is a measure of the frequency of the response class represented by the series, the operation of addition being necessary to combine the measures of the single instances into a measure of this dimensional quantity. Similar demonstrations can be generated for the measures of other dimensional quantities of a multi-instance response class, including celeration IRT, and so forth.

It is tempting to compare like measures of two or more classes within a repertoire by forming ratios among them. For example, the ratio of the average duration of one response class to the average duration of another may be calculated and taken as a measure of relative duration. Unfortunately, this operation causes the units to cancel, as it should, for relative duration is not a dimensional quantity of behavior, there being no unitary instance in a sense comparable to a unitary instance of a cycle.[3] Such quantities as relative duration, relative count, relative frequency, and so on, are said to be *dimensionless* and are, therefore, of little or no utility in the descriptive measurement of behavior. This shortcoming applies to all relational measures derived from division of measures of like dimensional quantities and forms the basis of the discussion of the weakness of the various percentage measures that appears later.

Topographical Measurement

Finally, before discussing the tactical implications of strategies of identifying units of behavioral measurement, it is important to dwell briefly on the special considerations for behavioral measurement imposed by topographical definitions of response classes. Topographical definitions allude to motion as a property of any behavioral instance as anticipated in Chapter 3. In those special cases in which the *form* of the response is the predominant focus of experimental interest, measurement must be performed with reference to those dimensional quantities descriptive of motion. Newtonian mechanics provides an extensive array of such dimensional quantities, including velocity, acceleration, momentum, inertial force, and so on, which are composites of mass, distance, and time. The units specifying amounts of these dimensional quantities have likewise been designated and will not be recited here.

The availability of this complete system of measurement invites the possibility of creating a discipline of behavioral mechanics, much as Descartes apparently envisioned in his *Traité de l'Homme* (1662). Vigorous contemporary activity of this sort is typified by the work of Gideon Ariel who combines computer technology with biomechanical analysis to analyze sports performances with astonishing precision (Moore, 1977). It should be clear from earlier discussions that although such a discipline might contribute to

---

[3]This difficulty can, in principle, be circumvented by a process of derived measurement typified by use of a thermometer. A dimensional quantity characteristic of the instrument yields units, usually in the form of time, distance, or electromagnetic measures. In the case of response classes, the derivation of such units requires applying vector analytic techniques to standard chart displays and is beyond the scope of this presentation.

several technologies, it would necessarily fall far short of the aims of a fully developed science of behavior, in that it would speak only indirectly of behavior as a recurrent phenomenon defined primarily by its effects on the surrounding environment.

Measurement of the mechanical aspects of responding necessarily invokes the dimensional quantities of distance and velocity, which may easily be confused with countability and frequency as dimensional quantities of any response class. This matter is readily clarified by recalling that the unit of countability is the cycle, which is not an expression or transformation of any distance unit. Thus, frequency as a measure of recurrence is not akin to velocity as a measure of motion, because motion occurs with reference to the dimension of distance whereas cycle repetition occurs only with respect to time. The fact that any movement of any organism may be described with reference to spatial displacement of all or part of the organism has no bearing on the property of repeatability of the movement. It is this property, of course, which is of central significance in the conception of behavior as an adaptive process and is a major facet of our scientific understanding of the phenomenon.

Finally, measurement of physical dimensional quantities implied by topographical considerations must be distinguished from efforts to differentiate quantitatively among *magnitudes* of responses. Specifying response magnitude is conventionally achieved by measuring changes in some environmental effect of the response (e.g., the distance by which an object is displaced). Although such measures may exhibit high correlations with measures of topographic features, it must be recalled that variation in effect on the environment constitutes the basis for defining differentiated functional classes (see Chapter 6). Magnitude is thus a definitional property, not a dimensional quantity, of behavior and should not enter directly into the measurement process.

IMPLICATIONS FOR MEASUREMENT TACTICS

Confronted with behavior as a natural, recurring phenomenon, the investigator must either select one or more dimensional quantities for measurement and analysis or evade the issue and attempt quantification in terms of some relative, dimensionless quantity. The advantages of measuring with respect to dimensional quantities reside primarily in the absoluteness and universality of the corresponding units, but certain practical problems of specificity and precision becomes correspondingly magnified. Accordingly, it is important to understand thoroughly the tactics underlying measurement of each dimensional quantity so that an informed selection can be made.

Measurement of Dimensional Quantities

Countability.   The most fundamental, almost tautological fact about the occurrence of a single instance of a response is that its cycle count is unity. Thus, counting cycles provides a measure of the dimensional quality of countability whether for a single response or responses within a class. A series of responses can be conveniently represented as an event record with time transformed into distance units from left to right on the display. Figure 7.1 is a hypothetical instance of such a record and is typical of those to which reference is made throughout the following discussion. An upward deviation in a solid line denotes the initiation of a response, whereas a downward deflection denotes its cessation. The measure of the countability of the set of responses depicted in Fig. 7.1 would be "three cycles." It is immediately obvious that this measure is indifferent to the dynamic temporal variation among the three responses shown in Fig. 7.1 and is, therefore, of limited sensitivity. Vastly different interpretations of the datum "three cycles" would be entertained if the time span represented is 10 minutes as opposed to 10 months and the responses are sexual. Cycle count becomes sensitive only if all temporal parameters are held constant, an experimental limitation often impossible to achieve. For this reason, it is usually essential to allow temporal variation to come into play in determination of an appropriate dimensional quantity.

Time ⟶

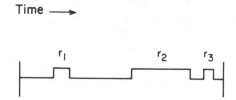

FIG. 7.1.   Diagrammatic representation of three responses in time.

Duration.   Perhaps the easiest temporal dimensional quantity to visualize is the duration of a single response instance. Duration is the dimensional quantity representative of the property of temporal extent that is readily represented as linear distance with the aid of a recorder operating at a constant speed.

In Fig. 7.2, the duration of r_1 is indicated by the span of time corresponding to d_1. Measurement of duration is singularly appropriate in those instances in which variation among the durations of a series of responses is of interest, especially if there is an overriding need to make the behavior more efficient (reduce the duration) or augment endurance (increase the duration). Combining measures of duration of a number of responses can be

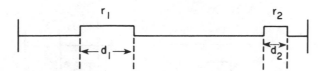

FIG. 7.2.   Diagrammatic representation of the durations of two responses.

accomplished by addition, but the result is often of limited utility if the cycle count is ignored. For example, the information that a child spent 30 minutes working on math problems is far less useful than would be the fact that in 30 minutes the child solved 75 problems. For this reason, it is preferable to define the *duration measure* of each response, r_i, as $1/d_i$; when these measures are combined algebraically,[4] the count indicator of the numerator is preserved and a more complete description of the temporal extent property of the series is achieved. In the math example, this would require taking the measure of the duration $(1/d_i)$ of working each math problem, then combining these into an aggregate measure of some kind, perhaps a total (75 cycles/30 min.) or an average (1 cycle/.4 min.). Of course, in the case of any single response, the count is trivially unity and all information about the value of the dimensional quantity is contained in the denominator.

Latency.   Figure 7.3 is a diagram of three responses in a series showing the three types of latency that reflect temporal locus as a property of behavior. Recall that temporal locus refers to the temporal location of the onset of the response with reference to other events, environmental or behavioral. Accordingly, three differently appearing latencies are possible: two genuine latencies and a pseudolatency. The first, designated l_1, is the pseudolatency and locates the onset of r_1 with respect to an arbitrary nonbehavioral event, the beginning of timing. The first response in any measured series within an operant class appears on the record some measurable distance after the beginning of timing. The time l_1 thus represented is a portion of a true latency in that it locates the first response relative to either a preceding response or an environmental event, one cannot say which. The second measured latency, l_2, locates r_2 with respect to the cessation of r_1, a behavioral event. Finally, l_3

---

[4]In making such combinations, care should be taken to maintain the separation of numerators and denominators, because they are separate dimensional quantities and possess different units. Thus, numerators can be added and denominators can be added, but the ratios (with their compound units) cannot. (See the earlier derivation of the frequency measure for a response class for an elaboration of this practice.)

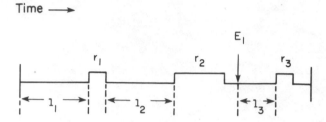

FIG. 7.3. Diagrammatic representation of the latencies of three responses.

locates the onset of r_3 in time relative to the occurrence of environmental event E_1. Suppose that r_1, r_2, and r_3 in Fig. 7.3 represent the responses of working the first three math problems from the previous example. The time between the beginning of the math period (when the teacher starts timing) and the child's starting the first math problem is the pseudolatency, l_1. The interval between completing the first problem and beginning the second (during which the child may have sharpened a pencil and gotten a drink) is designated l_2. After the second problem is completed, the teacher may give a direction such as, "Try to work faster." This event is denoted by E_1 and anchors the latency (l_3) of the next response (r_3). Because every response has a temporal locus, it has a latency, and the measures of individual response latencies give a precise picture of part of the dynamic character of behavior as it flows through time.

Just as in the case of duration, we define a *latency measure* as $1/l_i$ and thereby recover the count, however trivially, in the single instance. Again, algebraic combinations of latency measures preserve the time units as well as the countability factor and are sometimes of value in describing a series. In practice, explicit selection of the dimensional quantity of latency usually occurs when the experimental interest is with the temporal relation of responses to discrete environmental events (l_3). Summaries of latency measures are often used to describe this dimension in the case of a response class defined as a discriminated operant (see Chapter 6). In the case of free operants, l_2 forms the basis for measuring temporal locus and is discussed below.

Interresponse Time (IRT).   A series of latencies of the type represented by l_2 in Fig. 7.3 is displayed for a hypothetical free operant series in Fig. 7.4. The point at which timing begins for each such latency, l_{2i}, is the moment of cessation of the immediately preceding response, r_{i-1}, thus the occurrence of r_i is located in time with respect to another behavioral event. Because two behavioral events are required to define l_{2i}, this dimensional quantity is properly viewed as representing a property of a response sequence of length two and has come to be called the interresponse time. It should be clear from Fig. 7.4 that the IRT for a particular response is the time separating its onset

Time ⟶

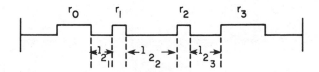

FIG. 7.4.   Diagrammatic representation of the interresponse times ($l_i = IRT_i$) of four responses.

from the cessation of the previous response; the response designated r_0 has no measurable IRT, although it may be said to have pseudolatency as discussed previously.

As is the case with other temporal measures of behavior, there is value in working with an *IRT measure,* defined as $1/IRT_i$. This permits algebraic summation and scalar multiplication while retaining the measure of countability. As a measure of the dynamic temporal characteristics of a response sequence, an aggregate of IRT measures ignores the dimensional quantity of duration, which may or may not be a limitation in specific research situations. Regardless, duration and IRT are not wholly separable, because for a given finite period of time, the longer the duration(s), the less time will remain for distribution among IRT's. In other words, while a response of a specific duration is in progress, another response (with its own IRT) is prevented from occurring.

It is instructive to perform a dimensional analysis on an aggregate of IRT measures. Summing such measures ($1/IRT_i$) over a series of N responses yields $N/\Sigma_{i=1}^{n} IRT_i$, where N is the count of the cycles in the series. Because IRT_i will be a measure involving time units, the dimensional quantity of the term $N/\Sigma_{i=1}^{n} IRT_i$ will have as its unit "cycles per unit time." This is the unit designator for the dimensional quantity of frequency, and the intimacy of the relation between the dimensional quantities of interresponse time and frequency becomes apparent.

Frequency.   The behavioral properties of repeatability and temporal locus combine to yield an important dimensional quantity characteristic of any multi-instance class, its frequency. The various latency measures discussed earlier reference the property of temporal locus and are, therefore, implicit participants in the measurement of frequency. However, the dimensional quantity of frequency primarily represents the property of recurrence or repeatability, and quantitative estimation of the "true" frequency of a behavior should place differential emphasis on excluding all but those latencies involved in the IRT measures of temporal locus. It follows that

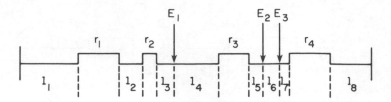

FIG. 7.5. Diagrammatic representation of four responses in relation to various latencies. The subscripts in this figure serve only to designate the various elements by their serial position.

$N / \Sigma_{i=1}^{n} \text{IRT}_i$, the linear sum of the IRT measures occurring in a series, is the best quantitative estimate of the true frequency of instances within a class.

The problems posed by this consideration are illustrated in Fig. 7.5. The compound unit appearing in any measure of response frequency is of the form *cycles per unit time,* and the measure is obtained by enumerating the cycles, cumulating the time (latency) measures, and performing the indicated division. Thus, the frequency measure that would result from the occurrence of 50 cycles in an aggregate latency period of 20 minutes would be 2.5 cycles/min. The question with reference to Fig. 7.5 is, which latency values would be aggregated to form the time component for the denominator of the frequency measure descriptive of this series of four responses?

First, there is the question of whether or not to include l_1, the pseudolatency associated with r_1. If the series were substantially denser with respect to countability, the proper tactic would be to exclude from consideration both l_1 and r_1, because error is introduced by the arbitrary location of the starting point. In this instance, however, excluding r_1 is tantamount to discarding 25% of the behavioral sample, so both r_1 and l_1 should be retained. In doing so, we recognize that l_1 inflates by some unknown amount the estimate of the true frequency because $l_1 \leq \text{IRT}_1$.

The IRT for r_2, designated l_2, will obviously be included and requires no further comment. The occurrence of an environmental event (E_1) between r_2 and r_3 separates the IRT of r_3 into two parts, l_3 and l_4. If l_4, the latency of response r_3 to E_1, is of experimental interest, arrangements should be made to determine its value separately, but it should not be allowed to substitute for or act as an estimate of the IRT of r_3, which is properly defined as $l_3 + l_4$. Similarly, l_3 may be of experimental interest, particularly if E_1 is an environmental event such as the delivery of a reinforcing stimulus, but it should still not be excised from the measure of the IRT of r_3 because r_3 *could,* in principle, have antedated E_1, making its IRT a real value less than l_3.

The same argument generally applies to l_5, l_6, and l_7, the sum of which is equivalent to the IRT of r_4. However, l_6 may pose problems in certain investigations because its extent is defined by two environmental events with no interceding occurrence of a measured response. The criteria for inclusion of l_6 rests, oddly enough, with the nature of E_2; if E_2 acts to remove the opportunity for the response to occur and that opportunity is restored with the occurrence of E_3, l_6 should be excluded and the IRT of r_4 would reduce to $l_5 + l_7$. The question of including l_6 must be decided on the basis of whether or not a response could occur during that period, not whether or not it does occur.

Finally, there is the problem of l_8. Because there is no r_5 for l_8 to estimate the IRT of, l_8 should be discarded. Often, however, because the end point of l_8 is arbitrarily located by the offset of the timing device, it is difficult to estimate its extent accurately. Including l_8 in the aggregate denominator of the frequency measure will deflate the estimate of the true frequency by an indeterminate amount. In practice, it is not uncommon to include both l_1 and l_8 in the belief that the amount by which l_1 underestimates the IRT of r_2 is offset by the amount of l_8. It should be clear that this practice introduces error and is, therefore, not to be encouraged; however, if circumstances force inclusion of l_1, further inclusion of l_8 reduces the error by some unspecified extent.

The net effect of this analysis is to suggest that frequency is measured by adding all real and estimated interresponse times and dividing the number of cycles observed by that sum. In practice, efforts to accomplish this often take the form of continuously timing the entire observation period during which cycle counting occurs, performing the indicated division and attaching the unit *cycles per unit time*. From Fig. 7.5, it is clear that this procedure will systematically underestimate the actual or true frequency by an amount proportional to the sum of the duration measures. The seriousness of this distortion varies with a number of factors. First, consideration must be given to the scientific purpose of the measurement. If response frequencies are being obtained for the purpose of comparing the effects of various treatment procedures on this dimensional quantity of behavior, the effect on eventual interpretation may be minimal, providing one is assured of the absence of a concomitant effect on duration. Often, however, a treatment that reduces frequency simultaneously increases duration, and the degree of measurement error correspondingly increases. Estimates of the magnitude of the treatment effect based on a comparison of frequencies will then be exaggerated without the experimenter's knowledge.

Again, a child doing math problems furnishes a convenient context for illustrating this point. Suppose that the teacher's primary concern is with the frequency of errors. A procedure such as early recess for fewer errors may be introduced and the result may be that error frequency indeed diminishes. It might be unnoticed, however, that fewer errors occur because fewer problems are attempted with inordinate amounts of time being spent on each problem. The direct effect of the early recess contingency might thus be on the duration of each response, and the conclusion that frequency was reduced would, in an important sense, be spurious.

If the purpose of obtaining an estimate of the true frequency of responding is to generate as nearly exact a quantitative description of the response as possible, the effects of the distortion imposed by inclusion of the duration measures may be cataclysmic. There are many situations in which measures of this type are used descriptively for diagnostic or evaluative purposes, and an exact measure is required. For example, if a given frequency estimate of a child's performance in mathematics is judged to be low, the remedial action indicated may vary according to whether long IRT's or long durations are responsible. A proper estimate of the frequency based only on IRT's would remove the ambiguity. If the estimate then remained low, attention would be focused on events during the interresponse intervals. But, if the estimate increased substantially, details of the performance topography would be modified in an effort to reduce response durations. In general, true frequency and duration measures reflect dynamic properties of behavior that are essentially independent, and behavioral measurement practices that fail to reflect this independence are of questionable descriptive utility.

Finally, it might be argued that the timing precision urged by this analysis is compromised by the difficulty of identifying the beginning and ending of responses. Although this is sometimes true in practice, it is important to realize that two different issues are involved. Specifying the onset and offset of responses is a matter of when to time, whereas the present issue concerns what periods should be timed at all. Precise measurement will be facilitated by addressing these problems separately; in the next chapter, we discuss behavioral observation in detail.

Celeration.   Implicit in the behavioral properties of temporal locus and repeatability is the complex dimensional quantity of celeration that references the characteristic of changeability over time. In many technological applications of behavioral science, measuring celeration is of prime importance, because behavior change is usually the technological objective. The importance of measuring celeration is fundamental to the basic science in that describing and investigating any dynamic functional relations presupposes the existence of an absolute, universal measure of behavior change.

Obtaining a measure of celeration requires determining the mathematical function relating a series of sequentially obtained frequency measures to real time and computing its first derivative. In practice, curve fitting procedures of estimation may be used to determine the function (see Chapter 17); the function is then differentiated with respect to time, yielding a measure whose units are of the form *cycles per unit time per unit time*. The most fully developed methods for rapid approximation of celeration measures involve graphically determining the slopes of linear functions best fitting a semilogarithmic display of frequencies against time (Pennypacker, Koenig, & Lindsley, 1972; White, 1974; White & Haring, 1976). As with any methods relying on linear trend estimation, however, these yield approximations that are often insensitive to meaningful nonlinear local variation among the frequency measures. More exact procedures involving actually differentiating the complex function will yield measures of frequency change that are maximally accurate at every point along the time dimension.

Dimensionless Quantities

It should be apparent that the basis of descriptive measurement in science lies in accurately quantifying the dimensional quantities of natural phenomena. As mentioned earlier, it is possible to form ratios among pairs of measures of any given dimensional quantity and generate values that have a certain comparative utility. Unfortunately, this process removes the units from the resulting measure, leaving only a number descriptive of a dimensionless quantity. For example, a talking duration of 15 minutes divided by an eating duration of 10 minutes yields the quotient 1.5, which indicates that the ratio of talking time to eating time was 3 to 2. For descriptive purposes, such numbers are simply unacceptable, for they have no referent in a natural dimension or property of behavior. The source of this limitation becomes obvious when one considers that any specific ratio can be the result of an infinite number of divided pairs: 2 equals $8 \div 4$, $10 \div 5$, etc. Thus, such a quantity is not uniquely descriptive of a behavioral event. However, if presented in the company of the dimensional measures that comprise the ratio so that no information is lost (e.g., 15 minutes/10 minutes), measures of this type can often assist interpretation.

A more general illustration of this point is furnished by so-called measures of time allocation. Suppose we are considering two response classes, R and S, and both are occurring during a period of observation. We can determine a total duration measure for each class by summing the duration time values of all r_i and s_i. Letting $d(R)$ and $d(S)$ represent these respective sums, we can form the ratio $d(R)/d(S)$, which expresses the proportion of time spent engaging in one class relative to the other. Finally, the ratio $d(R)/[d(R) + d(S) + d(\overline{RUS})]$ is the fraction of total time available occupied by responses of class R with ($\overline{RUS}$) representing all behavior outside classes R and S.

No matter which ratio is calculated, the information contained in the original duration measures is lost, and it becomes impossible to trace sources of variation in a series of such ratios. For example, if the ratio $d(R)/d(S)$ increases, this may be due to an increase in $d(R)$ alone with $d(S)$ remaining constant, a decrease in $d(S)$ with $d(R)$ remaining constant, or a combination of the two. Any influence from the experimental operations must change the magnitude of the ratio in one of these three ways (through direct contact with a dimensional quantity of behavior), yet it is impossible to discern from changes in the ratio alone which class is being affected. For example, if the talking duration ÷ eating duration ratio changes from 1.5 to 2.0 as we move from a bacchanalian evening feast to breakfast the following morning, we cannot tell if the increase is due to a decrease in eating resulting from lingering gastric distress or an increase in talking occasioned by a need to repair established social relationships.

A further limitation inherent in this practice is typified by ratios in which $d(R)$ appears in both the numerator and the denominator. Unnatural ceilings are imposed on possible values of such ratios, because they can approach, but never exceed, unity. As this limit is approached, variation that may be of substantial scientific importance is obscured, and its causes can easily escape detection.

The foregoing discussion and caveats apply equally to dimensionless quantities formed by ratios of measures of countability, latency, or frequency. Common percentage measures such as the "percent correct responses" so widely used in educational applications are usually dimensionless quantities formed from measures of countability alone and are, therefore, totally insensitive to important variation exhibited by the temporal characteristics of the performance. This is especially unfortunate in "mastery learning" situations in which the artificial ceiling imposed by the upper limit of 100 % obscures important variability that can be recovered by using the ratio of the frequencies of correct and incorrect responding as an index of performance quality. Again, however, such a ratio is much more potent descriptively if one or the other of the absolute frequency measures is also reported. For example, the statement that the correct response frequency was 3.6 responses per minute and was 9 times greater than the incorrect response frequency communicates far more quantitative information of importance about the behavior than does the phrase 90% correct. Of course, these points are equally valid in the full range of noneducational settings in which relative, dimensionless quantifiers are used to attempt to describe behavior. In all cases, the underlying issue is measurement sensitivity, which is a major consideration in choosing a dimensional quantity.

Choosing a Dimensional Quantity

Ideally, every attempt at measurement of behavior should contemplate complete and accurate quantification with respect to all dimensional quantities so that no information of potential value will be inadvertently missed. Although allegiance to this ideal should comprise at least one paragraph of the sworn oath of every behavioral scientist, it is inevitable that a variety of exigencies will frequently force observance in the breach. In addition, there are a number of further considerations surrounding measurement of certain dimensional quantities that can curtail the desirability or even the necessity of their measurement in a specific instance. Among these considerations are the specific experimental question under investigation, the manner in which the response class is defined, the probable nature of the resulting data, and various fiscal and social constraints surrounding any experimental undertaking. Overriding all of these, however, are the scientific demands for sensitivity and precision of measurement, for unless these criteria can be met with assurance, the balance of the effort is likely to be for naught.

Sensitivity.   Sensitivity refers to the capability of measured variation in the dimensional quantity to reveal changes in the phenomenon of interest to the investigator. Any dimensional quantity (such as duration) for which the underlying property is continuous has such sensitivity, limited only by the capabilities of the measuring instrument or the observer. It should be obvious that both countability and frequency are *not* continuous and never can be, because integers must be used to represent the count of response cycles occurring in discrete instances. Nonetheless, the time parameter of frequency may be almost infinitely adjusted to achieve any desired level of sensitivity. In other words, adjustments in the sensitivity of the frequency measure are made by changing the sensitivity with which IRT's (the temporal component) are measured. The limit of sensitivity is not set by the dimensional quantity itself, but by the smallest change in average IRT that can occur or that is of interest to detect. If the average IRT of a series is 1.5 seconds, for example, we may say that the frequency of that behavior is one cycle per 1.500 seconds, or 40 cycles per minute. If we use the minute as the time unit, the next hightest value possible is 41 cycles per minute, or 1 cycle per 1.463 seconds, because a fraction of a movement cannot be recorded by integral counting. In other words, if we pick a time unit, t, to use in the measure of frequency, we limit the sensitivity of the scale to $1/t$ as the smallest detectable change in the average IRT. The measurement scale then becomes a series of discrete values ($1/t$, $2/t$, $3/t$, ..., etc.), and values falling between these values cannot occur.

Suppose we select the second as our time unit, t. We can discriminate 10 cycles per second from either 9 cps or 11 cps, but finer graduations are not available, because there is no behavioral meaning associated with the quantity 9.3 cps. Increasing sensitivity is a matter of increasing the time unit; if 1 response/minute, 2 responses/minute, ..., etc., is not sufficiently sensitive, then changing to hours gives us 60 responses/hour, 120 responses/hour, ..., etc., as the converted values and also permits all the intervening integral values (61 responses/hour, 62 responses/hour, ..., etc.) to occur.

Appropriately, selecting t therefore becomes critical and is analogous to selecting microscope lenses to achieve the correct resolving power (Skinner, 1953b). One can select t as small as one wishes, but once selected, differences less than $1/t$ are beyond the sensitivity of the scale.

There are two practical consequences of the fact that the frequency scale is adjustable but always discrete. The first is that the issue of *significant digits* must be faced when reporting behavior frequencies. Suppose that responding is recorded for 6.0 minutes and 16 cycles are observed. The resulting frequency calculation would be 16/6 or 2.667 cycles per minute. Had either 15 or 17 cycles been recorded, the resulting frequencies would have been 2.500 cycles per minute or 2.833 cycles per minute, respectively. In the case of estimating to the nearest minute, only the first digit to the right of the decimal is significant, and reported results should be rounded accordingly. This constraint becomes especially important in describing the results of any algebraic combination of frequencies. The practice of reporting significant digits as an indication of the precision of measurement obtained has a long tradition in the natural sciences and may be expected to contribute greatly to the clarity of communication in a natural science of behavior, once it is understood.

The second implication of the limited continuity of frequency concerns accuracy of *estimation*. Apart from the question of sensitivity, there is always the question of how accurately true values of dimensional quantities are estimated by observed sample values. Because frequency is an invariant dimensional quantity of the response class, every attempt to measure it may be construed as an attempt to estimate a true value. The true frequency of a particular response of a particular organism could only be determined by observing and counting all instances of its occurrence throughout the organism's lifetime. Because this is rarely done, any frequency value based upon a lesser time of observation is necessarily an *estimate* of the true frequency. This poses a special problem when, in t units of time, observation does not reveal a single occurrence of the behavior. The estimate of the true frequency must then be zero, a result that is not only less than satisfying, but awkward for many subsequent mathematical operations.

The problem is easily solved if it is recognized that the measurement procedure (not the measure) is unsatisfactory. Getting a satisfactory estimate of the true frequency requires that the time of observation be extended until at least one instance of the behavior has occurred. For example, suppose that the true frequency of a certain response is one per hour. Observing for 10 minutes will probably fail to turn up even one instance. Is it justifiable to say that the frequency is zero? To say that it is zero implies that it is less than one per hour, less than one per day, less than one per week, etc. In fact, the observational procedure only permits the conclusion that it is less than one per 10 minutes, and the results of the measurement should be reported accordingly (frequency $< .1$ per minute). This certainly brackets the true frequency at the upper end while relieving the implication that the response never occurs.

Although the foregoing arguments are couched mainly in terms of measuring frequency, they apply equally to aggregate measures of latency and duration. The discontinuity imposed by integral counts of cycles and the limitations on precision of estimation engendered by inadequate temporal sampling are inherent in all measures of all such combinations of dimensional quantities. As is the case with measures of frequency, however, any resulting restrictions on interpretation can be accommodated through informed forethought.

Relevance.   The issue of sensitivity is closely related to the problem of measuring variability and, ultimately, to the role of variability in the subject matter of the science. Variability and tactics for analyzing its determinants are discussed in detail in Part III of this volume, but one simple fact must be stated here: Variability cannot be analyzed if it cannot be detected and measured. Although there is no differential sensitivity inherent among the various dimensional quantities of behavior (with the possible exception of countability), in any given experimental case measurement of one is likely to reveal the presence of greater variability than would measurement of another. Responding within classes, for example, may occur with highly stable frequencies, but exhibit considerable instance-to-instance variation in duration. Most respondents exhibit this characteristic, and interest is rarely directed at their frequency of occurrence. Moreover, the operation of selected experimental variables may be expected to exert differential influence on variation in one dimensional quantity as opposed to another.

Selecting any dimensional quantity that does not reflect variability of experimental interest is contrary to the objectives of scientific inquiry. Many investigators report stability in a behavioral phenomenon when they are, in fact, responding to the inappropriate use of a particular dimensional quantity for that experiment. For instance, repeated measures of duration may become stable while frequency is still exhibiting orderly but undetected fluctuation. Thus, the task of every investigator is to select for measurement those dimensional quantities that will show whatever variation in responding will be of experimental interest throughout the entire experiment. There may often be substantial risk in assuming that a single dimensional quantity will adequately serve this function. At the least, choosing only one dimensional quantity precludes serendipitous discovery of other forms of variability.

The solution to this problem does not lie in inventing *ad hoc* a vast array of synthetic, usually dimensionless, measures and applying them serially to the results of an experiment until one is discovered that reveals both variability and order. Although the fallacy underlying this tactic may not be detected for some period of time and the intermediate increment in publication likelihood may prove irresistible, the fallacy nonetheless exists and creates a situation inimical to the long-range objectives of the science. Simply stated, the fallacy is this: Any set of data will exhibit some structure from which a certain order can be inferred and described after the fact. There is no implicit guarantee that such a structure is replicable, however, or even that it resulted from the planned imposition of experimental operations. It is unlikely the reliability and generality of any result purporting to describe a natural process will obtain if such a result is even in part the consequence of an unnatural measurement practice. By adhering closely to the strategy of behavioral measurement that requires selecting natural dimensional quantities of behavior, the likelihood of reporting nonreplicable and nongeneralizable "false positives" is greatly reduced.

The objective should always be to obtain the most sensitive measures available so that we may be exposed to the maximum possible richness (complexity?) of our subject matter. We are always at liberty to discard or ignore variability of a certain type if we have first observed it, but it is impossible to understand the lawful workings of the organism–environment interaction if we cannot see, and later modify, variations in that interaction. This point is analogous to the extension of a person's visual sensitivity by the invention of the microcope; the discovery of "a whole world nobody knew was there" also occasioned the development of several new branches of science that sought to systematize the relations in that world. So it must be with the science of behavior. Sensitive measurement in terms of natural dimensional quantities will reveal "a whole new world" that was not obvious with earlier measurement techniques.

8 Observing and Recording

Observers, then, must be photographers of phenomena; their observations must accurately represent nature. We must observe without any preconceived idea; the observer's mind must be passive, that is, must hold its peace; it listens to nature and writes at nature's dictation.

—Claude Bernard

INTRODUCTION

Quantifying some dimension of a response class and creating a record of that information are crucial components of the entire process of behavioral measurement and, thus, of behavioral research. Detecting and notating the amount of the selected dimensional quantities are the first occasion on which the more abstract considerations of the previous chapters are tactically realized. The particulars of defining response classes and selecting dimensional quantities and their units of measurement must be strong sources of influence on the experimenter's early procedural decisions. The

145

consequences of these initial tactical choices will permanently determine the character of the data that must eventually be assessed with reference to the intractable criteria of stability, accuracy, reproducibility, and generality.

It is important to remember that any sources of measurement-imposed variability resulting from procedural decisions at this stage cannot be unequivocally distinguished from variability that is treatment induced, regardless of experimental design, statistical machinations, or interpretative myopia. The purity of the phenomenon prior to investigation may be likened to a glass container of clear water. As the various components of the measurement process are designed and implemented, any attendent sources of variability that are incorporated may be represented by drops of red coloring added to the water. A few drops will hardly change the water's color, but too many will gradually tint the liquid pink and then red. The exact shade of the metaphorical water must be continuously evaluated by the experimenter, as well as by scientific peers. Individual researchers must have their own means for testing the color of the water, as well as their own criterion for deciding when it is getting red enough to say "stop."

It should become clear that this chapter encourages a distinction between the experimenter's responsibilities of observing and recording. The goal of observation is to arrange conditions so that man or machine will react sensitively to the defined dimensions of the subject's behavior. The function of recording is to create an accurate and permanent translation of this reaction, usually in analogic or symbolic form.

STRATEGIC OBSERVATIONAL ISSUES

Characteristics of the Response Class

It is imperative that observation procedures be strongly influenced by the characteristics of the behavior to be observed. The simplicity of this dictum is deceiving, however, because different definitional tactics must necessarily influence observational procedures in different ways. For example, a functional response class definition will require that the observational procedure take account of the antecedent and consequent stimulus conditions that define the class. On the other hand, a topographical definition will necessitate observation of the mechnical properties of the response class and will depend heavily on the clarity of the stated limits of form. When temporal parameters are added to the definition, observation will have to incorporate precise measurement of time as well. Observation of response products would seem to demand only that the products be counted; however, such procedures must also be responsible for guaranteeing response authorship and numerical correspondence between responses and products. If interest is focused on the behavior of a number of individuals forming some kind of group, observation is likely to be complicated by the necessity of monitoring the behavior of more than one individual.

In addition to the implications for decisions regarding observational tactics emanating from the formalities of response class definititon, there are other characteristics of responding that may influence the measurement process. The suspected frequency with which the response occurs, for example, may influence a variety of logistical decisions prerequisite to establishing an observational procedure. In cases in which the use of human observers is unavoidable, the social significance of the behavior of interest may introduce a special source of error as a result of an uncontrollable interaction of the behavioral event with the observer's personal history. These and other considerations arising from extradefinitional characteristics of behavior are discussed later in conjunction with the tactics designed to ameliorate their effects.

Sampling by Sessions

The ultimate goal of any observational strategy is the production of a record of the observed phenomenon that meets certain criteria of reliability and accuracy. This means that the observational procedure should guarantee acquiring a sufficiently large sample of behavior to ensure representativeness without, at the same time, distorting the phenomenon or contributing extraneous "noise" to the variability of the eventual data. These considerations have traditionally been advanced as justification for the practice of performing a single observation on each of a large sample of individuals and then attempting, with the aid of statistical techniques, to estimate the "true" value of the dimension under consideration. Aside from the logical difficulties with this approach in general (discussed elsewhere in this volume), it is not justified as an observational technique simply because more appropriate methods are available. There is no need to estimate and eliminate "noise" statistically if such noise is excluded in the first place as a result of well-designed observational procedures. In designing such procedures, serious thought must be given to the questions of how often and over what period of time observation must occur in order to reduce attendant sources of error to a minimum.

The question of how often the periods of observation should occur and how long they should last is a question of accuracy of estimation. Except in ideal situations in which all occurrences of the response are being observed, one must sample from a total population of defined responses. As in every measurement problem, an observer is interested in obtaining a value that is the best possible approximation of the true parameter of the phenomenon. That is, one wishes to observe the occurrence of the response under any prevailing temporal restrictions on observation in such a way that the obtained measure of the dimensional quantity of the sample will closely approximate that for all responses in the class. If the dimensional quantity of interest were stable throughout the day or over long periods of time, the decision of how frequently sampling must occur and how long each session should be would be relatively easy. The investigator would merely sample the behavior during intervals of varying length, note the variability associated with each, and select the interval for which further reductions in variability were either miniscule or unimportant. However, there is often substantial evidence that a dimensional quantity is differentially influenced across times and settings by variation in controlling environmental stimuli. For example, for many coffee drinkers, the IRT's of drinking cups of coffee are quite short in the morning and, for a variety of reasons, become much longer as the day progresses. A sample of morning IRT's would clearly not provide a good estimate of the overall population of coffee-drinking IRT's.

The solution to this dilemma partly depends on the eventual goals of the research project that the measurement is to serve. For example, it is often true that the aim of the research is only to establish the effect of a particular treatment on otherwise stable responding. In such cases, it may be necessary only to observe a stable dimensional quantity rather than to determine its stability in the total population of responses in the class. The first step is to probe or sample responding at different times under different conditions or to measure all responses temporarily. This information will permit a more educated decision by showing how much the dimensional quantity varies and to what extent it does so consistently under what circumstances, thus revealing the location and duration of periods of relative stability. It may be observed that responding is consistently stable across times and settings, requiring only the measurement of a reasonable and convenient proportion of the population. However, it is dangerous to assess stability by assumption, because probes may show that responding differs systematically under two or more conditions. If it is not feasible to remedy the problem by measuring all responses in the class, it may be necessary to observe separately during different conditions or times. Whether or not the data from these separate observational periods are later combined or maintained as separate will depend on the research question and the data themselves. However, it is important to recognize that an unavoidable loss of information and a misrepresentation must result when data with different characteristics from separate observation periods are combined. The influence may be so small as to be unimportant, or so large as to seriously mislead the experimenter and the audience.

One source of influence over these fundamental observational decisions is sufficiently important to merit special mention. In deciding how often and how long to observe, the frequency of responding must be a major consideration, regardless of the dimensional quantity selected. Generally, the lower the frequency of responding, the greater must be the duration of observation periods.[1] This principle becomes clear in the case in which only two or three responses are emitted per day. Obviously, observation must go on all day in order to detect these few responses, and sampling during the day is out of the question.

Sampling Within Sessions

Thus far, our discussion of the initial decisions regarding how long the observational periods should last and how often they should be scheduled has assumed that observing and recording are continuous when they are occurring. The intermittency that results from periods of continuous observation separated by periods of nonobservation is often a necessary solution to logistical problems and can usually be arranged with no ill effects in the form of error in the actual data, although generalizing to periods of nonobservation will have the usual inferential risks. On the other hand, intermittency that is designed to occur when observational procedures are in effect (that is, within an observation interval) is usually unnecessary and is attended by serious consequences. We have already pointed out that most dimensional quantities reflecting behavioral properties are continuous, and any intermittent observation of responding necessarily imposes some artificial discontinuity on the results of the observation process. In addition, incomplete observation during observational periods almost forces sampling error to some unknown degree. Such sampling error is a major contributor to measurement-induced variability, which then becomes thoroughly confounded with treatment-imposed variability, severely compromising the accuracy and generality of experimental interpretations.

The incomplete observational practices under criticism here take many forms, and some categories have even been defined. Time sampling refers to procedures in which recording of all responses is continuous when observation is in progress. However, the duration of observational periods is usually relatively brief (less than 1 minute or even momentary), and the resulting intervals of nonobservation are relatively lengthy (often 10 minutes to an hour or more) during observational sessions. Thus, the actual cumulative time of observation for a session may often be only a small fraction of the session length, even though the episodes of observation may be regularly spaced throughout the entire session.

---

[1]This is not to discourage increases in the frequency of observation periods as well, but is intended to underscore the fact that responding occurring at low frequencies cannot be accurately observed without continuous periods of long duration.

A contrasting class of incomplete observational procedures has been labeled interval recording. Although the source of error here is somewhat different than that from time sampling, the effects on the stability and accuracy of measurement are unfortunately the same. In interval recording, the continuous period of time that constitutes the observational session is divided into brief intervals of arbitrary length (usually 10 seconds to 1 minute). Observers are then instructed to indicate with a symbol whether or not the response of interest occurred during each interval. The record can show only an occurrence or no occurrence; information that is in any way more exact is not included. Thus, an interval may in fact contain any number of occurrences greater than one, but the record will only indicate "at least one." Not surprisingly, interval recording is frequently combined with time sampling for the worst of both worlds.[2]

The ubiquity of within-session sampling in much behavioral research (especially in field settings) is weakly defended on a number of grounds. One such argument refers to the long tradition that this class of incomplete measurement practices has. However, tradition cannot be accepted as a defense here any more than the vaganotic tradition (see Chapter 4) can be an excuse for its unfortunate scientific consequences. Another argument is at least sometimes valid—that continuous measurement during sessions often meets greater logistical difficulties than within-session sampling. However, in science, convenience cannot be defended at the expense of full and precise measurement of the subject matter. This is especially awkward as a defense when the logistical difficulties are the unfortunate result of definitional and observational tactics that themselves have serious deficiencies. Perhaps the ultimate retreat for defenders of incomplete measurement is the argument that complete and accurate measurement is not necessary, that the degree of error attendant to within-session sampling does not justify efforts to arrange continuous measurement. It is certainly true that the consequences of incomplete measurement can be balanced against the costs of complete measurement. Overlooked in this compromise, however, is the fact that this comparison cannot be accomplished by assumption. The error of within-session sampling depends on the particular procedures used *and* the nature of the responding that is under observation *at any moment in each case.* Continuing changes in various aspects of the response class within and across sessions dictate that any empirical evaluation of the error of within-session sampling procedures must be continuing. This requires complete and continuous measurement, making clear the defenselessness of incomplete measurement procedures.

---

[2]Because these two procedures are discussed here only for the purpose of examining within-session sampling, we refer any interested readers to Hall (1974) for more detailed descriptive examples.

In spite of occasional attempts to justify these incomplete observational practices and even less frequent efforts to minimize sampling error by designing them to approximate as closely as possible the ideals of completeness and exactness, these procedures must still be characterized by the error that they almost inevitably ensure. Because the experimenter must contend with an ample variety of sources of variability that are beyond reasonable efforts to control, it is imperative that problems not be further compounded by unnecessarily adopting loose observation procedures with known undesirable consequences.

The conclusion to this discussion of the temporal dimensions of observation, as for most areas of research methodology, is that there are no prescriptions or formulas to direct the researcher. The decision of how often and how long to observe behavior may be guided only by strategic understanding, not by procedural rules. There is the overriding principle that ideal observation is both continuous and complete, leaving no opportunity for the encroachment of sampling error in any form. In practice, observational procedures should be manipulated in the direction of this goal; this is accomplished by increasing both the frequency and duration of observation periods whenever and however possible. The benefits that accrue in the form of increased accuracy and precision of measurement must be balanced against any actual increase in costs of observation. In weighing these factors, however, the investigator must remember that any error introduced as a result of faulty observational procedures is irretrievable and will remain to haunt efforts at analysis and interpretation throughout the entire course of the research.

Ensuring Access to Responding

The influence of observational requirements of the experimental setting in which the behavior of interest occurs may restrict or facilitate observational access. The observer is usually primarily dependent on visual (and, to a lesser extent, auditory) contact with the subject, and it is characteristic of applied settings that observers are faced with a myriad of factors that interefere with optimal visual contact. The behaver's movements may remove the response under investigation from view (or hearing), or the activities of others in the vicinity may produce the same effect. Even when the response of interest is easily discernable, observation may be further complicated by the occurrence of other behaviors that make detecting responses in a particular class more difficult. Even the frequency of the response itself can provide problems by being sufficiently high that discriminating separate response instances becomes difficult, thus complicating accurate counting. These difficulties are only exacerbated when the observer's influence on responding is such that the observer's presence or actions must go undetected.

Another way in which observation can be complicated by the experimental setting is for conditions in the setting to serve to restrict the frequency and/or duration of opportunities for observation. Even though the behavior may occur during all waking hours, opportunities for observation may be limited to relatively brief periods of time and/or to occasions that are too infrequent for adequate sampling. The sources of such restrictions are of little consequence if the limitations are intractable.

Fortunately, restrictions are not always beyond amelioration, and it is important in designing observational procedures to recognize the nature and sources of any inhibitions on ideal scientific observation from the research setting. The remedy may lie in improving the detectability or the availability of the response, and this may occasionally require that some degree of environmental engineering be undertaken before observation is actually attempted. One class of widely practiced engineering tactics involves attaching automatic detection and transmitting devices to the subject so that all instances of a particular movement can be registered. Several considerations surrounding the use of such devices are discussed later.

The laboratory use of highly confining experimental spaces for research on animal behavior is another illustration of premeasurement environmental engineering; restricting the sphere of activity of the organism ensures its continued availability for observation and keeps it in the vicinity of any stationary, mechanical recording devices in use.

Physical constraint is not always practical or desirable with people, so behavioral preparation may be required. A kindergarten teacher of our acquaintance[3] nicely solved the problem of obtaining daily individual measures of the academic behavior of each of her 150 charges by first programming a period of small group, seatwork activities that would keep everyone occupied, but from which individuals could absent themselves for a brief period. Once this operation was functioning smoothly and her attention was no longer required to maintain the activity of the large group, she was able to call each child over to a space in the corner for a one-to-one interaction that formed the context for observing and recording academic responses.

A variation of this strategy involves pretraining the subject with the aim of providing a behavioral context within which the response of interest will likely occur. In contrast to the above example in which the environment was rearranged in order to enable the response of interest to occur and be observed, the tactic here is to modify the person's behavior through training, so that a particular response class is more probable. For example, a speech therapist conducting articulation therapy with a small group of young children might spend a number of preliminary sessions teaching the children a

---

[3]Mrs. Connie Sneed, W. T. Moore School, Tallahassee, Florida.

variety of games chosen for their value in promoting a great deal of verbal behavior, a response class required for therapy.

OBSERVATIONAL TACTICS

In light of the foregoing strategic issues raised and discussed, it is possible to arrive at some general tactical principles that can loosely guide designing and implementing observational procedures. It is useful to understand that observation is closely akin to the process of transduction—transforming an event from one form to another. Any event being observed affects the transducer, which thereupon generates an output according to the principles of its design. In other words, given an exact specification of the output and knowledge of the details of operation of the transducer, the corresponding characteristics of the input are completely specifiable. Ideally, this may be said of a good observational system; from examining the record of the output, the experimenter should know exactly the nature and extent of the dimensional quantities of the observed behavior (input). The overriding tactical problem becomes that of ensuring the highest possible degree of correspondence between the characteristics of the behavioral events observed and the recorded products of the observational process. Two general classes of observational transducers are available to the behavioral researcher— machine and human[4]—and the special tactical considerations surrounding the use of each are discussed in this section.

Before proceeding, however, a seemingly trivial, but actually fundamental, point must be clarified regarding the role of observing and recording in defining a response class. It should be obvious that a response instance (and thus the class) is not actually defined until it is observed and a permanent record results, regardless of any other intentions and efforts on the part of the experimenter. It is imperative that the experimenter be especially careful in determining the extent to which any discrepancies may exist between the formal response class definition (to which the observational procedures are presumably sensitive), the definition that actual observational operations determine, and the definition that the resulting data record reflects. This care is necessary in order to assure optimum accuracy and generality when the

---

[4]The astute and contentious reader may assert the possibility of infrahuman organisms serving as observers of the behavior of other organisms, even including humans. Many examples of this capability may be cited, such as the barking of a sentry dog occasioned by the approach of a stranger, but there has been little development of appropriate record-making devices. The capacity of a pigeon to transduce physical events has been developed for the ingenious industrial application of detecting defective diodes (Cumming, 1966) and drug capsules (Verhave, 1966) moving by on a conveyor belt.

experimenter describes the research method and the resulting interpretations to scientific peers.

Observing by Machines

When the behaver's responses are detected by a mechanical, electrical, or electronic device, the procedure may be termed machine observation. (In a later section, we discuss the use of such devices to create a permanent record of behavioral events.) As pointed out previously, this practice also automatically ensures definition of the response class by the observational apparatus. It thus becomes imperative that the detection device be narrowly sensitive to those characteristics of the response that the experimenter intends to investigate. To illustrate, a device commonly used to record the occurrence of speech is known as a voice operated relay (VOR), consisting of a sensitive microswitch activated by sound pressures transduced by a microphone. Unfortunately, a characteristic of early models was that any sound, including coughs, throat clearings, belches, and extraneous sounds in the environment, as well as verbal utterances, would trigger them. Newer versions have incorporated band pass filters that screen out all but the frequency range that includes human speech, thus accomplishing detection of a class of events that much more nearly approximates the true interest of the researcher.

Effectively using machine transducers requires paying close attention to *calibration* procedures. When an investigator relies on an electronic or mechanical device to detect and report the occurrence of events of interest, it must first be determined that the device is properly sensitive to those events, and then assurance must be maintained that it does not begin failing to detect all occurrences. For example, many battery operated devices lose sensitivity to events of low magnitude as the batteries run down, creating the possibility of falsely portraying a gradual decrease in the frequency of the event when there has only been a decrease in sensitivity of the device. Furthermore, the device must remain sensitive to only those events in the defined response class. Drifts in sensitivity in either direction may cause the device to begin detecting events outside the defined class, with the result that the subject matter of investigation changes gradually through the course of observation. Mechanical pedometers (devices that count gross bodily movements, especially steps) are usually worn near the waist; if they drift in the direction of oversensitivity, they begin recording the girth movements that accompany laughter. Once such a device is placed in operation, its sensitivity must be periodically evaluated to ensure that its definition and detection of instances of a response class remain unchanged through the course of the research. This outcome can be assured only through frequent human monitoring of the observation process, coupled with periodic checks on sensitivity according to the calibration procedure. Adding a machine transducer to the observation process eliminates human observer bias; it does not eliminate the requirement for human vigilance. The solution to these problems lies in prevention through a combination of sound design, quality controlled manufacture, and proper field use. As automatic behavioral transduction devices become more widely available, a highly competitive industry will emerge, and it is the responsibility of investigators to ensure that the marketplace rewards quality.

The use of machine observation does not abrogate the use of human observers, although their role will be somewhat circumscribed. In fact, machine observation appropriates the task at which human observers are least proficient, promoting people to the performance of detection tasks for which designing machines is exceedingly difficult. Machines are ideal for the observational requirement that the same behavioral event (and no other) be precisely and reliably detected again and again with no sources of unprogrammed influence modifying detection; as a result of their conditioning histories, people usually execute this requirement very poorly. On the other hand, because of that same conditioning history, human beings are very sensitive to the widest variety of behavioral and environmental events in an experimental setting and their possible importance to the conduct and interpretation of the experiment; machines equal to this important observational task have not and ultimately cannot be invented. Thus, the necessity of human observation in this broad and complex role is only magnified by using machines to detect the repeated occurrence of single behavioral events. Ideally, human and machine function in tandem to ensure that observation is not only accurate, but complete.

An interesting example of machine transduction under seemingly difficult circumstances may be found in a research project by Azrin, Rubin, O'Brien, Ayllon, and Roll (1968). They were interested in developing means for controlling body posture (specifically "slouching") of normal subjects in their natural environment. This objective required a practical procedure for measuring the relevant aspects of postural behavior under a wide variety of conditions. Instead of employing platoons of trained observers under limited and infrequent conditions, they chose to develop a simple apparatus capable of continuously transducing the required features of postural behavior in terms of absolute units under virtually all daily circumstances. The apparatus defined slouching as an increased distance between two points on the back. This was transduced with a snap action switch taped on the subject's back at the level of the second thoracic vertebra. The switch was attached to an elastic cord also taped to the back, so that rounding the back caused the switch contacts to close. An alternative method of mounting the switch and cord used a light harness. In order to eliminate switch closures due to normal activities (such as looking over the shoulder, reaching, or bending over), a mercury tilt switch was adopted that blocked posture switch output when the torso was tilted forward more than 10 degrees. In addition, the definition of slouching was further refined as an uninterrupted switch closure for at least three seconds. The cumulative duration of slouching was recorded by a miniature elapsed time meter wired in series with the posture switch. A small programming device (2 × 4 × 6 centimeters and weighing 60 grams) allowed current to pass through the time meter only after the posture switch was closed for three seconds. The timer was read by magnifying it through a photograph that provided a permanent record that could be measured at a later time. Calibration showed that measurement error was only about one-fifth of 1% (about 30 seconds) at the 4-hour time range used for most subjects. In addition, the apparatus contained a small speaker and a transistor circuit that could sound a 500 cycles per second tone at 55 decibels when so programmed by the experimenter (this function was for control rather than measurement purposes). All apparatus was worn under regular clothing. The development of these observing and recording techniques allowed experimentation on variables influencing posture to procede with confidence that the data upon which further experimental decisions and interpretations would be based was continuous during observational sessions, satisfactorily accurate, and not subject to any of the complications usually accompanying human transducers.

As the science of behavior and its accompanying technologies develop, it seems inevitable that maching observation of behavior will become routine, facilitated by the products of substantial support industry.[5] Present levels of instrumentation will appear crude and will rapidly become obsolete. Although the potential for such advances is probably well within the current state of the art in engineering, behavioral science and technology have only just begun to place even simple demands on this source of highly sensitive and sophisticated instrumentation. The faltering nature of this early progress is probably largely due to reluctance to abandon traditions that glorify the human observer who dares enter the observational arena shielded only by a recording form, and armed only with a sharpened pencil. The impetus for shedding this tradition must come from behavioral scientists; we cannot expect our brethren in the engineering sciences to both state and solve our measurement problems. The behavioral scientist will be required to confront each problem of observation with the question, "What element in the environment changes as a result of each response and how can the change be transduced physically?" Answering the first part of this question is solely the responsibility of the behavioral scientist; a precise statement of the transduction required specifies the problem for the design engineer in the event the necessary transducer is not yet available. In light of our traditions, it will require vision and imagination for the investigator even to state the

---

[5]A provocative discussion of machine technology for both measurement and behavior change may be found in Schwitzgebel (1976).

question clearly. Too often, we accept the imprecise alternative by default, because it does not occur to us that a physical solution might be possible. However, as noted in Chapter 2, it is quite probable that advances in instrumentation will uncover vast new domains of behavioral phenomena possessed of a high degree of order and regularity that cannot be apprehended under the constraints of our present crude observation tactics.

Observing by Humans

It was stated earlier that observation involves the sensitive reaction of human or machine to the defined dimensions of behavioral events. These words were carefully chosen to communicate the idea that when humans are used as observers of behavioral phenomena, they serve as transducers upon which responses of interest must have a highly specific impact in order to become data. The human as transducer has many channels or senses for detecting events, and one or more of these must be stimulated by the defined dimensions of the target behavior. The act of observing is a response itself, and accurate observation is a matter of bringing this response under the necessary degree of control sharply exerted by the subject's behavior as a class of stimuli. This perspective toward observation using humans as transducers is crucial in designing suitable observational procedures when machines are unavailable. This section should make it clear that successfully using humans as observers of behavior itself presupposes an effective behavioral technology.

Selection.   The first issue that should be addressed after the decision has been made to employ human observers concerns who will be selected to perform the duty in the specific case. The necessary qualifications of individuals to serve as observing transducers will vary from one experimental situation to another, yet only rarely are efforts made to manipulate the accuracy and completeness of observation through informed prior selection. It has been repeatedly stressed that a major difference between a machine and a human observer is that the machine lacks the unique personal history that contributes heavily to the behavior of the human. Whether this history will facilitate or impair the development and maintenance of proper observing behavior is a question the investigator should weigh carefully as observers are selected. Former classroom teachers, for example, are likely to have a much different history with respect to the observation of children's behavior than will undergraduate students.

A second factor in selecting observers is the presence of extraneous behavioral contingencies that may impose limits on sensitivity of detection. A shop supervisor whose compensation may partly depend on the safety record of the employees in his or her charge will likely be far more sensitive to instances of safety rule infraction than would one of the employees elected democratically by voice vote. Using double blind procedures in medical observation is a familiar tactical response to this concern.

Finally, there is the fundamental sense in which a functional definition of some response classes all but requires certain persons to serve as observer-transducers. A classroom teacher who is disturbed by a child's talking out must, almost by definitional necessity, act as observer and recorder of that behavior, for it is the teacher's response of becoming disturbed that partially defines the behavior of interest. A somewhat different class of responses would almost certainly be detected by a trained, nonparticipant observer stationed in the back of the room, for that observer would respond to any and every verbal emission that met some arbitrary criterion of loudness and duration, whether or not it disturbed the teacher.

Training.   Proper training of the observer candidate is a complex and demanding process. A common tactic is deploying a number of minimally trained observers (see the discussion of multiple observers later in this chapter) and relying on statistical techniques to cleanse the data of impurities injected by their lack of behavioral preparation. Acquisition of an exact and proper observing response is a problem in behavioral control requiring a fully developed behavioral technology for its solution. In essence, certain specifiable aspects of the observed behavior must come to function as prompting stimuli for explicit responses on the part of the observer, the topography of those observer responses being determined by the amount of some dimensional quantity actually present on each occurrence of an event in the target response class. Furthermore, the functional relation between the stimulus properties of the subject's behavior and the observer's responding must remain stable throughout the entire investigation.

Achieving this degree of behavioral control first requires that the observer candidate possess or develop certain facilitative requisite skills, such as sitting still, focusing on the target subject, ignoring distractions, etc. Next, the observing or detecting response itself must be shaped to a stable topography and adequate frequency so that its occurrence in the eventual observation situation is fully functional. Careful consideration must be given to the topographical requirements of the observing response, since its temporal requirement for occurrence must be well below the temporal parameters of the response class to be measured. For example, no observer of a self-abusive child can furnish a full written description of each of a series of face slaps that occur at a frequency of 10 cycles per minute.

After the topography and frequency of the observing response have been established, the next step is to bring the occurrence of that response under the control of the relevant stimuli that will be present in the eventually observed target behavior. The technical procedures for establishing stimulus control should be brought into play at this stage, it being usually insufficient to rely on verbal instruction to mediate the appropriate functional relations.[6]

Calibration.   Once the observing response has been shown to occur reliably in the presence of, and only in the presence of, the relevant aspects of the training stimuli, the observer can be adapted to the experimental environment. After a period of time has elapsed to permit habituation to the novel or distracting features of the experimental environment, practice observation should begin and field calibration measures taken. The observer's skills should be adjusted at this stage to the levels of accuracy required for the eventual investigation. Brief episodes of on-site retraining may be required to ensure performance at this level.

Practice observing and calibrating sessions typically require the use of bogus, nonexperimental subjects. Measuring and adjusting accuracy implies the availability of either a known input signal (behavioral episode for which the values of the dimensional quantities to be observed are predetermined) or a means of establishing "true" values after the fact. The latter tactic is usually easier and can be expedited with the aid of videotape equipment or automatic transduction apparatus.

There are two generic procedures for calibrating a human observer on site. The first involves spot checking the products of the observer's behavior against a record produced mechanically or by dirct comparison with any products of the subject's responding. For example, in a program of research on personalized instruction, it might be necessary to train observers to monitor on-line the verbal interchange between students and proctors in order to record the correct and incorrect academic responses of the students. Unobstrusive tape recordings constitute a permanent record of the products of selected interchanges and can be used as a reference value for calibrating the observer. There are at least two deficiencies in this approach. One is that it is likely to be expensive and/or disruptive to arrange for machine transduction; otherwise, that procedure would have been elected in preference to a human observer in the first place (e.g., logistical limitations would preclude using tape recorders as the sole means of response transduction). The second deficiency is that accuracy or correspondence can only be assessed for the range of values actually observed; no measure of the observer's sensitivity to the full range of of observable values is available. It is important to realize that prolonged observation in a situation that does not provide the full range of values the observer was trained to detect is likely to

---

[6]The referenced techniques including fading, induction through behavioral contrast, differential reinforcement scheduling, and a variety of other procedures used in discrimination training. For a description and survey of these procedures, the reader is referred to Reynolds (1975).

alter the observer's repertoire, because this recent behavioral history may override the influence of the earlier training.

The second general method of calibrating a human observer avoids the problem of limited range, but does not expressly incorporate independent measures of the true values. This method involves the introduction of known sources of variation in the phenomenon being observed so as to provide assurance that the observer continues to detect the full range of possible values. One means of achieving this is to instruct a bogus "subject" to respond in an extreme manner and note the extent to which the observer's report reflects this condition. An alternative is rearranging the experimental environment in ways that have a high likelihood of producing substantial variation in the observed properties of the responses of the target subject, again inspecting the observer's responses for evidence of such an impact. For instance, in an industrial setting in which workers are serving as their own observers, major variations in the pace at which components to be assembled move into the work station must influence the number of components assembled and should be reflected in worker performance reports. If a means of obtaining true values is available, it can be used to provide reference data for an accuracy check. Lacking such means, this method is relatively crude, but will at least ensure that the observer remains responsive to major variations in the dimension of interest.

The details of this tactic must be closely geared to the behavior of experimental interest, so that an intervention is arranged that will almost certainly produce a known effect. One way of doing this is to reproduce an effect that has previously been observed with that subject. Used in this way, the environmental rearrangement constitutes a probe and is ideally of no greater duration than necessary to establish calibration of the observer. Prolonged alteration of the environment is likely to have lasting and possibly detrimental effects on the behavior of interest; these effects will then become major contaminants of the entire experiment. Should this happen, the subject is best "sacrificed" for purposes of the experiment. The experimenter must realize that although such a price seems high, the need for continued assurance that observation is accurate may justify it.

In many cases, advantage can be taken of natural, unplanned environmental contributions to extraneous variation and such events can be used as calibration checks. It frequently happens, for example, that institutionalized retarded subjects sustain unanticipated changes in their drug regimens or activity schedules, and major changes in behavior immediately ensue. Under such circumstances, investigators are likely to wax indignant, fuming at their inability to control external factors. They might pause briefly in their fulminations and recognize, especially if the observer produced the first indication that a change had occurred, that nature has just provided a calibration check and that the observer is still accurate, at least within limits.

Whenever calibration checks are made, there should be as little associated disruption in the observer's environment as possible. This means that the observer should be unaware that calibration is in progress, because knowledge of that fact could render the results of the calibration procedure unrepresentative of observational accuracy at other times. The investigator should never lose sight of the fact that a human observer is a highly sensitive and delicate instrument, likely to be influenced by a much wider range of occurrences than would a machine. The variability that constitutes the subject matter of the science of behavior is the major limitation of using humans as observers for the observational chores under discussion.[7] For this reason, frequent calibration checks are necessary and should be planned as an integral part of any experimental procedure relying on human observers.

There is an unfortunate tendency to separate the training and performance phases of an observer's experience, assuming that if the former is done correctly, the latter will remain satisfactory. This is demonstrably not the case, for training in the behavioral sense continues whenever the acquired skill is being practiced, and the same principles that were formally deployed in the training procedure are free to operate in the posttraining environment of the experiment. Consequently, it is imperative that the observer's behavior be monitored rather frequently for evidence that additional "training" is gradually altering the effects of the original procedure. A systematic calibration procedure not only meets this objective, but provides timely opportunities to formally retrain and thus adjust the sensitivity and accuracy of the instrument to the required tolerances. The data from such continuing calibration will further be available to scientific peers as evidence of the accuracy of observation (see Chapter 10).

A relatively detailed example may give the reader a practical perspective on the methods and importance of calibrating human observers. A significant public health problem in the United States is the high incidence of undetected breast cancer in women. As part of a broad effort to reduce the mortality figures resulting from this disease, there have been a number of attempts to induce women on a mass scale to submit to screening examinations. Early detection, while the carcinogenic lumps are still small, leads to a highly favorable prognosis. The behavioral problem centers on training screening personnel to detect small lumps, then ensuring that these people remain fully proficient while they perform their duties in clinics and mobile detection centers.

In attempting to bring behavioral technology to bear on this general problem, the Gainesville Behavioral Medicine Study Group developed a life-like breast model containing small lumps that were connected electronically

---

[7]Of course, human observers are superior for more broadly defined observational tasks, and we earlier encouraged their use in supplementing maching observations.

by means of pressure switches to various recording devices. This model proved highly effective in training the skill of breast palpation for lump detection (Adams, Goldstein, Hench, Hall, Madden, Pennypacker, Stein, & Catania, 1976; Hall, Goldstein, & Stein, 1977). The individualized training procedure allowed the observer to palpate the model following brief verbal instruction. Each time the observer reported detecting a lump, it was possible to examine the automatically transduced record to see if a pressure switch had closed. Thus, the model provided the true values against which the observer was calibrated. If a lump was properly located and reported, an independent record of that fact was produced by the machine. Training continued until the observer could detect all lumps greater than or equal to 2 mm in diameter in a series of models of varying sizes and textures. The observers were then assigned to field duties, palpating the breasts of women who presented themselves as part of the screening program. By taking the model into the field for follow-up measurements, the investigators were in effect recalibrating their observers to ensure that their accuracy remained high, regardless of the range of actual tissue configurations they encountered in their regular screening duties.

Subject Self-Observation.   It may prove enlightening to apply the above recommendations to the case of subject self-observation. We will consider here the use of the subject as observer of public behavioral events.[8] By public behavior, we mean those responses that are potentially observable by both the subject and others. The reasons for such a selection of an observer are usually related to the advantage of accessibility to the behavior of interest that the subject has over the other possible observers. Thus, the subject can observe the designated response class for extended periods of time (i.e., all waking hours per day) and across all settings that may be encountered in his or her daily schedule. In this manner, responses with low frequencies of occurrence can be adequately sampled, and observations of responding under different settings may be separately examined.

Although it may seem surprising in light of present day practices, the preceding discussions in this chapter have suggested that self-observation by the subject should in no way be considered different from observation by any other single observer. The same strategic goals and tactical procedures apply in both cases, and the "closeness" of the subject to his or her own behavior can only be considered an advantage. Any observer will be influenced by personal history and by present contingencies in ways that may be contrary to the goals of the observational task, but the unique situation of subject-observers does not in any manner make them an inherently inferior choice. The same training procedures already discussed must be applied in either case toward the goals

---

[8]Chapter 9 covers in detail the measurement of private behavioral events.

of assuring satisfactory reliability and accuracy of observation. The subject who cannot be adequately trained for the task must be replaced, as would any inferior observer.[9] If the subject is not a disadvantageous choice for the observer, then the greater access to the target behavior may often be preferred over that of other observers. The subject's access to his or her own behavior may actually solve otherwise difficult observation problems, such as the duration and frequency of observation periods.

Multiple Observers.   The perspective that human observers are transducers in the same sense as any physical observational apparatus is pervasively useful in its implications. For instance, the above discussion of observer training and calibration has in no way suggested the need for the use of more than a single observer for any one observational task. Because the use of multiple observers in social science research is an honored tradition, now elevated nearly to the status of a requirement, this discrepancy requires careful examination. We can determine only two reasons for using multiple observers—accuracy and believability. Before probing the legitimacy of these rationales, it is necessary to make the fundamental point that using two or more observers to detect behavioral events cannot provide any information about the reliability of any one observer's judgments. Reliability refers in this context to the stability of the responses of a single observer over repeated presentations of the same stimulus complex, and it can *only* be determined by comparing repeated observer judgments to each other over a series of presentations of an identical transduction of subject responding (e.g., a videotape).

In order for the stability of the correspondence of the observer judgments in relation to the observed events to be evaluated, the constancy of the dimensional quantities of the events must be known. A second observer is clearly irrelevant to this requirement and consequently provides no information by which reliability of the first observer can be determined. After all, reliability is a characteristic of the interaction between a single observer and a known part of the environment; additional observers are of no help in evaluating an intraindividual phenomenon. Therefore, reference to a second observer as a "reliability" of the first observer is improper (see Chapter 10).

If multiple observers can provide no information about the reliability of a particular observer, can they be used to determine or enhance the accuracy of

---

[9]In training the subject self-observer, it is usually prudent to develop the initial topography and frequency of the observing/recording response chain using a response class other than the eventual target. This eliminates the only serious special objection that might be raised with regard to using self-observation—that somehow the training alters the target behavior in unspecifiable ways. Any other impact of the observational process on the target behavior is as manageable as in the case of another human observer.

that observer's judgments? It should be immediately clear that in order to evaluate whether or not the responses of an observer are accurate transductions of some behavioral event, it is both necessary and sufficient to know the true value of the chosen dimensional quantity of the event. If a second observer cannot be shown to be more accurate than the first by this procedure, he or she is again a superfluous addition to the experimental setting. On the other hand, if the second observer has been shown to be accurate, he or she will suffice as the sole observer.

Using true values to calibrate human observers presupposes access to some means of determining the true value of the chosen dimensional quantity of the calibration event. By "true" value, we mean a measure determined independently from which all possible bias and random measurement error have been removed. The word "true" is used in a relative sense; even the most precise scientific measurement only approximates, however closely, the absolute true value of the phenomenon. "True" values used for calibration purposes must be of this type and cannot be supplied by an observer acting alone, because there is no way to ensure that all sources of bias and error have been eliminated in the case of a human.

There are two basic ways to obtain serviceable true values of behavioral dimensional quantities—by machine transduction or by measuring available response products. The proper approach to designing observational procedures will first throroughly examine any opportunities for using machines for observation, because they are preferable in principle. Even if this examination determines that machines are not feasible as the sole means of observation, this search will have the auxiliary benefit of unearthing any possibilities of using machines on at least a periodic basis for calibrating the necessary human observer. If machine transductions are too costly or otherwise unobtainable, one can revert to the tactic of acquiring response products.

Providing they are available, using response products has many advantages. They can be evaluated off-line, at leisure, and as often as necessary to establish the required true value. In many cases, continued collection and analysis is too disruptive and costly for response products to serve as the sole basis for all measurement, but their occasional use for observer calibration is feasible. Suppose, for example, an observer is recording the performance of the workers in the packing area of a shipping department. The observer counts each item as it is wrapped and placed in a carton. By selecting and unpacking a carton on a periodic random basis, one can check the accuracy of the observer's counts; one would not unpack all cartons, however, to ensure continuous accuracy. After opening the carton, any observer (the original observer, a second observer or the experimenter— it makes no difference) can determine the true value of the count of items in the carton. The special utility of this procedure for getting true value lies in the fact that it is performed off-line, at leisure, and as often as necessary to assure the investigator that the true value for each event (e.g., each carton) has been determined.

Although a second observer cannot be used to evaluate accuracy (again, an intraindividual characteristic), it is possible under some stringent limitations to use a second observer to *improve* the estimates of the true values of the dimensional quantity of a behavioral event over the estimates that might be available from a single observer. There are two distinguishable ways in which this outcome can be arranged.[10] First, it is possible (although certainly not necessary) that using two observers can improve accuracy if their independent but collective reactions are required to define the occurrence of each behavioral instance; that is, each observer must observe and in some way indicate each response occurrence. The response will be recorded as having occurred only if both observers independently agree that it did so. This requirement may improve accuracy by decreasing the chance of false positive judgments, but it is equally possible that it may increase the chance of false negative judgments. The difficulty with this procedure is that independent knowledge of the truth about the response occurences is unavoidably required in order to determine whether the use of the second observer results in any augmentation of accuracy over the reactions of the first observer alone. Of course, if this truth is available by some means, then the use of a second observer again becomes unnecessary, because the known true information can and should be used properly to train, calibrate and maintain a high level of accuracy in a single observer.[11]

---

[10]It should be apparent that this analysis only considers the simultaneous use of multiple observers of a single class of behavioral events occurring in one setting during the observational session. Whenever instances of a class occur in more than one setting over time, the sum of the judgments of single observers in each setting will obviously yield a more accurate estimate of occurrence for all such settings than would be available from one observer who was restricted to only one setting. For example, the collected observations of a teacher who stays in the classroom and an aide who stays on the playground will likely constitute a better estimate of the total occurrence of a kindergarten child's behavior of hitting other children than would the observations of either adult alone.

[11]Use of multiple human observers in this manner is certainly infrequent; the most ingenious example used pigeons as observers. During World War II, Skinner conducted a research project that had as its goal the use of pigeons to guide the trajectory of a large bomb called the Pelican (Skinner, 1961). Pigeons were trained to peck at the image of an object such as a ship as it appeared and grew larger in a viewing window. The nose of the bomb was constructed with a small space for each of three pigeons, so that they could see the target as the bomb fell. The clear windows on which pigeons pecked were designed to detect the spatial location of the peck of each bird and to transduce this information into changes in trajectory. However, the apparatus was constructed so that any adjustments in trajectory required that the location of two of the three birds' pecking responses at the image of the target be in agreement. It all apparently worked quite well.

A second means of improving the accuracy of observational judgments using more than one observer assumes that the error in the judgments of each individual observer is some constant value and, furthermore, that such error is randomly distributed across any collection of observers. If these assumptions were valid, averaging the judgments of multiple observers would serve to improve accuracy, with more observers yielding better estimates. However, both assumptions about human observing responses are difficult to justify empirically.

In addition to these limited means of improving accuracy, it is possible to phrase a defense of the use of multiple observers in terms of the *believability* of the resulting data. Believability is the propensity of the experimenters and their colleagues to accept as true any features of the data that are under examination. In the case of measurement variability, believability refers to the extent to which the data are assumed to be accurate representations of what actually occurred. There are certainly many features of the conduct of experiments that exert control over the interpretative behavior of experimenters and their peers. Chapter 18 on interpretation examines this perspective in detail.

However, using multiple observers to produce some quantitative description of interobserver agreement is widely acknowledged as a means of convincing all concerned about the "goodness" of the observational procedures used. Because we have already shown that the use of more than one observer of a series of behavioral events cannot possibly provide any logical evidence regarding either reliability or accuracy of observational judgments, the use of the indistinct term "goodness" is intentional and appropriate. In fact, this amorphous "goodness" seems to refer to an evaluation of both reliability and accuracy, the defense of which, if not deductive, must be inductive. This "logic of experience" tells us that if two independent observer's total session measures of the countability of a response during repeated observational sessions are always within plus or minus one of each other, then it is likely (to some unspecified degree) that those counts are reliable and "therefore" accurate, or that they are accurate and therefore reliable, measures of the true values. The more independent, simultaneous, and consistent observations are made of the same event, the more convinced we usually are of the event's actual occurrence. Even though this conclusion is not required and may not even be true, our conditioning histories are generally such that we find the data from a variety of multiple observer procedures to be convincing estimates of true values. The logical fallacy upon which our reasoning is based is the familiar *affirmation of the consequent,* and takes the following form:

1. If *A* is true, *B* is true.
2. *B* is true.
3. Therefore, *A* is true.

And in the present context:

1. If the observer's judgments are accurate, then a second observer's judgments will agree.
2. The second observer's judgments are made and do agree.
3. Therefore, the first observer's judgments are accurate (and consequently reliable).

It may be recalled from Chapter 2 that such reasoning is fallacious because it is not required that A is true *if and only if* B is true, so that B could be true even though A is false. This reasoning is examined in detail in subsequent chapters (e.g., 14), in which its central role in experimental reasoning is clarified. However, dependence on this reasoning as a justification for the use of multiple observers cannot be strongly defended for two reasons. First, the usefulness of affirming the consequent lies in examining a number of different consequents of the truth of the antecedent. This would suggest the use of as many observers as possible (because each observer's judgments can affirm or disaffirm the antecedent), but this is inadvisable for other reasons. Most uses of multiple observers include only two observers, forcing the experimenter into a weak inductive position. Second, dependence on this reasoning when it cannot be fully exploited is all the more difficult to defend because there are usually available alternatives of superior merit; this chapter has already discussed these tactics.

Nevertheless, it is important to recognize that long-standing convictions about the value of multiple observers have led to an honored, if naive, tradition in which multiple observers are considered *de rigueur*, even in situations in which they are clearly unnecessary. For example, if the response under study creates a relatively permanent product, then the product (if not used directly for measurement) can often be used to train and calibrate a single observer. One published study (which will go unidentified) exemplifying the present confusion examined contingencies intended to improve spelling accuracy in a school child. In spite of the existence of the products of the child's responses on paper, a second observer was used to assess the "reliability" of the teacher's scoring of the spelled words as correct or incorrect! The proper tack would have been for the experimenter to use the child's handwritten words to verify the correctness of the teacher's scoring. Any publication of the experiment should merely have reported the experimenter's verification. If we cannot be convinced by the experimenter's report under such circumstances, then we cannot accept similar reports of the other facets of experimental method and results, an obviously untenable position.

A final limitation of using multiple observers is logistical. The use of more than one observer requires additional efforts in finding, keeping, training, and calibrating observers. These efforts are disproportionally large for the increments in believability that may result. The possible effects of the presence of multiple observers on the behavior of the subject raises an area of further difficulties that are antithetical to the purposes of experimentation.

Given these various analyses, what, then, can be concluded about using multiple observers? Such procedures can only be seen as a choice of last resort; once the use of human observers is deemed unavoidable, every effort should be made to arrange observational procedures that will be successful with a single observer. Redirection of the resources that are too often squandered in the relatively unproductive grappling with the complexities of multiple observers toward the tactics suggested earlier for single observers will often satisfy the highest standards of reliability and accuracy of measurement. Only when evidence of these data characteristics is clearly too costly to obtain or insufficient in quantity (*not* quality) should multiple observers be considered. Their use should first be consistent with the legitimate but restricted means by which accuracy can be augmented. Only after these tactics fail or are found inapplicable should multiple observers be used in the blatant (and announced) attempt to encourage the acceptance of data as reliable and valid on the sole basis of our experiential conviction that if two people reported seeing the same thing, then it probably happened.

This discussion of strategies and tactics of observing behavior has recommended major revisions in observational procedure as now practiced by those who conduct research on human behavior. In particular, contemporary reliance on human observers is slavish at a time when mechanical, electrical, and electronic technologies have attained a state of near wizardry. The use of unassisted human observers can only be seen as the Stone Age of behavioral observation. The last quarter of the 20th century will certainly see dramatic advances in our capability to transduce behavioral events accurately.

RECORDING OBSERVATIONS

As stated earlier, a response is not actually defined until it has been observed and a record made of that information. It is at this point that what were heretofore only *facts* become *data*. The guiding strategy of recording is to create a permanent and accurate history of observations for future examination. The transduction of the ongoing behavior under investigation into data most often eventuates in some kind of numerical description. Although there may be an intermediate stage, such as audio or video taping, the effects of the responses on the machine or human transducers are eventually put into the precise language of all sciences—numbers and units. This is, however, only an interim stage between observation and the later data displays. The initial recording must preserve as much information as possible (without interfering with the task of observation) to facilitate the tasks of data analysis and professional dissemination. In other words, the observational record is only for the private use of the experimenter, and it should describe the results of observation as fully as possible in order to permit later uses.

Recording by Machines

The use of instrumentation to create a record of observations usually accompanies the use of machines for response definition/observation. The general superiority of this tactic becomes especially evident when the nature of the response and its setting present difficult definitional and observational problems. A study by Barrett (1962) furnishes an excellent illustration of such problems, and the tactics used to accomplish scientific measurement are exemplary.

The patient was a 38-year-old man in a Veterans' Administration hospital whose problem was extensive multiple muscular tics. These spasmodic movements included major contractions of his neck, shoulder, chest, and abdominal muscles, head nodding, bilateral eye blinking, opening of the mouth, and some additional minor facial movements. Even in the relatively restricted hospital setting, these behaviors presented obvious problems for accurate measurement. Barrett's solution used a swivel-tilt armchair in which the patient sat comfortably. A large U-shaped magnet was attached to the back of the chair top and allowed to hang freely. An induction coil was nested in electrical tape strung between the poles of the magnet and was adjusted so that the patient's larger movements (regardless of locus or amplitude) created a movement of the coil in the magnetic field. The resulting current was amplified with an EEG recorder to operate a sensitive relay, activation of which defined a response. The amplifier gain was set such that tics of sufficient duration and amplitude operated the relay, and after initial adjustments the setting remained constant. The relay stepped a cumulative response recorder that provided a continuous record of responses. All recording and other equipment was located in a separate room.

These procedures, supplemented with monitoring of the equipment and human observation, effectively dealt with the numerous difficulties presented by this case and was the basis for research demonstrating the stimulus control that could be exerted over the muscular tics, resulting in their virtual elimination for extended periods in the chair. The general tactics with which this problem was approached have equal utility in the widest variety of research settings.

Recording by Humans

Performance by a human in the role of observer/transducer can and should be facilitated by arranging for instrumented recording of the observer's responses. Unfortunately, the task of making a record of observer responses usually falls to the observer, and herein lies the most difficult aspect of designing recording procedures. It is crucial that the demands placed upon the observer by both observing and recording duties be successfully balanced so that one is not less adequately performed than the other. Highly sensitive observation is of no benefit if it prevents a full and accurate record from being created. Likewise, careful recording procedures are of little utility if they chronicle unnecessarily flawed observations. Thus, the goal of designing accurate recording procedures is a system compatible with the needs of precise observation; this requires assisting the observer by minimizing the duration and complexity of each recording response with no loss of accuracy.

With these requirements established, it is clear that a detailed examination of the functional and topographical requirements of the recording response is necessary. Because it is common that an observer is engaged in direct visual observation and is required to record the occurrence of each response, we can use this context to suggest appropriate tactics in designing recording procedures.

Making the recording response should not require the observer to break visual contact with the subject. It therefore becomes necessary to use a recording response that does not require eye–hand coordination for its execution. Although simple, inexpensive push-button devices are widely available and should obviously be used, malfunction may necessitate resorting to paper and pencil recording. In that event, making tally marks on a blank pad is inevitably superior to use of any prepared form that requires the observer to look away from the subject. When timing is a part of observing and recording, supplementary auditory or visual stimulation that minimally interferes with a visual observation can usually be arranged. If the observer must concurrently look at a stopwatch and the subject, then interrupt contact with both to make a recording response, there is likely to be some loss of accuracy resulting from the incompatibility of the three responses.

To recapitulate, recording is the terminal event of a complex series that begins with defining the response class of interest, proceeds through observing, and culminates in creating a permanent record of the behavior. It is imperative that the events that constitute the recording procedure in no way be allowed to vitiate attainment of the high standards of accuracy and precision that invariably characterize good scientific measurement. The permanent record that remains after defining, observing, and recording have taken place is the only evidence that measurement actually occurred, and the quality of the entire process cannot exceed the characteristics of that record. Moreover, the collection of such records defines the data base of the research. It is upon this base that the researcher and the audience must ultimately rely for the truth of any assertion concerning natural laws of behavior.

9 The Problem of Limited Accessibility

I. A general strategy
   A. Historical perspective
   B. Accessibility continua
      1. Public stimuli and responses
      2. Public stimuli and private responses
      3. Private stimuli and public responses
      4. Private stimuli and private responses
   C. Further strategic considerations
II. Measurement tactics
   A. Definition of response classes
   B. Dimensional quantities and units
   C. Observation and recording
   D. Stability, accuracy, and believability

With respect to each individual, . . . a small part of the universe is private. We need not suppose that events which take place within an organism's skin have special properties for that reason. A private event may be distinguished by its limited accessibility but not, so far as we know, by any special structure or nature.

—B. F. Skinner

A GENERAL STRATEGY

Previous chapters have assumed that those portions of behavior and environment that are of scientific interest are public or accessible by more than one person. However, the experimenter's interest may sometimes lie with investigating functional relations between responses and environmental events either or both of which are private or accessible by only the subject.[1] These special circumstances present some serious problems for a scientific approach to experimentation that is built upon replication. The extremes of

---

[1]The conceptions in Chapter 17 of Skinner (1953a) are basic to this chapter.

caution in this area that are prevalent among some behavioral scientists today are perhaps a justifiable reaction to the abuses that characterized earlier approaches to the study of private events and that are still widespread in the social sciences.

Historical Perspective

Owing to its origins in philosophy and its special inherited concern with the epistemological problem, 19th- and early 20th-century psychology is largely defined by attempts to study private events and various attendant "phenomena"—consciousness, the mind, awareness, etc. An overview of this mammoth effort (e.g., Boring, 1950) makes clear that attention should be focused on two principal aspects—content and method—and that, whereas little lasting illumination has been cast on the chosen subject matter, certain methodological considerations have substantial bearing on contemporary behavioral approaches to the study of private events.

The distinction between method and content is perhaps best typified in the work of E. B. Titchener (1867–1927). According to Boring (1950), Titchener recognized that a particular stimulus would occasion different observational reports depending on the point of view the observer took. If the observer took what might be called the "physical" point of view or set, the stimulus event was described in detached, objective terms. Lacking this set, the observer described the stimulus event in more subjective terms, including reference to feeling quality. Verification of the operation of these different sets was obtained in tests of two-point thresholds, in which a blindfolded observer was asked to report whether one or two needle points were being applied to the skin. At a given physical separation of the two points, the subject responded differently when asked to report what "is" from what "it feels like." Recognizing this characteristic of human observers, Titchener could train his observers to report only what "is" and thus act as neutral transducers of the sensory consequences of controlled stimulus events. This is closely akin to the demands imposed upon an observer of private stimuli and is, of course, exactly the demand placed on any scientific observer of public events, be they instrument dials, cells on a slide, or response instances.

A second methodological characteristic of certain early psychological traditions bears a close resemblance to the inferential practices of modern physics. Although Wundt's "mental chronometry" mentioned in Chapter 3 did not produce data of unimpeachable interpretability, it was, nevertheless, an attempt at descriptive measurement of phenomena whose existence and influence can only be inferred from effects observed under carefully controlled experimental conditions. A physical illustration of this strategy is furnished by Millikan's well-known oil drop experiment (Miller, 1972), in which the charge of a single electron is measured as a deductive consequence of careful measurement and control of all but one variable, whose effects are then quantified in terms of variation in the known parameters. Somewhat more simply, electrons themselves are known only by their effects on photographic plates and cloud chambers, not by direct observations, yet the operations by which these effects are detected are sufficiently controlled and replicable as to leave little doubt as to the existence and reliability of the underlying phenomena. Of course, the precision of idemnotic measurement in modern physics is sufficient to make the existence of an event such as an electron a compelling inference for the sake of completeness and parsimony. As we have previously indicated, the early attempts at quantitative demonstration of various mental phenomena did not partake of the benefits afforded by precise idemnotic measurement, and the scientific status of these phenomena remains in dispute to this day.

These two strategies, proper training and instructing of the observer and deductive inference from observable functional effects, hold promise as components of a natural scientific strategy for the study of behavioral events whose accessibility may be severely limited. In order to consider properly the role of these components in such a general strategy, it is first necessary to explore more thoroughly the dimensions of the problem posed by limited accessibility.

Accessibility Continua

In order to facilitate discussion of strategic management of the difficulties inherent in investigating functional relations between behavioral and environmental events whose occurrence may be difficult to detect, it is useful to propose a public–private continuum of accessibility for both behavior and the environment. These continua are depicted graphically in Fig. 9.1. In our usage, the concept of accessibility is a combination of the probability that the event exists at all coupled with the difficulty of observing it, given that it does exist.

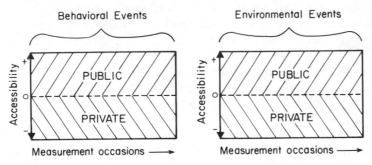

FIG. 9.1.   Schematic representation of accessibility continua for behavioral and environmental events over measurement occasions.

Describing behavioral events and environmental events with reference to an accessibility continuum underlying the discrete categories of public and private provides a dimension (susceptible to at least ordinal measurement) for analysis of a problem that has previously been viewed as largely semantic or philosophical. The terms "public" and "private" refer to adjacent nominal regions of the accessibility dimension, much as the terms "hot" and "cold" are descriptive of portions of the dimension of temperature. Even though for any single observer a particular event at any point in time either is or is not detectable, over a number of measurement occasions the accessibility of the event in question may vary within or across public or private regions for a variety of reasons.

One contributing explanation for this variation in accessibility lies in our conditioning history; we may not detect certain events because we have not been conditioned to respond to a particular class of stimuli. A skilled worker such as an inspector in a manufacturing plant has been explicitly trained by the employer and conditioned by the natural environment to detect and respond differentially to stimuli that are indeed public, but which others would not be able to detect in the absence of such a conditioning history. In another case, a class of events such as the behavior of swallowing may fall in the public region for any observer who is present (movement of Adam's apple invariably accompanies the internal movements that we call swallowing), but it would certainly strain the devotion of the most ardent observer to remain in a position to see every such movement by a subject for extended periods of time. The limitation on accessibility here is clearly only logistical, but it remains a limitation nevertheless. Finally, Skinner (1953a) points out the third justification for the schematic representation in Fig. 9.1: "The line between public and private is not fixed. The boundary shifts with every discovery of a technique for making private events public [p. 282]." Advances in scientific measurement technology repeatedly expand the accessibility of the universe of events by augmenting our sensory capabilities through magnification (in a generic sense) of some aspect of the event. Many behavioral events that occur inside the skin are routinely made public by measurement advances originating in medicine. This should be appreciated as a revealing area of support for expanding the frontiers of the science of behavior.

It should be clear, then, that the public or private nature of a behavioral or environmental event is not a characteristic of the event itself. Rather, it is a statement about the probability of an observer's behavior of detecting or responding to the event. The fact that an event is not being or cannot under some circumstances be detected does not mean that the event is inherently different from events that are or usually can be detected, nor does it mean that the event has the "property" of being private. Indeed, the most parsimonious assumption is that the "private" event is in no way different from "public" events and that any supposed difference lies only in the degree to which we have access to it.

The major benefit of this perspective lies in the enlightenment it offers to the strategies guiding the investigation of events whose occurrence is difficult or presently impossible to detect. Because the assumption is that such events are not different in their basic nature but merely raise problems of detection, the measurement problems forced by selecting such phenomena for study are not in any way different, regardless of traditional or a priori assumptions about the phenomena or the reasons for their inaccessibility.

Figure 9.1 suggests that the public and private regions of accessibility apply to both behavioral and environmental events. There are, thus, four possible circumstances of measurement distinguishable by this analysis, and each requires a somewhat specialized strategy for achieving accurate measurement and functional analysis. Let us now examine these strategies individually.

Public Stimuli and Responses.   When both the subject's movement and the part of the environment to which it is related are observable by the experimenter and others, there are no special difficulties other than the considerations discussed in previous chapters. It is indeed fortunate that public events have been the predominant focus of research interest in the early evolution of the science and that the demands for technology have been of a similar nature.

Public Stimuli and Private Responses.   When the functional relation of interest involves stimuli that are public but responses that are private, scientific investigation might seem impossible. In fact, the most careful of all behavioral researchers using infrahuman subjects in highly controlled laboratory settings routinely measure private behavioral events without hesitation. They ask a pigeon or a rat or a monkey to report what it sees or hears, and they accept the resulting data as accurate measures of private visual or auditory responses in spite of their inaccessibility to the experimenter. This is accomplished by teaching the animal to make a particular public response to experimenter arrangements of the relevant environment. Confidence in the accuracy of the public report is gained by the orderliness of correlations between the emission of the public reporting responses and successive rearrangements of the environmental stimuli. For example, a pigeon may learn that pecking a key results in the occasional presentation of grain only if the key is green; if the key is red, no grain ever appears no matter how much pecking occurs. Once this pattern is established and the pigeon only pecks when the key is green, we may safely infer that the private response of "seeing green" is occurring. The experimenter may then gradually change the color of the red key (holding other dimensions such as intensity constant) until its wavelength is very close to green and note when the pigeon resumes pecking. In this fashion, the pigeon's ability to differentiate colors in the spectrum can be assessed. This tactic is now commonplace, and through it we have learned about the sensory capabilities of various species in precise detail (Blough, 1966).

The tactic is used in an identical fashion to measure the same private responses to auditory and visual stimuli in humans of all ages. We teach a public response (such as hand raising or vocalizing) appropriate to the subject and the task and vary different characteristics of the stimuli (intensity of auditory stimuli or size of visual stimuli) in a systematic sequence. We trust the resulting evidence of the unobserved private responses (hearing and seeing) enough to prescribe prosthetic devices (hearing aids and glasses) that could be harmful if improperly fitted.

There is, then, an underlying strategy for investigating behavioral events of limited accessibility that has demonstrated success with animals and humans: First, train or bring under stimulus control a public reporting response appropriate to the subject and the task; then arrange to bring that response under the control of a particular stimulus accessible to both the subject and the experimenter. The demonstration that the resulting public responses are indeed accurate reports of the private responses is produced by the orderliness of the resulting data in relation to repeated manipulations of the public stimuli.

Private Stimuli and Public Responses.   The third combination includes responses of interest that are public but stimuli that are inaccessible. As before, this does not present an insoluble problem to the investigator. The tactic already well respected is to take advantage of the relation between the private environmental event and a public one. An example of this approach may be seen when a patient reports to a physician the repeated occurrence of migraine headaches. The physician is interested in minimal use of pharmacologic agents, and must therefore have confidence in the functional relation between headache pain and the patient's reports of the pain. After noting that aspirin and other mild drugs do not change the patient's reports of pain, the physician takes advantage of the fairly well-known effects of morphine by administering a substantial dose under controlled conditions (taking care not to inform the patient of suspected effects). If the patient then reports that the pain is no longer present and reports its return consistent with the time course of the drug, the physician's confidence in the relation between the reporting response and its prompting private stimulus is increased.

It is extremely important to caution here against falling into a trap. Successfully applying this strategy requires a known and demonstrable relation between some public environmental event and its private counterpart (in this case, morphine and its effects on pain). Certainly, this is not always available, and the researcher must never be in the position of hypothesizing the relation or, worse yet, the private stimulus itself in the absence of any such knowledge.

Private Stimuli and Private Responses.   Finally, we may consider the case in which the investigator is primarily interested in functional relations between responses and stimuli, both of which are not observable by anyone but the subject. If this were truly an unalterable situation, it would indeed pose a problem at present not approachable scientifically. The tactic in the two previous cases in which either environmental or response events were inaccessible was to make them public by applying measurement technology or by selecting other stimulus or response events whose correlations with the private events are either known or can be clearly demonstrated. Compounding those tactics may move doubly inaccessible relations into the scientific arena so that they can be subjected to the quality of analysis as are other behavioral phenomena. An especially creative and rigorous attack on the problem of inaccessibility of both stimulus and response events is furnished by the following laboratory example.

In a highly ingenious and elaborate series of experiments with rhesus monkeys, Adams and his co-workers (Adams, Hall, Rice, Wood, & Willis, 1975) have succeeded in reproducing by electrical means the private stimulus correlates of specific public stimulus displays. These investigators developed a complex procedure of which the following is a simplified variation: Monkeys are initially taught to respond on one of three different levers depending on whether one, two, or three dots appear on a screen. If anything else, or nothing, appears on the screen, the animal pushes a fourth lever. Appropriate lever responses are reinforced with food. At this stage, the experiment resembles the pigeon experiment mentioned previously, in which the private response of seeing is publically reported in the form of key pecking. Adams and his colleagues go further, however. After the monkey is trained to a high criterion of accuracy (always pushing the correct lever corresponding to the number of dots displayed), a blackout condition is arranged and patterns of mild electrical stimulation are applied directly to the animal's visual cortex. Varying the pattern of this stimulation produces lever responses previously correlated with dot displays, supporting the inference that the private event previously produced by dots can be reproduced by cortical stimulation. The availability of the fourth lever allows the animal to report that whatever it "sees" is not dots, thus increasing our confidence in the existence of the private correlate of public dots. It should be noted that a two-stage inference is involved here, supported entirely by the amount of control over the animals' lever pressing established in the training phase of the experiment. First is the inference that the same private response of "seeing dots" is occurring in the blackout condition; second is the inference that the private event evoked by the electrical stimulation at least closely resembled that which previously occurred when dots were presented before the eyes in normal light. The fact that differential lever responding is observed in the absence of light but only in conjunction with cortical stimulation supports both inferences. Incidentally, the purpose of this research is to develop an electronic prosthesis for the blind; refinement of the technique may lead to the ability to transform the signals generated by a miniature television camera into cortical stimulation that will elicit private visual experiences that are tightly determined by what the camera "sees."

The strategy underlying this research is closely akin to that used to investigate subatomic particles in modern physics. The private events that the monkey "sees" are not formally assumed to exist beforehand; their existence is the most parsimonious explanation of certain experimental effects observed under conditions that render any other cause unlikely. In physics, when certain data can be reasonably explained only by positing the presence of an electron of a specific charge, then that electron is identified by its effects. Similarly, the private stimulus "two dots" is identified by its effects on the monkey's behavior, it being unlikely that the monkey would, given this experimental history, strike that lever if any other event were the result of the specific cortical stimulation.

If a problem of double inaccessibility remains unapproachable by the tactics just described, then it may be time to call a temporary halt for purposes of regrouping while gathering reinforcements or planning a flanking movement. Reinforcements in this context might include developing new measurement technology or new tactics for describing correlations with public events. A flanking movement might embody redefining the problem of interest so that the question can be approached in a slightly different manner that will still provide valuable information. A cogent illustration of such a tactical redirection of efforts is exemplified by the work of M. K. Goldstein and his associates at the Gainesville, Florida, Veteran's Administration Hospital. A persistent logical problem in the remote delivery of health care services involved attempting to monitor patients in their home and work environments to verify that they are complying with medical instructions ("Get more exercise, take one of these three times a day, etc."). Traditionally, this monitoring has been attempted through haphazard and infrequent contacts with the physician, usually initiated by the patient in response to renewed distress. Alternatively, some psychologists have relied on systematic verbal reports, either by mail-in questionnaires or telephone conversations, both necessitating an ill-founded inference of correspondence between the verbal report and compliance behavior. By approaching the verbal report itself as the initial phenomena of interest, Goldstein has begun an experimental analysis of its determinants leading to development of techniques for establishing controlled calibration so that eventually, by exclusion, the only determinant of variability in the verbal report will be the actual details of the recent behavioral history (Goldstein, Stein, Smolen, & Perlini, 1976; Stein, Goldstein, & Smolen, 1976). In other words, correspondence between the public verbal report and the less accessible behavioral history is being arranged experimentally rather than assumed or taken for granted.

Whatever alternatives are pursued, behavioral scientists must not be embarrassed at the necessity of a temporary halt in the face of measurement limitations; it has been a long and respected tradition in the history of science. It is one thing to be on the leading edge of one's science, but it is quite another to be beyond it. It is far preferable to admit the present limits of our knowledge and measurement technology than to ignore such limits and begin abandoning the strategies and tactics that have brought us this far.

Further Strategic Considerations

Although there are some superficial similarities, the general strategy expounded here for investigating phenomena of limited accessibility is very different indeed from that of Wundt, Titchener, and the other early investigators whose legacy remains evident in the modern social sciences. The problem of limited accessibility was so pervasive that the 19th-century founders were easily convinced that an entirely different subject matter had emerged, occasioning abandonment of the established methods of the natural sciences. With hindsight, it is clear that this was an incautious overreaction to a problem of degree, not of kind. The troublesome demands of limited accessibility do not relieve the requirement of firm adherence to all other demands of careful natural scientific investigation discussed in the accompanying chapters. The basic strategy rests firmly on a scientifically sound technology of public measurement and dictates only supplementary cautions, not variations in basic conceptions.

The active investigation of less accessible behavioral phenomena has also properly lagged well behind the study of public behavioral events. This has allowed a considerable body of secure, basic knowledge about behavior to emerge and become available as a foundation for research on less accessible events. The importance of this chronology lies in the empirical support that has been acquired for the parsimonious scientific assumption that private behavioral events differ from public ones only in their accessibility (Skinner, 1953a). This cautious position would have to have been relinquished only with the utmost reluctance, and such an abandonment now seems quite unlikely.

The exposition of a strategy for the scientific investigation of less accessible stimuli and responses given in this section will no doubt be misinterpreted by some, and some cautious respect for difficulties inherent in this kind of research must be promoted. The central complication obviously stems from the obstacles to observing less accessible stimuli or responses, and the successful solution to this problem will be attained only after the expenditure of a more strenuous effort than the same investigation of more public phenomena would require. The general propositions discussed in this chapter must be accompanied in practice by special efforts at the various stages of response definition, observation, recording, and experimental design.

As a final caveat, the investigator should carefully consider whether an encounter with the problems of limited accessibility is an absolute requirement of the research interest. An honest and searching examination of the research question will often lead to an alternate phrasing for which the implied goals can be achieved through experimentation with public phenomena. Meaningful human behavioral research is difficult enough without borrowing unnecessary complications.

MEASUREMENT TACTICS

The balance of the chapter primarily concerns problems of measuring responses of limited accessibility, regardless of the accessibility of the environmental events to which they are functionally related. This is in no way intended to diminish the obviously fundamental importance of precisely specifying such stimuli. It is normally assumed in behavioral research that the public stimulus dimensions of the experimental environment under investigation will be adequately described, because this is usually a relatively easy task. To the extent that descriptive measurement of completely inaccessible stimuli is required, it is obvious that such specification can be induced only from the results of eventual measurement of public responses. Thus, considering response measurement tactics becomes both necessary and sufficient for dealing with the tactical consequences of the limited accessibility of stimuli. Moreover, in the event that both stimulus and response are fully inaccessible, the distinction becomes largely theoretical, and the term "private event" may be used to designate the functional entity.

Definition of Response Classes

Although defining less accessible response classes requires some special considerations, the basic tactics discussed in Chapter 6 with respect to publically observable responses fully apply here. The additional considerations stem from the fact that even though the researcher may have some conception of the behavior of interest, satisfactory access to its features and limits cannot be gained. This will hinder not only applying proper definitional tactics, but the adequate training of the observer who must also serve as subject.

Although the ultimate solution to these difficulties rests with technological advances that will make such responses public, there are some special tactics that can ameliorate the situations in the interim. The first of these is to define the response class as clearly, simply, and thoroughly as possible so that each instance will be maximally obvious to and detectable by the subject. For example, a detailed definition of "smiling" will likely facilitate far more accurate self-observation than will a definition of "presenting a positive self-image." Second, if the experimenter can also define private responses that have some kinds of public behavioral accompaniments, there will be the advantage of a source of corollary evidence about the occurrence of the behavior. For instance, the occurrence of a flatus emission may or may not be aurally detected by others depending on topographical features on the response and/or the ambient noise level in the surrounding environment; however, there are inevitably malodorous byproducts whose public detectability is attested to by a variety of reactions on the part of those in the immediate vicinity.[2] A third tactic is to define the inaccessible response class in such a way that the experimenter can arrange some kinds of tests to probe for verification about the definition the subject is using (as well as the occurrences of the behavior itself). To illustrate, a dental patient's personal definition of "cleaning teeth" can easily be evaluated with the use of plaque disclosing tablets that tint any plaque on the teeth so that it is easily detectable by the dentist. Because the dentist has little or no access to the patient's teeth cleaning behavior, it is necessary to arrange a probe for the effects of that behavior that will be accessible by both patient and dentist so that communication will have a shared, objective referent. These three general tactics are all means by which society teaches the individual to respond to their own private events, and the researcher may use the same tactics to provide supplementary information about the definition of the private event that the subject is using.

In all cases in which the target response still remains essentially inaccessible, it becomes necessary to train a publically observable response with which the subject can report the private event. The characteristics of this public reporting response are of the utmost importance in ensuring that the correlation between private and public responses is high. The general tactic is to arrange the environment of the subject such that the emission of the private response (and no other event) becomes the occasion for the emission of the public response. The tactics here are somewhat different than in the more common case in which one wished to bring a public response under the control of some public stimulus that precedes the response because the private event that will serve the stimulus function is inaccessible to the experimenter,

---

[2]For a more thorough discussion of this phenomenon, particularly those aspects bearing on detectability, see Carlin (1973).

thus preventing reinforcement of the public response in the presence of only the desired stimulus.[3]

Criteria for selecting the public reporting response to be brought under the control of the private event are that it be simple, discrete, clearly defined, and exclusively under the control of the private event. It should also be physically easy to emit with as little cost to the subject as possible. For example, recording responses on paper requires the subject not only to have a pencil and paper available at *all* times, but also to get them out and make a notation each time the defined event occurs. On the other hand, pushing a button on a mechanical counter worn on the wrist is comparatively easy. Selecting a public response that involves such mechanical or electrical assists can be important in facilitating acquisition of control by the private event and, ultimately, accurate reporting. The constant presence of a counter worn on the wrist, for example, can serve as a stimulus prompting the subject to observe the private events that comprise a part of the functional definition of the public counting response. Furthermore, the topography of the selected recording response should be distinctive, to endow it with an extremely low probability of occurrence except in the presence of the targeted private event. If, by virtue of special history or training, the reporting response is likely to be made to other events, either public or private, a substantial loss of measurement accuracy is almost inevitable.

Dimensional Quantities and Units

The discussion in Chapter 7 of the dimensional quantities of behavior and their corresponding measurement units is fully applicable to behavioral events of limited accessibility. The properties of repeatability, temporal locus, and temporal extent are characteristic of all behavioral events, regardless of how readily they may be observed. Nonetheless, from a tactical perspective, certain dimensional quantities may be preferable in the case of less accessible events because of the general requirements of ease and simplicity of the public reporting response. Selecting a temporal dimensional quantity, for example, may occasion the need for timing devices and procedures that are unjustifiable if simple counting would suffice in meeting the experimental needs.

Observation and Recording

The special problems surrounding observation and recording of behavioral events of limited accessibility emanate from the fact that the same individual

---

[3]The reader should note the strategic communality with the situation discussed earlier in which the stimulus (the inaccessible response event) is private and the reporting response is public.

who is to perform the observation and recording functions happens to be the author of the behavior as well. The general range of tactics requisite to good observation and recording practices (see Chapter 8) are fully relevant in this situation, but there must be special concern that implementation does not encroach on the individual's role as behaver. Because most humans are accustomed to fulfilling a variety of role functions simultaneously, this requirement is not insurmountable if approached knowledgeably and cautiously.

It is imperative to select subjects/observers who have a source, direction, and degree of motivation to participate that is compatible with the nature of the project and to take great care in arranging the many contingencies that inevitably accompany the conduct of an experiment to maintain this motivation. Some subjects may be inclined to produce the kind of data they think the experimenter wants to see; therefore, the initial training and all subsequent interactions with the experimenter must be carefully designed to avoid encouraging any kind of observer bias. Thorough efforts must be made to ensure that all consequences that unavoidably follow any observer behaviors are consistent with the goals of accurate observation and must not be differentially related to any quantitative features of the data. For example, the subject should not feel uncomfortable in reporting that she didn't feel like observing one day or that he forgot his counter. A special consequence of observing/recording that must be carefully managed is the permanent response product of the whole procedure—the data themselves. From the standpoint of maintaining bias-free observation, it is usually necessary to restrict the subject/observer's access to any permanent or cumulative rendering of the data. This tactic may even extend to covering the dials on a counter so that information the subject would not otherwise have concerning the day's cumulative performance is not available.

Stability, Accuracy, and Believability

Having proceeded this far in an investigation of functional relations involving stimuli or responses of less than desirable accessibility, the inevitable question of the stability and accuracy of measurement must be squarely faced. The discussion of multiple observers in Chapter 8 has already pointed out that assessing these data characteristics unavoidably requires knowledge of the true values of the dimensional quantities being measured for comparison to observational values. Such true values may often be available in experiments discussed in this chapter when the source of the limitations on accessibility is primarily logistical in nature. For example, when response products resulting from the behavior of interest are public but logistically difficult or costly to measure routinely, subject self-observation data may be compared to periodically obtained measures of the response products for a proper assessment of stability and accuracy. There may be many such instances when special, intermittent measurement efforts can be used to determine true values for this purpose; the next chapter considers the resulting assessment of stability and accuracy in detail.

However, the limitation on accessibility by the experimenter to the events of interest may be complete, precluding any evaluation of stability and accuracy. As Chapter 8 described, the only remaining tactic available to the experimenter is to arrange for the collection of supplementary data that will augment the believability of the original data. That is, data must be gathered that will serve to enhance the confidence of the experimenter and others that the subject-collected data constitute acceptably accurate and stable representations of the unknown true values. The reasoning by which such data become convincing again involves the logical fallacy of affirming the consequent, introduced at length in Chapter 2 and discussed in this context in Chapter 8. Because the reader is already familiar with this tactic, an extended demonstration of its uses in an actual research program will adequately illustrate the various issues and procedures involved.

The focus of the research program was various aspects of the study tactics college students use in preparing for tests over typical textbook material (Johnston, O'Neil, Walters, & Rasheed, 1975). One of the reasons for the paucity of empirical information concerning what is probably the single most important behavioral determinant of academic performance is that study behaviors occur at the choice of the individual in a wide variety of physical settings at all hours of the day and night. Even under ideal conditions, only some of what is usually called studying is publicly observable. Arranging for frequent public observation would have required using a study hall setting and restricting availability of materials to only that room. Not only was this a logistical impossibility, such an atypical condition would probably have altered the quantity and quality of the student study activities. Moreover, most study behaviors remain inaccessible to others regardless of the nature of any arrangements for external observation.

These facts necessitated approaching this investigation by developing a technology for measuring both public and private study behaviors via observing and recording by the individual student. A reporting form was developed over a period of two years; versions of it were used every academic quarter in a variety of courses with many hundreds of students with major and minor revisions made continuously on the basis of the resulting data. Throughout this lengthy process (during which no experiments using this evolving measurement technology were conducted) efforts were constantly made to construct the Study Report Form (as it came to be known) so as to increase the likelihood that it would occasion accurate reporting responses of both public and private study behaviors. This effort produced many changes in the form, sometimes of a seemingly subtle and sometimes of a more obvious nature. This process is too lengthy and complex to chronicle here (see

Johnston et al., 1975), especially because the Study Report Form was only one component of the eventual technology. The procedures for training students in the use of the form and the contingencies designed to facilitate their proper use of it were of equal importance to the form itself. These procedures included arranging appropriate consequences simply for completing the form as well as for making errors that were publicly detectable.

During the latter part of this development period, the tactic of affirming the consequent was used to augment believability in the validity of the obtained data. The assertion that the measurement system was producing valid reports of inaccessible study behaviors constituted the logical antecedent, and a number of consequent statements that had to follow from the truth of the antecedent were investigated (O'Neill, Walters, Rasheed, & Johnston, 1975; Walters, O'Neill, Rasheed, & Johnston, 1975). At least four classes of such antecedent–consequent relations were available for examination in this case. First, if the form was soliciting valid reports of study behavior, then a certain class of possible errors should be seen rarely if at all. For example, in their successive attempts to meet criterion on each unit, students should never have reported "rereading" the text assignment as a study tactic until they had first reported "reading" the material on the same or a previous attempt. An examination of the data from two academic quarters in one course showed that in 849 instances when "rereading" was reported, it never preceded the reported occurrence of "reading."

Another kind of consequent required by the asserted validity of the measurement technology stemmed from the design of the individualized, repeated testing-to-mastery style of the courses serving as a research vehicle (Johnston & Pennypacker, 1971). Given the nature of the teaching methods, it would have been highly unlikely that certain types of study behavior listed on the form would be reported. In these courses, such improbable study behaviors included writing multiple choice questions (all testing was with fill-in questions), rereading and transcribing lecture notes (there were no formal lectures and tests covered only text material) and using audio-visual materials (none were available to the student). The examination of many thousands of Study Report Forms showed that these behaviors were either not reported at all or in less than one-half of 1% of all possible instances.

A third consequent of the validity of the data was available in the patterns of academic performance exhibited by students. If there was a sound relation between test performance and study behavior and if study behavior was being properly reported, then this correspondence should be evident in the case of unusual patterns of academic performance. One such pattern that was occasionally observed was termed a reversal; when three or more quizzes were taken in the attempt to meet the 90% correct criterion, sometimes the score on the second (or third) quiz was markedly poorer than on the previous and

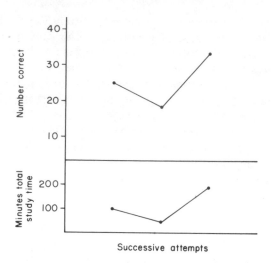

FIG. 9.2.   Corresponding reversal between correct performance and total study time for one student (adapted from Walters et al., 1975).

subsequent attempts. A number of such patterns were examined along with the corresponding reports of total study time on each quiz attempt; Fig. 9.2 shows one such comparison.

A fourth kind of prediction follows from explicit manipulation of variables in the academic environment that should exert predictable effects on the reported study data if the students' observations are valid. One experiment that followed the development of the measurement technology investigated the effects of size of each unit of course material. Eight successive units in one course were arranged into lengths of 30, 60, or 90 textbook pages. Such major variations in the curriculum to be studied should result in corresponding variations in the total time spent studying each unit. Even greater correspondence should be seen in the time reported as spent reading the text material for the first time in each unit (assuming nearly constant reading speeds across all units). This prediction was evaluated in two separate experiments with different unit size sequences and was consistently confirmed. The data for one individual are shown in Fig. 9.3.

It should be clear from earlier discussions of affirming the consequent that the data examined in an effort to affirm as many consequents as possible did not *prove* the validity of the measurement technology. However, a number of consequents that could have disproved the antecedent were shown to be false, thus increasing confidence in the asserted validity by some unspecified degree. Exactly how many consequents of the truth of the antecedent must be successfully shown to be true is, of course, unknown and dependent on many influences, such as available literature on the question, the investigator's experience in the area, the details of measurement procedures, the nature of

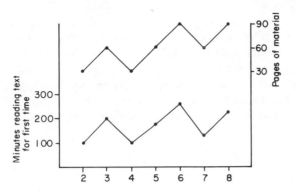

FIG. 9.3.   Time spent reading the text for the first time and pages of material
across units for an individual student (adapted from O'Neill et al., 1975).

the research question, and the characteristics of the reported data. However,
this remains as an extremely useful tactic for building believability in the
validity of data resulting from procedures designed to measure events to
which accessibility is limited.

The development of this measurement technology permitted for the first
time the experimental investigation of not only those variables directly
influencing study behavior but also the effects of controlled variations in
study behavior on subsequent academic performance. The investigation was
able to replace the traditional assumptions about the role of study behavior
(arrived at by *post hoc* interrogation of highly successful and unsuccessful
students) with replicable functional relations, thus opening a new area of
educational research to close empirical analysis. The strategies and tactics
underlying this entire program have demonstrated a level of robustness
commending their adoption in other areas involving human behavior, much
of which may be logistically or generically inaccessible. Generally speaking,
one gains precise experimental control over those relevant variables that are
accessible, and then the inaccessible phenomena reveal themselves, if only by
their effects. Canons of parsimony are not violated by a demonstration that a
major determinant of experimental variability can be *controlled,* even if not
directly observed.

We may confidently expect that the barrier of limited accessibility, once
penetrated, will crumble rapidly in the not too distant future. Skinner (1953a)
has reminded us that no description of behavior will be complete without an
account of events occuring inside the skin of the organism; the skin evolved to
protect the organism from infection, not from investigation. The rapidly
advancing technology of bioelectronic instrumentation is opening new
avenues of experimental access to numerous physiological state variables on
which internal behavior surely depends. Our enhanced ability to identify,

measure, and control these hitherto inaccessible independent variables permits even greater versatility in isolating the behavioral phenomena that are the result of such processes. As research embodying this strategy becomes commonplace, the traditional inventions of mentalism will lose whatever explanatory utility is now claimed for them. In their place will appear functional explanations of those phenomena that, because of their limited accessibility, have posed problems of interpretation that are more apparent than real.

10 Stability and Accuracy of Measurement

Although this may seem a paradox, all exact science is dominated by the idea of approximation.

—Bertrand Russell

INTRODUCTION

The reader who has followed us carefully to this point is undoubtedly aware that issues bearing on the stability and accuracy of the eventual results of measurement arise throughout the entire measurement process, from initial definition of the response class through design of the recording system. If the problems posed by these considerations are addressed squarely and solved effectively at their inception, the final products of measurement will necessarily be as stable and accurate as the available technology will allow. Furthermore, quantitative evidence of the degree of stability and accuracy achieved will be continuously available in the form of the results of calibration probes, obviating the need to collect the entire set of experimental data before coming to grips for the first time with the question of reliability.

Because the several strategic and tactical issues bearing on stability and accuracy of the products of measurement are generally either poorly understood or ignored entirely in favor of a welter of complex statistical techniques, it seems prudent to collect and review them in a separate chapter, which concludes the entire section on measurement. These issues are crucial to experimentation, and if their iteration here underscores for the reader the pervasiveness of their influence at all stages of the experimental process, the purpose of this chapter will have been well served.

SOME FUNDAMENTAL ISSUES

The goal of any scientific measurement operation or procedure is to arrive at the best possible estimate of the true value of some dimensional quantity of a natural phenomenon. To the extent that this goal is achieved, it is said that the measurement is accurate or valid. Accuracy or validity of the results therefore becomes the yardstick for gauging the quality of any measurement procedure. For purposes of clarity, *accuracy* may be defined as the extent to which obtained measures approximate values of the "true" state of nature, perfect accuracy being obtained when equivalence is demonstrated. It should be immediately recognized that perfect accuracy is a limit condition, unattainable in any practical specific instance, but approachable with ever diminishing error.

Both the design and evaluation of any measurement procedure are largely predicated on the extent of knowledge about the true state of nature. Three possibilities exist logically: (1) the true state exists and independent measures of it are available; (2) the true state is known to exist, but cannot be measured independently; or (3) no true state of nature exists apart from the results of a measurement operation. Let us consider and dispense with the last of these possibilities first.

The lengthy discussion on the origins of vaganotic definition and measurement attempted to clarify the pitfalls and consequences of defining and measuring phenomena *solely* on the basis of variability obtained through measurement of some other phenomenon. With variability as a starting point, phenomena were defined into existence as necessary anchors for the "error" that was assumed manifest in the observed variability. Thus did Quetelet comfort himself concerning the existence of "natural ideals" as the targets at which nature aimed, but randomly missed, in producing bell-shaped distributions of physical characteristics in various populations. Fechner refined this tactic by attempting to create units of measurement of similarly defined emergent phenomena out of obtained variability, and the mental measurement movement, spearheaded by Galton, created not only the phenomena but entire scales by which they could be measured out of variability observed in other measures. The ultimate testament of this tradition is embodied in the oft-quoted statement, "intelligence is whatever is measured by intelligence tests" that evokes in most listeners a mordant distrust of extreme operationalism that can be overcome only by prolonged training in the philosophy of science. However, it must be understood that the existence of a noun in the natural language does not guarantee the existence of a referent in nature, notwithstanding the tenacity with which the contrary belief is held by all who labor in the vaganotic tradition. Verifying the existence of a natural phenomenon requires more than a set of numbers that purport to be measures of that phenomenon, regardless of the eloquence with which such an existence is advocated.

There are, however, many events and processes in nature whose existence can be empirically demonstrated but that cannot be directly and independently measured. Often, only effects can be measured, as is the case with electrons and various magnetic phenomena, including gravity. It is instructive to consider the reasoning that underlies attempts to measure (not define) such phenomena. As we do so, we will deal with the second case mentioned above, that in which true values exist in nature, but cannot be independently measured.

Measurement of temperature as a characteristic of matter provides a convenient context in which to explore this case. Suppose we do not have a thermometer and our task is to invent one. Suppose further that we have noticed that things expand as they got hotter and we therefore elect to attempt to measure temperature by taking advantage of this fact. We might even be fortunate enough to start by filling a graduated cylinder with mercury, although that is not essential. What is essential is that whatever substance we select, we begin by demonstrating the reliability of the measurement. *Reliability* refers to the capacity of the instrument to yield the same measurement value when brought into repeated contact with the same state of nature. Thus, this meaning of reliability is concerned with the *stability* of measured values under constant conditions. We can establish this for our "thermometer" by repeatedly bringing water to a boil and, just as it starts to bubble, noting the level attained by the expanding substance in the glass tube. Even though we do not yet even have a measurement unit, we can determine the reliability of our "thermometer" at one end of the scale by simply recording the distance by which the substance expands each time and comparing the variability of those measures with the total distance traveled. Repeating the process at the other end of the scale (when ice begins to form) establishes the reliability of the instrument for the two extremes of water in liquid form.

Having satisfied ourselves that our instrument reliably (stably) yields these measures (in terms of length), we can use the arithmetic means of our "boiling" and "freezing" measures as our best estimate of a true value of the distance on our measuring instrument at which water boils and freezes. If we then divide the distance from the freezing measure to the boiling measure into 100 equal subdivisions, we will have created a graduated thermometer with something closely akin to the Centigrade scale as its metric.[1] These values are, of course, arbitrary but not fictional, because water boiling or freezing can be verified without a thermometer. The resulting true values (100 degrees and 0 degrees) are therefore *valid* measures of states of nature and can serve as

---

[1]Our sample procedure says nothing about the reliability of measures obtained at the middle ranges of the scale. To get such data, one would have to apply repeatedly a known amount of heat to ice at the melting threshold, thus producing a series of water samples of nearly constant temperature.

reference values against which to validate other measuring devices as well as intermediate graduations along the scale.

The term *valid* is used here to connote the extent to which measurement is actually of the object, event, or phenomenon purportedly being measured. The correspondence between independently induced changes in the state of nature (applying heat to the water) and the state of the instrument (expansion of the column) serves to validate the instrument in the absence of independent measures of true changes in the state of nature. In both the theory and practice of psychological measurement, distinctions are made among various kinds of validity (concurrent, construct, face, content, etc.), but all share the property of being statements about a quality of measurement that cannot be established in terms of correspondence to an independently known true value. Because such correspondence *can* be established in the case of measurement of dimensional quantities of behavior, the term *accuracy* is used instead to refer to that quality of measurement reflected by the correspondence between measured and true values.

It should be clear that the assertion that our thermometer yields valid measures is predicated on its demonstrated reliability. The figure of 100 degrees, or any other reading, would inspire little confidence if in our series of insertions of the instrument into boiling water we obtained a wide range of readings. In this case, then, validity is obviously bounded by reliability; a valid estimate of the value of a dimensional quantity in nature cannot be expected from a device that cannot yield stable measures when the dimensional quantity is independently held constant.

The third case, in which the true state of nature exists and can be independently measured, follows closely from the previous discussion. Once we have an instrument that has been validated in the manner of our thermometer, it can serve to provide independent measures of true states of nature for purposes of calibrating other unproven devices or procedures. In developing such instruments or procedures, *accuracy* (correspondence with the true value of a state of nature as yielded by the reference device) becomes the standard of design. If the device displays consistent accuracy, its reliability is assured, and unless it displays consistent accuracy, its utility is suspect no matter how reliable it appears. Sticking a ruler in a pot of water as the temperature is raised will yield highly reliable measures of the depth of the water, but will tell us very little about the changing temperature, particularly if the coefficient of expansion of the ruler material is similar to that of water. Thus, measures of temperature furnished by the ruler will be highly reliable but inaccurate, because no correspondence with an independent measure (thermometer reading) of the changing state of nature can be obtained.

Measuring the dimensional quantities of behavior most nearly resembles the case in which true states of nature can be independently determined and measured, with the measures used as standards for determining validity.

Therefore, accuracy becomes the criterion, and any obsession with reliability is likely to beg the basic issue. The contemporary undue concern for reliability of behavioral measurement procedures is probably a holdover from traditions of psychological measurement wherein only reliability could be demonstrated in the absence of general agreement as to whether or not a true state of nature even existed, let alone whether it could be independently measured.

ACHIEVING ACCURATE BEHAVIORAL MEASUREMENT

Several tactics of maximizing the accuracy of behavioral measurement have been discussed. Issues surrounding this problem arise at every stage, beginning with the conceptualization of the subject matter of the investigation. Admitting hypothetical states and processes almost ensures that measurement will be inexact, and questions of validity (not accuracy) will certainly arise. On the other hand, restricting inquiry to directly observable events allows advantage to be taken of the idemnotic measurement strategy that, in turn, forces careful election of relevant dimensional quantities and their standard, absolute units.

The care and precision with which the response class to be studied is defined contributes directly to the eventual accuracy of measurement. Broad, vague definitions present relentless problems of detection, particularly if human observers are involved. An ideal standard is furnished by the automatic functional definition in which definition and detection are both the result of activating an automatic transducer in the environment; if the transducer operates, a response has been detected, and the requirements for the operation of the transducer constitute the definition of the response class. Under these conditions, error resulting from vagaries of definition is restricted to drift in the sensitivity of the transducer and can be reduced to a clear minimum.

Selecting a particular dimensional quantity (latency, duration, frequency, etc.) for measurement fixes the choice of the unit and occasions considering tactics for reducing sources of measurement error inherent in the use of each. The discontinuity of integral counting, for example, requires that attention be paid to the significant digits in any obtained estimate of frequency, since frequency estimates are always based on a finite time sample (see Chapter 7). Selection of a single time-related dimensional quantity, such as duration, may induce a lack of sensitivity to important variation in another, e.g., IRT. Furthermore, because time measures are essentially continuous, it is important that any estimate of a temporal value be obtained with a device whose precision and accuracy are known in advance, because instrument errors are harder to detect after the fact in the case of continuous dimensions.

Probably the single greatest source of measurement error is introduced at the stage of actual observation. To minimize such error, it is necessary to concentrate on prevention at the time of design and manufacture in the case of machine transducers or during selection and training of human observers. Even if all feasible precautions have been taken prior to actual observation, it is still necessary to conduct frequent calibration checks during the course of data collection. Continuously assessing both stability and accuracy is the only way to ensure that initially determined standards apply to all data collected. Of course, the process generates substantial amounts of data as it unfolds, obviating any need for *post hoc* assessment of the quality of measurement. The investigator should be satisfied as to the accuracy of measurement at the moment the last observation is recorded and should be able to proceed with confidence directly to analysis and interpretation.

ASSESSING MEASUREMENT ACCURACY

It has been stated and restated that the procedures necessary to assess the accuracy of measured data are a subset of the procedures required by the effort to ensure accurate measurement in the first place. That is, evaluating the extent to which attempts to obtain accurate data are successful is a natural, integral, and inevitable consequence of the design and conduct of good idemnotic measurement practices. However, following the earlier definition of accuracy, the extent to which observational data are accurate can be assessed *only* if the "true" values of the observed behavioral events are known. If such knowledge is available, then the evaluation of stability and accuracy is simultaneously performed by comparing the observer's responses to the true values. Accuracy can be assessed by comparing these two values for a single behavioral event. Assessing accuracy for a collection of behavioral events (such as for the number of responses in a single observational session) also depends on the requirement of assuring perfectly instance-by-instance correspondence. This may be difficult to arrange, and the experimenter may be limited to the position of merely comparing the observer's report of the sum of the measured dimensional quantities for a session (e.g., total number of response cycles, total duration of responding, or response frequency for the entire session) with the known true composite value for the session. Even if the two values agree, accuracy has not technically been demonstrated, because response-by-response correspondence was not examined. In such a case, only an inferential statement can be made about accuracy, because the responses detected by the observer were not necessarily the same ones that contributed to the composite true value for the session. The experimenter has only the affirmation of the consequent reasoning discussed earlier to support a personal conviction and to convince colleagues that the observer made judgments only about the target behavioral events and detected all of those.[2] Because this reasoning becomes more convincing as more consequents of the truth of the antecedent are shown to be true, it behooves the experimenter in this dilemma to make as many such evaluations of accuracy as possible.

Assessing the stability of observer judgments is most easily accomplished if a constant behavioral event can be repeated, presented, and observed. However, it can also be evaluated by comparing observer responses with true values over a series of observations of different behavioral events, providing true values are available. Of course, if such comparisons show perfect agreement, then stability is an irrelevant consideration. However, if these repeated comparisons show less than perfect correspondence (i.e., are less than accurate), the stability of the error becomes a legitimate question. The nature of the deviations of observer reports from true values is of fundamental importance to the further conduct and interpretation of the experiment, because instead of being random, they may show a stable or consistent bias that requires ameliorative action or must influence interpretation.

As we pointed out in the last chapter, the comparison of observational data with true values occurs naturally in the course of calibrating the machine or human observer. The results of these comparisons made prior to and throughout the experiment fully constitute the necessary evaluation of stability and accuracy. Reporting or displaying such results may take many forms depending on the nature of the stability and accuracy data and the display format of the experimental data. It may be sufficient to merely report the calibration operations (in the case of machine observation, perhaps), or it may be necessary to plot the calibration data on the same chart as the experimental data (as might be the case when frequent calibration checks are made throughout the entire course of experimentation). Of course, the guiding strategy here is to display the stability and accuracy data so as to enhance its influence on the interpretative behavior of the viewer.

This brief discussion of evaluating the stability and accuracy of measured data should have encouraged the realization that although stability and accuracy can be clearly distinguished by definition at a strategic level, the means by which they are achieved and assessed at a tactical level are usually identical. The sufficient task is to determine the correspondence between obtained measures and true states of nature, and the stability/accuracy distinctions arise depending on the nature of the correspondence. In the unlikely event that perfect accuracy is demonstrated over repeated

---

[2]The reasoning is as follows: If the observer's composite session report is accurate for all instances, then the composite report will agree with the composite true value. It is found that there is such agreement. It is therefore concluded that observation is accurate for all instances.

comparisons, stability exists by definition. If perfect stability but imperfect accuracy is exhibited, interest lies in the size and direction of the error. If neither perfect accuracy nor perfect stability are available, the characteristics of the error variability become crucial to further experimental decisions and interpretative reactions.

We have previously made the point that stability and accuracy can be simultaneously assessed only when the true values of the dimensional quantities of interest are known. Thus, when true values of the dimensional quantities of interest are not known (the second case discussed earlier), it is by definition incorrect to pretend that such determinations can be made. Although Chapter 8 discussed two restricted means by which accuracy could be improved with the use of multiple observers, evaluating the existence of any such improvement would be impossible in the absence of evidence of true values available from other sources. That same discussion introduced the sole tactic open to the experimenter in such a dilemma—to attempt to augment believability or confidence in the accuracy and stability of observations. The use of independent multiple observers providing additional sets of reactions to the generally same behavioral events can in no way provide the true values necessary for the assessment of accuracy and stability, but the independent judgments of a second or third observer can increase by some idiosyncratic extent the confidence one places in the degree to which the responses of the first observer are representative of what actually occurred. Such believability can also be enhanced by evidence of correspondence between an observer's reports and information from any other sources bearing on the occurrence of the behavior of interest. For example, the last chapter showed that major variations in the environment that must inevitably (or nearly so) produce variations in responding can be of some utility in repeatedly examining consequents of the assertion that the primary observer's reports are accurate.

Using this or any other tactic forced by the inability to determine the true values of the behavioral events in question raises a further question regarding the style in which any evidence on the believability of the single observer's judgments is publicly reported. Of course, the guiding strategy that should already be apparent (and is treated at length in Chapter 16) requires presentation of such data in whatever format most effectively contributes to reader interpretations having good generality. This strategy should lead to appropriate data display decisions in most instances; however, there are some traditions accompanying the use of two or more human observers that merit special comment. There is a distressing tendency to report correspondence between the judgments of a primary and a secondary observer in the form of a single percentage summarizing all such pairs of observer reports (usually erroneously termed interobserver reliability scores) for the entire experiment or, at best, for each experimental condition of the experiment. This practice is distinguished by all of the pitfalls associated with statistical summarizing, which we discuss elsewhere (e.g., Chapters 11, 16, and 17). Aside from the means by which such percentages are calculated, any reader must be especially cautious about the value of such figures when the number of observational sessions on which the secondary observer was present represents a small fraction of the total sessions. It must be recalled that the logically fallacious reasoning that constitutes the sole justification for using multiple observers becomes useful only when many consequents of the antecedent can be shown to be true. When a great many such pairs of observations are available (such as for every session), then summarizing these data only serves to hide important information from the reader.[3]

The strategy of measurement recommended throughout these pages rests heavily on the availability and determination of true values. A virtual guarantee of their availability is furnished by the conception of behavior as the subject matter of a natural science. All phenomena studied by the methods of the natural sciences are possessed of truly quantifiable dimensional quantities for which true values exist in each and every specific case. To deny this possibility is to deny the legitimacy of the strategies of the natural sciences for the study of behavior, or even to deny that behavior is a natural phenomenon.

Once availability is assured, the problem of determination remains. In the light of present traditions, many are likely to take *a priori* the position that determining true values is sufficiently difficult as to be impractical; however, we have suggested several tactics by which the problem can be effectively approached. In undertaking this effort, the investigator should remember that "true" is always used in the relative sense of a limit that is approached and realized only by degrees. There is always the possibility of error in any empirical measurement, and no one can ever be certain that a true value has been determined. However, the effort should always be in the direction of improvement, and the investigator who accepts this challenge will often be pleasantly surprised at how easy it is to produce estimates whose accuracy is beyond reasonable contention.

---

[3]At this point, the reader should be convinced that it is rarely necessary to be in the position of needing to summarize multiple observer data with a single score. However, in view of the frequency of such practices as reported in the current literature and notwithstanding the persuasiveness and veracity of the arguments in this volume, some readers might wish to consult excellent chapters by Hawkins and Dotson (1975) and Johnson and Bolstad (1973) that are both cautious and thorough in their treatment of these matters. An exposition of such procedures in these pages might be construed by some as an inconsistent and unwarranted breach in the conviction with which alternative strategies are endorsed.

Part III DESIGN

11 Variability

I can, if the worst comes to the worst, still realize that the Good Lord may have created a world in which there are no natural laws. In short, a chaos. But that there should be statistical laws with definite solutions, i.e., laws that compel the Good Lord to throw the dice in each individual case, I find highly disagreeable.

—A. Einstein

THE IMPORTANCE OF VARIABILITY

No two objects or events are ever exactly alike. Furthermore, a given object or event changes with the passage of time, so that any basic Law of Identity applies only instantaneously in the real world, however valid it may be in the abstract. The physical universe is an infinitely complex arrangement of constantly changing phenomena. Variation is the rule, not the exception, of all that exists.

Confronted by this metaphysical inevitability, many thoughtful humans have sought to explain or impose conceptual order upon the universe by

201

appealing to extranatural constants as agents of cause, order, and design. The philosophical and religious systems of thought that characterize nearly all cultures may be viewed as a manifestation of this distinctly human characteristic. Alternatively, however, the rise of science has provided a strategy for organizing and understanding natural phenomena that not only accommodates but takes full advantage of the universal characteristic of variability. As we have so often mentioned throughout this volume, measurement provides the key to this strategy, for it is by means of measurement that differences among objects or events may be more exactly discerned. Once identified, these differences form the basis of orderly systems of description and explanation. Differences exist by degree; certain sets of objects or events may be discovered to be more similar than others and may consequently be grouped and classified. Moreover, variation often permits prediction and, under certain conditions, a specifiable degree of control.

In the most general sense, the subject matter of all science is variability. Specific sciences differ according to the subdivision of the natural universe chosen for unified investigation, but all share the task of investigating the variability characteristic of all natural phenomena. Without variability, there would be no science, as there would be no need for classification and organization and nothing to explain.

The overriding and unifying function of science is to measure and explain variability. This responsibility is discharged through a bewildering variety of approaches and techniques that have selectively evolved in each of the subject matter disciplines by relentless application of a simple criterion—orderliness and a generality of the data. From the scientifically primitive practice of stating "co-relations" among uncontrollable but measurable phenomena to the highly precise and exacting methods of the biophysicist or nuclear chemist, the goal is the same: to account for variability in observed phenomena in terms of other observed phenomena. When a certain domain of variability can virtually all be accounted for by identified sources or determinants, new areas of investigation are embarked upon where fresh variability awaits analysis. The new domain is often the product of a major change in observational perspective, as when the electron microscope revealed the details of variable phenomena not previously known to exist.

Like all other natural phenomena, behavior displays variability, and, like the other sciences, the science of behavior has as its task the explanation of that variability. For a variety of reasons, recognition of this mission or even acceptance of its possibility has been slow in coming. The fact that behavior is variable and the observation that behavioral variability serves the adaptive needs of organisms in dynamic environments has led many to the conclusion that behavioral variability is somehow an intrinsic property of the organism and is, therefore, inaccessible to conventional tactics of scientific analysis. It follows from this assertion that behavior itself is a phenomenon to which the usual strategies of sciences are not applicable and that must, therefore, be understood in extrascientific terms, if at all. This position must be examined in considerable detail, for it is often advanced as a basis for misgivings about a natural science of behavior.

TRADITIONAL ARGUMENTS
FOR INTRINSIC VARIABILITY

Most philosophical and religious explanations of behavior, particularly human behavior, rest on an implicit assumption of intrinsic variability. It is not our intention to explore the issue of free will versus determinism in detail, but we must mention that this persistent philosophical dispute is but an unnecessary restatement of the question of the nature of behavioral variability. Lacking a strategy for analyzing the determinants of variability even in simple physical phenomena, early cultures appear to have consistently assigned the causes of such variability to contrived entities such as gods, spirits, and demons. As the physical universe began to yield to the search for order through experimentation, the distinction between physical and nonphysical phenomena became more crucial to the maintenance of the social order (see Chapter 1). It was indeed fortunate for the doctrine of indeterminism that mathematical statistics had reached the level of development it had by the early 19th century; otherwise, Quetelet and others could not have salvaged a scientific credibility for intrinsic variability by making it a springboard for measurement. As it was, however, the impact of the publication of *The Origin of Species* was probably dulled somewhat by the simultaneously growing practice of allowing assumed intrinsic variability to form the basis of measurement scales. Measurement of this type (vaganotic) permitted the "scientific" study of a wide range of human characteristics, including behavior, while retaining the perspective that the variability encountered was inherent or intrinsic and therefore beyond the purview of experimental analysis.

The assumption of intrinsic variability has become almost indispensable to the research methods of modern psychology, education, and the social sciences. To a considerable degree, there is a requirement for "error variance" against which to assess the variability imposed by treatments. The dogmatic insistence in some quarters that all experiments be performed on large samples almost seems to be a statement tactically reifying intrinsic variability in order to preserve the legitimacy of prescientific conceptions of the causes of behavior. It is revealing to observe the frequency with which presentations of data describing human behavior from which virtually all unexplained variability has been experimentally removed are dismissed as "trivial," "irrelevant to the real world," or insensitive to the "real underlying causes of behavior."

By Analogy to Physics

A popular argument on behalf of intrinsic variability in behavior is frequently couched in an analogic comparison to the frontiers of modern physics. It is contended that because physics has been forced to a position of stochastic or statistical indeterminism in the theoretical treatment of certain quantum phenomena,[1] a similar interpretation of the variability evident in behavior is justified. This argument may or may not ultimately prove to be correct. At some future date, the determinants of behavior may possibly be traced through a series of lawful connections to a phenomenal level coextensive or equivalent to that currently under investigation in physics. If, at that time, physics remains committed to a principle of final indeterminancy, it may be appropriate to conclude that the principle is valid for all natural phenomena, including behavior.

To advance this argument as a justification for perpetuating the practice of relying on statistical inference for the analysis of molar behavioral phenomena is, however, to ignore both the history of physics and the almost total lack of comparability of the present behavioral measurement and control procedures with those of modern physics. By the end of the 19th century, physics had advanced to the state of a fairly complete, quantitatively exact science with respect to the known range of detectable phenomena. In other words, almost all known variability had been explained. Only because, in effect, the limits of measurement precision in physics exceeded the limits of natural variability did 20th-century physics discover new domains of phenomena that appeared indeterministic. Claiming this degree of sophistication for a science that has only within the last quarter century identified its basic measurement units and begun practicing idemnotic measurement appears unduly immodest, particularly on the part of those who have yet to participate even in this advance. Had the advent of mathematical statistics antedated the development of a deterministic mechanics, it might well have been that the science of mechanics would not have been developed to set the stage for quantum physics. Galileo would have employed the techniques of large sample, vaganotic measurement to a population of balls rolling down planes, derived acceleration as a property inherent in the balls, and invented a metric for scaling their animate force.

---

[1]The term "indeterminism" as used in contemporary physics refers to a *methodological* limitation on our knowledge of the behavior of basic particles imposed by Werner Heisenberg's discovery that the position and momentum of a particle cannot be simultaneously determined. As a result, quantum mechanics utilizes a system of stochastic models to describe the effects of large populations of particles with statements of probability being assigned to describe the motion, or path, of any single particle. Because this practice arises from an apparently inherent limitation on measurement, it should not be construed as empirical support for the *metaphysical* concept of indeterminism that asserts *a priori* that some events are without antecedent causes.

History makes it clear that the opposite occurred. A well-developed, highly quantitative science of mechanics evolved without the aid of stochastic measurement, and unexplained variability was reduced to trivial levels of measurement error. From this science has emerged fully functional technologies that have been shown capable of controlling variability (reducing error or unpredictability) to virtually any extent required. The degree of exact prediction and control over real phenomena underlying the successes of the space program are not the result of laboratory reliance on conventional application of confidence interval statistics. In eventual engineering applications, such figures serve only to describe any residual predictive error that results from known tolerances of measurement precision in manufacturing; they are not the basis for establishing certitude about the underlying physical processes.

A final point must be made with respect to the argument for indeterminism by analogy with physics: Theoretical acceptance of an indeterminancy principle in physics has been forced by highly reliable data obtained through measurement techniques that are above suspicion. The principle is, therefore, a consequence of the data and remains subject to revision pending the acquisition of new data. For the social sciences, however, it appears that intrinsic variability (analogous to indeterminancy) is an *a priori* assumption that thereafter guides experimentation and methodological development in the manner of a self-fulfilling prophecy. If it is assumed that behavior is intrinsically variable, it is unlikely that methods of analysis will be refined so that it is possible to address empirically questions concerning the nature of behavioral variability. Premature acceptance of the indeterminancy analogue will, therefore, consign the science of behavior to a level of scientific and technological inferiority that promises little of benefit to mankind and delivers less.

From Genetic Variability

An entirely different argument on behalf of intrinsic variability in behavior emerges from carefully considering the role of variability in natural selection. It has been observed that in order for organisms to reproduce, they must adapt to the environment in which they exist for a sufficient period of time to reach maturity and reproductive capability. For many organisms, this process of adaptation is essentially behavioral, and behavioral variability therefore becomes a necessity for successful adaptation to a constantly changing environment. It is argued that many species became extinct because the range of their behavioral repertoires was insufficient to permit adjustment to some rapid environmental change. From this deduction, it is but a short step to the assertion that natural selection occurs with respect to behavioral variability in some genetic sense, and that the variety of behavioral topographies exhibited by a complex mammal is solely a product of its genetic endowment, inaccessible to analysis except through phylogenetic reconstruction. In this argument, behavioral variability becomes an innate characteristic of the organism—a product of its evolutionary history. Certainly the phylogenic origins of a particular organism provide the morphological limitations that will characterize that organism's interaction with its environment. Furthermore, these limitations are clearly a product of the success the organism's ancestors enjoyed in adapting behaviorally to their circumstances. In other words, the *potential* for a given range of behavioral variability is undoubtedly determined genetically as a result of evolutionary selection pressures. Nonetheless, it does not follow from the foregoing observations that the *actual* variability observed in the individual case is genetically determined. Equally plausible is the assertion that the organism's genetic endowment determines what it can do whereas an entirely different set of variables determines what it actually does.

There is no question that behavioral variability mediates adaptation and is, therefore, intricately involved in the process of natural selection. Saying that such variability is exclusively the result of natural selection, however, confuses function with cause—an error easily made by those not thoroughly familiar with the details of the evolutionary process. For example, movements of birds' wings enable them to fly, but this function does not explain the evolution of wings in any causal sense. Wings did not evolve in order to provide contemporary avians with the opportunity to enjoy flight. Rather, it is probable that wings are the result of a selection process whereby possessors of slightly elongated lateral appendages had a somewhat greater advantage in securing food and escaping predators than was enjoyed by those not so endowed. With differential selection favoring continued variation in this characteristic, it is easy to see how certain species gradually acquired the morphological requisites (not the behavior) of flight. Flight as behavior is acquired by each individual in the species and, of course, dramatizes the role of behavior in the selection process; young birds who depart an elevated nest and fail to exhibit the proper motor patterns rarely get a second chance. Under different environmental circumstances, however, this pressure is modulated so that such species as ostriches and penguins do not fly, although their vestigial wings are involved to some extent in surface locomotion. In the evolution of these species, there has evidently been very little selection pressure against nonflying wings, with differential survival value placed on size and aquatic mobility.

The conception of behavioral variability as intrinsic flows naturally from the observation that different species exhibit variation in behavior that certainly correlates with their variation in morphology. Because both types of variation are clearly functional in the adaptation of species, it is tempting to conclude that both are the product of natural selection and can be explained by genetic factors. In contrast, the upcoming discussion of variability as extrinsic addresses the question of the evolutionary significance of behavioral variability from the perspective of its determination by variation in the environment. This shift in focus is subtle but important, redirecting attention from the function of variability toward a search for its determinants.

Implications of the Intrinsic Argument

It is unlikely that science will ever completely resolve the issue of whether or not, or to what extent, behavioral variability is inherent or intrinsic. We have reviewed two of the more commonly enunciated justifications of the position that it is intrinsic—the analogy with quantum phenomena in physics and the traditional argument from biological evolution—and found neither overly compelling. Scientific resolution, however, would require incontrovertible proof of the truth or falsity of the assumption that variability is intrinsic, and this should not be expected. The methods of empirical science lend themselves, as Sidman (1960) point out, not to proof of the null case, but only to demonstrations of the plausibility of the alternative. Evidence favoring the assumption of behavioral variability as intrinsic is currently scanty, albeit extensively buttressed by tradition.

Regardless of one's philosphical preference on the matter, there are certain strategic consequences of the assumption that behavioral variability is intrinsic that must be understood. As we have pointed out, an immediate corollary of this assumption is that identifying determinants and eventual control is an *a priori* impossibility. Endorsing this position fosters an attitude toward the subject matter that adversely influences virtually every decision the researcher makes. The form and content of the experimental question will reflect the assumed futility of precise external control, substituting hypothetical relations among complex inner states for concrete predictions of the effects of specific experimental operations upon observable properties of behavior. Thereafter, all measurement decisions and the ensuing tactics are such as to ensure sufficient variability for affirmation of the original assertion to be inevitable. The design strategies necessitated by the uncritical adoption of vaganotic measurement procedures not only preclude identifying functional relations through controlled replication, but foreclose all but the crudest interpretative alternatives afforded by the inferential testing of statistical hypotheses.

Clearly, the experimental strategies and tactics that issue from the assumption of intrinsic variability are consistent with and confirming of that assumption. Firm commitment to that position can be the only justification for perpetuating a research style that is so obviously inexact and inefficient. The reader whose philosophical proclivities favor interpreting behavioral variability as extrinsic, but who, for reasons of training or tradition, nevertheless approaches behavioral research from the intrinsic perspective, must just as surely live with the empirical consequences of such actions. Fortunately, an entirely different set of consequences flow from relaxing the assumption that behavioral variability is intrinsic, and it is to these that we now turn.

THE CASE FOR BEHAVIORAL VARIABILITY AS EXTRINSIC

The fact that behavior displays variability is disputed by no one. However, the sources and uses of such variability are at the very heart of the divergences in strategy and method that differentiate various disciplinary approaches to the understanding of behavior. Having just discussed the strategic and tactical limitations of the assumption that variability is intrinsic, we will now explore the complementary benefits that derive from the assumption that behavioral variability is extrinsic—that is, describable, predictable, and explainable with reference to variation in other phenomena, either organismic or environmental. In this regard, it is important to remember a few of the details of our definition of behavior (see Chapter 3). Behavior constitutes a portion of the *interaction* that transpires between organism and environment; it is, therefore, evident that variability in behavior may be a reflection either of variability in the organism, variability in the environment, or both. Implicit in this definition is the corollary that behavior is *not* a property or attribute of the organism and is, therefore, not solely the result of the organism's genetic history or physiological status. In other words, because behavior is not intrinsic to the organism, neither is behavioral variability.

This conclusion is not inconsistent with either the theory or facts of evolution by natural selection. Rather, it offers a somewhat simplified account of the role of behavior in natural selection, because it does not presuppose a direct genetic account of behavioral variability. It is commonly agreed that the behavioral process is instrumental to survival and reproduction; organisms do not reproduce at the moment of birth, but must exist in an environment for varying periods of time until reaching maturity. It is also understood that no organism exists in a completely static environment. The environment of any organism constantly changes, usually imposing a requirement for corresponding change on the part of the organism if it is to survive. By responding to such requirements, organisms cause further change in the environment. If these environmental changes mediate or promote survival, such as when distance from a predator or proximity to food is increased, the organism enjoys an increased chance of contributing to the gene pool of the species. This by no means implies that organisms act in order to enhance their contribution to subsequent phylogeny, only that the evolutionary effect of their action is ultimately mediated genetically.

It is variability in the environment that becomes the sufficient cause for variability in behavior. We say sufficient rather than necessary because no one has ever created a variation-free environment in which to observe the occurrence of behavior in the absence of simultaneously occurring environmental variability. Apparently, environmental variability is a universal condition to which all organisms must adapt and survive; the behavioral details of this adaptation are clearly dependent on the nature of environmental variation that prevails. In some instances, either naturally or experimentally produced, environmental variation exceeds the repertoire of the organism, and it perishes. However, other members of the species who, by virtue of a more fortunate morphology or behavioral history possess a larger repertoire, may survive an extreme instance of environmental variability, and the gene pool of the species is accordingly modified. Fascinating examples of this process are found among the rat populations inhabiting certain sections of large cities. Upheavals in their habitat imposed by politically inspired variation in the frequency of garbage collection creates conditions under which those that are to survive must move indoors and feed on humans. It is probable that litters birthed indoors are more likely to emit such behavior than are those reared on the shipping docks, because the former possess a more compatible behavioral history.

Of greatest importance is the fact that many aspects of environmental variation can be controlled by experimental means, and the ensuing variability in behavior may be measured and correlated with any environmental independent manipulations. Changes in behavior that are regularly and repeatably produced by specific operations on the environment can hardly be said to be the result of intrinsic variability. This illuminates the basic strategy of the science of behavior—to exert control over selected aspects of the environment and to observe the resulting changes in behavior.

In any experiment, this strategy takes two concurrent forms: reducing or eliminating variability in behavior by isolating and controlling those extraneous factors in the environment responsible for it and enlarging the remaining variability in behavior by deliberately arranging for occurrence of variation in some independent variable. The goal is to account for observed variability in behavior by its relation to known and controlled variation in the environment. The scientific enterprise thus becomes the search for the determinants of observed variability. Successful results of this search take the form of convincing demonstrations of controlling relations between manipulated environmental variables and resulting change or variation in behavior. Again we see that variability functions as the basic grist of the scientific mill—the raw material from which relational statements are made and verified.

This concludes our brief examination of the two contending assumptions (and their scientific implications) concerning the origins and nature of behavioral variability. It should be clear that the assumptions one makes concerning behavioral variability may extensively condition the approach one takes in attempting to understand it scientifically. It may also be convincingly argued, however, that one's philosophical position on this issue is irrelevant if the day-to-day conduct of a science of behavior is methodologically sound. Our purpose in raising the issue is to apprise the reader that the fundamental methodological differences characterizing the social and natural scientific approaches to the study of behavior are derivable from discrepant basic positions on this fundamental issue. Although it is no doubt the case that many of the more vigorous proponents on either side of various methodological disputes have never even considered the underlying philosophical questions, it is also true that the influence of tradition and training on one's strategic proclivities can eventually determine one's convictions concerning the nature of behavioral variability. Individuals with extensive personal histories in the broadly traditional approach to behavioral experimentation may, if pushed, adopt the view that behavioral variability is intrinsic, if only to maintain consistence with their past practices. Of course, even if one takes the position that behavioral variability is partly intrinsic and partly extrinsic, the proper strategy is to exhaust by experimentation the sources of extrinsic variability before succumbing to the strategic dictates of intrinsic variability.

Regardless of philosophical stance, one cannot ignore the accomplishments in description, analysis, and understanding that have resulted from 40 years of intensive behavioral investigation guided by the strategies issuing from the premise that behavioral variability is extrinsic. It is with studied regard for this perspective and its achievements that the present volume confidently seeks to extend these strategies and their corresponding tactics to the entire domain of human behavior.

SOURCES OF BEHAVIORAL VARIABILITY

The successful search for sources of extrinsic variability leads naturally to an attempt at classification. The result of any such attempt will necessarily be a system of major categories of independent variables to which behavior is functionally related. Every classificatory system is to some extent arbitrary, and subdivisions discussed below often were chosen primarily for didactic convenience.[2]

---

[2]In Chapter 19, we discuss the extent to which similarly arbitrary systems of classifying the independent variables of a science of behavior serve as the basis for organizing institutions of higher education into disciplines and departments. Always ignored, of course, is the commonality of the dependent variable.

Organism

Not all variability that occurs in the transaction between organism and environment is imposed directly by the external environment. The other major factor in the interaction, the organism, also houses sources of behavioral variability that are subject to experimental manipulation. We have already noted that an organism's genetic and physiological endowments set limits on observed behavior. Within these limits, however, the complex dynamic processes that comprise the physiological functioning of an organism contribute to behavioral variation over time. It is important to consider these processes as belonging to the internal environment, maintaining the clarity of their status as independent variables in the science of behavior.[3]

Among the intraorganismic variables that contribute to variation in behavior are the whole range of *cyclic physiological processes* that determine homeostasis—energy consumption, oxygen depletion, water balance, and so forth. As shifts in these states occur, behavioral events transpire that include among their consequences restoration of an optimal level of one or more state variables. As a simple example, variation in the frequency or duration of drinking responses correlates with time since the previous drinking episode, mirroring the cyclic nature of water balance.

A closely related source of intraorganismic variation derives from the fact that merely behaving engenders changes in the economy of the internal environment. Even in a relatively static external environment, an extended series of behavioral acts will display variation due to the effects of what is usually called "fatigue." The effects of the controlling variables may be studied indirectly by imposing external controls that pace the behavior or otherwise modify its frequency or intensity, such as when breaks are programmed into a work schedule. Such variables may also be studied by direct intervention in the internal environment by administering various chemical substances that either depress or magnify the degree of behavioral variation. In any case, the effect on behavior is of primary interest, and this effect is seen through the lens of variability.

There is another large class of intraorganismic variables that may be termed *developmental.* All else being equal, changes in behavior can be shown to result from an orderly series of noncyclic physiological changes that take place in any organism with the passage of time. Unfortunately, little is known

---

[3]Identifying variables as belonging to the internal environment does not imply that any resulting variability is intrinsic. The intrinsic–extrinsic distinction refers to the nature of sources of control, not to their location. Many sources of extrinsic behavioral variability are found in the internal environment.

concerning the exact contribution or operation of these variables in determining human behavior, because they are rarely studied in well-controlled environments. A great many "scales" have been derived by developmental psychologists that estimate various ages at which certain types of behavior may be expected to appear, but these are merely statistical compilations of the ages at which the behaviors do appear and should not be taken as minima imposed by the genotype. Under conditions of explicit and direct control over environmental contingencies, for example, it is probable that functional speech could be shaped in very young infants, even though it ordinarily does not occur until 8 or 9 months of age. Careful control over the environment and close management of complex contingencies has produced swimming behavior in 3-month-olds, although there is little likelihood that walking could be produced at that age because of insufficient muscular development.

Behavioral changes are also observed that are dependent on physiological changes that accompany aging. These changes are very often the result of changes in the capacity of the individual to receive stimulation from the environment, as when audition or vision begin to fail. The functional influence of the environment is altered in these cases in that events that once directly affected behavior no longer do so. Equipping the individual with "behavioral prosthetics" (Lindsley, 1964) can sometimes restore functional behavior by specifically adjusting the environment to suit the individual. Hearing aids and spectacles are familiar examples of behavioral prosthetics, as are wheelchairs, moving sidewalks, and inclinators. The importance of such devices to the natural science of behavior rests with their function—they are instances of the general class of environment rearrangements that magnify the dependence of behavior on the environment.

Intraorganismic sources of behavioral variability are among the most difficult to isolate and control experimentally. Because they are not directly accessible and are not as conveniently manipulable as are events in the external environment, the temptation has been great to regard them as inherent and, therefore, sources of intrinsic variability. As discussed earlier, this is tantamount to foreclosing experimental inquiry on the grounds that any detected variation is beyond explanation and must remain the result of unalterable intrinsic properties of the genotype. Research then becomes focused on attempts to describe the particular genotypic property, inferring variation in it as a logical necessity of observed variation in behavior. What should be an independent variable thus becomes the object of inquiry, and the search for knowledge of the determinants of behavior is forsaken.

The presence in the natural language of such nouns as "memory," "intelligence," "ability," and so on, only exacerbates the false sense of contentment that arises when some variation in behavior is "explained" by referring to some intrinsic repository of its determinants. To these common terms have been added a great many new and more technical terms that also refer to hypothetical processes or capacities that are little more than elaborate disguises for our collective ignorance. The practice of invoking a hypothetical process, such as inhibition or retention, to describe an orderly set of behavioral data does not explain these data, although many people are easily persuaded to the contrary. The current popularity of parent action groups formed to cope with the elusive mysteries of "learning disabilities," "dyslexia," and "minimal brain dysfunction" serves primarily to divert this unlimited force for educational improvement away from simply meeting the behavioral needs of children whose academic performance displays uncommon variability.

Unfortunately, not only the laity but young scientists often uncritically accept as real the existence of such explanatory fictions and waste a great deal of time and money attempting to refine our understanding of them. It is curious that even though we may be publicly amused by Descartes' efforts to locate the soul in the pineal gland, we become deadly serious if our belief that "language ability" resides in the left hemisphere of the human brain is assaulted. Of course, the data support no such contention. For example, verbal behavior is clearly disrupted by accidental injury or surgical stimulation of the left hemisphere. That is a behavioral fact that does not require the invocation of an "ability" for its interpretation. More importantly, if the "ability" explanation of the behavioral change is eschewed, it is more likely that environmental means will be sought to restore the behavior to its earlier functional level. Success in this venture will isolate the behavioral processes involved and eventually shed light on the actual contribution made by the nervous system.

Experimental Setting

In any investigation, the behavior of interest takes place in an environment composed of many potential sources of observable variability. Usually, one or two such sources are the focus of deliberate experimental attention and constitute the independent variables of the study. The remaining environmental sources of variability are traditionally grouped under the heading *"extraneous"* to signify that they occupy a position of secondary interest to the investigator. Regardless of the degree of disinterest the investigator may profess in these variables, however, they remain potent sources of influence on the data, and care must be taken to manage their collective effects in a manner that benefits the research goals. To the extent that sources of extraneous variability operate in a capricious, systematic, or in any way nonconstant fashion, their effects may become hopelessly intertwined with the planned effects of the independent variables, making it impossible to isolate and assess the latter. If the goal of the research is to describe the effect of a particular planned variation or behavior, its actual attainment will always be modulated by whatever unchecked influence extraneous variables are allowed to have. Unfortunately, there is no way to separate or even recognize the contribution of extraneous sources of variability in behavioral data after the fact. Efforts to cleanse the data with statistical lixiviators offer little relief because they involve a chain of reasoning from empirically unlikely assumptions that cannot be independently verified. Consequently, such sources of variation must be confronted prior to or during data collection and their influence either brought under control or eliminated entirely.

Generally, the requisite experimental strategy calls for selecting and/or designing an experimental environment that will provide the clearest possible background against which to impose planned independent variable manipulations. Repeatedly measuring the target behavior in the absence of planned intervention provides useful information concerning the ambient influence of extraneous variables and furnishes a crucial source of feedback by which the investigator can evaluate and adjust tactics for minimizing these factors. A full discussion of the tactics by which this general strategy is implemented throughout an experiment is presented in Chapter 12.

Basically, there are two generic alternatives available to an investigator confronted with the problem of managing extraneous sources of variability in the environment. One can either attempt to gain operational control over the contributing variables so as to hold them constant (or nearly so), or one can try to eliminate them entirely. There are advantages and disadvantages (both tactical and logistical) to both of these approaches that we do not elaborate here. However, mention should be made of the fact that control by elimination frequently involves a highly specialized environment, such as a sound- and lightproof chamber, that may introduce its own peculiar, though constant, influence so as to limit generality of the findings to more natural, uncontrolled settings. On the other hand, the sacrifice may be worthwhile if the relation of experimental interest can only be examined *in vitro*.

There is a continuum of specificity along which either of these alternatives can be implemented. At one extreme, the investigator can identify and control, one-by-one, sources of extraneous variation until all that might have contributed ambiguity to the findings have been dealt with. This is usually somewhat time-consuming, but actually more economical, because trivial factors that would not be cost effective to control are left free to vary. At the other extreme, all possible variables are either controlled or eliminated, regardless of their potential impact. This is usually the more costly but conservative approach, because it is predicated on no suppositions or irrevocable bad guesses about the wisdom of leaving some variable uncontrolled. On the other hand, the price of this blunderbuss approach to control may include the loss of potential sources of serendipitous findings;

controlling all present sources of variation may preclude the appearance of additional future sources that would have been welcome.

How does an experimenter decide how much control is enough? This must be a pragmatic decision subject to review at any time. Basically, enough control is operating when the relations of interest can be viewed clearly against residual background noise and when there is little or no doubt as to what constitutes the functional independent variable. When one or the other of these conditions cannot be satisfied, more control is indicated, and the investigation should not proceed until it has been achieved. In many cases, it will prove sufficient to control yet another extraneous variable—time of day, response history of the subject, observer training, etc. In others, a wholesale redefinition of the experimental environment may be called for, forcing the decision to move the research to a fully controlled laboratory setting. In each instance, the investigator must weigh all the pros and cons and take the best action available for the case at hand.

Measurement

A substantial amount of extraneous variability can also be traced to the various aspects of the entire measurement operation: response definition, unit selection, observation, and recording. In general, real extraneous variability in the subject matter is of two types; it may be *imposed* inadvertently or it may be a *residual* consequence of inaccuracy or imprecision in the measurement process (or inadequacies of experimental design or execution). For example, permitting an observational situation in which there is substantial reactivity to the observer imposes variability in that target behavior. Residual variability would result from a poor response class definition that, unbeknownst to the experimenter, actually contained two or more functional response classes that are differentially influenced by the treatment variable (see the following section). In either case, it must be understood that it is within the investigator's power to preclude contaminating the data with either type. These sources of variability result from acts of either commission or omission by the experimenter, and evidence of their influence in any set of data can immediately be construed as an indication that the investigator does not fully understand or care about his or her methodological responsibilities. Good experimental practice requires that such variability be eliminated, whether by anticipating and avoiding sources of unnecessary imposition or by ensuring that each decision involved in measurement is calculated to eliminate an already existing source of extraneous variation.

It is also useful to distinguish between *real* variability that actually exists in the phenomenon under investigation, whether imposed by the experimenter or retained as a residual effect of uncontrolled sources, and various forms of *illusory* or artifactual variability that do not exist in the subject matter. The latter category includes variability in the data that is due entirely to flaws in the measurement procedure, such as undetected observer bias, or drift in sensitivity. It is impossible to isolate this type of variability on the basis of inspection alone; it can be done only by controlled management of all facets of the data-gathering procedure. It must be managed, however, because its impact on correct interpretation is as profound as any source of extraneous variation.

The major decisions required at each step of the measurement process and the source of variability each decision is designed to eliminate have already been discussed in previous chapters. A brief review here is intended to highlight the relevance of these tactics to the overall experimental strategy of arranging for the variability imposed by the manipulated independent variables to stand out in the sharpest possible relief against a quiet, homogeneous background.

Response Class Definitions.   The first possibility of measurement error arises from the definitional actions that are or are not taken by the experimenter. The discussion in Chapter 6 of the various tactics available here and the nature of the variability that can be incurred was extensive and need not be repeated. However, one consequence is such a pervasive possibility and is of such sufficient import that a brief reiteration is mandatory. Many experimenter decisions at this stage can easily result in a single defined response class that in fact includes more than one functional class. The reader will recall that the importance of a functionally defined response class lies in the generic homogeneity of the functional relations among behavioral events in the class and determining stimulus events in the surrounding environment. Not only does this ensure investigating and interpretating a single, functionally unitary, behavioral phenomenon, it means that variability resulting from otherwise fully accurate measurement is the consequence of variation in only one set of functionally related environmental events. When this is not the case—when the defined class includes responses actually in two or more different functional classes—variation will be observed in the total defined and measured class that may result from: (1) variation in only one of the actual functional classes; (2) variation in the different functional classes in different ways under the control of different external sources; or (3) variation in the different functional classes in different ways under the control of the same stimulus event, whether it is an extraneous or a controlled independent variable.

In other words, variability that is likely to result from improper definitional practices will obscure the clarity with which true functional relations between an independent variable and a single functional response class may be detected. Even more likely is the possibility that interpretations will be erroneously drawn about the effects of the independent variable on a unitary behavioral class that is, in fact, not functionally unitary at all, thus assuring limits on the generality of the conclusions that will be discovered only after subsequent, costly replicative failures. The time to ensure against such misfortunes is at the moment of original definition; careful pursuit of the tactics suggested in Chapter 6 will ensure distinct functional classes.

Dimensional Quantities.   Following definition, the investigator must select a dimensional quantity (and its associated measurement unit) that is sensitive to the variability in which there is experimental interest. For example, the selecting of countability (and cycles) for measuring a response class being investigated with an experimenter-paced trials procedure would indeed show variability in responding, but countability would probably not be a sensitive indicator of experimentally important variability. Any variability in countability could trivially be accounted for by the trials variable, whereas rich variation in latency might go undetected. A comparable situation may exist for any dimensional quantity in each case, although the means of identifying such situations may not be obvious. Any behavior can be described with the complete range of dimensional quantities. Assuming that such measurement is accurate, sensitivity is subjectively defined by the experimenter depending on the question under examination. That is, whereas it may be possible to observe variation accurately in a number of different dimensional quantities describing various aspects of behavior, it may be that only one dimensional quantity will show variation that is relevant to the experimenter's interest. This dimensional quantity would then be described as sensitive under those circumstances; however, a different experimental interest in the same behavior might define some other dimensional quantity as the most sensitive.

Thus, assuming proper definition of the dimensional quantity and otherwise accurate measurement, the most likely means by which experimenter actions can result in unwanted variability is through selecting a dimensional quantity in which variability is irrelevant, subject to control by variables that are themselves uncontrolled, or influenced by nontreatment variables that may be intentionally or inadvertently controlled by the experimenter. Whichever the case, ignoring such possibilities will encourage the assumption that observed variation (or lack of same) is the result of variation in the independent variable, thus guaranteeing interpretations of limited generality.

The discussion has thus far assumed the selection of a true dimensional quantity, an assumption that has less contemporary justification than might be desired. Choosing a dimensionless quantity (such as relative duration) ensures further barriers to detecting and clearly describing independent variable-induced variability and is discussed at length in Chapter 7. However, adopting the vaganotic measurement practices detailed in Chapter 4 must hold the honor of constituting the most severe and intractable collection of unit-related problems. The multiple sources of variability inevitably resulting from vaganotic measurement first preclude the identification of all but a hardy and select few of the functional relations existing in nature and then limit the description of those relations to only the crudest level of clarity.

Observing and Recording.   The consideration of variability arising from observing and recording practices is a minor industry in science. The possibilities for observational error are sufficiently obvious to most that arguments for their existence are unnecessary; Chapter 8 details the range of actual difficulties. It should be emphasized, however, that except for the problem of reactivity of the subject's behavior to the observational procedures, the variability that results from improper observation is artifactual or illusory rather than extant in the phenomenon itself. This is an important acknowledgment both because it may serve to motivate efforts to distinguish between real and illusory variability in the behavior under study and because it may augment the caution with which eventual interpretations are tendered. The real danger, of course, is that the proper distinctions may not be made, encouraging the assumption that the results of the observational process solely reflect variation in the phenomenon, when, in fact, a major agent of the obtained variability is an inherent characteristic of the measurement procedure that has nothing to do with the phenomenon being measured. For example, a less than fully trained observer will probably improve in observational accuracy during the early course of experimentation. This change will appear as a change in the data, and it is impossible to ascribe it to observer drift without reference to independent calibration results.

The conglomerate of sources and types of extraneous variability just reviewed is often simply categorized as "measurement error." This phrase harkens back to the 19th-century custom of calling any unanalyzed variability "error" and relying on statistical procedures for its description and management. As the foregoing discussion indicates, variability arising out of the activities that collectively comprise measurement is not "error" in the technical sense, and can largely be either controlled or eliminated, but there will remain some variability reflecting the fact that less than perfect accuracy of measurement has been achieved. Chapter 10, on stability and accuracy of measurement, discussed rather thoroughly the criteria for scientific measurement and strategies for meeting these criteria with human behavior. In practice, however, these criteria are only loosely approximated, and residual variability ("error") will exist. The investigator thus needs a set of tactics for recognizing such error and keeping it at a minimum. Residual error of measurement may be classified as either *random* or *systematic*—an important distinction, for the ensuing effects on interpretation will be quite different in each case. Random error merely adds "noise" to the data in the form of variability that does not appear related to or explainable by any known process. It is this type of variability that is often thought of as intrinsic or irreducible beyond some level as a result of inherent biological limitations. Many investigators are content to treat random errors of measurement statistically, asserting that the effects of random error will be distributed equally across all conditions of observation and that strong experimental "signals" will be detected against such background noise.

There are two problems with this approach. First, true randomness is a statistical concept that is rarely observed in reality; the great expense to which modern casinos are forced in keeping roulette wheels unbiased attests to this fact. Treating such variability in accordance with the assumption that it is random in the mathematical sense introduces a potential interpretative error that may be costly. Evaluating treatment differences against a so-called "error term" that is assumed to be random may prompt overconfidence in the generality of the result, especially if the error term is artificially reduced by the operation of some unknown, and hence unreproducible, source of bias or constancy in the measurement. Of course, failure at attempted replication should bring this possibility to light, but the eschewal of replication among investigators who rely on statistical induction of experimental generalities should not encourage serious reliance on this safeguard.

The second problem with assuming that residual measurement error is "random" and therefore manageable by statistical means is that its masking effects are not eliminated. The accuracy of measurement must always exceed the differences to which the measuring instrument must be sensitive. When this condition is not met, basic and lawful changes in the phenomenon being studied will escape detection because they are overpowered by either insensitivity or error in the measurement procedure. A good illustration of this principle is furnished by weight scales. If a person goes on a diet to lose 10 pounds, a bathroom scale that regularly displays an error as large as ±25 pounds when subjected to a 150-pound weight will be of no help in tracking the orderly variability that occurs as weight begins to decline. The fact that the error appears random does not relieve the problem. On the other hand, a scale used to weigh trucks at highway patrol stations may be calibrated to well within the necessary limits of accuracy when tons are the unit of measurement, but will generally be incapable of detecting a one or two pound change. The necessary sensitivity is clearly lacking, and an appropriate measure of accuracy cannot be obtained. One must, therefore, be assured of the highest possible accuracy of measurement consistent with the magnitude of measured differences it is necessary to detect. If measurement is known to be accurate within prespecified tolerances, it is certain that observed variability falling outside that range is not due to measurement error, and it becomes prudent to instigate an experimental search of its causes.

Systematic measurement errors are also a source of variability, but one that may not be so troublesome. A systematic error is one that is not random, but due to operation of some source of bias, often undiscoverable or extremely difficult to remove. Of course, it is preferable to remove the source of error by adjusting or recalibrating the measurement system. If, for some logistical reason, this cannot be done, *and if the extent and variability of the error can be exactly specified*, its influence can be removed from the data by algebraic correction. Again, the scale analogy is useful. The dieter can happily detect one or two pound weight changes even if the scale has a systematic error of 15 pounds. All that is necessary is that a fixed correction be applied if it is necessary to estimate the true weight. In the case of behavioral measurement using frequency or a time unit, systematic errors can be tolerated providing, again, they can be determined and a correction applied to those instances in which an exact measurement is necessary. Most systematic errors of this type should not influence the sensitivity of measurement and therefore the ability of the measuring procedure to detect change, providing the error is additive and its source does not interact with a treatment procedure or some other independent variable. For example, an observer who consistently misses a random 10% of the responses that might otherwise be included in the functional class under analysis will not adversely affect the data used to evaluate the impact of a planned treatment providing that on the occasion of introduction of the treatment the error does not increase to 20%. However, it is usually harder to be assured of this degree of independence than to remove the source of error in the first place.

Experimental Design

The next four chapters deal extensively with the strategies and tactics of designing experimental protocols whose sole purpose is to isolate and explain sources of behavioral variability. At this point, however, it is desirable to gain an advance perspective on this material from the general vantage point of isolating sources of extraneous variability, whether real or artifactual. One source of variability in particular—the fact that all organisms do not behave identically—merits special discussion, because it embodies the central problem that statistical approaches to experimental design and analysis have attempted to solve.

The evolution of experimental design in psychology and education has been implicitly guided by the existence and changing conceptualizations of *intersubject variability*. Viewed essentially as intrinsic, intersubject variability has been generally construed as an uncontrollable source of "error" suitable only as a reference value for vaganotic decision metrics. Adopting this assumption, whether by intention or default, places the investigator in the untenable position of having to "live with" variability that is not only irrelevant to the purpose at hand, but that persists as a nuisance and source of contamination at every phase of the research through final dissemination. There is no gainsaying the high degree of sophistication and elegance that characterizes the modern approach to statistical management of intersubject variability; it is sufficient to point out that these techniques are largely unnecessary, because intersubject variability is usually imposed by the experimenter at great cost and inconvenience.

To understand why intersubject variability is properly viewed as extraneous, the reader need only be reminded that the subject matter of the discipline is the behavior of individual organisms (see Chapter 3) and that the grand goal is the elucidation of general functional relations between such behavior and controlling independent variables. As a matter of definitional and logical necessity, intersubject variability has nothing to do with the description of, nor can it ever be used to explain, the behavior of any single organism. The fact that two organisms may behave differently says nothing whatever about why either behaves as it does. On the other hand, an adequate account of why each behaves as it does will necessarily be sufficient to explain any differences that are observed between them. A science of behavior must obviously be able to account for differences in behavior that are observed among individuals, and to do so will require that the generality of its basic functional relations be explored, established, and specified. This requires that the functional relations must first be discovered, a task made all but impossible by premature insistence on the type of artificial generality that is believed furnished by experimentation on large groups of subjects.

The intersubject variability that is the inevitable accoutrement of what might be referred to as a "groups design" is managed, to the extent that it is managed at all, by statistical averaging techniques. Lamentably, using an average does not eliminate or explain the variability; it merely produces a number with respect to which the variability is balanced or cancelled. It is often mistakenly argued in support of large-group research that if the average comes from a large enough sample, its representativeness is somehow assured. This argument is consistent with the view of variability as intrinsic and uncontrollable and is correctly used to support the desire for accurate estimates of population parameters from sample statistics. It is absolutely true, for example, that the greater the size of a random sample drawn from a specific population, the more closely will the sample mean approximate the true value of the population mean.

Unfortunately, a science whose aim is to isolate and identify real causes of variability has little or no occasion to estimate population parameters from sample statistics, and as a representative measure of the individual case, the arithmetic mean is usually not very good. One can only evaluate the accuracy of the mean as representing the individual cases by comparing it to the measure for each individual case. It will quickly be discovered that increasing the number of cases will not increase the proportion of such cases that happen to be equal to the mean, and it is a rare occurrence when even one individual measure happens to coincide exactly with an average derived from the data of many other individuals. The security afforded by a large sample is therefore illusory and artificial on the matter of representativeness of the individual case and should not be mistakenly viewed otherwise.

Another, more elaborate, justification for imposing intersubject variability through a groups design involves using that variability as an "error term" against which to assess the variability imparted by experimental treatments. The reader who has followed the argument to this point surely realizes that "error" is never an appropriate standard against which to evaluate anything, least of all the major outcome of a research investigation. Moreover, the usual "error term" calculated from variability between subjects within groups is not error at all; it is an extraneous source of variability that is enlisted primarily for its statistical utility. The requirement that group or cell sizes exceed a certain minimum is an acknowledgment that a certain amount of such variability is necessary in order to perform the statistical tests and that it must be obtained from somewhere. Once admitted, however, it must be contained; paradoxically, the way to contain it is to admit more so as to justify its treatment with large-sample statistics that assume randomness. From that point on, any treatment difference of nonzero magnitude can be shown to be "significant" by sufficiently augmenting the sample size. Of course, the amount of variability in the behavior of any single subject accounted for by the treatment has not increased, nor has any real generality been established, because it is not immediately evident whether the effect "observed" statistically holds for even one subject, let alone several. The general tactic is clearly reminiscent of the early attempts of automobile manufacturers to meet air pollution standards stated in parts per million. Rather than reduce the absolute number of polluting parts emitted, they contrived blowers to add additional clean air to the exhaust of the vehicle, thus bringing the ratio down to stated limits and creating the illusion of having made exhaust emissions "cleaner."

Notwithstanding the peculiar and rather futile use made of intersubject variability in "groups designs," the fact that different subjects behave differently cannot be ignored by a science of behavior. Neither should this fact be allowed to occupy a position of priority in an enterprise seeking to establish the functional determinants of behavior that will hold in each and every case. It is of immediate interest only insofar as it sets limiting or boundary conditions on our explanations of behavior. To the extent that intersubject variability can be controlled and accounted for, we are able to specify the limits of generality of our findings across individual organisms.

The problem of intersubject variability should be regarded as a problem of generality to be addressed through replication (see Chapters 15 and 19).

Typically, an experimental procedure will produce a set of relations between measured behavioral events and certain controlled variables in the environment. The behavioral measures are made on a single organism at a time. The question of generality may then be asked, "Will the same relations be observed if a second organism is substituted for the first?" The only way to arrive at an answer is to replicate the procedure on a second organism, then a third, a fourth, and so on. With each replication, differences in the exact quantitative properties of the relation will undoubtedly appear. If it can be established that little or no variation in explicitly controlled experimental manipulations occurred from one replication to another and that various sources of extraneous variability have been controlled or eliminated, it is reasonable to conclude that the variability observed among the experimental relations has something to do with the fact that different organisms were involved. The investigator now invokes the usual strategy and attempts to track down experimentally the causes of these differences and may begin by asking, "What variables must be added to Subject A's environment to cause the data to resemble that of Subject B?" The experimenter is now using the tactic of imposing variability in an effort to change the behavior of Subject A in a specified way. If successful, a major step will have been taken toward quantifying the differences between Subjects A and B in terms of controllable variables. A simple example of this process occurs whenever eyeglasses are fitted: A change (lenses) is made in an individual's environment such that the variation in behavior (reading an eye chart) from a standard is eliminated. Eliminating that variability establishes its source (e.g., myopia), in addition to permitting it to be quantified in terms of measurable characteristics of the lenses needed to remove it. By repeating this process for a suitable number of subjects, it is possible to identify a variable that accounts, at least in part, for the intersubject variability initially observed. In all probability, this variable is an important determinant of behavior, and our scientific mission is advanced.

Display and Quantification of Data

Finally, the experimenter must transform the results of observations under the arrangements of the independent variable demanded by the experimental design into stimuli that will guide subsequent analytic and interpretative behaviors. The central issues involved in this facet of research and the range of possible transformations that are available are discussed in Chapters 16 and 17. For the moment, it is important to point out that experimenter decisions regarding different display and quantification practices may distort the appearance of the real variability as it existed in nature and was detected by observation. Clearly, no machinations with the data can in any way change the real variability that was present and observed in the phenomenon.

Nevertheless, to the extent that this real variability is not faithfully retained in all transformations (illusory variability may be created or real variability may be hidden or lost), the variability that is apparent in any transformations is likely to be assumed to reflect variability in nature accurately. This highly dangerous assumption is avoidable by the experimenter, because he or she has access to all previous transformations of the data all the way back to the observer's judgments. However, scientific peers who can only react to the final published transformations are in the disadvantageous position of either making that same risky assumption, attempting transformations of their own based on limited information, or guessing about the true variability in the absence of necessary portions of the data. It is easy to understand the seductiveness of the assumption that the variability that survives display and quantification operations is real, for that is the sole source of information that the viewer has available. This perspective should, therefore, heighten the importance of forthcoming discussions of display and quantification of data.

Independent Variables

Whatever sources of behavioral variability are not serving as the independent variable under investigation are generically considered to be extraneous, and our discussion of variability arising from the organism's physiology, the experimental environment, and measurement and design decisions by the experimenter has assumed this to be the case. All of the efforts to minimize the effects of extraneous sources of variability are required by the goal of arranging events so that virtually all subsequent variation in the dependent variable is the result of variation in the independent variable, carefully imposed by the experimenter. Implementing this tactic will facilitate the strategy of examining unambiguous functional relations between the independent variable and the dependent variable. The remaining chapters in this section are devoted to a detailed exposition of how this strategy is realized.

12 Steady States and Transitions

Manipulation of new variables will often produce behavioral changes, but in order to describe the changes, we must be able to specify the baseline from which they occurred.

—M. Sidman

THE STEADY-STATE STRATEGY

At the heart of good behavioral research is an intimate understanding of the typical characteristics of the behavior under study when no treatment is being administered. The obvious function of this information is to permit comparisons with the same behavior when under the influence of an independent variable in order that any changes can be detected. The more detailed and accurate this information under both nontreatment and treatment conditions, the more exact will be the resulting knowledge of the relations between the independent and dependent variables.

Increments in accuracy and fullness issue from each additional observation of responding under each condition. In human behavioral research, a single observation, no matter how accurate, invites the question of how typical or representative the observation is of the same subject's responding at other times under the same conditions. The answer *cannot* be derived from observations of other subjects under the same conditions; such a procedure only raises the further question of how similar the other subjects are to the first subject, a far more difficult issue to address.

A second observation of the behavior of the single subject again suggests the question of representativeness: Assuming that the two observations are different, which is the more representative of all unobserved occurrences of the behavior? This question in turn provokes a third measurement, and then a fourth, and probably even more. As the number of observations begins to accumulate, the clarity of the answer to the original question concerning the typical characteristics of the behavior under present conditions is enhanced, but a number of other questions are likely to emerge. These questions will be suggested by the emerging characteristics of the behavior being repeatedly measured under as constant a set of conditions as can be arranged. It may now be possible to detect cycles, trends, and other fluctuations that enlarge the relatively simple question of representativeness into a host of questions concerning the variables influencing the behavior. It may even be necessary to address some of these questions before being able to answer fully the underlying question of representativeness.

For example, suppose Fig. 12.1 represents the results of an effort to describe the baseline occurrence of a particular response. After the first three or four data points have been collected, it is clear that responding is not stable, but appears to be decreasing. Why is this? Is the measurement procedure reactive? Is a natural process such as extinction in progress? The next several observations reveal increasing variability, and a four-unit cycle seems to be emerging. What is the cause of that? Is it reliable? By the time all of the data have been collected and plotted, it appears that the high points are getting higher, the low points are getting lower, and the intermediate values are becoming less frequent. Is it possible that two separate functional classes are involved? What are the controlling variables driving these measures apart? What will be the limits reached by the highs and lows? Will they reconverge? Clearly, some of these questions must be answered satisfactorily before the planned investigation can be undertaken. Tracking down these answers may even turn out to be more rewarding than answering the original experimental question.

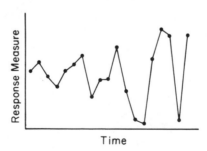

FIG. 12.1.   Hypothetical baseline responding.

This discussion began with a statement of the importance of an understanding of the characteristics of responding under nontreatment conditions; however, the reasoning outlined here clearly applies to responding under any set of constant conditions in the course of an experimental program. For example, all of the questions raised concerning the data of Fig. 12.1 could be asked with equal cogency if Fig. 12.1 represented the data of a treatment phase rather than an attempt to capture an initial baseline. The question of representativeness under some treatment condition is the familiar yet deceptively simple one concerning the effect of the manipulated independent variable (or more accurately, the nature of the functional relation between dependent and independent variables). The deception encouraged by this question lies in the temptation to consider any few observations made after the treatment is initiated as an adequate assessment of its effect on responding, especially if the change actually observed was anticipated. In fact, it is necessary to make repeated observations beginning with the implementation of the independent variable and continuing for an extended period of time thereafter to determine when the treatment began to have an effect, the characteristics of the effect as time progresses, and the nature of the effect after its influence has stabilized. Thus, the question is not just the basic one of determining whether or not a change in responding from previous conditions has occurred, but the more demanding ones concerning the nature of whatever change occurred and what its enduring features are.

The characteristics of the "state" of the behavior being investigated under any conditions may be crudely described as either stable or unstable, and responding is said to be in a steady state or transition state, respectively. The study, understanding, and use of these relatively defined behavioral states is a crucial strategy in the science of behavior. The power of within-subject comparisons in experimental designs rests on the precision of control that this tactic facilitates. This control is demonstrated and monitored by means of the strategies and tactics described in this chapter; abrogation of these responsibilities can crumble the keystone upon which the experimental edifice is constructed.

STEADY STATES

A steady state may be generally defined as a behavioral state in which the behavior of interest exhibits relatively little variation of its measured dimensional quantities over a period of time. A full exposition of the meaning of this definition follows in a later discussion on the tactics of implementation, but it seems proper to first consider the basic functions served by steady states.

Uses

A successful effort to establish conditions generating stable patterns of responding is inevitably highly informative. Following careful response definition and measurement, continued observation for an extended period of time under relatively constant environmental conditions (whether treatment or nontreatment) will allow the experimenter to identify the characteristics of responding that prevail under those conditions. Characteristics refers here to the dispersion of the response measures over time and the relations of variations in any such distribution to minor or major changes in accompanying environmental events. The above reference to maintaining "relatively constant environmental conditions" means only that the experimenter is not knowingly producing uncontrolled variations in functionally related environmental events. It certainly does not mean that surrounding conditions are constant, however; there may be substantial changes of obvious importance, as well as more subtle changes that might be unnoticed. It is important to remind the reader that any observed variation in the measures of responding is assumed to be the product of variation in some controlling variable that is subject to independent isolation and control. The presence of such variation should therefore serve as a signal that a potentially powerful independent variable remains to be identified and explored.

Just how much environmental change can occur under the rubric of "stable" conditions may seem arbitrary. The presence of a substitute teacher is a natural change in stimulus conditions that might seem likely to have major effects on much behavior of a school child serving as an experimental subject. Stable conditions might still be said to prevail, however, if the effects on the child's responding are slight or not detectable. Assuming little measurement-induced variability, the demonstration of steady-state responding often but not necessarily means that the events controlling the response are relatively stable. This definition is not circular but functional. If trends, cycles, or other forms of variability are observed in the data, it is a safe inference that certain controlling stimuli are influencing the behavior in a nonconstant or unstable manner. Thus, the "steady" in the phrase "steady-state behavior" indirectly refers to the assumed steadiness (at least of their composite influence) of controlling environmental conditions as well. Other aspects of the environment not functionally related to the behavior may vary markedly, but, although such variation may be highly conspicuous, it has nothing to do with the designation of stable stimulus conditions.

It is precisely such uncontrolled natural variation that is likely to aid in identifying possible controlling relations between particular events and the response of interest. If Dennis' misbehavior is unusually frequent on those days when Sandra sits behind him in school, a possible (not proven) controlling relation has been suggested. Such observations alert the experimenter to certain extraneous factors that may influence responding when the treatment manipulation is implemented. If steady state responding has not been achieved before the independent variable is manipulated, the experimenter may be unaware of these extraneous variables and their possible contaminating influence on the data. Establishing stable responding is thus an index of the rigor of experimental control. If sufficiently stable responding cannot be obtained, the experimenter is in no position to add an independent variable of suspected but unknown influence. To do so would be to compound confusion and lead to further ignorance. Separating the effects of any experimental manipulation from the effects of uncontrolled or unknown variables requires a clear empirical statement that such other variables are not present or are being held constant, and the steady-state demonstration furnishes such a statement.

One of the most important reasons for establishing stable stimulus conditions that produce steady state behavior prior to introducing the experimental variable is to permit the treatment effect to be evaluated by comparison to the same individual's behavior under otherwise identical nontreatment conditions. Another way to attempt this assessment is to compare the performance of one subject who is under treatment conditions with that of another subject who is not. The earlier problem of representativeness is transformed from one of experimental control to one of statistical deduction by ignoring controlling stimulus relations, adding the required large number of subjects to the bare minimum of two, and regarding the averages of the subject's reactions (one group under no treatment and one group under treatment) as representative effects. The most serious problem raised by this tactic in the present context is intersubject variability, discussed at length in the previous chapter. That is, the variability in the data that comes from the different effects of the independent variable on each subject in the experimental group is condensed into the group mean, which represents the effect of the manipulated variable on a nonexistent average subject. This measure is compared to that from the control groups that similarly combines the differing reactions of other subjects to the nontreatment condition. The eventual comparison made between group means is based entirely on intersubject variability, both in the numerator and denominator of the test statistic (t, F, etc.). This intersubject variability is not a characteristic of the behavior of any individual, has no part in the interpretation of behavioral processes, and is therefore completely extraneous.

In contrast, using steady states instead of control groups avoids the problem of intersubject variability while at the same time augmenting experimental sensitivity to the impact of the manipulated variable. This increased sensitivity to treatment effects results from reduced contamination by the effects of other variables and by increased awareness of the presence and influence of all such extraneous variables. Such increased awareness derives from the intimacy of the experimenter's acquaintance with the behavior of the subject acquired during the demonstration of steady state responding.

The sensitivity and control engendered by this tactic facilitates identifying unambiguous functional relations between controlling variables and behavior and enhances the generalizability of the experimental findings. Using steady states in this fashion is perhaps one of the most important features of the proper scientific study of human behavior. The benefits of this tactic are numerous and pervasive in their influence, and a thorough understanding of its implementation is a prerequisite to the conduct of good research. In order to enjoy these benefits, the researcher must be prepared to take an active part in inducting a steady state should it fail to occur naturally. Establishing stable states of responding frequently requires the exercise of an effective technology of behavior control, just as good research in any discipline requires control over those variables that influence and determine the natural state of the dependent variable. Fortunately, the last 40 years of behavioral research have witnessed the development of an impressive array of reliable behavioral control procedures that are fully applicable to research on human behavior.[1] Mastering these procedures and their uses should be an integral part of the training of any serious student of the science of behavior.

Identification

The experimenter who begins collecting data under either baseline or treatment conditions must soon consider how to recognize or identify steady-state responding. It has already been pointed out that all definitions of steady states are relative; there are no fixed rules or criteria that can assist the researcher in discharging this obligation. Nevertheless, the importance of properly identifying steady states remains undiminished if their full utility is to be realized.

Trends.   Identifying steady-state responding involves considering two major aspects of variability—direction of change and range. We first discuss the direction of change characteristic of behavioral data that takes the form of trends over time. In most cases, stable responding is characterized by a relative absence of consistent changes in the data in either a generally increasing or decreasing direction. Not surprisingly, identifying such trends in the data is also unassisted by any simple rules and requires that the investigator have experience with similar behavioral data. The variety of possible trends is endless, and they must always be considered in conjunction with other aspects of variability. Figure 12.2 shows a few typical features of trends.

---

[1] Perhaps the most exhaustive compendium of this literature is Honig and Staddon's edited volume, *Handbook of Operant Behavior* (1977).

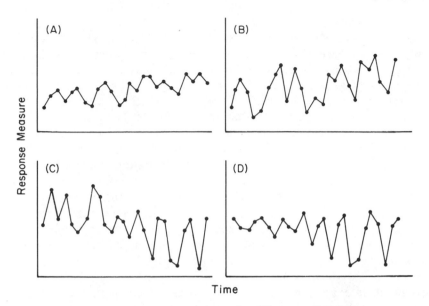

FIG. 12.2. Hypothetical data showing different trend patterns.

Panel A shows an increasing trend characterized by a very gradual but consistent increase in the data. In panel A, the range of variability is fairly constant, as it is in Panel B. However, the larger range in B may mask the fact that the linear trend has the same slope in both cases. In Panel C, the majority of the data points fall within a central range and show a horizontal slope. The existence of a downward trend may be seen in the fact that the early portion of the data shows a number of high peaks that are gradually replaced by a number of low data points in the latter half of the panel. This is similar to data in Panel D, in which most points fall within a central range. Although low data points appears with increasing frequency, the remaining data points continue to fall in the original range.

The importance of an adequate number of observations over an extended period of time may be seen by placing a piece of paper over all but the first five or so data points in each panel. When this is done, in no case does the available evidence suggest a trend. Now slowly slide the paper to the right, gradually exposing additional data points. How many of the 25 data points in each record are necessary to identify a trend? Of course, the answer will differ for most readers, depending on their own experience and training. If these records represented the behavior of subjects in a research setting in which the reader had a great deal of experience, the answer would probably be further qualified. The point, however, is that identifying a trend in a set of data inevitably requires collecting an adequate number of observations. The only way to confirm or disconfirm a suspected trend is to make additional measurements under the same conditions.

Both Panels C and D (and, to a lesser extent, A and B) illustrate patterns that hint strongly of multiple or complex determination. Whatever variables might be influencing the occurrence of high and low points, their effects are not stationary over time. The reader should become sensitive to the fact that a single set of behavioral measures plotted against time rarely reflects the operation of a single independent variable. Variations in the range seen in successive segments of the data are often a clue to the presence of multiple determinants whose influences are asynchronous. When the trends associated with the extreme values (highs and lows) across segments are nonparallel, the result is immediately obvious in the form of variation in the range. Clearly then, detecting trends in data cannot be accomplished without simultaneously evaluating the pattern of changes in the range.

Before leaving this discussion of trends in behavioral data, it should be added that under limited circumstances, it can be acceptable to treat trends as stable states. This can be done only when the trend itself is stable or is the only conspicuous aspect of variability in the data. It must be remembered, however, that any trend cannot continue indefinitely. Therefore, using trending data as a reference for experimental comparisons presupposes secure knowledge of the limit of trend.

Range.   The second aspect of variability that is involved in identifying steady-state responding is range, specifically, the absolute values (and the pattern) of deviations among collections of points. We refer here to collections of any size, from pairs of adjacent points to the entire set. The data portrayed in Fig. 12.3 will facilitate discussion.

Generally, stable responding is characterized by a relatively constant range of variation whose values are otherwise acceptable in the context of the research project. Both Panels A and B in Fig. 12.3 show a nearly constant range of variability, and either might be acceptable or too large depending on other aspects of the study (see Chapter 11). The data in Panel C fall mostly within a fairly constant central range. The five low data points show no sign of increasing or decreasing in density and are of approximately the same value. Such a pattern might be acceptable in some circumstances and unacceptable in others. For example, the low points might be easily explained by a known change in the experimental setting; this fact would then require a decision as to whether control of that variable was warranted under the circumstances. On the other hand, the absence of an obvious explanation should suggest the need for manipulations designed to identify the factor responsible before proceeding with the experiment.

Panel D shows two kinds of changes in local variability. An initially narrow range is followed by a relatively sudden increase in high and low values. This is abruptly followed by the return of the original narrow range, which is then followed by a rapid increase in the upper values. Faced with this pattern of locally changing ranges, the experimenter must acknowledge uncertainty

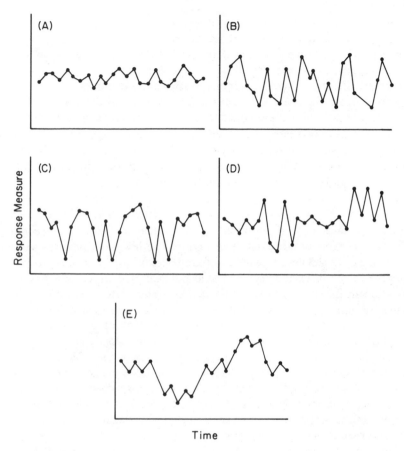

FIG. 12.3. Hypothetical data showing different ranges and patterns of variability.

about the patterns to follow and address the question of what variables are influencing the subject's responding.

Panel E shows a different pattern of local ranges still. The data show an initially small central range abruptly followed by the same locally narrow range displaced to a lower region of the scale. After another cluster of data points in the central range, the data jump to a higher level with the same relatively narrow range. This is finally followed by another group of points in the original portion of the scale. The aggregate reveals five clusters of data points, each with the same narrow local range, but representing three different levels of responding. Again, the experimenter must admit a poor basis for predicting future levels of responding and must take steps to ameliorate this limitation prior to manipulating the independent variable.

It may again be enlightening to uncover each panel in Fig. 12.3 slowly. In no case do the early data points reliably forecast future patterns of variability.

At what point does one become sufficiently confident about the stability or instability of the data either to predict a continuation of the same pattern or to judge it too unstable for confident prediction and therefore in need of experimental improvement? Of course, such a decision is impossible with hypothetical data gathered under unspecified circumstances and displayed on unscaled axes. However, even with full knowledge of the scales of the axes and the conditions of data collection, the experimenter who is confronted with patterns like these must still make the go–no-go decision without complete certainty about the correctness of the judgment. It should be clear, incidentally, that display techniques are crucial in assessing the stability of data. Chapter 16 treats this topic in detail.

Cyclicity. So far, we have been considering fairly simple cases of instability as a way of illuminating the considerations that are part of identifying stable or steady-state behavior. The few basic patterns shown in Figs. 12.2 and 12.3 are in reality only examples of an almost infinite range of possible forms of variability. It should be clear that observable patterns of variation in direction and range usually combine to form complex patterns that may make steady-state identification more difficult in the real case.

There is a particular class of complex patterns of instability that may sometimes actually be considered indicative of steady-state responding. When the subject's responding produces a locally unstable but repeating pattern, that pattern can be described as periodic or cyclical. The periodicity of the cycles may be either irregular (or at least unspecifiable) or regular, but the responding may be regarded as stable if both the cycle and period are regular and if the period is short enough that a sufficient number of cyles can be observed under all experimental conditions. For example, a cycle commonly observed in applied studies follows the periodicity of the 5-day work or school week. If the experimental phases are of sufficient duration to allow exposure of the various conditions during a number of full cycles and if the 5-day pattern is consistently observed and therefore comfortably predictable, then designating responding as steady state is justified. Panel A in Fig. 12.4 shows stylized data exemplifying such a situation.

The situation becomes more intractable when the cycle is irregular and/or the period is of long duration. For instance, if the period reveals a quarterly fluctuation during the year and if experimental phases are considerably briefer, the different conditions of the experiment are likely to fall on different phases of the cycle. Not only would this present purely interpretative difficulties, but one or more of the variables under investigation might also interact with the determinants of the phase of the cycle during which they were imposed, partially obscuring the effect of the independent variables. Panel B in Fig. 12.4 shows graphically the interpretative difficulties posed by a cyclical pattern whose period extends across three experimental conditions.

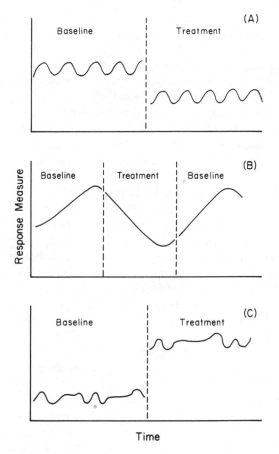

FIG. 12.4.   Stylized hypothetical data showing various cyclic patterns across phases.

Ignorance of this pattern would almost guarantee interpretative error, whether or not there was any actual interaction between the treatment variable and the variables responsible for the cyclical process.

The cycle may be predictable in form but not in frequency of appearance. This can be an extremely disquieting instance of failure to achieve steady state, for it leaves the investigator with virtually no way to differentiate the effects of planned interventions from those resulting from the sporadic occurrence of the variables determining the cyclic variation. In such cases, if the degree of variation in the cycle is sufficiently small compared to the variation due to other extraneous variables and compared to the variation imposed by the experimenter, the cyclicity may be safely ignored. Furthermore, if the cycle is sufficiently brief that a number of periods will occur within each experimental phase (even though irregularly), it may again be possible to proceed without special attention to the fluctuations. Both of these situations are true in Panel C.

Frustrations resulting from the appearance of cyclic variability in the effort to obtain steady-state responding cannot be relieved by any of a class of tactics that have in common manipulating data collections and display procedures instead of manipulating determining variables. The reader will recall that the former can only lead to "changes" in variability that are only illusory, whereas the latter can lead to changes in real variability that result in illumination of its source and, consequently, control or elimination.

One such tactic involves taking measurements over large enough observational periods so that the cyclic fluctuations are effectively obscured through summation. For example, the day-to-day variation that defines a weekly cycle can be eliminated if the recording interval is expanded from daily to weekly. Expanding the interval to include an entire month obliterates any variability due to any periodicity of the occurrence of the weekly cycle. These relations are illustrated in Fig. 12.5. Clearly, the offending variability is not eliminated; it is merely hidden from view. The effect may always be achieved by averaging the results of shorter, more frequent recording periods and displaying the results against larger time units. A rather sophisticated variation of this tactic involves computation of "moving averages," which allows retaining the finer divisions of the time scale (see Chapter 16) while statistically distributing the variability associated with that level of magnification. Whatever the variation, these tactics have the effect of hiding and possibly misrepresenting potentially valuable data. Done on a small enough scale, the loss may be insignificant in the overall context of the study; however, it tends to be all too easy to convince oneself that there is no loss when in reality there is. These methods of smoothing out cyclic instability are abused when the loss of information results in a misrepresentation to the experimenter (and readers) sufficient to make either unaware of real variability and thus of true experimental effects.

Sometimes the cyclicity may itself be the focus of the investigation, whether as the original goal or forced by its overwhelming presence. The student of the science of behavior should recognize that isolating the variables responsible for the production of any orderly pattern of behavior (e.g., circadian rhythms, estrous cycles, as well as environmentally induced behavioral cycles) represents a sizeable advance in the program of the science. When cyclicity is encountered, it should be regarded as something more than an annoying impediment to establishing steady-state responding; cyclicity presents an opportunity to isolate and gain control over the determinants of an important form of behavioral variability. A digression from the originally anticipated course of experimentation may yield handsome returns in the form of eventual control if a new, manageable independent variable is discovered.

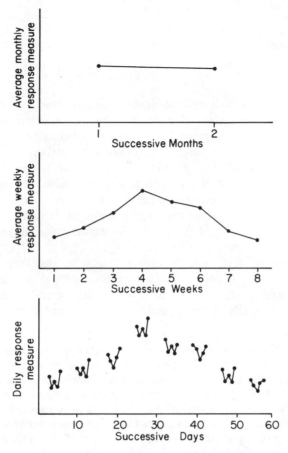

FIG. 12.5.   Hypothetical data showing the loss of variability resulting from averaging over successively larger units of time.

Research generated by such a strategy may well be among the most prolific sources of future knowledge about the determinants of behavioral phenomena.

Finally, this discussion of identifying steady states must consider the inappropriate inducing of stability in the data by any of a variety of measurement decisions. Such experimenter-imposed restrictions can result from placing artificial limits on the sensitivity of the response to variables of interest, or they can be a consequence of the insensitivity of measurement procedures to actual variation in responding. The former case is illustrated whenever the response selected is too heavily under the control of variables extraneous to the basic experimental question; the latter results from selecting the wrong dimensional quantity for analysis. In either case, the apparent stability can only be misleading, because it suggests a degree of experimental control that does not correctly represent the experimenter's knowledge about and manipulation of controlling variables.

Criteria

The previous section considered the identification of steady-state responding by discussing generic classes of instability that do not characterize stable responding. The broad statement that steady-state behavior must be defined by the absence of certain forms and degrees of variability is obviously inadequate. In practice, this principle must be translated into a specific decision to maintain present conditions, rearrange conditions to obtain better stability, or implement a new set of conditions. A variety of loose rules or criteria have evolved to assist the experimenter in arriving at the proper decision with a minimum of subjective bias and a maximum of predictive confidence.

Not surprisingly, these criteria are quite crude, and their proper use demands a thorough understanding of the role of steady states in experimental design and more than a little training and experience. The importance of properly selecting and using a stability criterion is clearly described by Sidman (1960):

> The utility of data will depend not on whether ultimate stability has been achieved, but rather on the reliability and validity of the criterion. That is to say, does the criterion select a reproducible and generalizable state of behavior? If it does, experimental manipulation of steady states, as defined by the criterion, will yield data that are orderly and generalizable to other situations. If the steady-state criterion is inadequate, failures to reproduce and to replicate systematically the experimental findings will reveal this fact [pp. 257–258].

It should be clear that the experimenter who makes a decision to implement the next set of conditions is acting on the basis of some kind of criterion, even if it cannot be stated formally. That is, at the very least, the decision is based on the history, acquired as a student and researcher, that gave the unspoken criteria upon which to act. However, these conditions allow too much opportunity for the exercise of other past and present influences of which the experimenter is also unaware. Carefully considering the appropriate criteria will help to clarify those factors that should play a role and minimize the influence of those that should not.

This does not mean that the criterion decision is an *a priori* one; this requirement might guarantee its erroneousness. Only if the researcher has considerable experience under similar experimental conditions or if pilot studies have preceded the ongoing investigation would it be wise to specify steady-state criteria before collecting data. Usually, enough data must be available that all of their features are recognizable before an educated decision can be made.

One kind of criterion involves a simple statistical description of stability (see Chapter 17). It should be noted that this is very different from a statistical evaluation of stability. As Sidman (1960) points out, a stable state may meet a statistical standard without having any experimental utility, as the case when the range and patterns of variability are experimentally unacceptable although showing statistically nonsignificant differences over time. The crucial concern is with the degree of experimental control and the clarity of obtained functional relations that the criteria encourage.

Statistical criteria generally specify the amount of variability that will be permitted over a specified number of data points. Such criteria might describe the maximum range for so many sessions (e.g., no point may deviate by more than 5% from the median of the last five sessions), or they might impose a limit on the difference between the means or ranges of two successive series of sessions (e.g., the means of two consecutive sets of 10 points may differ by less than 10% of the total range). The possible specifications of such criteria are nearly endless and may provide any degree of stringency desired. One qualification is appropriate when the variability changes as a function of different experimental conditions; in such cases, an adjusting criterion based on predicted or observed variability should be used. A case commonly observed involves a wide range of baseline variability being replaced by a much narrower range under the powerful influence of treatment conditions. A fairly stringent criterion for baseline data may be immediately met in the treatment phase, thus possibly not allowing sufficient exposure to those conditions so as to fully assess their effects. An increase in the stringency of the criterion in the treatment phase based on the changes in variability would avoid this situation.

A second kind of criterion specifies primarily temporal requirements by setting an *a priori* limit on the number of sessions of experimental conditions, with some number of the final sessions arbitrarily constituting the steady state. The limitations here are obvious; considerable experience with responding under similar or identical conditions is prerequisite to making an educated judgment about the number of sessions that will indeed be required. In addition, if more than one subject is involved, they probably will require different periods of exposure to the various conditions before stable responding is observed. The time limit must accommodate the slowest case.

It is important to clarify that this kind of criterion must be specified by the experimenter solely with reference to the influence of experimental conditions on the subject's behavior, and the criterion must not be determined by other features of the experimental environment. In most applied settings, there are social, institutional, or financial limitations on the amount of time available for experimentation; however, these considerations cannot properly contribute to defining steady-state criteria.

A third kind of criterion is based on unassisted visual inspection of the data. Visual inspection here means looking at the data as it is being produced on-line without preconceived notions of the level of stability one is looking for. We call the criterion used in this situation the Supreme Court standard: "I can't tell you in advance what it is, but I'll know it when I see it."[2] Although not quantifiable *a priori*, certain features of the data display, when they appear, will evoke the response, "stable" on the part of the experienced investigator. These features are numerous and subtle, but include such factors as the overall range, local variability, trends, and various facets of the experimental situation. Although it may initially appear otherwise, using this procedure is not entirely a subjective process, for the investigator will be able to specify exactly what characteristics of the data are prompting the judgment. For this reason, visual inspection can only be employed in conjunction with standard measurement and display procedures with which the researcher has thorough familiarity and experience.

The potential of visual inspection for sensitive and stringent definition of stable responding therefore depends heavily on the training, experience, and intellectual honesty of the researcher; at the same time, the inherent potential for abuse of visual inspection is considerable. There is a natural tendency to look at the characteristics of one's hard won data in a favorable light, and visual inspection may result in erroneous or questionable judgments of stability for that reason. It should be clear, however, that the impact of this tendency on the generality of the findings of some investigators is not an indictment of the basic method of visual inspection. Valid use of this method presupposes thorough familiarity with the many subtle criteria that are available for consideration, as well as an experienced understanding of the properties of the behavior being investigated and the conditions of measurement. This facility is only acquired as a result of rigorous training and experience. Researchers who bring such a history to the problem of visually determining stability rarely, if ever, allow their wishes and hopes to color their interpretation of empirical reality, knowing full well that to do so only postpones an inevitable reckoning through replicative failure. Of course, successful replication of the observed functional relations by other researchers will also lend encouragement about the adequacy of one's judgments.

Although it may seem that so far the discussion of steady-state responding has focused on establishing it under baseline conditions, the reader is reminded that no distinctions are made regarding its utility under any and all experimental conditions, including those in which a treatment is in effect. In some ways, it is even more critical to demonstrate stable responding when the nature of the effect of a treatment condition is in question. It is important to assess fully all effects of an experimental change, including extended as well as initial influences on responding. Implementing a treatment condition will

---

[2]Based on the well-known statement of Justice Potter Stewart in his concurring opinion in the Supreme Court's pornography decision in *Jacobellis* v. *Ohio, 1964.*

likely initiate a transition in responding, completion of which must be clearly determined in order to describe thoroughly the effect of the independent variable. An early change in a desired direction to a markedly different level of responding may suit the preconceptions of the experimenter, but terminating the treatment phase at that point may preclude the opportunity to observe whether responding continues to change further in that direction or quickly returns to pretreatment levels. Whether a new or the original steady state is eventually obtained, the full nature of the transition will be of considerable interest itself and cannot be determined in the absence of a terminal steady state. Furthermore, steady-state responding must be obtained under any treatment phase, because that phase will often be the baseline from which a subsequent condition will be assessed.

TRANSITIONS

The understanding of transition states is inextricably bound up with a thorough knowledge of steady states. A transition state is one in which responding is changing from one steady state to a different steady state. In the researcher's study of the controlling relations between human behavior and the environment, a comfortable intimacy with transition states is no less important than with steady states.

Concern with transition states will often be primarily tactical, as the researcher examines other characteristics of the data or merely tries to engineer maximum change in the level of responding in minimum time. On the other hand, fully analyzed transition states are of general interest as the empirical basis of any effective behavioral technology. With rare exceptions, the intent of any application of scientifically established principles of behavior is to engender *change* in some property of a specified class of responses made by a designated individual or population. Successfully inducing such a change is equivalent to successfully inducing a transition state. The concept of change as applied to behavior necessarily involves transition from one state or condition to another, and any developed technology for engineering change will necessarily depend on a body of established scientific knowledge describing the general phenomena of behavioral transition. In particular, more is required than mere technique for inducing rapid or pronounced changes in responding.

Identification

Whatever the nature of the inquiry, the investigator must be able to identify the boundaries of any transition state, and this effort clearly requires identifying the stable states preceding and following the transition. Identifying the end points of a transition state invokes fundamental

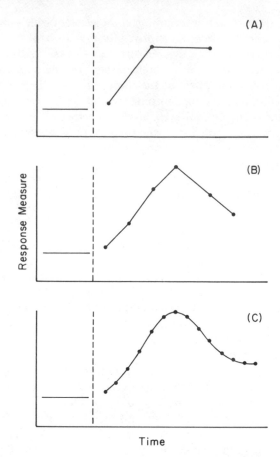

FIG. 12.6. Hypothetical data showing the graphic results of varying frequencies and numbers of measurements of a transition state.

considerations of behavioral measurement, especially frequency of measurement. The more often observations are made during the course of a transition, the more information is available and the more precisely the boundaries of the transition state can be specified. Although difficult to achieve in many instances, continuous measurement is thus the ideal. Conversely, the more widely distributed in time the observations of responding, the less confidence we may feel concerning the completeness of the transition picture drawn by the data points. Figure 12.6 illustrates this point. The same hypothetical transition is depicted in all three panels, but the infrequent measurement shown in Panel A gives a false impression that stability has been achieved at the level of the second data point. Increasing the number of measurement points as shown in Panel B begins to capture the true form of the transition function, but fails to locate the point at which stability again appears, marking the end of the transition. This deficiency is remedied in Panel C in which sufficient additional measurements are made to ensure an accurate picture of the transition and to identify its end points.

A common source of transitions is the experimenter's arrangement of a change in the environment that is intended to affect responding. Because such a treatment-initiated transition is properly attempted only after establishing stable responding under nontreatment conditions, the beginning of the transition presumably should be easy to identify. However, the change in the independent variable implemented by the experimenter may not come into contact with the subject's behavior until some time after the experimenter's action. Until that first contact with the new condition, responding will remain under the control of the preceding steady-state variables. This demarcation will more accurately separate behavioral characteristics under the control of steady-state variables from those under the control of transition variables, but the moment of impact may be logistically difficult to observe. Furthermore, the effect of the change on responding may not be immediately detectable because of limitations in the sensitivity of measurement.

It may be useful to illustrate these points with a familiar example. The effects on classroom deportment of a change in the daily schedule of activity periods (e.g., switching math and physical education during 6th and 7th periods) will certainly not be felt during the first five periods of the day of the change. The first actual contact any pupil will have with the change occurs somewhere near the scheduled beginning of 6th period, depending on whether the student is tardy, etc., but a noticeable change in outburst frequency may not occur until late in 6th period or possibly even the next day.

This general point warrants a brief though important digression. The knowledge that the experimenter-manipulated treatment variable may not come into contact with the behavior for a period of time after the change was implemented can be abused. It is certainly not sufficient license to label *any* transition occuring at some point after the beginning of the experimental condition as the effect of the independent variable. There are many instances in the literature in which a transition abruptly began some considerable time (often a number of days) after the experimental phase was begun and certainly well after the treatment variable contacted the behavior. To interpret such a transition as exclusively due to the independent variable may be quite risky and is likely to prevent the search for the unknown variables actually responsible. The stable state attained after such a transition cannot be assumed to be solely the result of the treatment variable. The delay between initiating the experimental phase and the actual point of contact of the independent variable with the behavior is usually quite brief and often clearly specifiable. The further from that point that transitions are observed to begin, the more cautious the experimenter must be in identifying them as treatment variable dependencies.

One kind of end to a transition state is the resumption of steady state responding. Prior to the introduction of a treatment condition, responding is under the control of the prevailing conditions. Initiating an independent variable arrangement is expected to inaugurate some influence on responding, thus disturbing the steady state that had been present. This instability may continue until the influence of the previous condition has dissipated and is replaced by control from the new conditions; stability may still not be observed until the new set of conditions has exerted sole influence for some time.

Unfortunately, not all transition periods conveniently end in recovery of stable responding; a secondary, unplanned transition may follow immediately with no intervening period of stability. Such secondary transitions may be identified by a departure of trend and/or range from that established during the initial transition and are almost always a sign that new variables have become operative. Secondary transitions may thus be highly informative, albeit a source of unending annoyance in the conduct of a research program. When a secondary transition period occurs, the investigator is faced with three basic options: (1) temporarily redirecting the program toward identification, analysis, and control of the variables responsible for the secondary transition; (2) manipulating additional variables in an attempt to suppress the influence of the suspected variables; or (3) simply enduring the secondary transition period and awaiting the reappearance of stability.

In any case, specifying the end of a transition state involves the definition of steady-state behavior discussed at length earlier. One tactical value of an adequate steady state definition, then, is to prevent the initiation of further experimental manipulations while a transition is still in progress. Failure to achieve the termination of a transition state is likely to result from insufficiently prolonged exposure to various experimental conditions such that new environmental changes are begun in the midst of the transition. This guarantees obscuring not only the effects of conditions that produced the transition, but the influence of the new conditions as well. The questions left unanswered by such untimely interventions (see Fig. 12.8) are numerous: What would have been the later characteristics of the transition? Was the transition merely one in which the original steady state would have eventually been recaptured (see the following discussion)? What would have been the stable effect of the interrupted condition? What were the details of the interactions between the two sets of independent variable arrangements? Which of the effects of the new condition may have been due to this interaction? The lack of an empirical resolution to these questions leaves the impatient researcher in a disadvantageous position from which to draw accurate and useful conclusions about the influence of specific independent variables.

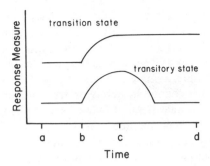

FIG. 12.7. Schematic representation of transition and transitory states.

Transitory States

The discussion has thus far centered around changes from steady-state responding that were the result of experimental manipulations of independent variables and that eventually resulted in a new steady state. Of course, many influences beyond the knowledge or control of the experimenter may initiate similar transitions. However, an infinite variety of controlled or uncontrolled sources can also produce temporary changes in responding followed by the eventual reestablishment of the original stable state. Such transitions have been termed *transitory states* (Sidman, 1960) and are distinguished from transition states only by the fact that the original, rather than a new, level of stable responding defines their termination.[3] This distinction is represented graphically in Fig. 12.7.

The ability to distinguish empirically between transition and transitory states is of enormous tactical importance in behavioral research. With reference to Fig. 12.7, the steady states (from *a* to *b*) and the initial transition stages (from *b* to *c*) are the same for both curves; at point *c*, the experimenter cannot determine which type of transition has been encountered. In order to make this determination, the investigator must refrain from further action until at least point *d*, by which time stability had been recovered in both cases.

The implications of this distinction become clear when the consequences of prematurely terminating the experimental condition associated with the transition are considered. If the present phase were ended at point *c* in Fig. 12.7, the interpretation that the increased level of responding constituted the full effect of the new condition would be correct in the case of the transition state but quite incorrect in the case of the transitory state. Only by extending

---

[3]The term "state" is used throughout this chapter in a manner consistent with that established by Sidman (1960). As such, it connotes only characteristics of portions of the data; the denotative implication of constancy is obviously excluded, especially in the case of transitions.

the phase until steady-state responding is clearly obtained (point *d* in the figure) would any certainty about the conclusion be warranted.

It should be clear that transitory states can legitimately result from planned experimental operations as well as from the presence of extraneous sources of variability. For example, a single administration of a drug may be expected to result in a temporary change in behavior from which recovery is full and complete. However, regardless of what is expected, the effect may be permanent, resulting in a genuine transition state. The converse of this situation is probably more prevalent and certainly more serious—a transition state is expected (but not verified), when, in reality, the treatment produced a transitory state that is mistakenly assumed to be a transition state in the absence of a suffient period of exposure and measurement. The effects of many training procedures may be suspect on these grounds, particularly if no follow-up measures of proficiency are obtained to substantiate the claim that the behavioral changes induced by the training are reasonably permanent.

Interpretative Problems

The foregoing discussion dramatizes the need for adhering to the entire experimental agenda embodied in the steady state strategy. In particular, allowance must be made for such prolongation of observation under each treatment condition as is necessary to demonstrate unequivocally whatever steady state constitutes the final outcome. A broader discussion of the tactical implications of implementing planned experimental interventions in the absence of reliable stability can now be properly undertaken. Regardless of the origin or nature of the determinants of any transition or transitory states, the interpretative complications guaranteed by imposing treatments on nonstable baselines must be fully grasped and appreciated. Figure 12.8 illustrates a series of the most common empirical ambiguities that result from insufficiently attending to the dictates of the steady-state strategy.[4]

Panel A in Fig. 12.8 shows an increasing baseline trend followed by a similarly increasing trend in the treatment phase (beginning at the dotted line). In the absence of further manipulations, it is impossible to determine if the slight increase in slope was produced by the manipulated variable or is merely the result of cumulated effects of the variable response for the initial trend. A further possibility is that the treatment phase trend is the product of some interaction of the two sets of variables.

Panel B illustrates a baseline trend similar to that of Panel A, but which is instead followed by a contrasting downward trend in the experimental phase.

---

[4]As the next two chapters clarify, these two-phase "mini-experiments" are used here solely as illustrations and in no way depict the results of complete experiments worthy of interpretative attention.

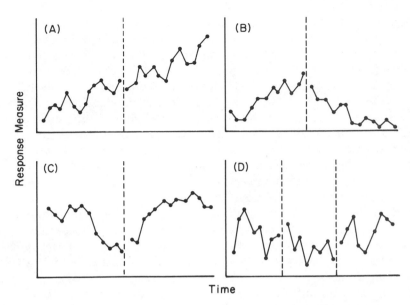

FIG. 12.8. Hypothetical data from experimental phases following an unstable baseline.

Although the reversal in trend renders a conclusion of an experimental effect more attractive, this must be considered an equally unjustified interpretation. Both Panels A and B reveal only changes in trends between pairs of adjacent, unstable phases; that one involves a change in direction as well should best be viewed as irrelevant. The variables responsible for the trend observed under baseline conditions must be considered as possible, if not likely, influences on behavior in the treatment phases, and the nature of that influence has yet to be clarified. Compared to the observed patterns, pure effects of the treatment variables (uncontaminated by the possibly persisting effects of the variables responsible for the trend) might have appeared as enhanced, diminished, neutralized, or changed in some other manner. Even worse is the possibility that no treatment effect is actually present and that the timing of the treatment introduction in Panel B happened accidentally to coincide with the peak of a cyclic process. The availability of a powerful variable overriding the noise of unstable responding is fortunate, but its true nature cannot be determined if it is used as a substitute for obtaining steady-state behavior. The greater believability of the inference that some effect is indeed demonstrated in Panel B merits even more stringent insistence on a proper and complete experimental analysis of its nature and determinants, a task that is grossly impeded by any unchecked operation of trend-inducing variables.

In Panel C, a high followed by a lower cluster of data points represent baseline responding. The increase in responding shown in the treatment phase could again reflect the influence of unknown variables producing the baseline variability, a relatively pure treatment effect, or an interaction of baseline and treatment variables. The data in no way inform us of the correct alternative.

Finally, Panel D shows three phases in which the number of sessions in each condition is quite limited. Given this restriction and the relatively large range, there is no hint of steady-state responding in any phase. Although there might be a tendency to infer a decrease in responding in the second phase, there is also considerable overlap in ranges across phases. As a matter of fact, if the phase change lines were removed and all data points were connected, no trends or other experimental effects would likely be suspected. A limited number of observations simply cannot define a steady state, especially in combination with any strong pattern of instability.

The basic strategy of experimentation that relies on demonstration of control through steady-state responding is at once uncompromisingly exacting and extremely powerful. Our entire discussion of steady-state strategies has perhaps sometimes seemed to imply that stability is always eventually earned as a reward for patient measurement. In theory, it is always obtainable, but only infrequently as a result solely of prolonged measurement. In fact, this approach to experimentation is highly demanding of the investigator's entire range of skills requisite to the unmistakable demonstration of experimental control, and this approach can only be seen as more arduous than the traditional alternative of statistical control.

In practice, the costs of obtaining steady-state responding may even occasionally be prohibitive. Sometimes the impediments may be beyond the ability of the experimenter to circumvent, and sometimes the solutions may be available, though at a price. The experimenter must then weigh the consequent costs and benefits in reaching a decision. That decision may be to put aside temporarily the original question for the purpose of beginning an investigation of the variability. This strategy has a long and honored tradition in science and is often fruitful. The alternative is to coexist with the greatest degree of stability that can be arranged by redesigning some facets of the experiment to accommodate the undesirable variability. This accommodation might necessitate modifying the experimental design in order that the resulting data will permit the most accurate and generalizable interpretations justifiable under the unavoidable constraints.

The power inherent in the general strategy of obtaining control by establishing stable reference levels of responding resides chiefly in the clarity with which experimental results may be manifested. When an experimental effect is seen against the backdrop of controlled, stable responding, the investigator naturally has greater certainty as to its causes. Although considerably more experimental labor is inevitably required than is occasioned by any attempt to manage extraneous variability statistically, the benefits of increased reproducibility and generality of the products of experimentation that accrue would appear to justify the effort.

13 Strategies and Elements of Experimental Design

So far as I can see, I simply began looking for lawful processes in the behavior of the intact organism.

—B. F. Skinner

INTRODUCTION

Convincing experimentation within any domain of natural phenomena may be conceptually reduced to exploiting the soundest possible measurement strategy in order to examine the delicate interplay between stable states of nature and those changes that are the product of experimentally imposed control over selected independent variables. For most investigators, the decisions required in conducting a program of research are not as obvious as the above quote suggests; however, once the basic strategies have been mastered, the tactics of experimentation are remarkably reasonable and straightforward. The plan of attack providing the context within which a succession of experimental decisions is made is known as the experimental design. The purpose of the present chapter is to unravel such experimental decisions by discussing general strategies that dictate and explain the design of experiments. An even more molecular examination is then made of the basic elements of design. Intimacy with them is prerequisite to their management in the decision making we call tactics of experimental design, the topic of the next chapter.

249

The importance of clearly appreciating the function of experimental design within the more global context of overall research strategy can scarcely be overestimated. If not thoroughly understood, this facet of experimentation can severely restrict the scientific value of conclusions drawn from otherwise sound research. A provocative idea, sound measurement procedures, and forceful control of relevant variables can unite in producing an ambiguous or trivial result if they are brought to fruition through an overall design that is incompatible with the fundamental strategies of experimentation.

STRATEGIES

Meaning of Design

What do we mean when we talk about experimental design? Actually, there is a continuum of meanings ranging from molar to molecular. In the broadest sense, reference is made to one's overall perspective toward experimentation, implying or at least encouraging inferences about a philosophy of science and a conception of the subject matter in a particular field. In this sense, this entire volume concerns experimental design, even though only three chapters share the specific appelation. The reader must realize that this characterization is not inaccurate, because all of the chapters are inextricably related to the content of these three.

Moving further along the continuum, design can also be used in the sense of arranging the conditions of a particular experiment. This meaning tends to encompass the entire program of tactical decisions an investigator makes, including the statement of the question, measurement procedures, the experimental operations, and interpretation of data. Sometimes, however, this usage of design is allowed to connote the notion of a rigid structure that, once selected, determines a set of rules governing decisions at all stages of the investigation. This meaning imparts the implication that a static package or formula is being selected from a reference catalog that predetermines the basic tactical components of the research and into which all existing characteristics of the behavior, its environment, and any relations must be fitted (see Chapter 5).

At the molecular end of the continuum, the phrase experimental design can refer only to the particular arrangements of different independent variable conditions, exclusive of measurement and interpretation considerations. In this sense, a single experiment may be viewed as a number of successive designs that are collectively necessary to clarify relations between independent and dependent variables. Thus, some design decisions might be made in response to the data unfolding as the investigation progresses. This sense of design encourages the experimenter to pursue in more dynamic fashion the solutions to problems of experimental control immediately upon their emergence.

The various broad and specific meanings of experimental design have their place in useful communication, and our concern is less with the molar-molecular continuum than with other connotations and implications of the phrase. It is most imporant that the design of whole research projects in general, their component experiments, and the particular manipulations within each experiment be viewed from a *dynamic* rather than a static perspective. It is unnecessarily limiting to ignore the subtleties and complexities of the many experimental design decisions by selecting a structure, package, or formula that forces predetermined and stringent control over the variety of other decisions that are a part of scientific research. The inflexibility compelled by this perspective presupposes so many features of the subject's behavior, its environment, and the effects of independent variables that the investigator in effect wears blinders that restrict from view any features of the phenomenon that are not consistent with prior design requirements. This static approach discourages the researcher from exhibiting many of the most valuable characteristics of scientific activity, such as modifying planned tactics as data or hunches suggest or discovering and pursuing serendipitous findings. Any story of scientific achievement has as its subtheme the sensitive flexibility characterizing the investigator's style of scientific inquiry.

In its most extreme form, the static conception of experimental design really has little to do with experimentation, but focuses on interpretation. When research is conducted in accordance with the assumptions and dictates of a mathematical or statistical model in terms of which the eventual data will be analyzed, most tactical design decisions are preempted by these nonempirical considerations. In essence, the term "design" here refers to the structure or component arrangement of an array of spaces to be filled by the quantitative results of observation. This structure can be thought of as a program for performing those algebraic operations on the data that are required by the analytical model. The task of experimentation thus becomes one of filling the spaces in a fashion that leaves inviolate the assumptions of the model. Such design decisions as are made conform to the demands of the model, not to the demands of nature, and the utility of the eventual result rests entirely on the degree of correspondence between the model and the actual state of nature. It is disheartening to observe students acquire skill in suppressing their curiosity about, and eventually their sensitivity to, variations in observed phenomena that are not anticipated by the preselected "design." They learn to dismiss such variations glibly as "experimental error" on their way to mastering designs sufficiently complex that all traces of any but the most blatant mismatches between nature and the model are forever hidden by the algebraic camouflage of "error variance."

In contrast, the dynamic approach to experimental design may be illustrated by an analogy between a scientist and an organmaster. The sounds that issue from the thousands of pipes of a large cathedral pipe organ are controlled by stops, couplers, manuals, and other controls that must be selected and managed by the organmaster. Faced with any particular composition, the organist can create a unique and flawlessly appropriate blend of sounds by the many decisions and actions made both before and during the performance. The investigator should be able to sit down to the myriad features of the research problem and, with an intimate knowledge of all facets of the strategies and tactics of scientific investigation, create a unique blend of design characteristics that he or she will continuously adjust as new dimensions of the problem are encountered during the course of the study.

This dynamic perspective on experimental design should not be misunderstood. The investigator must make a number of preliminary decisions upon which initial actions are based; it cannot be denied that certain assumptions and expectations as well as existing information influence each of these decisions. In addition, it should be clear that any decisions will have implications for future actions and the evidence upon which those actions are based. For example, early decisions must be made about how response classes will be defined. This activity will be at least partially determined by the general experience of the investigator with the behavior of interest and by previous studies on closely related phenomena. Once made, such decisions implicitly force the presumption that the response class will exhibit certain characteristics compatible with the definition and that those features will remain satisfactorily stable throughout the study. These features of the response class definition will exert a strong influence on the dimensional quantities selected, the observation and recording procedures created and the variability of the resulting data.

Other necessary decisions will be based upon equally tentative assumptions and expectations. It is because the effects of such decisions are incompletely predictable that the perspective toward design as dynamic, flexible, and adjusting is so valuable. Instead of having a single, static design decision force the experimental results and conclusions into a predetermined mold, the ideal is to uncover the natural relations that are present in a way that shows them with maximum clarity, whatever modifications in design may eventually be required. This strategy clearly presupposes confidence that any questions carefully asked of nature will yield informative and useful answers, whether or not those answers match the preconceptions of the experimenter. The worst consequence of a static approach to design is the all too frequently seen case in which the data resoundingly support the design at the expense of answering the empirical question. Although not inevitable, this outcome is encouraged when the experimenter initially asserts that "this should happen when" instead of asking "what will happen if?" This difference may seem subtle, but the implications are often profound.

Functional Relations

The touchstone of all scientific research is order. The orderliness of relations between variables is at once the operating assumption upon which the experimenter proceeds, the observed fact that permits doing so, and the goal that continuously focuses experimental decisions. The task of the behavioral scientist is to so arrange the various features of the experimental environment that an orderly relation between manipulations of a single feature of the environment and variations in the measures of the chosen response class is convincingly demonstrated. This requires that only one feature of the environment at a time be allowed to impose variations in responding with other features being held as constant in their influence as possible. This tactic facilitates demonstrating that variation in responding is a direct function of variation in a specific aspect of the environment; this relation, properly demonstrated, is termed a *functional relation* (see Chapter 2).[1] The uncovering of functional relations may be seen as the superordinate strategy guiding design decisions to which all other efforts discussed in this and the following chapter are appropriately subservient.

Demonstrating a functional relation is not equivalent to asserting that the independent variable causes the effect in the dependent variable. The traditional terms of "cause" and "effect" imply that the ultimate questions of *how* the experimental manipulations produced their influence on responding have been answered. In practice, a functional relation merely shows that the examined environmental and behavioral events were observed to occur together in a certain way under particular conditions. Why the relation exists is not answered by showing that it does exist; this problem simply stimulates an additional series of questions and experiments now permitted by the original demonstration.

Actually, the "co-relation" that a functional relation demonstrates is just that, a correlation. Even the most penetrating experimental design can show only that the independent and dependent variables are correlated to some

---

[1]This requirement has been frequently misinterpreted as supporting a simplistic conception of the determination of behavior. In fact, the details of multiple determination can only be investigated through the controlled production of interactions between classes of independent variables followed by detailed analysis of the effects of each variable in the presence of controlled constant values of the others. Complex, static designs that are useful in identifying statistical interactions are not helpful in either analyzing or explaining the workings of behavioral interactions, because the dynamic nature of behavior changing over time is not satisfactorily accommodated (see Chapters 5 and 17).

degree in particular ways under specified circumstances. Causation or a cause–effect relation cannot be demonstrated by a single experiment, no matter how elegant the design, but can be addressed only by the accumulated evidence of a number of well-designed experiments. The ability to demonstrate causation is not a property of a design itself; rather, it is approximated by accumulating a number of thematically related and reliable functional relations, each of which was the product of a design that permitted the experimenter to show the thoroughness and precision of his or her understanding of the determinants of the phenomenon by exercising an ability to create predictable variations in it. Claude Bernard (1865/1957) captured the essence of this strategy over 100 years ago when he wrote:

> The object of the experimental method . . . consists of defining the conditions necessary to the appearance of the phenomenon. Indeed, when an experimenter succeeds in learning the necessary conditions of a phenomenon, he is, in some sense, its master; he can predict its course and its appearance, he can promote or prevent it at will. An experimenter's object, then, is reached; through science, he has extended his power over a natural phenomenon [pp. 65–66].

It is obvious from the foregoing that the limitations of correlational research designs geared to a statistical interpretation of the eventual data are not due to the fact that the resulting evidence consists "only" of a correlation but to various characteristics of that approach to research. The best functional analysis also yields "only" a correlation, but the emphasis on demonstrating control relieves the more serious limitations of most statistical designs. The complex experimental designs that yield data satisfying a statistical model for analysis achieve a sort of static control through randomization, counterbalancing, nesting, and so on, that exists, if at all, only within the specific data set under examination. On the other hand, experimental control exploits valid behavioral *processes* to achieve the same effect, but the generality of those processes assures the generality of the relations they help illuminate. Such generality cannot be reasonably expected from a strategy that places primary emphasis on sample size, thus forcing tactics of response definition, measurement, and analysis that inevitably preserve extraneous intersubject variability, itself an uncontrolled random variable.

A final terminological note is necessary at this juncture. The term "control" has acquired unsettling social connotations that are totally unwarranted by the nature and tactics of behavioral research and technology. The control over responding that uncovers a functional relation resides not with the experimenter but with the treatment variable. It is improper to say that experimenters (or therapists) control behavior. They only control some part of the environment, and that part of the environment may exert orderly influences on responding. The word "control" in this context is even less definitive than it sounds. It properly refers only to the independent variable side of the correlation discussed previously and implies neither causation nor explanation; it merely assists in describing a relatively high correspondence between specific states of the independent variable and accompanying measures of behavior. It is even technically incorrect to say that control resides with some aspect of the environment, because ultimately any environmental manipulation interacts with the biological characteristics of the organism to produce behavioral phenomena (see Chapter 3; see also Morse & Kelleher, 1977). If order emerges in measures of the organism–environment interaction called behavior, it can only mean that the biological parameters of the relation are also subject to lawful influence, as is indeed suggested by the evolutionary requirement of survival through adaptation. Complete details of this influence are beyond the scope of our present knowledge, but the very fact that organisms are both sensitive and responsive to those features of their surrounding environments instrumental in their survival suggests that a part of the explanation of the ability of the environment to exert lawful control over behavior ultimately resides in the biology of behaving organisms.

Number of Subjects

The sources of influence on the number of subjects used in an experiment are both multiple and obscure. One school of thought holds that large numbers of subjects in an experimental sample are necessary to assure representativeness and thus generality of the result to some even larger population. A contrary position asserts that a small number of subjects is all that is required to demonstrate the functional relations that a behavioral science seeks and that generality is more easily obtained through replication based on sound functional relations. In any case, the number of subjects used in an experiment has crucial effects on almost all other research strategies from defining responses to observing and recording to designing experiments to interpretating data. A number of chapters present discussions relevant to this topic; the present comments constitute only a brief summary of some of the more salient points.

The purpose of any experimental design is to organize the production of variability in the dependent variable as a result of experimenter-arranged changes in the independent variable. In order to maximize the clarity of these relations, it is always necessary to minimize all other influences over the dependent variable to draw unequivocal conclusions about the effects of the particular independent variable under study. The various measurement operations are carefully designed and managed to ensure that no unnecessary variability is imposed on the data. It is mandatory that we not counteract these considerable efforts by adding the known and major source of variability (intersubject) that arises from selecting as data the collective effects of the independent variable on the behavior of a number of different subjects.

This is not to say that differences in the effects of a variable on the behavior of different subjects are unimportant, but their explanation may be less crucial than is often assumed. The proper occasion for considering interorganismic differences arises with the attempt to establish limits or boundary conditions on the generality of described functional relations. Thus, the significance of these differences is an empirical matter requiring exploration at that point in the scientific program when the issues of generality are addressed. Establishing a critical role for individual differences by assumption has generally only obscured the more basic issue of generality. In any case, the determinants of between-subject differences observed under some constant condition are not uncovered by using large numbers of subjects in groups comparison designs. Worse still, the variability imposed by the manipulated independent variable will inevitably be obscured to some degree when it is quantitatively homogenized with intersubject variability; this is perhaps the most disastrous result of comingling inter- and intrasubject variability. That obfuscation is easily averted by insisting that all experimental effects be clearly demonstrated on the behavior of one organism at a time with its single environmental history. The question of the representativeness of the effect for other subjects in the population (subject generality) can then be easily and effectively approached by succeeding investigations with other subjects. In Chapter 19, this topic is pursued in even greater detail.

In addition to avoiding contamination by intersubject variability, experiments designed for conduct with single subjects have other advantages. Experimentation with single subjects gives the investigator greater flexibility than is afforded by investigations involving large groups of subjects by removing the penalties for changing conditions in unplanned ways suggested by on-line data analysis. If not preoccupied with the purely logistical demands forced by the management of a battalion of subjects, the investigator can be more sensitive and responsive to the need for managing all relevant environmental variables that is imposed by the rigid criteria of clarity that the results must satisfy. Moreover, the uninspiring administrative requirements of subject acquisition (even from a pool), permission and consent documents, individual attrition, and eventual debriefing will sap the energies of even the most devoted experimenter.

In practice, researchers using single-subject designs often select two or three or occasionally some larger number of subjects for a variety of reasons. For instance, it is important to protect against the considerable loss that would result if the sole subject was unable to complete the project for any of the multitude of reasons that plague human behavioral research. It is also in the interest of experimental economy to derive the maximum utility from the laboriously arranged experimental conditions by initiating efforts at intersubject replication of the findings. Furthermore, a few additional subjects make it possible to probe loads that emerge from the original data with different subjects now having a common experimental history. There are even cases in which it may be necessary to work with a larger collection of individuals;[2] however, regardless of the number of individuals exposed to experimental conditions, each is always considered and treated as the subject of a separate, self-contained experiment. This means that many of the tactical decisions that this book discusses are made separately for each subject (with certain exceptions that are discussed later). In particular, data analysis and interpretation is conducted independently for each subject, and there is no quantitative integration of the data from different subjects required for identifying experimental effects. Either the effect is evident in most, if not all, of the individual subjects' records, or it cannot be said to have been demonstrated. An effect that emerges *only* after individual data have been combined is probably artifactual and not representative of any real behavioral process.

Replication

One of the strategies guiding the use of a small number of subjects is replication. Because replication is considered at length in a broader context in the last chapter of this section, the purpose of the present comments is only to relate replication to its influence on experimental design. Thus, replication is considered here only with reference to a single study or an experiment using a single subject. Replication refers to repeating experimental manipulations in an attempt to reproduce functional relations that assist in establishing generality. The repetition can be as nearly an exact duplication of certain prior conditions as possible, or it can incorporate varying degrees of deliberate variations.

Facilitating the repetition of particular experimental manipulations with the same subject (intrasubject replication) is one of the major strengths of using within-subject designs. To the extent that a relation between the independent variable and the response measure can be repeatedly demonstrated, the experimenter and the eventual audience can be more thoroughly convinced of its existence. If the experimental design shows that

---

[2]A possible source of extraneous variability, situational reactivity, can be effectively avoided in instructional settings, hospital wards, prison cell blocks, and so on, if the investigation is carried out unobtrusively in that environment and all indigenous personnel automatically participate. Of course, there are often nonscientific, social reasons for collecting data from large numbers of individuals as well, particularly when it is suspected that an experimental manipulation may result in some humanitarian benefit to any who receive it.

the effect of the manipulated condition on responding can be selectively turned on and off by the investigator with a considerable degree of precision, the reliability and generality of the functional relation is enhanced. Using designs that require only one, or at most a few, subjects makes any number of such repetitions both practical and convenient, particularly because no assumptions of equivalence of randomly sampled sources of extraneous variability need be met.

The number of such repetitions thus becomes a relevant consideration—two is better than one, three is better than two, and so on. The quality of the reproduction of the functional relation is important as well. Obviously, an exact duplication of previously obtained results is ideal; however, generating at least the same *kind* or *form* of relation is minimally necessary to term a replication successful. When variations in some aspect of the independent variable are involved in additional repetitions of the experimental procedure, an exact quantitative duplication of earlier results is not anticipated, but again, the same form of the relation should be observed.

These are only the most basic considerations of the role of replication in experimental design, as the next chapter shows. Evaluating the effects of the independent variable in more than one setting, with more than one behavior, or with two or more subjects, quickly adds complexities to the basic tactics of replication, although leaving the underlying strategies unchanged. Even in the most complex studies, however, the investigator tries to clarify the full nature of obtained functional relations, and replication is an indispensable tool.

ELEMENTS

All experimental designs are constructed of certain common and fundamental elements, the understanding of which is central to comprehending adequately the subtleties of experimentation. The characteristics of each of these components as they are imposed upon or selected by the investigator completely define the features and limitations of any and every experiment. The task of the researcher is thus to decide how to arrange these elements in a flexible design that presents the greatest number of opportunities for detecting functional relations while placing the fewest restrictions on interpretation. It may be surprising to realize that there are only three basic elements in any experimental design: the behavior under investigation, the environmental setting in which it occurs, and the independent variable.

Behavior

An obvious basic element of experimental designs using human subjects is the dependent variable, behavior. Earlier chapters have dealt with this topic in detail, and our present purpose is to consider the number of response classes that can be used in design. It should be clear that in a single experiment, the investigator can define and use one response from one subject or more than one response (two in the simplest case) from one or more than one subject. This could mean minimally two responses in one subject or one response from each of two subjects.

There are a number of consequences that accompany this decision. The tasks of observing and recording are certainly simpler with the selection of a single response class. The use of more than one response in a design requires that all of the dimensions of measurement already discussed be successfully contended with at least twice, including the demands of controlling those variables that influence each response. Using multiple responses also requires that a condition of independence exist between them, at least with respect to the effects of the independent variable imposed on any of them. Failure to obtain this independence vitiates the experimental reasoning that the design would otherwise permit, as the following chapter details. This independence must be assumed whether the multiple response classes are selected from one subject or from each of two (or more) subjects. If the data make clear that the two responses selected are independent—that is, if variation experimentally imposed on one is not accompanied by corresponding variation in the other— then it is of no consequence for design purposes whether the two responses are generated by the same subject or are examined singly with a pair of subjects. There is a greater prior likelihood that the responses of different subjects will be independent, but it is by no means assured, especially when certain classes of independent variables are publicly manipulated.

Experimental Setting

The environment in which the behavior of interest occurs can be divided into two parts for purposes of understanding the design of experiments. The systematically manipulated independent variable can be distinguished from the experimental setting, the latter including all aspects of the environment except the treatment variable. The investigator can choose (unless circumstancs force otherwise) to incorporate only a single setting in the design or elect to use more than one setting (usually only two or three). The consequences of this decision are similar to those discussed above with regard to selecting one or more than one response. The use of a single setting is simplest from a logistical point of view but provides less design flexibility than might be necessary to satisfy demands for generality. As with choosing between one or more than one response, neither option is inherently better or worse with respect to any criterion of believability. As usual, there is no simple rule to invoke in deciding whether to use one or more than one experimental setting in conducting a given piece of research. The proper choice depends on the details on the question being addressed, the experimental environments, and the anticipated power of the independent variable.

If two or three experimental settings are a designated part of the design, the investigator then faces the task of arranging for measurement in each setting, even if the same response is being measured. At the same time, he or she must contend with identifying and controlling those variables in each setting that require management in order to establish a steady state in each response. In particular, it is important that the stimulus conditions of each setting not exert any appreciable influence on the response of interest in the other settings. For example, suppose we are interested in examining the effects of an incentive system on tardiness in grade school children. We might easily decide to employ two successive class periods in two separate rooms as settings, introducing the incentive program in the first, but not the second period. For the second classroom to serve as a setting in which to collect tardiness data for comparison with similar measures from the first classroom, it is necessary that other activities in the first classroom (such as prolonged assignments, fatigue inducing activities, or highly exciting events) be prevented from confounding the effect of the incentive plan by spuriously increasing the measure of tardiness in the second classroom. Separating two settings spatially and/or temporally does not offer any unqualified assurance that their impacts upon a common response are functionally independent; such assurance must be garnered empirically.

Independent Variable

Any changes in the experimental setting are made with the goal of minimizing and/or holding constant its influence on responding. In contrast, changes in the independent variable are arranged by the experimenter in order to maximize and systematically vary its influence on responding. Whatever the nature of the independent variable in an experiment, the investigator must make design decisions about the order and timing of its systematic variations during the course of the research. At the simplest level, decisions must be made regarding the mere presence or absence of the variable for every period of time encompassed by the experiment. Thus, the investigator must decide on the temporal arrangements of various treatment and nontreatment conditions across designated behavior/setting combinations. These arrangements exhaustively reduce to either *sequential* or *simultaneous*; in the course of a single experiment, both arrangements can be used in a coordinated manner. The use of one response from one subject in one setting permits only a sequential arrangement in which a baseline condition is followed by a treatment condition. Any simultaneous change requires at least two behavior/setting combinations. For example, an experimenter using two settings might arrange baseline followed by treatment phases for the response in both setting 1 and setting 2, simultaneously introducing the independent variable in both settings. Both sequential and simultaneous arrangements might also be used in an experiment that studied two different response classes in the same setting with baseline, treatment, and then baseline phases for each response. If initiation of the treatment phase for the second response followed by some period of time after its onset for the first response and if the beginning of the final baseline phase occurred at the same time for both behaviors, the design would consist of a sequential change followed by a simultaneous change. Clearly, there is an almost limitless number of variations possible on this theme; selecting a particular arrangement depends on the exact comparison required by the reasoning to be supported by the experiment. These matters are fully discussed in the next chapter.

Generality of Design Elements

These dimensions—the behavior (dependent variable), the experimental setting, and the treatment (independent variable)—are the building blocks of all behavioral experimentation. Regardless of the intricacies and subtleties of the most complex experiments, these elements in combination constitute the core of every experiment, and their arrangement (whether or not intentional) completely defines the design, which in turn influences interpretation of the findings. The generality, moreover, extends to all cases in which experimental comparisons are made statistically between or among sets of data collected from groups.

The exhaustive reduction of so-called "groups design" practices to various combinations of the three basic elements is a straightforward exercise. Essentially, the distinctive features of groups designs result from the selection of the response class; multiple responses (usually one from each of a number of subjects) constitute the phenomena under investigation, and the tactical complexities insinuated by that decision have already been fully discussed. The implications of all necessary decisions regarding single or multiple experimental settings and the control and timing of independent variable manipulations are essentially common to all designs, whether of the single-subject or of the multiple-subject variety. Thus, the requirement for controlling extraneous variation through establishing and maintaining equivalence and independence of multiple behavior/setting combinations is not removed by involving multiple subjects, although the temptation to substitute statistical partitioning as a means of after-the-fact control becomes stronger when data are available from a large number of subjects. However, as we have discussed elsewhere, deliberately confounding intersubject variability with a variety of other extraneous, poorly controlled sources and then attempting to remove the entire conglomerate by appealing to assumptions of independence and additivity of variance constitutes poor behavioral research technique, regardless of the design strategy involved.

Manipulating the independent variable again reduces to the decision (with attendant control requirements) of whether it is to be present or absent during any specified period of experimental time for each and every subject. A "control group," in the classical sense, is defined as those subjects who, at a given time, are not exposed to the conditions that the other subjects experience. For them, the independent variable is absent at exactly the time it would be present if they were in the experimental group; all other sources of variation are assumed equivalent for both groups.

The major difference, then, between experimental strategies that rely on single subject/behavior combinations and those involving multiple subject/behavior groupings distinguished by treatment variations is not one of basic design elements, but of the interpretative reasoning afforded by differences in elemental arrangement. This topic is discussed at length in the next chapter.

NOTATION OF DESIGN ELEMENTS

The preceding discussion suggests the need for a notational system for describing the arrangement of the basic elements of experimental designs. Such a notational system can provide graphic, symbolic, shorthand communication of the primary features of all designs, regardless of their complexity. This facilitates comparing different designs from completely different experiments in terms of the basic elements common to all experiments without resorting to the static and restricted perspective encouraged by the use of generic terms crudely summarizing classes of designs. A good notational system promotes a dynamic and flexible approach to experimentation by encouraging consideration of a greater variety of elemental arrangements than is traditional, each sensitively matched to the peculiarities of particular experimental situations. However, perhaps the most important benefit is a careful examination of the manner in which the basic elements are arranged in an experiment and of the resulting effects that such arrangements have on experimental reasoning both while the experiment is in progress and during the final interpretation of the data. Finally, this notation will permit us to examine in detail the tactical intricacies of experimental design.

The symbols in Table 13.1 denote the major features of research designs. These symbols can be combined in an infinite variety of ways to describe any experimental design. The following hypothetical examples are offered for the purpose of more fully illustrating the use of the notation in the description of various designs.

In Fig. 13.1, the notation tells us that for the behavior of talking by Subject 1 in the home, an initial condition in which the independent variable is not implemented (but measurement is occurring) is followed by a second

TABLE 13.1
Symbols for Notating Elemental Arrangements

————	A solid horizontal line indicates that the independent variable briefly described underneath is arranged to be in contact with the behavior while measurement is also in progress. In a parametric study, the different parameter values are noted in parentheses below the independent variable description.[a]
- - - - - -	A dotted line indicates that the independent variable is arranged to be *not* in contact with the behavior, although measurement is in progress.
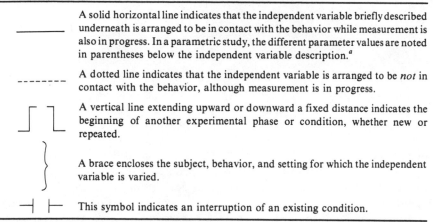	A vertical line extending upward or downward a fixed distance indicates the beginning of another experimental phase or condition, whether new or repeated.
	A brace encloses the subject, behavior, and setting for which the independent variable is varied.
—┤ ├—	This symbol indicates an interruption of an existing condition.

[a]The term "parametric study" refers to an experiment in which a full range of values of the independent variables is investigated. As an example, a parametric study of the effects of a certain drug on responding would examine a number of different doses or concentrations, ranging from very light to the maximum safely allowable.

condition in which token reinforcement is introduced. This second phase is followed by a reinstatement of the first condition. The passage of time in which events are sequentially ordered is indicated by arranging the symbols from left to right. An independent variable label is not repeated after the first phase in which it appears and is identified; any horizontal line drawn at the same level denotes a repetition of that same condition. The length of all horizontal lines indicating the durations of conditions is constant in all cases in which the actual duration is either not known or not a matter of design interest. Finally, the amount of detail provided in the description of the subject, behavior, setting, or independent variable should be determined by the degree of specificity required for the intended audience.

Figure 13.2 shows a parametric study using the response of working problems in the classroom for Subject EM. Because the initial condition is one in which the independent variable of token reinforcement is already in effect, the first horizontal line is solid rather than dotted. In addition, the different schedules of token delivery (the varied parameter) are indicated

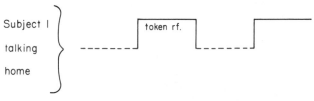

FIG. 13.1.   An example of a simple within-subject comparison.

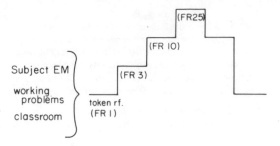

FIG. 13.2.   An example of parametric variations as part of a design.

below the lines in each new phase; this also means that each phase is a variation of the parameter with the scheduled event (tokens) remaining unchanged. For this reason, the treatment description is not repeated at each new level.

Not every condition change in an otherwise primarily parametric study involves a variation in the parameter under investigation. The notation in Fig. 13.3 shows an experimental condition (following a baseline phase) in which a parametric value of one day is noted, thus forecasting future changes in that parameter. The second treatment phase introduces a new condition unrelated to the parametric study that consists of a relatively minor change from the previous phase. However, any planned variation in controlling conditions nevertheless constitutes a different condition and must be so indicated. The third treatment phase is described only with a new value of the parameter first identified, thus indicating the reintroduction of the transaction delay condition (without phone calls). The final phase examines a further value of the parameter.

Figure 13.4 shows three different variables separately administered in alternation with nontreatment phases. The experiment begins with an

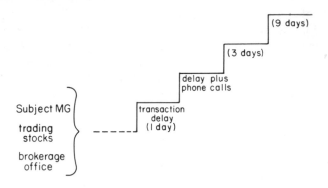

FIG. 13.3.   Notation for a parametric study also involving nonparametric conditions.

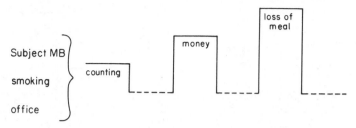

FIG. 13.4.   Notation for alternating treatment and nontreatment phases.

experimenter manipulation that is followed by a baseline condition in which that procedure is removed. Except for this one circumstance (the baseline phase is a new condition), new conditions are always indicated by upward excursions, and there are no downward deviations below either the initial level used or (as in this case) the nontreatment level.

The example depicted in Fig. 13.5 uses the same response in two subjects in the same setting. Any combination of multiple subjects, responses, or settings would be diagrammed in a similar manner, with only the nonrepeating elements listed in the subsequent braces. In this case, the second subject encountered both the first variable and the return to baseline after their respective introductions to the first subject; however, both subjects began and ended the fourth phase simultaneously. Note that independent variables do not need to be labeled for the second subject; each level indicates the same condition originally described at that level for the first subject/behavior/ setting combination. Again, in the absence of a real time line at the bottom of the diagram, the relative location of vertical deviations indicates only an

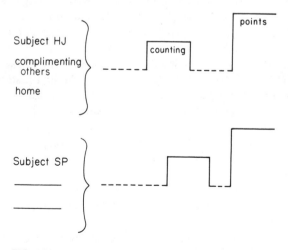

FIG. 13.5.   Notation for a design involving two subjects.

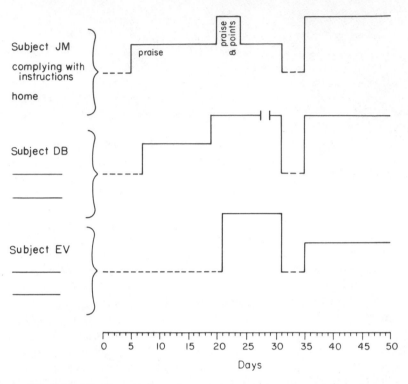

FIG. 13.6.   Design notation using a real time scale to locate independent variable changes.

ordinal relation in time (i.e., earlier than or later than), and all horizontal lines are of a constant length. The sequential arrangement of treatments is thus depicted by placing the vertical excursion indicating introduction of a phase in the middle of the horizontal line denoting the matching phase. As a result, it will often be the case that the length of a subsequent phase line will be arbitrarily either shorter or longer (by multiples of 2) than the standard length (as in the case of the second baseline phase for Subject SP). Simultaneous arrangements are obviously represented by exact vertical alignment of the related excursions.

The format discussed thus far is appropriate for diagramming symbolic temporal relations in planning an experiment when the actual durations of phases are not yet known. However, when diagramming completed experiments, much greater precision is available if an equal interval time scale (days, weeks, etc.) is used to locate all vertical steps indicating changes in independent variables.

In Fig. 13.6, the phase changes are located with reference to the real time scale at the bottom. This indicates the exact duration of exposure to each condition, thus permitting the viewer to see the precise temporal relations between phases. One effect of this addition is that it is possible to show the actual proximity of all sequential changes. For instance, although the shift to the praise plus points condition occurs on different days for each subject (and is thus technically a sequential change), all subjects begin that phase within a period of three days. This information is important because of differences in the reasoning permitted by sequential versus simultaneous changes, which is discussed in the next chapter.

Finally, it should be clear that few of these largely arbitrary notational conventions are sacred. For example, phases could be designated by letters in the conventional fashion (*a b a, a b a c,* etc.) with a legend to describe their referents. In fact, this may be a convenient way of verbalizing about some facets of particular notated experiments. However, some aspects of this notational system should not be compromised because of their heuristic value. For instance, replacing the vertical steps component of the system with a series of lines on one horizontal plane and indicating differences between conditions with letters would remove the stimulus value of the present graphic conventions that emphasize temporal relations among conditions.

The full potential of this notational system becomes apparent in the following chapter as it is used in discussing design tactics. However, it is important here to reiterate the goal of this system: It is intended to describe only the arrangement of the basic design elements for the purpose of facilitating an examination of the influence of such arrangements on the interpretative reasoning that the arrangements allow. As we shall see, the particulars of the arrangement of the three basic design elements completely determine experimental reasoning, and by depicting only the nature of such arrangements in an experiment, this notation becomes a kind of a graphic representation of the reasoning that each arrangement permits. As such, one strength of the notation is that it does *not* describe any other aspects of an experiment, including the nature of the resulting data. Furthermore, the simplicity of the symbols and the rules guiding their use is important in encouraging practical and routine application; the fact that occasional experimental circumstances may not be anticipated by this modest set of conventions is only a minor inconvenience that will hardly disturb the experienced user. We should also note that other writers have proposed similar design schema that are undoubtedly of comparable utility to their purposes. It is not our intention that the present system be construed as a proposed replacement for any of these. Rather, we urge only that exhaustive schematic notation of design *elements* come to replace descriptive labels as aids to experimental reasoning; such terms as quasi-experimental, $N = 1$, nested block, multiple baseline, and so on, have very little genuine heuristic utility when compared to a display that locates all of the elemental arrangements relationally in time.

14

Tactics of Experimental Design

*Someone remarked to me once: "Physicians shouldn't say, I
have cured this man, but this man didn't die under my care." In
physics too, instead of saying, I have explained such and such a
phenomenon, one might say, I have determined causes for it,
the absurdity of which cannot be conclusively proved.*

—Lichtenberg

INTRODUCTION

This volume has now reached the point in the chronology of experimentation
when the investigator is ready to introduce a deliberate change in the
experimental environment. He or she has formulated the experimental
question to be addressed, specified the behavior of interest, defined the
response class to be measured, decided on the units of measurement, arranged
a means of observing and recording, verified the stability and accuracy of the
resulting measures, and obtained stable data under ambient conditions. As
discussed in the previous chapter, the experimenter has also decided (unless
circumstances preempt the decision) whether to work with one behavior in

one subject or multiple behaviors in one or two or more subjects. A similar decision will have been made regarding whether to arrange the manipulations in single or multiple experimental settings. Finally, at this point, the first of a series of decisions must be made regarding the temporal arrangements of the presence and absence of independent variable conditions across behaviors and settings; this is the topic of the present chapter. Here, we examine in detail this aspect of experimental decision-making by analyzing the reasoning underlying various elemental arrangements and then by using the resulting fundamental tactics to construct experimental designs that bring powerful assistance to the process of inquiry.

EXPERIMENTAL REASONING

Independent Variable Changes

Although it seems remarkably simple, there are only two kinds of changes that can be arranged with the independent variable: A new condition can be introduced or an old condition can be reintroduced. Although we could also speak in terms of adding or removing a condition, these terms are confusing because they often do not match what the experimenter actually does. The new condition added may involve the removal of some stimulus or the condition removed may require introducing or adding some stimulus. The terms old and new are related to the immediate experimental history of the conditions and are more useful in understanding the reasoning upon which interpretations will be based. The existence of these alternatives is readily accommodated by the notational system, as shown in Fig. 14.1.

Experimental designs are merely temporal arrangements of various new and old conditions across behaviors and settings in ways that produce data that are convincing to the investigator and the audience. There may be a

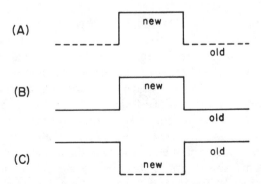

FIG. 14.1.   Notation for introducing new and old conditions.

number of different new conditions, but the reasoning behind such manipulations of independent variables is the same in each case.

Affirmation of the Consequent

When steady-state responding has been attained in one condition (for example, a nontreatment phase) and the experimenter is ready to implement a new (treatment) condition, an implicit prediction has been made. As is pointed out in Chapter 12, the experimenter is predicting on the basis of the stable responding that if additional observations were made under unchanged conditions, there would be no important changes in responding. In fact, it is a forecast that the investigator constantly makes and then verifies with data from continued exposure to the same conditions, whether nontreatment or treatment. When the investigator is convinced through the observed success of such predictions that no change in responding would occur if no changes in the environment were made, then introducing the independent variable while holding other influences constant obligates using the following reasoning: If the new condition is one that in fact has some control over responding under these circumstances, then a change in responding will occur coincidently with its implementation and maintained presence.

This kind of if-then statement and the reasoning that follows as data are collected under the specified conditions involve an important form of reasoning known as affirmation of the consequent. Affirming the consequent as an inductive strategy was first introduced in Chapter 2. The reasoning involved is as follows:

1. If A is true, B is true.
2. B is shown to be true.
3. Therefore, A is true.

Even though this reasoning is formally fallacious, discussions in previous chapters have shown the ubiquity of its power and utility in scientific inference.

The experimenter's reasoning following the manipulation looks like this:

1. If the new condition controls responding, changes will be observed in the data while it is present.
2. Changes are indeed observed in the data while the condition is present.
3. Therefore, the new condition controls responding (i.e., produced the observed changes).

It should be clear from earlier discussions that the observed changes in responding could have been due to influences other than those stemming from the new condition. Some changes in unidentified controlling variables could have occurred concurrently with the new condition and, unbeknownst

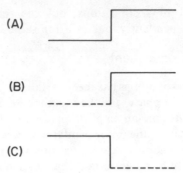

FIG. 14.2.   Notation of "one change" experimental designs.

to the experimenter, these extraneous variables could have produced part or all of the observed changes in responding. At this point, the experimenter's case is weak, but not without substance, because empirical evidence of the truth of *B* (the consequent) does say something about the truth of *A* (the antecedent) by eliminating one of the conditions that could have proved *A* false. Establishing the truth of this one consequent only constitutes a license to investigate further consequents of the truth of the antecedent. Thus, an experimental design of the generic type in Fig. 14.2 is quite weak, and confirmatory data must be considered only a starting point for further arrangements in the experiment.

We have thus far examined only the reasoning supporting an independent variable change to a new condition. The logic involved in implementing an old condition (whether following a new or another old condition) is of the same form, but with the important difference that there are two different antecedent statements in which the experimenter may have interest. The logic of the first looks like this:

1. If the present condition controls responding, then its termination will be accompanied by changes in the data.
2. Its termination is accompanied by changes in the data.
3. Therefore, the terminated condition controlled responding.

The reasoning by which the second available antecedent statement may be supported is as follows:

1. If the old condition controlled responding before, then similar responding will again be observed in the data when only that condition is present.
2. Similar responding is again observed in the data as a result of reintroduction of the old condition.
3. Therefore, the old condition controlled responding before, as now.

It should again be clear that in both cases the empirical truth of the consequent does not *prove* the antecedent to be true, because variables other than those constituting the antecedent could be responsible for the observed effects. However, as before, the observed change in responding following the termination of one experimental condition and the simultaneous reintroduction of a previous condition is not wholly uninformative. The experimenter's confidence in the truth of the antecedent is increased by some unmeasurable degree. When this evidence is added to that from other manipulations, the result may be a sufficiently clear and convincing picture to encourage the investigator to draw tentative conclusions about the experimental question.

It frequently happens that the experimental outcome fails to constitute affirmation of the consequent. That is, there is no clear effect of any kind in the data. In that event, the investigator is on the horns of a dilemma, logically speaking. If the absence of the effect is the result of lack of experimental control or measurement precision, no conclusion can be drawn and another experimental attempt should begin. On the other hand, to the extent that all experimental operations were of sufficient power to permit the effect to emerge if it was going to, then its absence constitutes valid disconfirmation of the antecedent according to the *modus tollens* form of deductive argument (if *A*, then *B*; not *B*; therefore, not *A*) outlined in Chapter 2. This is a most powerful outcome, because it is both logically valid and experimentally conclusive, but it clearly presupposes investigative skills of the highest order.

Reasoning from Independent Variable Changes

It is important to be clear that any single change in conditions always allows two similar but different sets of inferences to be made. Even though only one set of data is available, the experimenter may in principle be concerned with either the first condition or the second condition of an adjacent pair; usually, one is of greater interest than the other. For example, when the first phase is a nontreatment condition and the second involves some particular manipulation (Panel A in Fig. 14.3), the interest is usually in the effect of the independent variable manipulation, because there is no known isolated

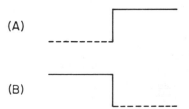

FIG. 14.3.   Notation showing a change from nontreatment to treatment (A) and from treatment to nontreatment (B).

variable of concern in the baseline phase, whose termination will be informative.

Likewise, when proceeding from a treatment to a nontreatment phase (Panel B in Fig. 14.3), the onset of baseline conditions is usually of less interest than the withdrawal of the treatment variable (because no specifically manipulated independent variable is controlling responding). When both adjacent phases involve an independent variable manipulation, the experimenter's attention may necessarily be divided between two equally plausible inferences: The observed effect is due to termination of the prior condition or instatement of the subsequent condition. It is important to note that there is still only one set of data available to affirm either of the two consequents. The fact that two (or possibly more) somewhat different inferences may be drawn about the effects of single change does not render a design any more illuminating than when only one inference is plausible or of interest. The power of the contribution of any independent variable manipulation lies in the nature of the data that are generated, not the number of inferences that may be derivable related to the experimental question.

The reasons for this position can best be illuminated by closely analyzing the following example (see Fig. 14.4) of an investigation of the incentive value of two different commodities for a retarded subject. Data collected under the stars condition may be used to examine an inference regarding either the effects of the prior cookies and juice condition or the stars condition. However, if these two phases constitute the complete experiment, it is clearly not legitimate to use any changes in responding associated with the stars phase to affirm both consequents, because each antecedent constitutes one possible source of disconfirmation of the other. That is, if the data observed under the stars phase show a change from the cookies and juice phase, it could be that the first phase was ineffective and that the changes in responding were entirely due to the stars condition. On the other hand, it could be that the stars condition is completely ineffective and that the changes in responding were due to the withdrawal of the cookies and juice. As it stands, this design cannot generate data that will allow an unambiguous selection of either alternative.

Although this argument is true for any pair of adjacent phases, the dilemma may be ameliorated by other aspects of design and experimentation. For instance, when one of the adjacent conditions is a baseline or nontreatment

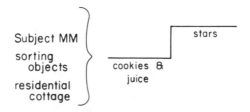

FIG. 14.4. Notation of a hypothetical design examining two incentive conditions.

phase, the experimenter's interest may understandably lie in the effects of the treatment condition (whether revealed by termination or initiation). However, the logical dilemma remains—any change may be due to either condition, regardless of the nature of the experimenter's interests or beliefs. The only real escape from this predicament lies in the experience and knowledge the investigator has with the same or similar design elements. This may become available through a variety of tactical maneuvers.

The experimenter might select the antecedent that appears more plausible in light of the experimental question and arrange independent variable manipulations that provide opportunities to affirm additional consequents of that antecedent. For example, in the experiment with the retarded subject, the investigator might elect to examine further consequents of the assertion that the initially observed change in responding was the result of the stars condition. The expansion in Fig. 14.5 of the design shown in Fig. 14.4 may provide the necessary information.

The alternation of different experimental conditions with repeated presentations of the stars condition creates the opportunity to assess the effect of the stars condition following the termination of a variety of other conditions. If the data generated by each successive presentation of the stars condition are substantially like those obtained under its first presentation, the experimenter may be somewhat more confident in asserting that the original change in the data was not due to the withdrawal of cookies and juice. In the process of arriving at this position, more will have also been learned about the influence of various other incentive conditions on Subject MM's sorting behavior.

Many readers will note that using nontreatment conditions in place of the praise, TV time, and playground time conditions would also have afforded the same information regarding the stars treatment. The benefit of examining these three new conditions was purchased at the risk that any of them might

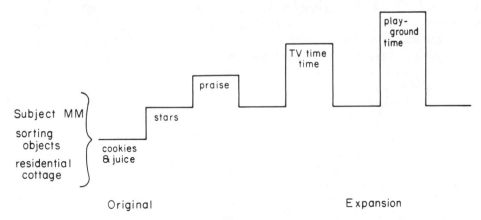

FIG. 14.5.   Expansion of the design in Fig. 14.4 to further examine the effects of the stars condition.

interact with the stars condition; however, the dynamic approach to design allows this risk to be continually evaluated along with the growing utility of the new manipulations. Had the data so indicated, the experimenter could have at any point imposed a nontreatment condition between successive stars conditions.

The experienced reader will also appreciate that this illustration was concocted for its value in illuminating certain aspects of experimental reasoning and would probably not constitute the most advantageous design with which to commence an investigation of the effects of various treatments on the behavior of the subject. Among other issues, the problem of sequence effects (discussed later in this chapter) would have to be addressed in any effort to evaluate such a range of independent variable arrangements.

Multiple Behaviors and Settings

To this point, we have considered the two basic types of independent variable changes and the reasoning that accompanies their use in research with a single behavior in a single experimental setting. However, as we saw in the last chapter, experimental designs may incorporate two or more response classes and/or two or more settings. Various combinations of multiple responses and settings do not change any of the foregoing points, because each behavior/setting combination should be construed as an independent experiment. In fact, as Chapter 12 pointed out, the multiple responses or multiple settings must be independent to avoid confounding variability due to interactions with that imposed by the independent variable.

However, if the two different behavior/setting combinations receive exposure to the same independent variable, further influences on the investigator's experimental reasoning arise. If they are to be considered part of the same experiment, the two behavior/setting combinations must each encounter the same independent variable condition at least once. This creates the requirement that the same experimental conditions must occur in some temporal relation to each other across the two behavior/setting combinations; Chapter 13 described sequential and simultaneous arrangements as exhausting the possibilities.

There are some important limits to designating multiple behavior/setting combinations that are intended to function as part of the same experiment. In order for the use of multiple behaviors and settings to be a part of the same design and thus augment the experimental reasoning, the general experimental conditions under which the two responses (whether two from one subject or one from each of two subjects) are emitted and measured must be ongoing concurrently (in other words, they must be in the same experiment). In addition, both behavior/setting combinations must be exposed to the same independent variable conditions at least once (and preferably several times). Although this exposure does not have to be simultaneous for the different behavior/setting combinations, it must be the identical treatment condition along with the associated extraneous variables that impinge on the two responses and/or settings. This is because the conditions imposed on one behavior/setting combination must have the *opportunity* of influencing the other behavior/setting combination at the same time, regardless of the condition that actually prevails for the second. The word "opportunity" has two subtly distinct meanings in this context. One refers to logical necessity; that is, there must be a second behavior/setting combination simultaneously undergoing measurement if any comparative statement is to be made. The other meaning refers to plausibility as described in the following chapter. Oddly enough, the strength of a comparison is inversely proportional to the plausibility of the results that are obtained. The following examples assist the discussion.

The notation in Fig. 14.6 shows a design in which the logical opportunity for the treatment condition for Subject 1 to influence responding for Subject 2 occurs during the span of time designated as a. The empirical opportunity in this hypothetical example might be based on a certain prior likelihood of a change in behavior of Subject 2 during period a; if no change is observed, the support is augmented for the reasoning that the design permits regarding the treatment effect on Subject 1.

These possibilities also exist in Fig. 14.7 (reciprocally for both behaviors) even though exposure to the treatment condition is never simultaneous.

However, in Fig. 14.8, measurement is not concurrently maintained for both subjects, thus precluding the logical opportunity to observe possible effects of the treatment on the responding of the other subject.

It follows from this discussion that using responses of two subjects each responding in different settings would not meet the requirement that there be

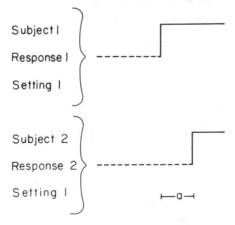

FIG. 14.6.   Notation in which a designates the opportunity for Subject 1's treatment to influence Subject 2.

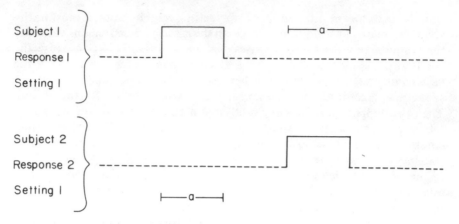

FIG. 14.7.   Notation in which *a* designates the opportunity for each subject's treatment condition to influence responding by the other subject.

a coincident opportunity for detecting the treatment effect. A treatment condition for one subject could not then come into contact with the responding of the other subject, because the second subject's responding would be occurring in an entirely different location. When the two response classes are of the same individual but occurring in different settings, the implications for experimental reasoning are not as unequivocal. Generally, the greater the plausibility that the two responses would be affected by the single treatment, the more powerful is the demonstration of experimental control evidence by data showing a change in only one behavior. Thus, if the two responses were topographically different but probably in the same functional response class (such as hitting and kicking in a young child), selectively induced changes in one response at a time would be a more

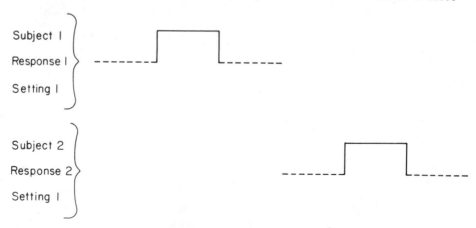

FIG. 14.8.   Notation of independent designs have no logical relation as a single design.

convincing demonstration of experimental control than if the responses were apparently unrelated functionally, although of the same person (such as complimenting one's spouse and writing journal articles).

Before examining the reasoning behind the use of multiple behavior/setting combinations, it is important to understand some additional reasons for their use in a design. Quite often, the influences on this decision are social in origin and beyond the control of the investigator. Conditions in the applied setting may make it necessary or advantageous to investigate more than one response or responding in more than one setting. For instance, those in charge of the subjects or setting may particularly want two subjects or two different response classes in one subject to be studied, and the propensity of the investigator to cooperate may have something to do with the cooperation he or she receives in turn.

Sometimes the nature of the behavior of interest and the conditions under which it occurs makes it advantageous to add this element of complexity. This is often the case when logistical factors or uncontrollable influences on the behavior may preclude returning to old conditions after certain treatment manipulations. For example, physical changes intended to influence pedestrian traffic patterns in a city park may be too expensive to reverse. Similarly, in studying the retail purchasing behavior of an individual, one treatment phase may produce collateral effects on responding (such as starting a savings account) that will make it difficult to reestablish the conditions of the previous phase. In both cases, working with a single behavior in one setting might saddle the experimenter with design limitations that could be partially relieved by using multiple responses and/or settings.

Perhaps the most common reason for using multiple behavior/setting combinations in a design lies in the strengths lent to interpretations of data generated in this manner. As the following discussion indicates, the stringent requirements for experimental control, which such designs incorporate, can augment the believability of the interpretations. Furthermore, the additional replications that accompany this tactic can strongly extend reliability and generality.

Simultaneous Changes.   These potential strengths do not automatically accrue to interpretations based on all designs using multiple responses and/or settings. The exact nature of the temporal relation between the same experimental condition across the two behavior/setting combinations has a considerable influence on interpretations that can be made. Independent variable changes that are arranged to occur simultaneously across two or more behavior/setting combinations do not take full advantage of the strengths that are possible. Consider the reasoning that the arrangement in Fig. 14.9 permits.

If the first behavior constituted the basis for the entire experiment, the reasoning would be as discussed earlier: Some interpretation could be made

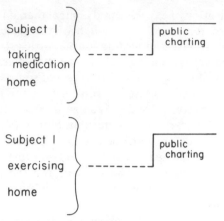

FIG. 14.9.   Notation for a multiple behavior design with a simultaneous change.

about the influence of public charting on the response of taking medication for this subject. The addition of the second response, assuming that it showed the same effects under the two conditions as did the first, would only permit the same reasoning to be repeated. The fact that the public charting procedure was followed by the same behavioral effects in two instances would constitute a useful replication across behaviors, but would not otherwise strengthen the evidence that public charting was functionally related to either behavior. The experiment can afford only limited support for the demonstration of explicit control, and the investigator must still rely on replicated affirmation of the single consequent statement already described. These same limitations hold for independent variable changes that return to an old condition simultaneously for two responses in the same setting or the same response in different settings. Because there is no dependence between the two replicated procedures in the experimental reasoning that they afford, they do not together constitute a single design, but two separate designs.

As an aside, it is precisely this state of independence among replications that is necessary to satisfy the assumptions of randomness underlying the statistical evalutions of the data arising from between-groups comparisons. To illustrate, the conventional two-group experiment is diagrammed in Fig. 14.10. If the subjects are randomly assigned to the groups, there is only one consequent to affirm, and that is done on the basis of the group means. The reasoning is as follows:

1. If the treatment is ineffective (A), the means will be the same (B).
2. The means are not the same (B'). [$p(\mu_1 = \mu_2 \leq .05)$].
3. Therefore, the treatment is not ineffective.

Of course, the means can be different (statistically) for any number of reasons having nothing to do with the effectiveness of the treatment, so the

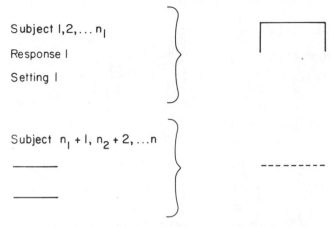

Subject I, 2, ... n_I

Response I

Setting I

Subject $n_I + I, n_2 + 2, ...n$

FIG. 14.10.   Notation of a conventional control group design.

logic of the null hypothesis test does not avoid the fallacy of affirmation of the consequent. This is easy to understand if we remember that the above argument is of the modus tollens form (see Chapter 2) and is deductively valid. That is, if the premises are true, the conclusion must be true as well. However, the *empirical* reasoning afforded by this argument actually begins with the conclusion that "the treatment is not ineffective." It takes the following form:

1. If the treatment is effective, the means will be different.
2. The means are different.
3. Therefore, the treatment is effective.

There is a major logical shift required as we seek to assert the truth of the premise from a demonstration that its negation leads to a valid conclusion. Although the demonstration is deductively valid, the further inference invokes the usual induction process associated with affirming the consequent. The point of this whole discussion is that, in spite of the great numbers of subjects that may be involved, there is at best only one consequent to be affirmed in Fig. 14.10, and that situation affords the barest minimum of reasoning opportunities.

Matching the subjects pairwise across the two groups does not increase the number of consequents to be affirmed, but it does afford the opportunity to reaffirm the same one as many times as there are pairs. Unfortunately, there is no way to do this statistically, because each subject usually receives only one observation, but consistent replication of $E_i > C_i$ builds confidence in the assertion that $\mu_E \neq \mu_C$.

The number of affirmable consequents in the two-groups design doubles if a pretreatment measure is made on each of the experimental subjects and this is compared with the during- or posttreatment measure, either statistically

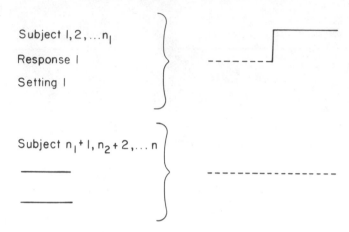

Subject I, 2, ... n_I

Response I

Setting I

Subject n_I + I, n_2 + 2, ... n

FIG. 14.11. Notation of a traditional mixed design involving two groups.

within the group using a test for correlated means or subject-by-subject. Figure 14.11 shows the notation for this design. Of course, if the subjects are paired, each pair again constitutes a replication, as was true in Fig. 14.10.

The utility of casting traditional between-groups comparisons in the present design notation lies in revealing the paucity of opportunities for experimental inference afforded by such tactics. As discussed in Chapter 2, all experimental inferences depend on induction from affirmed consequents; to the extent that these methods offer fewer opportunities to draw such inferences, they are scientifically inferior for behavioral research. However, as discussed in Chapter 5, in those cases in which only one inference is of interest, these designs are adequate although highly inefficient.

Sequential Changes.   Simply implementing the same changes to new or old experimental phases at separated points in time for the multiple responses or settings produces a significant benefit in the reasoning on which the investigator can draw. A design of the basic form shown in Fig. 14.12 serves as an example. As before, affirmation of the consequent reasoning for the effect of the ad lib break schedule on working responses is available for each manipulation independently. However, the temporal spacing of the treatment change can provide important evidence of experimental control. The additional reasoning is as follows:

1. If the ad lib break schedule controls responding (as opposed to control by other unknown variables that might be present), then changes will be observed only in the data for Susan.
2. Changes are observed only in the data for Susan.
3. Therefore, the ad lib break schedule controls responding (as opposed to control by other unknown variables that might be present).

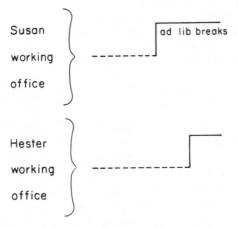

FIG. 14.12. Notation for a multiple behavior design with a sequential change.

Thus, a sequential arrangement such as this provides a basis for support of three contentions: (1) that the treatment controlled responding in the first behavior/setting combination; (2) that only the treatment produced the change; and (3) that the treatment controlled responding in the second behavior/setting combination. In addition, a sequential return to an old condition can provide the same benefits compared to a simultaneous change to an old condition.[1]

There is one caution that must be understood here. This reasoning is not available on an all or none basis. The degree of temporal proximity of the independent variable changes across the behavior setting combinations can modulate confidence in the syllogism formally outlined above. Although phase changes in adjacent time intervals (e.g., days) across multiple responses or settings are indeed sequential, the influence of unknown, concomitant, extraneous variables that might be present could still be substantial, even a day or two later. This problem can be avoided by demonstrating continued stability in responding for the second behavior setting combination during and after the introduction of the treatment for the first combination until a sufficient period of time has elapsed to detect any effect on the second combination that might appear. Thus, in the example in Fig. 14.12, ad lib

---

[1]As we pointed out earlier, the multiple behavior/setting combinations may involve two response classes from one subject or one response class each from two (or more) subjects. The latter case warrants brief comment for the sake of consistency. Readers who are distressed by our criticisms of between-subject comparisons inherent in groups comparison designs may wonder how we can encourage between-subject comparisons in this context. Actually, there is no question that a between-subject comparison is in principle a more ambiguous basis for inference than a within-subject comparison because of the unique histories of the different subjects and all that that entails. However, the impact of that limitation can be only slight in the approach to design described here but is enormous in the groups comparison tradition because of the other details of the ways in which between-subject comparisons are made.

breaks would not be implemented for Hester until it is unmistakably clear that Hester's working was not affected by the earlier introduction of the same break schedule for Susan. Of course, these points fully apply to cases in which the multiple responses and/or settings are investigated with the single subject.

To summarize, there are only three antecedent–consequent pairs that are ever available for empirical affirmation. These derive from the exhaustive set of experimental comparisons arrangeable on the basis of the presence or absence of any single variable. The independent variable can be introduced and the influence of its presence compared with that of its absence; the independent variable can be removed and the same comparison made; or, the effects of the presence and absence of the independent variable can be compared simultaneously by involving two or more behavior/setting combinations. Hence, one can evaluate the effect of a variable by introducing it, removing it, or comparing the effects of its presence or absence in two otherwise equivalent contexts.

If it appears that such a modest array of possibilities for implementing a mode of reasoning that is itself essentially fallacious constitutes a feeble platform for scientific inquiry, the reader should take comfort in the knowledge that such a perception is correct! In isolation, any of these contrivances permits only the flimsiest of inductive defenses, and then only to the extent that the data are free of ambiguities. Unfortunately, there is no alternative, notwithstanding the efforts of some (e.g., Hull, 1943) to warp the scientific method into conformity with formal, deductive logical systems.

The strategy of inquiry that embodies generally inductive tactics is legitimized only by the reliance on a number of requisite strategic goals and tactical practices that constitute the themes of the other chapters in this volume. Thus, requiring sound measurement, insisting upon verified steady states as empirical referents, and ascribing to high standards of reliability and generality achievable only through replication comprise the major empirical parameters of a system of inquiry in which inductive reasoning is fully justified by the breadth and quality of the resulting data.

DESIGNING ELEMENTAL ARRANGEMENTS

With a clear understanding of the strategies, elements and reasoning of experimental designs, we are now in a position to consider the many ways in which the strategies can guide the arrangement of the basic elements so that reasoning that leads to convincing interpretations of data is permitted. The basic arrangements that derive from new and old conditions of the independent variable for single or multiple behavior setting combinations

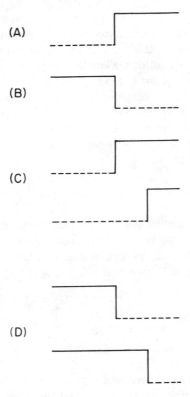

FIG. 14.13.   Notation of basic arrangements of the independent variable.

that (if multiple combinations) are varied in a sequential fashion are shown in Fig. 14.13.[2]

As complete designs, these four basic arrangements are clearly inadequate because of the weakness of the reasoning that accompanies their isolated use. Instead, the strategies governing experimental design dictate using compound elemental arrangements that result in an almost infinite variety of designs, each of which is uniquely suited to the needs of the particular case at hand. Of course, the primary function of any elemental arrangement is to address the experimental question by changing some aspect of the environment in order to observe any possible effects on the measured response classes. Which aspects of the environment are selected for

---

[2]Simultaneous changes have already been described as not constituting a basic design arrangement because no experimental reasoning is available from the simultaneous arrangement of the independent variable across the two behavior setting combinations that is not already permitted by the separate treatment changes for each.

manipulation and in what sequence they are addressed are questions whose answers are almost idiosyncratic to each experiment. In the absence of a scientific investigation of this facet of experimenter behavior, we can only delegate this source of influence on building experimental designs to the training and ingenuity of the individual investigator. Meanwhile, the design of compound elemental arrangements is further guided by two additional objectives: increasing the number of consequents that are examined and controlling for alternative explanations. These exert powerful control over scientific behavior because they augment the clarity of functional relations produced by that behavior.[3]

Simple Replication

One common compound arrangement results from adding a return to an old condition following some new condition (or some other old condition). This compounding is achieved by combining the basic independent variable arrangements shown in Panels A and B of Fig. 14.13. Figure 14.14 shows a

FIG. 14.14. Notation of a new followed by an old condition.

familiar form, which has been called a "reversal" design because the return (or reversal) to the original nontreatment condition should result in responding that again comes under the control of those conditions and "reverses" the experimental effect as well. It is a superior design to either of its two basic arrangements alone because of the additional reasoning discussed earlier that becomes available. In this arrangement, two consequents of the truth of the antecedent are empirically examined. This tactic can be repeated as desired in order to build confidence in the functional relation under examination. For example, the design in Fig. 14.15 permits repeated assessment of the same two

FIG. 14.15. Notation showing temporal repetition of the design in Fig. 14.14.

consequents examined earlier once more or as many times as are necessary. In other words, other considerations being equal, the more times each

---

[3]Throughout this discussion of compound designs, the reader should not lose sight of the points made earlier concerning design as a dynamic process in which each succeeding arrangement is determined in part by the data resulting from the previous arrangement. As the illustrated designs become more complex, it will be assumed that earlier data warranted each extension, not that the design was fully cast prior to the onset of experimentation.

consequent is tested in a design, the more powerful the design. The more times the consequent is affirmed by the data, the greater the confidence in the reliability of the relation.

Evaluation of Alternative Antecedents

Simple repetition of an experimental operation and reaffirmation of the attendant consequents does more than merely establish the reproducibility of the demonstrated relation; it permits weak inferences to be drawn concerning the necessity of the independent variable in the production of the observed effect. In the case of the two designs just discussed, each successful reproduction of the empirical relation adds some confidence to the assertion that the effect is not the result of some other variable whose presence may have accidentally coincided with the imposition of the independent variable. Isolating the actual determining variables participating in any functional relation constitutes another major objective served by experimental design. This objective is accomplished by systematically evaluating and eliminating alternative explanations cast in the form of logical antecedents whose consequents are then examined empirically. In order for the reader to develop a sophisticated comprehension of the role of compounding design elements in this process, it is necessary to elaborate our earlier discussion of experimental reasoning.

Logical Strategies.   By now, the reader is familiar with the general strategy of affirming the consequent as the reasoning device underlying virtually all experimental activity. If a particular hypothesized antecedent is true, certain consequents may be said to follow; the empirical demonstration that one or more such consequents are indeed the case lends credence to the veracity of the proposed antecedent, thus contributing to resolution of the original experimental question. However, as the reader may recall from Chapter 2, affirming a consequent supports only the "if," or sufficiency, aspect of the desired "if and only if" relational statement. The "only if" aspect gains inductive support to the extent that plausible alternative antecedents can be experimentally eliminated.

Conceptually, the strategy calls for identifying and either weakening or eliminating possible rival antecedents as accountable for the observed consequent. Ideally, it is possible to eliminate unequivocally a particular alternative explanation by showing that the observed effect is obtainable in its absence. This strategy reiterates the rationale underlying the various tactics of experimental control that generically reduce to efforts to ensure that variables that could conceivably affect responding are either held constant or eliminated. The following example illustrates this process of experimental reasoning.

Suppose, as part of a weight management program, a physician prescribes to a patient a diuretic to be taken three times a day in pill form. If the patient takes the pills (A), he or she will lose weight (B). The patient returns to the clinic and examination discloses that he or she has gained, not lost, weight. The plausible inference is that the patient did not take the pills; that is, observing B' (gain in weight) affirms the consequent of the antecedent A' (did not take pills). Although highly plausible, this inference is not a *necessary* conclusion from the data. It is still possible that, through operation of some rare metabolic disorder, the patient actually took the diuretic pills and nevertheless gained weight. To rule out this possibility, the experimental manipulation necessary would involve eliminating A' by experimental control through direct administration of the drug, either by forced administration of the pills or by injection. If the patient still gained weight, the alternative explanation would no longer rest on whether or not he or she took the pills, but would concern their metabolic effect on this particular individual.

Sometimes, it is impossible or impractical to eliminate an alternative explanation (A') experimentally. In such cases, a weaker but acceptable tactic involves showing the alternative antecedent to be implausible by arranging to disaffirm its consequent. The reasoning is of this form: If A', then B'. B' is sought, but not observed. Therefore, the plausibility of A' is weakened. On purely logical grounds, demonstrating anything other than B' should completely disconfirm A'. The logical form of the argument is again modus tollens and is deductively valid. In reasoning from experimental findings, however, greater caution is usually in order.

The source of risk in this practice is that the inference is usually based on the absence of an effect. A number of circumstances could occasion failure to observe an effect other than the fact that A' is not operating. The most common explanation for such an outcome rests with the measurement procedure; asserting the absence of an effect requires complete certainty that the effect would have been detected if present. Thus, enormous pressure is placed on the tactics of measurement, making it unwise to attempt disaffirmation of a consequent in isolation—that is, without corroborative evidence that the measurement operations are adequate. Earlier demonstration of experimental effects accompanied by measures of stability and accuracy obtained during calibration would augment the empirical evidence, as would simultaneous measurement of two or more responses, only one of which will be involved in the disaffirmation effort. The latter tactic is illustrated in Fig. 14.16.

Consider the incomplete design in Fig. 14.16 as it might be used to begin evaluating the effect of a self-administered program workbook on skill at doing fractions. The overall reasoning is as follows: If the programmed text is an effective specific learning aid (A), then an increase in an appropriate measure of working fractions will occur upon implementation of the programmed text (B). Alternatively, if other uncontrolled, concomitant environmental changes (teacher attention, etc.) are the influential variables

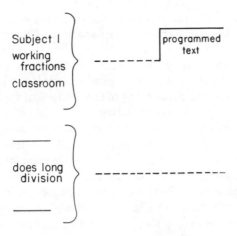

FIG. 14.16.   Notation of a design to evaluate an alternative antecedent.

(A'), then long division performances will change at the time the programmed text is introduced (B'). The desirable outcome would consist of a recorded change only in fractions performance with long division performance continuing as it did before the introduction of the programmed fractions text. This outcome would affirm the consequent of A while disaffirming the consequent of A', thereby supporting the contention that the fractions text is effective while weakening the alternative assertion that the change is the result of teacher attention, etc. Because the two response classes are measured concurrently, there is also some suggestion that failure to observe B' was not the result of undetected deterioration of the measurement process. Of course, if no change was observed in either response class, measurement may be at fault or there is simply no effect present in the first place.[4]

Evaluation of these alternatives is immediate: The possibility of measurement insensitivity should be dismissible by the outcome of calibration operations, leaving a weak or nonexistent effect as the plausible alternative. Finally, even if the hoped for effects are observed, this design only constitutes the beginning of the experimental inquiry. Subsequent manipulations would be required to establish the reproducibility of the impact of the fractions text, as well as to eliminate the possibility of hidden interactions with one or more uncontrolled variables before any reasonably firm statements could be made about the nature of the programmed text as a determinant of responding.

Before proceeding to a discussion of the tactical applications of these

---

[4]The careful reader will notice that this reasoning is the logical strategy underlying the sequential arrangement of independent variables over multiple behavior/setting combinations. The role of extraneous variables unintentionally associated with the treatment constitutes the alternative antecedent that the sequential arrangement evaluates.

logical strategies, it is useful to consider the notion of *plausibility* in the above approach to weakening alternative explanations. Plausibility refers to the subjectively assigned veracity of a statement (often taking the implicit form of a prediction) about some events made on the basis of some history of experiences with those events. The logical rationale for such statements or predictions regarding the plausibility of the relation of some event to another is probably both deductive and inductive but is rarely stated in any case. This lends embarrassingly subjective and nonscientific connotations to the term, and yet it is a ubiquitous and demonstrably useful facet of scientific reasoning. In general, when either an implausible effect can be unequivocally obtained or a plausible effect thoroughly shown not to occur, confidence in the results is augmented to a disproportionate degree (Sidman, 1960). As used in the situation referred to in Fig. 14.16, the plausibility of an alternative explanation of an observed effect is reduced by experimentally showing that one or more consequents of that explanation are not obtained. Like the affirmation of the consequent fallacy that it serves, the use of plausibility by working scientists can be successfully defended by its very utility in scientific method. A full explanation of its use will issue only from an experimental analysis of scientific behavior.

Tactical Applications.   The reader should now have a comfortable grasp of the style and function of the reasoning that underlies evaluating alternative explanations. In essence, the mechanism of consequent affirmation is used repeatedly to allow empirical statements of sufficiency of the relations between independent and dependent variables to converge on the condition of necessity. This goal is approached by empirically eliminating or rendering implausible alternative explanations of observed phenomena until, ideally, a single condition remains that is then regarded as both necessary and sufficient for the given effect. Efficiency and economy of experimentation are admirably served by those rare but ingenious experimental manipulations that eliminate numerous plausible alternatives with one stroke; the authors of such researches are properly touted for their methodological brilliance. Such manipulations usually have the effect of holding constant a large number of potentially influential variables while leaving only one free to vary and be investigated.

A distinction is made between two generic types of potentially influential variables that should be controlled by any experiment. The first class may be termed "natural cause" variables, and their control is the raison d'être of the experimental method. A phenomenon observed in nature may result from one or many variables. Experimental analysis of the sort described is required to isolate and identify them and the nature of their influence. This, of course, is the ultimate purpose of experimentation.

Unfortunately, there is a second category of variables to be controlled that are in some sense an artifactual byproduct of the experimental process itself, even though their influence on behavior is very real. These variables may be termed "artifactual cause" variables, because they only occur as a result of the activities that specifically define experimentation and are not mirrored by any known natural processes. For example, any parametric evaluation of an independent variable requires that separate values be manipulated and studied sequentially, an event not likely to occur in nature. The effect, if any, imposed by a particular sequence could easily be mistaken for the effect of the variable itself, an eventuality that must be detected by the machinery of design. Because behavior is such a dynamic phenomenon, the formidable problems of controlling for artifactual influences cannot be solved through the devices of traditional, static design principles, that presume single measures will be made of each behavior/setting combination. The extraordinary complex designs that abound in the educational and psychological literature are an attempt to address this complex control problem; unfortunately, it is often the case that a sort of pseudocontrol is imposed whereby the main effect is eliminated statistically along with everything else or is buried in a four-way interaction. The main function of any such design is to evaluate and remove artifacts induced by the requirements of large numbers of subjects each measured only once. Fortunately, a straightforward application of a single subject, continuous measurement strategy avoids most of these artifacts. Nonetheless, there are certain artifactual byproducts of any experimental process that must be controlled if the pure effect of the independent variable is to be evaluated. In order to discuss the tactics of arranging design elements to achieve this purpose, it is first necessary to establish clearly the meaning of the word "control," because it has been somewhat abused by the practice of preceding it with the word "statistical."

The reader will recall that the previous chapter pointed out that the phrase "control of behavior" is misleading and inappropriate, because the only option of the experimenter is to exert control over the environment. This point warrants extension in the present context, because many of the alternative explanations for a particular effect are removed from consideration as a result of environmental control. In other words, in addition to controlling the occurrence of the independent variable, the researcher controls other facets of the environment while gathering empirical support for proposed relational statements concerning the determination of behavior. The word "control" properly denotes only direct manipulation of some discrete aspect of the subject's environment. Manipulation includes production, maintenance, and withdrawal, whereas maintenance refers either to holding the variable constant at a given level or changing it from level to level at will. Control in this sense does not include *post hoc* determination that variation occurred and attempts to eliminate it by assumption and statistical estimation. Thus, the idea that sequence effects, for example, can be controlled by arranging for all possible combinations to occur and by assuming homogeneity and additivity of the resulting variation (thus permitting its exclusion as an "error term") is foreign to the concept of control espoused here. Estimating the effect of a variable is not equivalent to controlling that variable, no matter how elegant the estimation procedure.

Of course, not all variables can be directly controlled by the experimenter; in many cases, nature alone is responsible for the production maintenance, or withdrawal of an influence on behavior. The crafty experimenter enlists nature as a coinvestigator in these cases, arranging for measurement and manipulation activities to coincide with the natural occurrence of a particular level or state of interest (a tactic to which the science of astronomy is especially indebted). Fortunately, most of the common sources of extraneous, artifactual variability that plague behavioral experimentation are subject to direct control in the proper sense of the term. Before we identify a few of the more pervasive sources and illustrate the design tactics that permit excluding them as plausible explanations for obtained effects, one final terminological extension of the above point must be clarified.

Because "control" for explanations of the effect of the independent variable in terms of extraneous variables refers only to the experimenter's manipulation of such nontreatment variables and because "design" refers only to arrangements of the three basic elements—subject behavior, experimental setting, and the independent variable (and *not* extraneous variables)—it is incorrect to describe experimental designs as controlling for alternative explanations. Control can only be engendered by the experimenter, and any design can only serve as a means of detecting and assessing the effects of such efforts. Thus, any particular design does not have a permanent property of controlling for the effects of a certain class of extraneous variables, although generic features of certain elemental arrangements may serve a consistent evaluative function for the influence of extraneous variables of some type. The relation between control and design as two classes of experimenter behavior must be characterized in the following manner: Experimenter efforts to control extraneous variables constitute a necessary supplement to arranging the fundamental elements of an experiment in a design that will yield reproducible and generalizable data.

One class of alternative explanations that has already been mentioned in the above examples is commonly referrred to as *sequence effects*. The sequence of two successive conditions can influence responding when the first condition produces an effect on responding that interacts with the variables arranged in the second condition.[5] That is, the effects of the second condition on responding are dependent on the nature of the responding that results from the first condition. The possibility of such interactions is obviously

---

[5]A special case of sequence effects is created by those treatments that produce irreversible effects. True irreversibility (probably a rare phenomenon) would prevent recapturing baseline responding in subsequent conditions. This topic is discussed at length in Sidman (1960); however, its identification does not pose problems unanticipated by this section.

available in any within-subject design, and the facts of behavior make it clear that such possibilities may often be realized in some degree (Morse & Kelleher, 1977). Of course, the extent and importance of any sequence effect is a separate consideration; the behavioral possibility of such explanations of responding in no way guarantees either the existence of such effects or places limitations on the generability of the main effect when it does exist.

The only possible control for sequence effects is the arrangement of experimental conditions in such a manner that the sequence of concern is avoided entirely. If this tactic is compatible with other experimental interests and needs, no better recommendation can be offered. However, in the event that a particular sequence of conditions cannot be avoided, has already occurred and now warrants evaluation, or is of primary experimental interest, many designs of elemental arrangements can be created that will serve to identify the presence of effects uniquely due to a particular sequence and to assess their full extent. Before proceeding to a few illustrative elemental arrangements, it is of the utmost importance to remind the reader that any arrangements that are diagrammed in the remainder of the chapter are inevitably only parts of a infinite variety of more complex arrangements each suited to a particular experiment. Only a sample of the arrangements that might be useful in detecting and evaluating certain effects are presented, and these are in no way intended to support the suspicion some may hold that generic categories of design types exist and should be botanized.

One arrangement that has potential for illuminating sequence effects is shown in Fig. 14.17. The question addressed by this arrangement concerns whether or not the responding engendered by the second phase (*b*) for Response 1 is influenced by the effects of the immediately preceding condition (*a*). The arrangements for Response 2 allow the opposite sequence to occur,

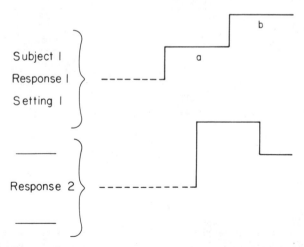

FIG. 14.17.   Notation of an elemental arrangement that can detect sequence effects.

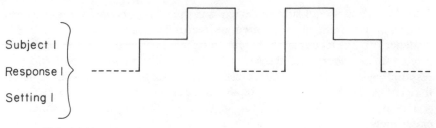

Subject I
Response I
Setting I

FIG. 14.18.   Notation of a within-subject design that can evaluate sequence effects.

thus inviting comparison of responding across the two *b* conditions. The temporally staggered introduction of the *a* and *b* phases across the two responses facilitates assessing the independence of the response classes (an especially important concern with two responses from the same subject) and provides additional consequents that can affirm that any change is due to the treatment and not to extraneous variables. The overriding concern with this collection of elemental arrangements is with the necessity of a comparison across response classes,[6] and the concern would be no different if the two responses were from two different subjects, rather than only one. The risk in either case is that treatment *b* might differentially affect the two responses for reasons related to their different histories, etc. Although this possibility is also assessible, it is a further complication that is not required.

This situation may be avoided by the following sets of arrangements shown in Figs. 14.18 and 14.19, which permit only within-subject comparisons. The design in Fig. 14.18 could be followed or even replaced by the arrangements notated in Fig. 14.19.

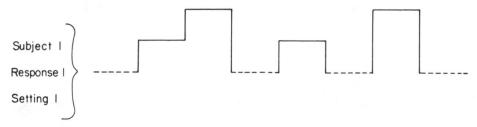

Subject I
Response I
Setting I

FIG. 14.19.   Notation of a within-subject design that can evaluate sequence effects.

In both cases, the tactic is to arrange for comparisons between responding under the treatment condition of interest with responding each time the treatment is preceded by different conditions. Applying this general pro-

---

[6]The reader is reminded that the focus of the comparison is at least initially on the reproduction of functional relations (the kind or form of the independent variable effect), not of narrow quantitative features of responding, although a science of behavior must eventually be able to reproduce those features as well.

cedure can result in a variety of arrangements that leave no hesitation about the effects of a particular treatment and the requirements for reliably producing them.

A second plausible explanation of suspected treatment effects is the operation of some *time-dependent process* such as maturation, fatigue, change in homeostatic level, etc. Whether factors are operating can usually be clearly established during the obligatory period of baseline measurement with the requirement that baseline measurement be virtually continuous and sufficiently extended to reveal any cyclic patterns, either short term or long term. If such patterns are detected, their sources can be controlled in one of two ways. First, a search can be made for the variables responsible, and they can be manipulated until reasonable stability is achieved and held constant thereafter. This is a common practice in the case of such time-related phenomena as the effects of drug regimens; the dosage is stabilized before experimentation begins and may even be augmented to remove cyclicity. Second, if the variables cannot be identified and/or the cyclicity not removed, it is possible to minimize their impact through timing of experimental manipulations to coincide with the occurrence of the same stage within each cycle. Running experimental sessions at the same time every day, for example, is often a sufficient control for the timing of meals and other activities that are usually governed by a regular schedule in an institution.

Verifying that control has been accomplished is a design problem that can be approached in a variety of ways. In essence, the problem is to arrange a comparison condition that encourages the appearance of any time-dependent influence that remains uncontrolled. If such an effect fails to materialize in the comparison condition, its simultaneous presence in the experimental condition may be deemed highly unlikely. The arrangements of elements in Fig. 14.20 permits that evaluation. This arrangement and the reasoning it

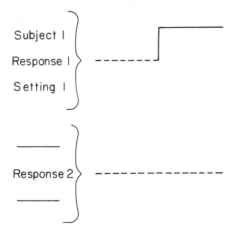

FIG. 14.20.   Notation of an arrangement that can evaluate the effects of time-dependent influences.

permits have been thoroughly discussed earlier with regard to Fig. 14.16, so those points will not be reiterated here. However, with respect to evaluating time dependent extraneous influences, two points should be stressed. First, it is imperative that Response 1 and Response 2 be independent, lest an effective treatment variable imposed on Response 1 exert a correlated influence on Response 2 that is mistaken for an extraneous effect. Such a correlation would encourage a mistaken interpretation about the influence of the extraneous variable in the case of Response 2 that would, in turn, raise doubts concerning the effectiveness of the treatment on Response 1. Thus, failure to assure independence of Response 1 and Response 2 can exact a double penalty. Second, the burden placed on the measurement procedure must always be considered when the absence of a change is to play a major part in the reasoning process. The arrangement in Fig. 14.20 should not even be considered for the present purpose unless it is supported by measurement procedures that exhibit sufficient sensitivity established by independent demonstration.

The problem of response interdependence in the assessment of time-dependent effects can be avoided with the arrangement in Fig. 14.21, wherein only one response is required and the treatment variable is reintroduced at various times likely to coincide with the influence of the time-dependent extraneous factor. If the time-dependent factor is operating (i.e., has not been controlled), the measured effect on responding will show variation from presentation to presentation of the independent variable. Conversely, if the effects on responding are highly similar across repeated presentations of the treatment condition, there is support for the inference that the extraneous temporal effect has been controlled. As before, this reasoning places a substantial burden on the measurement system, and the same caveats apply. Moreover, there is no explicit guarantee that any observed effects are not the result of a time-dependent extraneous factor, and the design per se cannot relieve this possibility. Deliberately timing the treatment introductions to coincide with *various* points on the observed or suspected cycle of operation of the extraneous variable will invite variation in performance. Therefore, care should be taken to ensure that the intervening baseline phases are of varying durations to increase the likelihood of detecting time-dependent variation if it is still present, thereby enhancing the plausibility of the

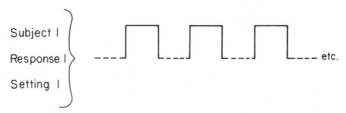

FIG. 14.21.   Notation of a design evaluating time-dependent effects with a single response class.

inference that it is absent in the event no such variation is observed. The careful investigator gives the alternative explanation every opportunity to be confirmed before discarding it.

One of the most pervasive classes of alternative explanation for observed effects of manipulated variables on human responding is described by the phrase *reactivity of measurement.* The assertion is that any observed change is not the result of the independent variable, but is simply due to the fact that the measurement procedure (itself a change in the surrounding environment) has exerted an effect on responding. To the extent that this is true, it may constitute an important fact about behavior and might be investigated separately. However, as a contaminant in the interpretation of some other experimental effect, measurement procedures are readily managed by the general tactic of holding their influence constant. This can be accomplished by extending the period of baseline measurement until stable responding is achieved before introducing the treatment variable. In the event an interaction is suspected between the treatment variable and the measurement procedure, it may be necessary to devise an unobstrusive measurement procedure or at least to vary certain aspects of the original measurement procedure while replicating the treatment condition. The arrangement in Fig. 14.22 suggests how this might be done.

To the extent that responding is similar under all applications of the treatment, any reactive effect of measurement may be assumed constant and not a source of further concern. The question of what the effect would have been in the total absence of measurement is a popular one that, like the sex of God, is not amenable to experimental evaluation. The question commonly arises in educational contexts in which formal measurement is an infrequent

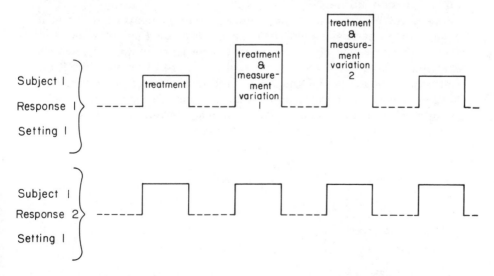

FIG. 14.22. Notation of a design for evaluating reactivity to measurement.

practice except in the service of research. People often wish to know whether a demonstrated effect will generalize to a measurement-free application, and, of course, any answer must rely on sheer speculation, because an empirical answer would presuppose measurement. Nevertheless, many assume the generality of specific treatment effects to measurement-free situations and thereby nurture a number of curious behavioral technologies that are devoid of measurement.

Other Considerations

The experimental question addressed by manipulating the independent variable, the goal of examining as many consequents as possible, and the need to assess the adequacy of controls for alternative explanations do not exhaust the influences on the experimenter's designing of elemental arrangements. Previous chapters have discussed the many constraints under which scientific investigations are conducted in a nonlaboratory environment, and some of these logistical, social, and ethical limitations can have effects on design decisions, too.

For example, a particular condition necessary to clarify the functional relation may be precluded by social considerations. The only solution will lie in the investigator's creativity in selecting and administering alternative conditions that may provide the needed information. If there are no useful options, the study must be reexamined in light of this limitation, and abandonment may be preferable to continuation with a weak design. The same decision may be forced when the limitation on the minimally necessary design stems from the lack of availability of the subjects and/or setting for a sufficient period of time.

One effect of limitations on elemental arrangements is to prevent reestablishing a particular condition of an earlier phase. Logistical, social, or ethical influences may often create this circumstance in applied research, making arrangements of the sort notated in Fig. 14.23 unavailable. If the nontreatment phases permit unrestrained self-mutilation of tissue-damaging force, the success of a punishment procedure would often make reinstituting the original conditions unacceptable on many grounds. However, the evaluation of the full effects of the punishment procedure may proceed

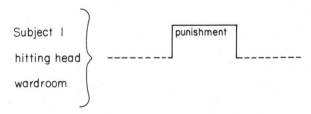

FIG. 14.23. Notation of a sequence of phases that may sometimes be unacceptable.

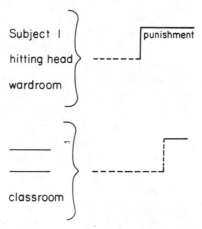

FIG. 14.24.   Notation of a more acceptable revision of the design in Fig. 14.23.

unabated if multiple behavior-setting combinations are used, thus removing the need for reestablishing the prior condition. Figure 14.24 shows such a design.

Another general consideration involves a variation on some of the procedures discussed in Chapter 12 on steady states. A special case of the elemental arrangement diagrammed in Fig. 14.25 approaches the goal of obtaining steady-state responding in a different manner than we have discussed thus far. Instead of maintaining each condition until stable responding is demonstrated before implementing the next condition, two conditions can be repeatedly and rapidly alternated. This tactic, which originated in the behavioral laboratory where each of the two conditions lasted only a few minutes or less so that a large number of each was administered in each daily session, can be powerfully convincing when the proper experimental control is available (Sidman, 1960). Rapid alternation of two conditions that control rapid alternation in levels of responding can remove the necessity for using two subjects and can furnish a highly believable demonstration of experimental control. However, the risks associated with this tactic can be serious when each condition lasts for an entire session, when the total number of exposures to each condition in the entire study is quite limited, and when that alternation constitutes the complete design. Such a

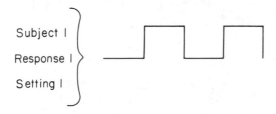

FIG. 14.25.   Notation of single alternation of two experimental conditions.

procedure can hide important instability that should be identified and controlled and can create a misleading illusion of stability. For instance, it could be that one or both treatments produce immediate changes in responding that are not representative of the stable effect that would be observed under continued exposure. In other words, an undetected transition or a transitory state may be initiated at each introduction of each condition. Although the repeated reintroduction of each condition may gradually change the initial level of responding observed, this is unlikely to be discovered when the total number of exposures to each condition in the experiment is quite limited. In addition, this arrangement may be highly suspect as a generator of interaction effects that might not otherwise occur.

These alternative explanations can be evaluated with the proper elemental arrangements. If the rapid alternation of conditions is treated as a single manipulation or phase, the proper solutions become obvious. This alternation condition should be preceded or followed by phases in which each treatment is administered alone until stable responding is demonstrated, thereby relieving concerns regarding the representativeness of the effects observed under brief exposure. This solution is depicted in Fig. 14.26.

We would like to conclude this two-chapter discussion of experimental design by contending that the reader who has a secure understanding of these fundamental strategies and tactics may lack only sufficient experience with the appropriate subject matter and setting to enable creation of an almost limitless number of designs that will assist the discovery of functional relations in nature. The means of addressing virtually every research problem that can be ameliorated by arrangements of the basic experimental elements is now available. The relative simplicity of the present analysis belies a capacity for complexity and breadth of application that will be quickly appreciated by the experienced investigator.

In spite of the power of this perspective, a few readers may be distressed that our discussion is closing without a formal taxonomy of experimental designs complete with convenient generic labels, guidelines for application, and rules for interpretation. By way of consolation, we can only reiterate our earlier declaration that such a "cookbook" approach to the major features, much less the subtleties, of experimental design cannot be justified either here

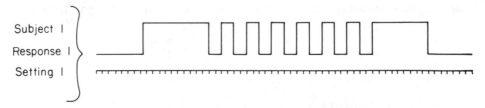

FIG. 14.26.   Notation of a design combining steady-state tactics with rapid alternation of conditions.

or even in more elementary texts, handbooks, or primers. Such codifications are only a misguided disservice to the readers, in spite of the apologies and rationalizations that usually accompany those efforts. The inevitable encouragement of classifications (whether brief and simple or lengthy and detailed) that today abound in descriptions of experimental designs leads to toward a rigid, static, narrow, and crude conception of an experimental repertoire that is actually flexible, dynamic, broad, and elegant. The distinguishing strength of the perspective we have attempted to describe lies in its superior enhancement of the critical experimenter skill of sensitively matching and adjusting the arrangement of experimental elements to the unfolding nuances of unique experimental situations. Not only can this advantage not be denied, it should not be compromised out of mere convenience.

15 Replication

```
I. Introduction
II. Role of replication
    A. Reliability
    B. Generality
III. Dimensions of replication
    A. Within session
    B. Within phase
    C. Within experiment
    D. Within laboratory or program
    E. Within area or field
    F. Across areas and fields
IV. Issues surrounding cross-experiment replication
V. A replicative history
```

... But before you found a law on this case test it two or three times and see whether the experiments produce the same effects.
—Leonardo da Vinci

INTRODUCTION

Replication means repetition, and repetition pervades every nook and cranny of scientific method. The fact that observation may be repeated under varying conditions makes possible a cybernetic or self-adjusting system that, over a period of time, results in cumulation of a relatively errorless scientific literature. Technically, the term *replication* refers to the repetition of independent variable conditions (with their associated measurement procedures) that wholly or in part are procedurally similar in some unspecified degree to conditions previously studied. Replication does not refer to the reproduction of the results originally observed; thus, the quality of the replication refers only to the extent to which equivalent environmental manipulations associated with earlier observations are duplicated. A replication that fails to generate the same effects on behavior may still be successful, especially if it is an alternative condition sufficient to produce the effect. Whereas replication refers to the specific management of the

303

experimental environment, the term *reproduction* is used to denote duplication of the dependent effect. Thus, one replicates procedure in an effort to reproduce effects.

It should also be clear that depicting experimental activity as replicative may be independent of the intent of the experimenter responsible for it. In fact, much actual replication at the level of whole experiments is not conducted explicitly for the purpose of replication. One experimenter is likely to design a study to address other questions that will increase understanding of controlling variables, and any replication of others' earlier work may be incidental. Or it may be that at some later point still another investigator examines the report of the experiment in the literature and is able to interpret it as a replication of even earlier work. Regardless of the original intent underlying replicative experiments, the role they play is central to the cohesiveness of scientific progress.

ROLE OF REPLICATION

The role of replication is manifested through the characteristics of reliability and generality revealed in the data. Replication provides information about the reliability of previous findings under the original conditions and about the extent to which they may be generated under conditions other than those that originally produced them. Unfortunately, this information is not available on an all-or-none basis. There are many other factors that will influence an investigator's interpretations of the outcome of a replicative effort; Chapter 18 treats this topic in detail. A fundamental consideration that is relevant here, however, is whether the measurement under repeated conditions is made with the same or different subjects.

Intersubject replication is usually performed (Sidman, 1960) "to determine whether uncontrolled and/or unknown variables might be powerful enough to prevent successful repetition [p. 74]." When the original finding was based on a single subject, repetition with another subject is not automatic. If the methods of the original experiment were adequate and the investigator has no special reasons to be uncertain of the conclusions, simple repetition for the sake of seeing if the original subject was abnormal is likely to be wasteful. If the original findings are consistent with the established literature, replication is not likely to be thought necessary. On the other hand, if the experimenter is inexperienced in some important aspect of the study, if there is reason to suspect some facet of the method, or if the data are at odds with existing literature, then there may be good reason to repeat the experiment in some way with another subject. In addition, it is frequently efficient for a study to involve two or three subjects concurrently. Because of the logistical difficulties of arranging field experiments and the uncomfortably high chances of losing subjects for the many reasons peculiar to such settings, it is merely a conservative judgment that dictates multiple subjects. Thus ensured against the regrettable loss of one subject, the investigator is not forced to start over and thereby prolong the duration of the entire project. Sometimes these additional subjects are part of the same design (see Chapters 13 and 14) and sometimes they are not, but each subject in a multiple subject experiment provides the occasion for some degree of intersubject replication.

It should be clear that intersubject replication is very different from intergroup replication. As Sidman (1960) points out, intergroup replication may provide information about reliability of the central tendency across groups of subjects, but it provides no information on intersubject generality as defined by the number of individuals the group data actually represent. Statistical consolidation of the data from any group of individuals, no matter how large, provides no evidence concerning the reproducibility of the findings across individual subjects. In any case, intergroup replication infrequently occurs within an experiment designed in accordance with traditional group statistical research (Sidman, 1960).

Intrasubject replication is an inevitable feature of the methods described in this volume and is an essential part of them. Intrasubject repetitions of independent variable conditions can provide powerfully convincing demonstrations of an effect and the experimenter's control over the variables that are sufficient to control the phenomenon. Orderly changes in the subject's behavior resulting from such manipulations yield valuable affirmative information about the stability of an effect. Intrasubject replication provides this information without the confounding influence of intersubject variability and, when accompanied by careful attention to the other features of within-subject methods, results in an elegant and convincing argument for the reliability of a phenomenon.

Reliability

With this understanding of the basic differences between inter- and intrasubject replication, let us examine the utility of replication in providing the experimenter with information on the reliability or stability of an effect.[1] The question the experimenter must ask concerns whether the effects of a procedure, technique, or variable are real and stable and will occur upon demand under highly similar conditions when they are again presented. The question is one that the experimenter usually answers within the confines of the same experiment or research program, because it is most easily and

---

[1]This must be distinguished from the reliability or stability of measurement discussed in Chapter 10. Unlike the reliability of an effect, measurement reliability cannot be safely inferred from the resulting data, but requires independent verification.

directly answered by attempting to arrange as nearly an identical repetition of procedure as is possible.[2] In fact, repetition of identical procedures even with the same investigator, setting, and subject is not possible, and there is no reason to spend an inordinate amount of energy in the attempt. However, endeavoring to assess the reliability of a new effect under substantially different conditions is risky in that if unsuccessful, there is no evidence about whether the failure lies in the unreliability of the phenomenon (as yet unexplored) or in the premature changes of other variables. Therefore, the stability of a sufficient relation across repeated instances is usually evaluated under reasonably constant conditions soon after the relation has been initially identified and before further experimental questions are addressed.

One of the important effects of successful demonstrations that an effect is real and stable and can be repeatedly produced at the demand of the experimenter is that the believability of the implied functional relation is powerfully augmented for both the investigator and the scientific community. With increasing confidence that there is indeed a functional relation that can be repeatedly produced, the experimenter can proceed to further empirical analysis and the scientific community can more confidently examine the resulting evidence and launch experimental reactions. One of the reasons for this believability lies in the alternative explanations that demonstrations of reliability through replication may illuminate. By repeating essentially the same conditions originally manipulated, one can to some extent evaluate the influence of unknown variables that might have been operating only during the original demonstration. Although the possible influence of all experimental artifacts cannot be addressed by simple replication, a natural suspicion about the influence of one-time variables can be somewhat diminished in this manner. Intrasubject replication can also evaluate the influence of time as an explanatory alternative by showing that the supposed functional relation can be produced at any point in time. This is an important capability that is inherent in complete within-subject designs and notably lacking in most between-groups comparisons.

A second consequence of showing reliability of effects through replication is of considerable importance to the literature of the area. Assessing the reliability of functional relations is one of the many procedures that are collectively responsible for the self-corrective nature of science. The fact that the scientific community highly values evidence of the reliability of phenomena and the availability of replication as a technique for assessing reliability have the effect of encouraging its use by the individual investigator. The experimenter then generates replicative data that may demand further experimentation to better identify, clarify, and understand the phenomenon in question, so that the interpretations that become a part of the literature are

---

[2]Sidman (1960) terms this kind of repetition "direct replication."

less likely to be misinformed than if replication had not been conducted. Then, other scientists may attempt to repeat the reported study, which in turn is likely to provide further information about the reliability of the phenomenon. This extension will either build further confidence in the effect or cast doubts on the original research. In both cases, more investigation will likely follow, either probing the generality of the effect or inquiring further into the conditions of its existence. This effect of evaluating reliability through replication is difficult to see without taking a historical perspective, because it is constantly in progress over long periods of time for any particular topic. But the effect of this cybernetic process on accumulating an increasingly accurate body of discovered knowledge should not be underestimated.

Generality

The second major role of replication is providing information about the generality of a functional relation over a wide range of conditions. As with reliability, this is a natural outcome of a moderate degree of repetition in subsequent experimentation. However, whereas reliability is sought by exactly duplicating the treatment of interest, generality is more likely to be pursued through repetitions in which a number of procedural differences are arranged.[3]

It should be clear that any replication can provide information about the reliability and generality of the phenomenon, regardless of the degree of procedural similarity to earlier experimentation. However, when reliability is the goal, the more changes that are incorporated into the replication, the more substantial is the risk that the effect is not general enough to be demonstrated under new conditions. When generality is the goal, the more similar the replication to the original experiment, the less informative will be the data regarding the universality of the phenomenon under varied conditions. If there is any reason for special concern about the original findings, it may be prudent to direct subsequent efforts at removing that doubt by repeating the same conditions. However, when the experimenter is confident about the research techniques, there may be minimal risk in attempting to establish both reliability and some generality by using the original data as the basis for a substantial departure from the original procedure.

Generality is discussed in detail in Chapter 19, but it is important to clarify here its contribution to the function of replication in the scientific enterprise. Whereas demonstrating reliability shows us the certainty of our knowledge, demonstrating generality actually increases our knowledge. It does this by

---

[3]Sidman's (1960) term for this tactic is "systematic replication."

showing that a functional relation can be obtained in spite of changes in a number of variables. Our knowledge is augmented in an important way when we know that a phenomenon can be shown to hold not just under condition *A* but across the widely varying conditions *B, C,* and *D.* Demonstrating generality through replication focuses, directs, and redirects research in an area by probing the nature and extent of phenomena and by showing the relations among phenomena. In this way, evidence about generality is a major systematizing force in an area of knowledge, and, as with reliability, the process of generating such evidence is a crucial element of the cybernetic system of scientific investigation.

A familiar example of this process is furnished by the use of tokens as conditioned reinforcers in both the animal laboratory and various applied settings. For many years, students of the behavior of laboratory animals had investigated the manner in which various stimuli such as lights and sounds could come to serve a reinforcing function by virtue of temporal association with known primary reinforcers such as food, water, escape from painful stimuli, etc. The generality of these findings was substantially enhanced when it was shown that the major functional effects could be obtained using tangible objects such as poker chips (Wolfe, 1936) and marbles (Malagodi, 1967). In particular, an important interspecies generality was established by Ayllon and Azrin when, in their now classic work *The Token Economy* (1968), they demonstrated the ability to replicate the major behavioral effects of using tokens with institutionalized humans. Although it can be argued that humans have behaved in orderly ways with respect to money for many centuries, the work of Ayllon and Azrin explicitly connected that behavior to a known body of fundamental behavioral phenomena, thus underscoring the potential for further investigation of economic phenomena within the context of a science of behavior.

DIMENSIONS OF REPLICATION

We have already seen that replication may vary from nearly exact duplication of experimental conditions to repetitions in which an earlier finding is taken entirely out of the context of previous research and is reproduced under very different conditions. In addition to similarity to previous experimental conditions, another major dimension along which replications may vary is temporal. Repetitions of measurement under similar independent variable conditions may occur a number of times within a single session or over a period of years across different fields of science. In fact, these two dimensions—procedural similarity and time—combine to give a comprehensive picture of the broad scope of replication that entitles it to such an important position in science.

Within Session

Many of the advantages of using individual subjects in the manner suggested in these pages have already been described. An additional benefit is that the effects of an experimental condition may be examined repeatedly within a single experimental session by frequent withdrawals and reintroductions of the treatment variable. However, if each time the variable is removed and reintroduced is to be used as a replication, corresponding portions of the data must be isolated for separate analysis, because the reasoning supported by replication would be lost if only the session summary data formed the basis for analysis. Successful reproduction at this refined level defines within-session steady-state responding and is most important, because failure here is often a good predictor of failure at other levels. However, successful within-session replication is more a necessary than a sufficient requirement for predicting successful replications at other levels, because the subsequent introduction of different variables may at any stage interfere with reproducing the original effect.

Within Phase

Repeated within-session withdrawal and reintroduction of a condition for more than one session also constitutes within-phase replication. In addition, when the treatment condition is continuous throughout each of a number of sessions, that and any resulting demonstration of steady-state responding may be viewed as replication and reproduction, respectively, across sessions within an experimental phase. In other words, exposing the subject to the same set of conditions in repeated sessions constitutes within-phase replication. For all of the reasons examined in the earlier discussion of steady states, the repeated exhibition of a stable relation between responding and some independent variable condition across sessions while other experimental conditions are held constant may be fundamental to the objectives of the experiment. The proposed duration of a treatment condition will usually exceed a single session, and data from within a single session, no matter how stable, cannot then provide the proper reference for comparison. Of course, demonstrating steady-state responding across sessions provides within-phase replication and reproduction.

Within Experiment

As Chapters 13 and 14 showed, the many possible arrangements of the basic elements of experimental design define the range of replicative formats. Within the course of a single experimental effort, the investigator may implement various new and old conditions in a way that achieves numerous replications of varying procedural similarity. Replication at this level is a routine part of within-subject experiments, and it provides the investigator with valuable data that continuously guides the selection of experimental manipulations in a more illuminating direction. Of course, repetition of various conditions in an experiment is the structural support for experimental reasoning that the data legitimize.

Within Laboratory or Program

Another level at which replication occurs is as a part of a series of related experimental efforts comprising the research activities of a single laboratory or research program. In the course of pursuing some experimental theme, the investigator will design replicative efforts consonant with the evolving data and the direction of the research. Such replications may take the form of nearly identical repetitions, but the experienced researcher working extensively in one area is likely to take advantage of increasing familiarity with experimental procedures and the problem of interest by building replications into the design of subsequent experiments, rather than designing experiments whose only value is simple repetition.

Within Area or Field

Replication within an area or field of investigation and across different laboratories and programs is particularly important because it involves different experimenters and research programs. Regardless of the thoroughness of replicative efforts by a single investigator or program, the credibility of any findings will remain limited until the functional relations are reproduced by other researchers. This dimension of replication is crucial because there are variables peculiar to any experimenter and research program that can have major and unidentified influences on the dependent variable, regardless of the purity of the experimenter's motives in fully identifying and describing all relevant factors in a study. The absence of these variables in other programs thus occasions an imperative test of the generality of research results.

Across Areas and Fields

Replication across different areas of investigation and fields of science is the zenith of the replicative process. Establishing generality at this level is an important part of discovering similarities in nature and thus of systematizing knowledge. For example, Skinner (1975) has suggested that the migratory patterns of various species may be viewed as a replication across phylogenic generations of the basic process of shaping by contingency adjustment that is so reliably seen at the level of the behavior of single organisms within species. As a necessary condition for this suggestion to have merit, specific patterns of continental drift that are anticipated by the plate tectonics theory of geophysics must be postulated. Under the assumption that certain portions of the Earth's crust slowly separated in specific directions, the conditions for gradual elongation of a species' habitual range would be met, and orderly change to a migratory pattern would result. Data provided by Carr (1966) and others confirm these predictions and, to that extent, suggest generalities that draw together the fields of zoology and geophysics with the science of behavior.

ISSUES SURROUNDING
CROSS-EXPERIMENT REPLICATION

The methods of replication across experiments (within-experiment replicative efforts have been discussed in the previous chapters of this section) involve a number of different but related questions, none of which have unequivocal answers. However, the reader should by now be comfortable with a general discussion of guiding strategies and facilitating tactics designed to produce a posture of informed flexibility when facing issues of technique at the level of experiment-specific decisions.

Perhaps the first general question concerns how to decide when specific replicative efforts are necessary. Important considerations here include the thoroughness of the literature concerning the relations under study, the experience the investigator has with the experimental procedures, the accuacy of available measurement, the stringency of the experimental design yielding the present findings, the congruence of the data with the existing literature, the possibility and plausibility of alternative explanations, the costs of replicative efforts under consideration, the importance of the findings, the uses to which they will be put, and the direction that future experimentation might take.

In light of some or all of the foregoing considerations, the experimenter assesses the reliability, generality, and believability of the existing set of results in the process of deciding whether or not to replicate. To illustrate, one may perform an experiment with fastidious adherence to all the canons of procedure, only to find oneself with a result that either has no counterpart in the literature or, worse, appears to contradict an accepted finding. Replication, probably on a broad scale, is clearly in order, if only to enhance believability. On the other hand, a set of results that were obtained under less than optimal procedures, but that are in general agreement with established findings and are not directly crucial to the next experiment, might be allowed to stand without further examination. The reader undoubtedly can concoct examples of the myriad other combinations of circumstances that would weigh for or against the decision to replicate, depending, of course, on the quality of the original data.

Whatever the decision, if an effect is characterized by insufficient reliability and very limited generality, data generated by later uses of the procedure by either the investigator or other researchers will eventually communicate this fact. Such results will appear in the form of some degree of failure to reproduce the effect that was suspected on the basis of the earlier study, and explanation of the failure will necessitate returning at least to some earlier replicative effort that was successful, if not to the original experiment. Replications must then be arranged in a more cautious sequence, lest the effect again be lost.

A related question discussed earlier concerns the very style of the replication itself—that is, the degree of similarity of the repetition to the original procedures. That discussion pointed out the influence that the goals of reliability and generality played in designing replications, and the same considerations that bear on the decision to replicate are again pertinent. However, although the variables influencing this decision are many, the answer may be immediate. For instance, if the finding is strongly at odds with the literature, a highly similar repetition may be obviously required to demonstrate reproducibility. If planned experiments already incorporate replicative procedures, no special deliberations may be necessary. As a further example, the previous chapter showed that a common motivation for conducting a replicative manipulation stems from the presence of a legitimate alternative explanation for the observed effect. The decision regarding the degree of procedural similarity to be built into the replicative experiment may be easily reached by simply eliminating or controlling the variable in question and otherwise duplicating the earlier method. On the other hand, the investigator may feel sufficiently confident in the results that proper management of the offending variable may be accompanied by further changes in procedure that are in keeping with the planned progress of the experimental program. In any case, the earlier list of considerations does not necessarily forecast a difficult decision so much as it does the need for careful reflection.

A futher question concerns the number of replications necessary to establish reliability clearly and provide at least some evidence regarding generality. This judgment, like many, depends on the circumstances surrounding the research. All of the considerations thus far discussed and summarized in the upcoming chapters on interpretation bear on the decision whether or not to engage in further replicative efforts of some kind. It may be that the planned experimental program already calls for further manipulations from which information on reliability and generality will become available; in such a case, no extra efforts may be necessary. On the other hand, it may be that the exigencies of applied settings are such that the question of reliability of the findings is a serious one that requires additional attention before proceeding any further. Certainly, the more questions that are raised by less than ideal measurement practices, the more the issues of reliability of both measurement and effect beg for additional experimental verification.

Another question asks exactly what constitutes a successful reproduction. Not surprisingly, the same interpretative considerations listed above are involved in the answer. In addition to evaluating the replicative study on its own merits, the experimenter must also compare the findings to those obtained from earlier research. The special criterion by which reproductive success is evaluated centers on the extent to which the original forms of the functional relations are reproduced. Exact duplication of the quantitative details of the original result is both highly unlikely and unnecessary to specifying a successful reproduction, but recovery of the form of the effect is essential. As is always the case, the investigator's interpretations will be evaluated with respect to the ultimate criterion of their generality.

It should be mentioned that the question of what constitutes a successful replication is often addressed by a researcher who is reviewing already published research performed by others. Because most studies may not be conducted for explicit replicative purposes, a later researcher may be the one who eventually defines the study as replicative in nature with respect to other experiments. In such circumstances, the interpreting scholar labors under the same disadvantage as all readers who do not have available to them the complete details of the study's method and findings. This handicap must encourage a greater caution in the conviction with which one interprets a study as replicative.

There is also the issue of what action to take when a successful replication does not reproduce the original effect. Of course, the experimenter's response will depend greatly on such variables as the quantity and quality of published literature on the topic, confidence in his or her own original research on the problem, evaluation of the entire replicative experiment in its own right, and the nature of the unsuccessful reproduction. If the experimental procedures were highly similar to those of the earlier study, there would probably be a greater tendency to examine experimentally the variables that might have been responsible for the original finding (perhaps it was an experimental artifact). In the event that a number of procedural changes were made in the second study, the obvious first step is to attempt an exact replication of the second study to ensure that its effects are reproducible. If so, it may then be appropriate to examine the effects of the variables that were changed. In any event, the only available course of action is further experimental manipulation of variables of potential influence in a gradual winnowing process that will eventually clarify the primacy of a few replicable variables.

Finally, it is important to understand that evaluating a series of replicative studies is not an actuarial problem to be solved by a statistical polling of the literature. Replicative failures and successes cannot be balanced or assessed in an electoral fashion. Neither is the final truth or falsity of conclusions dependent on the degree of confidence in them, although increments in confidence are all that can ever be obtained. Those increments can only be acquired with certainty by experiment, not by logic or statistics (Sidman, 1960).

A REPLICATIVE HISTORY

It is probably difficult to develop a full appreciation of the role of replication in science from didactic discussions such as this. Perhaps a more comprehensive understanding can be facilitated by stepping back to view the evolution of research on a particular topic from a historical perspective.[4] This will provide a unique account of the process of knowledge discovery in a selected area.

We have chosen for this extended example a paradigm popularly known as timeout (TO), because its research history is interesting, easily traceable, and illustrative of earlier points.[5] The studies referenced are those most important for present purposes, and the list hardly exhausts all publications on the topic. Most of the replicative efforts were aimed toward extending the generality of some aspect of an effect and were the works of different authors. A number of the references are to publications describing multiple experiments, each experiment including much replicative information. Many ancillary points of replication are not mentioned in this brief survey. The studies are organized into eight categories based on methodological similarities and are graphically arrayed in the form of a tree in which the categories are displayed as branches growing from a foundation literature serving as the trunk.[6]

The timeout paradigm can be generally described as a class of procedures in which a period of time (usually fairly brief) is arranged to follow some response and during which some reinforcement that is usually presented or earned is not available. The typical effect of this procedure is to decrease the frequency of the response, and it is thus commonly called a punishment procedure.

---

[4]The *Science Citation Index* is a very useful reference collection for this purpose.

[5]We would like to express our gratitude to Michael S. Rosenbaum and Phillip K. Duncan for their capable efforts in successfully developing this idea and writing the history upon which the present section is based.

[6]Our exposition of this genealogy, particularly the earlier elements, will necessarily entail the use of some technical terminology peculiar to the area of animal operant conditioning. The reader who may be unfamiliar with this vocabulary can comfortably ignore the technical details of various experiments without sacrificing an appreciation of the contribution of these studies to the supraordinate replicative structure of the literature defining the area.

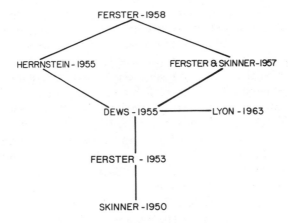

FIG. 15.1.   Foundation timeout literature.

We begin with a group of studies (Fig. 15.1) that establish the foundation of the research area.

Skinner (1950) first described the basic contingency, although the term "timeout" had not yet been coined. In a matching-to-sample experiment, an incorrect response produced a brief period of darkness. The same blackout procedure as a method of beginning and ending experiments with pigeons was used by Ferster (1953). This procedure was useful for adapting the birds to the experimental chamber prior to beginning the experiment and as a method of convenience for the experimenter, whose presence was no longer required at the termination of the session to remove the birds. Ferster noted that extinguishing the lights in the experimental chamber resulted in the pigeons' roosting. Thus, the pigeons could remain in the darkened chamber overnight without emitting many key pecking responses. Although the procedure was still not termed "timeout," Ferster's (1953) work constituted a replication of Skinner's use of the procedure in that the earlier procedure of preventing a response from having any effect within the session was extended to the beginning and end of each session.

Next, Dews (1955) used a 15-minute timeout as the intertrial interval for pigeons on several schedules of food reinforcement. This extended its usage to a method for defining discrete trials. Herrnstein (1955) investigated the effects of a 30-second pretimeout stimulus (warning signal) on responding during different variable interval schedules of food reinforcement. He found low rates of responding during this pretimeout stimulus as opposed to the higher rates that occurrred during the operation of the variable interval schedule, thereby extending the generality of the timeout dependent phenomenon. This effect opened a new area of research.

Ferster and Skinner (1957) were the first to define timeout explicitly. Their seven years of exhaustive research with schedules of reinforcement included investigation of several parameters of timeout in combination with several parameters of simple and complex schedules of reinforcement.

Ferster (1958) investigated the effects of a pretimeout stimulus, the interruption of a variable interval schedule by a response-independent timeout, the availability of two response keys (one producing reinforcement and the other avoidance of timeout), and the use of contingent timeout to differentially punish short interresponse times (IRTs). In replicating the work of Herrnstein (1955), Ferster's experiment with the pretimeout stimulus extended this line of investigation from pigeons to chimpanzees, thereby demonstrating the interspecies generality of the effect. The investigations of response-independent timeout replicated earlier work in which timeout was used only to separate trials. Ferster found that timeout used in this manner served to reduce shorter IRTs differentially, and that timeout for short IRTs produced longer IRTs. These studies extended the generality of timeout observed in rate of responding to the dimensional quantity of interresponse time. Finally, Ferster's (1958) monograph demonstrated that chimpanzees would avoid timeout when reinforcement was scheduled for responses on one key and timeout avoidance on the other key. This was apparently the first demonstration of timeout avoidance on a concurrent schedule, and it served as the basis for several further investigations of timeout avoidance that are discussed in the following paragraphs.

A successful replication of Dews' (1955) experiment was performed by Lyon (1963) using a 1-minute timeout, whereas Dews'(1955) study had used a 15-minute timeout as the intertrial interval. The demonstration that timeout is effective at both of these values adds generality to the observation that timeout reduces response rate. The multifaceted Ferster (1958) study served as the basis for research in a number of replicative directions; Fig. 15.2 schematically represents some work concerning timeout duration and schedule effects on accuracy of responding.

Ferster and Appel (1961) investigated the effects of various durations of response-contingent timeout on incorrect responding in a matching-to-

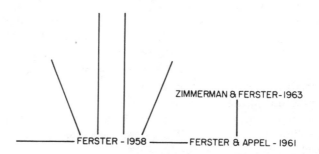

FIG. 15.2.   Timeout duration and schedule effects on accuracy of responding.

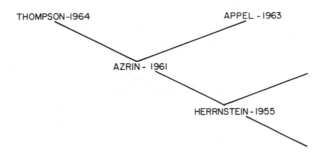

FIG. 15.3.   Timeout from aversive schedules of positive reinforcement.

sample procedure using timeout durations ranging from 0.50 to 600 seconds. A further extension of the matching-to-sample research was performed by Zimmerman and Ferster (1963), who investigated the effects of timeout durations ranging from 1 second to 600 seconds, with the schedule of timeout presentation ranging from fixed ratio 1 to fixed ratio 50. The Ferster and Appel (1961) study extended knowledge about timeout duration, and the Zimmerman and Ferster study provided information regarding the importance of the schedule on which timeout is delivered.

Another area of investigation concerned timeout from aversive schedules of positive reinforcement (Fig. 15.3). In extending Herrnstein's (1955) demonstration of the effects of a pretimeout stimulus on behavior maintained by a variable interval schedule of reinforcement, Azrin (1961) investigated the effects of increasing the ratio requirement of a fixed ratio schedule of reinforcement on the rate of timeout production. This research demonstrated that a high fixed ratio requirement can become aversive, in which case timeout may have the effects of a positive reinforcer. In a direct extension of Azrin's work, Thompson (1964) investigated the effects of ascending and descending ratio requirements of a fixed ratio schedule on the rate of timeout production. Again, the results showed that a high fixed ratio schedule became aversive, producing timeout responses (escape). This work supported Azrin's (1961) findings that an organism on a simple fixed ratio schedule would earn timeout via an operant response during the fixed ratio pause, and it extended the generality of the previous work by demonstrating that the organism would earn timeout during a mixed schedule. Appel (1963) partially supported Azrin's (1961) work by showing that simply changing the stimulus supported responding, thus demonstrating the possible importance of stimulus change in the time-from-aversive schedule studies. These studies furthered understanding of the broad nature of the phenomenon by showing that the timeout contingency is not inherently aversive or appetitive, but that its functional effect is determined by the immediate experimental context.

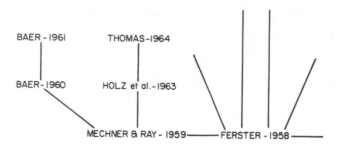

FIG. 15.4.   Avoidance of timeout.

A number of studies examined the use of timeouts in avoidance procedures (Fig. 15.4). Mechner and Ray (1959) used rats to replicate part of Ferster's (1958) work by showing that the organism's behavior stabilized at a specific IRT that allowed avoidance of timeout; they extended Ferster's (1958) work with chimpanzees in that interspecies generality was established. Baer (1960) investigated responses that escaped or avoided timeout and replicated earlier timeout studies with human subjects whose responses avoided timeout. This work extended the procedures for investigating timeouts, yet the rate at which these responses were emitted exceeded the minimum required to avoid timeout. Most important, interspecies generality was further established in that the avoidance of timeout procedure was extended to human behavior. Using a similar procedure, Baer (1961) demonstrated that timeout contingent on a previously reinforced response produced a decrease in responding. This study extends the generality of his 1960 study by demonstrating that even a previously reinforced response would decrease in frequency if it produced timeout. Holz, Azrin, and Ayllon (1963) showed that human subjects would avoid timeout by responding on a manipulandum producing reinforcement when it was available as an alternative to the manipulandum producing timeout. This work replicated that of Ferster (1958) and extended the generality of his results in that Holz et al. (1963) used a fixed ratio schedule. Thomas (1964) conducted research that extended Ferster's (1958) work by demonstrating that different patterns of avoidance responding were a function of widely differing parameters of variable interval schedules. Interspecies generality of avoidance responding was extended to pigeons in the Thomas (1964) study.

The Ferster (1958) study also served as the basis for some research concerning pretimeout stimuli (Fig. 15.5). Ferster (1960) extended his 1958 work by investigating the effects of a 50-second pretimeout stimulus and found that the rate of responding decreased during its entire presentation, even though responses emitted during the last 5 seconds were the only responses that produced timeout. Results similar to those of Herrnstein (1955) and Ferster (1958) were obtained using a multiple schedule and varying

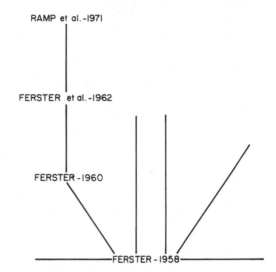

FIG. 15.5.   Pretimeout stimulus.

certain parameters of the pretimeout stimulus. Ferster, Appel, and Hiss (1962) found that a pretimeout stimulus increased the postreinforcement pause associated with fixed ratio schedules ranging from fixed ratio 85 to fixed ratio 250. In a second experiment, these authors demonstrated that low doses of several drugs resulted in increased response rates as the ratio requirement increased. These studies, in using pretimeout stimuli with fixed ratio schedules, replicated earlier work of Ferster (1958), Herrnstein (1955), and Ferster (1960). Ramp, Ulrich, and Dulaney (1971), working with a child, found that a 5-minute pretimeout stimulus immediately decreased disruptive behavior, even though the timeout itself was delayed. This study is a replication of previously mentioned studies concerning avoidance of timeout in that another value of the pretimeout stimulus duration was investigated; furthermore, interspecies generality was again estabished in extending this work to human behavior. Finally, the study by Ramp et al. (1971) represents the first instance in which a pretimeout stimulus was associated with a delayed consequence in a human behavioral engineering situation.

A number of studies addressed a variation of the timeout procedure with humans in which the reinforcer was physically removed (Fig. 15.6). Baer (1962) demonstrated that the contingent application of this form of timeout to thumbsucking decreased the rate of this response. The generality of Baer's 1961 results was extended in that the 1962 study used a novel response that produced timeout. In addition, the length of the timeout was not predetermined but simply equivalent to the duration of the target response. Tate and Baroff (1966) and Peterson and Peterson (1968) investigated the effects of timeout as a punisher to decrease self-injurious behavior in a psychotic and a retarded child, respectively. Both studies demonstrated that a

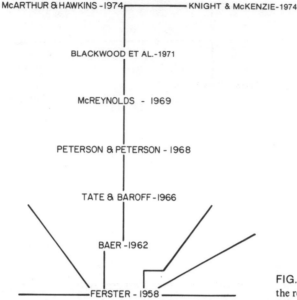

FIG. 15.6. Physical removal of the reinforcer.

decrease in such behaviors and a concomitant increase in non–self-destructive behaviors resulted from the contingent application of timeout. These two studies demonstrated generality of timeout procedures across experimental subjects and settings. In addition, generality of effective timeout stimuli was increased in that Tate and Baroff (1966) used withdrawal of physical contact, whereas Peterson and Peterson (1968) used food withdrawal.

The generality of the effect of timeout was further extended by its application to inappropriate speech (McReynolds, 1969), eating and vomiting (Blackwood, Horrocks, Keele, Hundziak, & Rettig, 1971), and out-of-seat behaviors (McArthur & Hawkins, 1974). In addition, these several authors investigated several different parameters of timeout from food reinforcement. Knight and McKenzie (1974) also punished thumbsucking with timeout from reading, thereby replicating the effects obtained by Baer (1962), who used timeout from viewing cartoons to decrease the same behavior. These two studies thus demonstrated the effectiveness of removing the opportunity to obtain conditioned reinforcers as a form of timeout. Also important to note in the Knight and McKenzie (1974) study is that timeout was applied by parents in the home, thereby demonstrating that the basic effect may be obtained by nonprofessionals. Finally, the studies presented in this section represent an important and often overlooked form of replication that occurs whenever a basic principle or procedure is successfully applied for therapeutic purposes.

Another group of studies investigated ignoring as a timeout from social reinforcement (Fig. 15.7). Timeout from certain forms of social reinforcement is naturally arranged when adults ignore instances of inappropriate behavior by children. Ignoring as timeout has been investigated in studies dealing with delusional speech (Richard, Dignam, & Horner, 1960); incorrect spelling and work habits (Zimmerman & Zimmerman, 1962); inappropriate crying, crawling, and isolate play (Harris, Johnston, Kelley, & Wolf, 1964); physical and verbal aggression (Brown & Elliott, 1965); inappropriate scratching (Allen & Harris, 1966); temper tantrums (Risley & Wolf, 1967); and incorrect responses to questions about magazine pictures (Barton, 1970). All of this research is thematically related to that of Ferster (1958), in that ignoring represents contingent removal or withdrawal of the opportunity to obtain positive reinforcement.

The demonstration that ignoring is effective as a timeout procedure with these various responses supports the general finding that timeout can be used as an effective punishment procedure. Furthermore, in these studies, timeout was applied either for the duration of the inappropriate response or for a

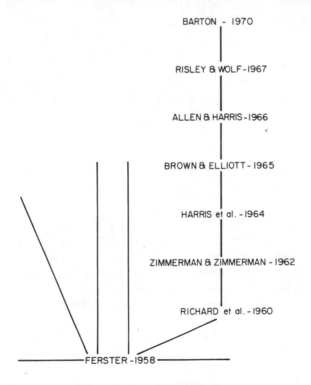

FIG. 15.7.   Ignoring as timeout.

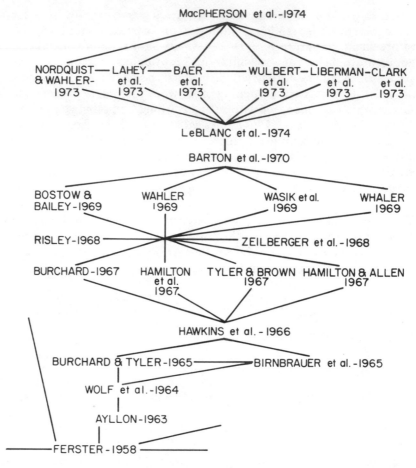

FIG. 15.8. Isolation as timeout.

predetermined period of time. That both procedures were effective adds support to the conclusion that timeout can be an effective punisher. Further generality of the effectiveness of timeout contributed by these studies arises from the fact that the studies were conducted in a variety of settings, often using parents as administrators of the timeout procedure.

The largest area of timeout literature concerns physical isolation of humans as a timeout procedure (Fig. 15.8).

The first instance in which timeout consisted of physicaly removing the human subject from a reinforcing situation was reported by Ayllon (1963). This study extended Ferster's (1958) procedure, which consisted of the contingent application of timeout for a specific response by again applying it to human behavior. In Ayllon's (1963) study, the inappropriate response (approaching another patient's table or eating unauthorized food) resulted in removal from the situation (dining room) for the remainder of the meal.

Several later studies used the physical removal of the subject, which terminated the opportunity to obtain positive reinforcement as a timeout in dealing with temper tantrums (Risley & Wolf, 1967; Wolf, Risley, & Mees, 1964); "unacceptable behavior" (Burchard & Tyler, 1965); general disruptive behavior (Baer, Rowbury, & Baer, 1973; Birnbrauer, Wolf, Kidder, & Tague, 1965; Burchard, 1967; Hamilton & Allen, 1967; MacPherson, Candee, & Hohman, 1974; Tyler & Brown, 1967); aggressive and/or oppositional behavior (Bostow & Bailey, 1969; Hawkins, Peterson, Schweid, & Bijou, 1966; Wahler, 1969a, b; Zeilberger, Sampen, & Sloane, 1968); inappropriate climbing (Risley, 1968); self-injurious and aggressive behavior (Hamilton, Stephens, & Allen, 1967); inappropriate mealtime behavior (Barton, Guess, Garcia, & Baer, 1970); autistic behavior (Nordquist & Wahler, 1973); failure to respond to questions (Wulbert, Nyman, Snow, & Owen, 1973); delusional speech (Liberman, Teigen, Patterson, & Baker, 1973); verbal tic (Lahey, McNees, & McNees, 1973); and aggressive behavior (Clark, Rowbury, Baer, & Baer, 1973; LeBlanc, Busby, & Thomson, 1974; Wasik, Senn, Welch, & Cooper, 1969).

The major commonality across all of these studies is that timeout consisted of removal of the subject from the setting. The effectiveness of this method of terminating reinforcing events further secures the generality of the effect of this timeout procedure. The generality of the general phenomenon of timeout is also extended in that timeout is shown to be effective for: (1) stimulus durations lasting from 1 minute to 3 hours; (2) different forms of isolation areas (e.g., classrooms, institutions, and homes); and (3) different agents who deliver timeout (e.g., parents, teachers, and therapists). It should also be noted that with the exception of four studies, all studies in this section involved concurrent reinforcement of appropriate behavior as part of the treatment procedure in order to facilitate a therapeutic goal.

The foundation trunk and the seven branch areas of research can be depicted as a tree showing the evolution of areas of research on this paradigm (Fig. 15.9).[7]

What is not immediately clear from our brief literature review is that all of the referenced studies are characterized by the same general approach to experimentation described in this volume. This means that there is an enormous amount of within-session, within-phase, and within-experiment replication that contributes greatly to the reliability and generality of this literature, as well as to the directions of ongoing development. The result is a body of discovered knowledge of considerable technological value that can trace its lineage directly to its basic science antecedents.

---

[7]Nowhere in the text of this section do we indulge in the variety of blatant clichés afforded by this metaphor. We have refrained from calling attention to the fruits of this tradition of research, the location of its roots in the lore of the animal laboratory, the unintended fertilizing effects of the outpourings of early critics, and even the fact that this section has added several leaves to this volume. We felt that to so indulge ourselves would be an instance of barking up the wrong tree.

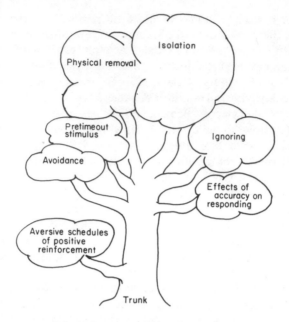

FIG. 15.9.   Areas of timeout research.

The extent of the replicative relations among studies in this literature was not fully known until this review, and many of the studies had no between-experiment replicative goals guiding their conception and conduct. However, because of their general adherence to the many facets of intrasubject design leading to clear functional relations, they have not only added greatly to our knowledge about timeout procedures but have illuminated the role of many other variables in the control of behavior. A similar group of 58 studies on any topic that used indirect measurement, intergroup design, and statistical analytical strategies would undoubtedly not have the same coherence and utility in both the laboratory and the field for the simple reason that the powerful role played by the cybernetic strategy of replication would necessarily be largely absent. The dimensions of replication outlined earlier can be realized only in the context of the entire array of methods addressed in this volume.

Part IV INTERPRETATION

16 Display of Data

Artists can colour the sky red because they know it's blue. Those of us who aren't artists must colour things the way they really are or people might think we're stupid.

—Jules Feiffer

INTRODUCTION

In popular usage, the word *data* refers to something given in the form of facts upon which an inference may be based. As such, bits of general information or imprecise statements resulting from some form of observation are often referred to as data. In any experimental science, however, the term *data* is typically reserved for the quantitative results of deliberate, planned, usually controlled observation. In other words, data result when scientific measurements are made in the context of some plan or design that is generated for the explicit purpose of inspecting some phenomenon or event. Data are therefore the quantitative manifestation of variability, whether natural or imposed, that is characteristic of all phenomena and that it is the business of science to explain.

In virtually all scientific endeavors, data in raw form consist of recorded results of observations—measurements made in accordance with a specified procedure and expressed in the form of numbers and units. In this form, data serve only one purpose: documentation. They exist in a permanent fashion after measurement has ceased and are available for off-line examination and analysis. In raw form, data are an important, but by no means the final, product of the process of scientific measurement. In order that their ultimate value may be realized, data must be processed, analyzed, and interpreted. It is the purpose of this chapter to begin discussing strategies and tactics for accomplishing this task.

Displaying data is a process of transforming the factual output of any investigation into stimuli whose function is to influence interpretative behavior. Not only raw data but also the results of any quantitative manipulation are transformed into some form of visual display that will serve as a stimulus both for the investigator and eventually an audience. It is crucial to remember that this transformation in no way changes the observed facts, and to the extent that variability is created through display techniques, it is purely illusory (see Chapter 11). Unfortunately, this aspect of the scientific endeavor receives only cursory attention in the formal training of behavioral scientists, perhaps because an adequate appreciation of the stimulus value of behavioral data for a wide range of extrascientific human behavior (e.g., policy-setting, administration, etc.) is only beginning to emerge. In other words, the facts and principles uncovered by a science of behavior will not by themselves influence any significant social or technological improvements. Data will contribute only to this end to the extent that they are composed into effective stimuli that help prompt actions that may eventually contact reinforcement in the form of demonstrable human benefit. A full discussion of the strategies and tactics underlying the creation of such stimuli is undertaken in the present chapter from the perspective of creating displays to influence the behavior, first of the experimenter and later, the audience.

STRATEGIES OF DISPLAY

Chronology

Scientists rarely respond directly to a natural phenomenon in a pure form; they respond to their data that are the result of the transformation engendered by measurement. The guiding strategy is to arrange for the data to present a configuration that, in the context of certain rules and conventions, accurately represents the measured natural event so that the effect produced on the interpretative behavior of researchers and their colleagues will faithfully reflect the generality of the event in question.

The role of data display therefore becomes most critical during the actual course of experimentation, because the interpretations that the investigator makes then may completely determine the scientific value of the results of the experiment. For this reason, highly sophisticated recording equipment is often mated with analogic display devices to provide the researcher with a real-time picture of the course of change in the phenomenon under investigation. Familiar examples of this tactic include the use of instruments for continuously monitoring vital systems in space flight, EEG recording polygraphs, and the cumulative response recorder. Mention was made earlier of the importance Pavlov attached to such equipment; provision of an on-line record of the saliva drop count allowed him to switch tactics in midexperiment as an unexpected result appeared that required different experimental tactics for analysis. Skinner also frequently commented on the value of the on-line cumulative record in providing a visual display of the course of behavior change during an experiment. As was the case with Pavlov, the availability of records of this type enabled Skinner to make timely adjustments in experimental procedures in response to characteristics of the data, thus maximizing the amount of information obtained per unit of experimental time and resources invested.

The importance of creating on-line data displays in assisting experimental decision–making becomes even more obvious when contrasted with the more conventional tactic requiring the investigator to await not only completion of the experiment but also a vast data reduction and statistical analysis before learning if the experimental hypothesis was confirmed. In view of the extraordinary investment of time and money that may predate a questionable or disconfirming result, it is not uncommon to observe heroic efforts at statistical resuscitation, followed, in the less fortunate cases, by extensive eulogizing either in the form of ritualistic recitation of the complexities surrounding behavioral research or reaffirmation of the general utility of the theory despite its embarrassment in the instant case. Investigators who have the opportunities to be influenced by their data as they are being produced hardly ever find themselves in this predicament. The data have more likely guided them in a series of on-line experimental decisions so that by the end of the experiment, the basic outcome is already relatively well established. At worst, this tactic may show them at an early stage that sufficient control is lacking to justify continued data collection until better control is established. They can then discontinue data collection, cut their losses in time and resources, and retool for more successful assaults. Under more auspicious conditions, however, they will revise experimental plans in light of whatever empirical exigencies emerge and proceed to an unambiguous and informative experimental conclusion.

Upon completion of data collection in an experiment, the data await further transformation into the variety of stimuli that will help determine the investigator's interpretations and conclusions. At this stage, quantitative summarization should occur concurrently with the creation of visual displays that pictorially amplify the information emerging from the quantification. It is at this point that investigators can and should indulge themselves in the luxury that their labors have afforded them: the opportunity to ask questions of data that did not previously exist. This should be a very private time, a time of intimacy wherein the procreator can leisurely explore every hidden detail and nuance of the progeny without ever having to make public any fantasies, insights, or misguided curiosities. It is also the time at which most great discoveries are either made or confirmed. It is tragic that most inexperienced investigators, in their zeal to obtain an answer to the original research question, never create the opportunity to savor the rich and fulfilling experience of a complete, unhurried interaction with one's data. As in amorous foreplay, the process of exploring one's data should proceed from the general to the particular, aided at every step by enhanced visualization. In particular, the results of each quantitative manipulation should be immediately graphed or charted and the result studied for clues as to the next step that should be taken in the process of total discovery. A coherent interpretation begins to take form as the investigator tests each succeeding rendering for consistency with its predecessors. "Well, if that's true, then we should see thus-and-such if we plot the data this way" typifies the verbal behavior that usually accompanies this process. The excitement produced by each successive confirmation or suggested revision of interpretations indicates the nature of the reinforcement that surrounds the creative act. This is especially true when a discovery is made that is so contrary to expectation that it occasions immediate planning for replication in anticipation of a whole new avenue of research.

When this private process has been completed, the researcher will have produced a series of visual displays that permit recapitulating the interpretative process for an audience. This is done by selecting from among these the ones that most clearly illustrate both the reasoning process and the features of the data that support the conclusions. Extreme care must be taken at this point, however, to ensure objectivity and rigor. The careful researcher uses the data to test as many alternative explanations as can be proffered, discarding each only after being convinced of its unworthiness. By actually daring nature to disprove a conjecture, an investigator can achieve far greater confidence in the correctness of any eventual interpretation than would result from accepting as satisfactory the first and only explanation suggested, even though the experiment may have been designed to confirm the correctness of that explanation. In the not uncommon event that the originally favored explanation fails to completely dominate each and every rival, it is incumbent on the researcher to report this fact rather than conceal it. Only if this principle is scrupulously adhered to can nature be allowed to communicate fully through the medium of experimentation. Filters imposed in the form of ill-conceived theories whose prosperity is given priority over discovery only serve to retard and confuse our efforts to discern order in the natural phenomena that captured our interest in the first place.

Finally, the time comes when the results of the research are to be reported to a wider audience. Issues surrounding this event are discussed more fully in a later chapter, but it is important to reiterate that stimuli will be created that are intended to influence the behavior of other people, often remotely in time. The nature of the eventual reaction is much easier to predict if the reaction to certain of the display components has been previously established. For that reason, standardization of the formats of data display in the behavioral sciences should be encouraged, much as it has generally come to be required in the older sciences. Standard calibration of deflections and paper speeds, for example, allow viewers of EEG records from any laboratory to respond directly to the data without first having to construct a unique interpretative context in response to a singular or unorthodox display format. The efficiency and effectiveness of communication among the early investigators of animal operant behavior was probably due in large measure to the standard nature of the cumulative records that were generated. Because the strategy is to encourage responses to the unique characteristics of the data rather than to the novelty of the display format, one tactic for ensuring that outcome is to preclude the occurrence of responses to extraneous novel stimuli by excluding such stimuli from the total display context. To the extent that standardization induces familiarity with the format, it enhances the discriminability of the novel and salient aspects of the data, and the aims of communication are better served.

Summarizing Data

Assuming that the researcher adopts the strategy of arranging for the data to communicate all of which they are capable, it is usually best to begin by arranging the raw data in sequential order of their collection. This step from on-line to off-line inspection does not involve distorting the data, only transforming the temporal dimension of the experiment. Care should be taken to keep the transformed temporal dimension intact in the event the subjects were not measured simultaneously. Now the experimenter looks for evidence of any time-dependent effects, including those associated with the introduction of the various treatment procedures. At the same time, the experimenter should be looking for evidence of effects other than those anticipated and noting whether they hold for all subjects, treatments, and so on, or occur only with special combinations of the various independent variables. Already, questions for future research will begin to take form, particularly if one or two odd configurations emerge from a large but otherwise orderly display. This may be the only opportunity the investigator has to ask, "I wonder what made that happen?" for soon summarizing will begin, concomitantly destroying the little nuances that are the protoplasm of serendipity.

As summarizing begins, information inevitably starts being lost. This is true even if the summarizing only involves transforming the data of a single session into a single data point. This loss of information is expected and poses no dangers providing that: (1) the information that is lost is redundant with the information that is retained; (2) no information of value is inadvertently or mechanically discarded; and (3) new information of an artifactual nature is not created and allowed to exert control over the investigator's behavior. Almost without exception, the process of summarizing involves combining data that were previously distinct into composites dictated by the investigator's conception of the relative importance of the several dimensions of the experiment. For example, continuous real time records may be condensed within an experimental phase and displayed against larger continuous time units such as the hour, day, or week. At this step, the variations in moment-to-moment responding become lost in the computed summary measure for each arbitrarily selected period of time. Presumably, the researcher has inspected the records in fine detail and has concluded that nothing of value is sacrificed by this consolidation and that something of value may be gained by inspecting the array with a different level of optic resolution. A next step might be to collapse the data across subjects in order to examine the effects of the treatments with any variation due to subject differences removed from the display. As discussed in the following chapter, it is imperative that at each step a measure of the discarded variability be obtained and displayed and that the data be preserved in their raw state so that a reconstruction can take place if ever required.

The researcher who successively collapses and displays the data in terms of decreasing numbers of determining characteristics will finally approach a display involving only the major variables of interest with all else having been subsumed by the process of combination. It is imperative at this point to select one of the original records and make a simultaneous comparison with the summarized display. If there is less than close similarity between the two, there may be good reason to believe that valuable descriptive information has been lost in the process of summarizing and that the propriety of the final display as a stimulus for interpretation may be questionable. The degree of similarity required is ultimately a matter for the experimenter's judgment. However, to the extent that the summarized display prompts interpretations of limited generality, that shortcoming will eventually be revealed by failure of an expected replication. Usually, one or two natural parameters of the data (subjects, sex, age, location, etc.) will turn out to have played a larger role in determining the variability of the data than was originally anticipated, and the data should be resummarized and redisplayed against this parameter. In all likelihood, recasting the data in this fashion will suggest the operation of an interaction among treatment and uncontrolled variables that may limit the generality of interpretation of the immediate results, but will certainly suggest the direction of the next experiment.

Selecting Representative Data

The process of summarizing data has thus far been discussed as an essentially private activity that is useful for gaining an interpretative perspective on the overall outcome of the experiment. It should *not* be assumed that the graphic results of this summarizing process constitute the best or only stimuli available for presentation to audiences. In fact, for this purpose, the tactic of selecting typical or representative records should be given *first* consideration. Such records preserve the nuances and irregularities of the phenomenon as directly measured in time and better represent the actual, observed empirical relations than a summary ever could. Presenting individual records is an especially convincing way of demonstrating that the experimental result is not the product of statistical averaging but is descriptive of the single case. The laws of behavior are statements of the relations between individual organisms and the environment, and any display resulting from a summary across individuals necessarily obscures or distorts the details of those relations. This remains true even when the summarized data show a "clearer" and more consistent effect than is detectable in the records of the majority of the subjects. A weak and inconsistent treatment effect can be strengthened only by manipulation of the experimental environment, not by *post hoc* manipulation of inadequate data. There is also considerable merit in presenting representative single records when communication with a relatively naive audience whose beliefs about behavioral processes are too often shaped by smoothed curves that are rarely encountered in nature.

In selecting typical records for display, a process of classification, even a taxonomy, is presupposed. The dimensions of this taxonomy may be imposed by the parameters of the experiment (e.g., levels of the independent variables) or they may emerge by induction on the basis of obvious characteristics of the records. In either case, a representative from *each* major taxonomic subdivision should be selected and its degree of representativeness of others in that category should be described, quantitatively if possible. For example, if the records group naturally into three categories with some showing the treatment effect very clearly, others giving evidence of it against a background of uncontrolled variation, and the remainder being uninterpretable, one record from each category should be selected for display.

The selection process is usually simplified if a small number of subjects are involved. The large number of records resulting from measurement on each subject over many sessions can then be classified in the manner described and representative instances selected. The careful reader will note that selection is conducted with regard to individual records, not individual subjects, unless for some reason only one record exists for each subject. An individual record may be defined as the result for one subject of one experimental session, one treatment phase, or the entire experiment; only in the latter case will the number of individual records and individual subjects be identical.

How does one describe and measure the degree to which the selected record represents the category from which it was chosen? For a long list of reasons, inferential statistics is ill-suited to this task, although it is possible that a goodness of fit technique could be devised that would be of some utility. A better procedure is to display range indicators (see Fig. 16.14), which portray the extremes of the collection and against which a visual comparison of the selected record is sufficient to communicate representativeness. Another method involves displaying a summary record for comparison with the individual record, but this can be easily abused if the summary record is used to guide the search for the "representative" individual record. If there is much variation among the records in the collection, the summary record may not resemble more than one or two individual records, and selecting one of them as representative would clearly be inappropriate. This error can be avoided if the individual record is selected independently on the basis of its similarity to the other records and then, if necessary, compared to the summary as a means of showing the extent to which all of the records are similar so that the composite closely resembles any individual. Accordingly, any summary display should only be used for a supplementary function and should not constitute the basis for any more than the briefest textual reference.

Discarding Data

When readying data for analysis and display, one may encounter a record of a session or an entire collection of records from a single subject that may legitimately be discarded from further consideration (see also Sidman, 1960). Research data are the property of the researcher, the subjects, and, arguably, the sponsor of the investigation. They are not in any sense the property of the scientific community until and unless a decision is reached to so confer them in the form of a publication. Throughout this discussion, emphasis has been placed on the conversion of raw data into stimuli that will first guide the investigator's interpretative behavior and perhaps later influence a larger audience. Investigators have a solemn obligation to themselves and to their discipline to ensure that their interpretations reflect the real state of nature with as little error as possible. In all decisions made throughout the conduct of the research, they should act to eliminate as many distracting, extraneous influences on interpretation as possible; this principle is not excepted at the stage of data display and analysis. Thus, irregular data can and should be discarded, provided the researcher does so with the conviction that nothing of potential value is thereby lost and the decision is reported and explained. For example, if an equipment malfunction, illness of the subject, unplanned modification of a drug regimen, etc., imposes sufficient extraneous variability as to render that portion of the data wholly incomparable with those collected under planned conditions, the investigator may properly exclude those data from further consideration. Of course, the aberrant data must not be of greater value than the remainder, for if they are, there should be an immediate attempt to replicate their effects, putting aside the original experiment. However, when this is not the case, contaminated data should not be allowed to confuse the investigator in the performance of the interpretative task, already more complicated than most people can easily comprehend. Nor should the investigator feel any obligation to burden the audience with pictures, descriptions, and accounts of such findings; it is usually sufficient to mention their existence and their fate.

It is important to complete the above perspective by describing its balancing accompaniment: If unplanned events occur during the experiment that must cast serious doubts on the meaning of the data, then the implicated records should be omitted from further analytical consideration *even if* they show no ill effects or comport with the experimenter's preferences. The general rule that covers both kinds of circumstances may be stated thusly: Whenever extraneous events transpire that seem to influence the responding of any subject, the affected portions of the records (or perhaps, the entire records) should not be communicated to a larger audience if the likely effect will be to detract from the accuracy and generality of interpretations, regardless of the extent to which such interpretations may match the investigator's preconceptions.

These considerations can never be used to justify the investigator's picking through the data to find the instances confirming expectations while blithely discarding the rest as being due to uncontrollable factors, even though these may be partially specifiable. "We'll throw George's data out because I don't think he liked the assistant, and anyway, his records look sort of funny," is not an excusable practice if the fact that George's data "look funny" cannot be unambiguously linked to a distinct difference in experimental protocol, however accidental. It is quite possible that the other subjects did not like the assistant either, and discarding George's data on the basis of such a specious rationalization will serve only to obscure the fact that less experimental generality was actually realized than will appear to be the case from inspecting the remaining individual records. As a result, a finding might be propounded that is impossible to replicate simply because the uncontrolled variable that made George's data "look funny" occurs with substantial frequency and must be controlled if the experimental effect is to be repeated. If such data are numerous and explainable, it is a sign that poor experimental control was operating, and an improved replication should be undertaken prior to any dissemination. Again, the experimenter can make this decision privately and should feel no obligation to publicize any findings until convinced of their merit and accuracy. Difficult though it may be to admit that an experimental effort failed for lack of sufficient control, it is far more difficult and costly to trace this source of confusion backward through time after an unreplicable result becomes part of the scientific literature. The inherent, self-correcting nature of science need not be overburdened by tolerating or encouraging abdication of responsible judgment prior to propagation of results.

As a postscript to this discussion of discarding data, we acknowledge that many readers may recoil in disbelief that such a practice would ever be condoned under any circumstances. There is an honored tradition of full disclosure in the social sciences, spawned in part by a well-nurtured sense of mistrust that is probably inspired by the advocacy nature of much social science research. In the context of this style of interpretation, the flawed character of the underlying measurement strategies and the persistent refusal to deploy adequate experimental controls become even more painfully obvious. The only relief for this discomfort is a spurious show of "total honesty," which cloaks the practice of presenting the bad with the good, usually indiscriminately. Because of the extraordinary value placed on honesty in the extrascientific culture, this strategy is rewarded at the expense of methodological refinement that would render honesty of the investigator incidental as a standard for evaluating scientific findings. The criteria of reproducibility and generality necessarily presuppose honest reporting of data but also impose methodological standards and practices that honesty alone cannot satisfy.

TACTICS OF DISPLAY

After considering what aspects of the data are to constitute the material for display, a general decision regarding display format must be reached. Basically, one can arrange quantitative data in either tabular or graphic form. There are numerous advantages and disadvantages associated with each tactic that should be considered as the investigator proceeds.

Tabular Format

Usually, the easiest way to arrange data for visual display is in tabular form. Measures or summary measures are grouped in accordance with the structure of the natural parameters of the experiment, and the result is viewed and interpreted. Creating tables is usually a good first step in the transformation process, for it leaves the data in raw form (unless already transformed from an analogic state) that is nevertheless convenient for subsequent manipulation and rearrangement. Tabular format is also excellent for purposes of data storage, because considerable spatial condensation can take place without loss of information, particularly with the aid of microfilm or microfiche. Many computer information storage and retrieval systems are designed for the purpose of filing data in tabular format, and the investigator who keeps hard tabular copy of data in exactly the format in which it is stored in the computer is well prepared to interpret the results of any computer-generated summary.

In addition to its storage advantages, a tabular format is convenient as a visual display for presenting a large amount of data to which frequent reference will be made in an oral or written discussion. It is especially suitable for presenting information that is purely descriptive as opposed to relational; descriptive characteristics of subjects (age, sex, years of institutionalization, etc.) and experimental procedures (sequence of treatments, values of independent variables, sessions times, etc.) can often be concisely communicated in a table, avoiding lengthy and tedious prose. It is also customary to present the results of complex statistical reductions in tabular form; there even exists within some disciplines a modicum of standardization regarding the presentation of such results.

Unfortunately, data presented in tabular format are robbed of most of their potency as a stimulus for subtle interpretative responses. Although tables facilitate inspecting large quantities of data, they almost necessarily preclude detecting relations (e.g., temporal) in the data, other than in very simple cases (such as when two columns of numbers are shown and both are constantly increasing). Even then, only the presence of a correlation is detectable; the form of the correlating function can be surmised only crudely, if at all. If, however, the form is unimportant, but there is a need to communicate exact corresponding values, a tabular array such as is often used to convert Fahrenheit temperature to Celsius presents the information in the form most convenient for visual processing.

Graphic Format

Detecting relations in the data or between the data and the independent variables almost always requires that the information be displayed in the form of a chart or graph. This format communicates relations most efficiently, providing care is taken to eliminate certain sources of distortion that are often unintentionally allowed to operate. The essence of any graphic display involves arranging representations (dots, lines, bars, etc.) of the data in such a manner that the intended relations are manifested by the spatial arrangement of the components of the display. However, histories of reinforcement with respect to visual stimuli then tend to predispose certain responses, whether or not such responses are justified by the data. It is, therefore, relatively easy to wittingly or unwittingly create displays that spatially misrepresent the relations of interest to an extent sufficient to invite or guarantee misinterpretation. Anyone making or viewing a graphic display should question every interpretation made on its basis in this light: "Is this interpretation warranted by the data or am I merely responding to a suggestion inherent in the spatial characteristics of the display itself?" Examples of such misinterpretations are described later in connection with each decision that must be made in preparing such displays.

In considering problems of representativeness of data displays, the reader should remember that the only veridical perception of a behavioral event occurs at the moment of observation. All renderings of such events in the form of data are the result of one or more transformation processes that must inevitably make their own contribution, however slight, to the viewer's reaction. This is especially the case in the conversion from numerical to spatial representation, when error is usually introduced and some information present in the data is likely to be lost. At the very least, transforming numbers into plotted graphic symbols incurs a loss of precision that is inversely proportional to the sensitivity of the scale, coarseness of the symbol, accuracy of the plotting technique, etc. It is certainly possible to process substantial amounts of data by this means, although the accuracy of interpretations can be severely compromised by the inevitable control exerted by each display. If, however, both creator and viewer are alert to these possibilities and carefully consider the influence of each of the decisions made in the course of preparing a visual display, graphic techniques can be highly effective as a medium of communication. These decisions, together with the caveats surrounding each, arise as each component of the graphic display is selected and are easily discussed in terms of the major components of every graphic display.

Horizontal Axis.   Most graphic presentations make use of the Cartesian convention (actually introduced by Hipparchus) of representing two dimensions by a pair of intersecting perpendicular lines.[1] The horizontal member of the pair is known as the x-axis and is traditionally used to represent the independent variable if a functional relation is to be displayed. In any display relating a measure of behavior to values of some experimental

---

[1]The terms *abscissa* and *ordinate* are often inappropriately used in the social sciences to refer to such lines. In proper mathematical usage, the term *abscissa* represents the first element of ordered two-tuples (x_i, y_i) in the case of two-dimensional representations. It is properly designated as representing the coordinates of the arguments, or domain values, of any functional relation. The ordinate designates the range (second) value of the two-tuple. Thus, the proper terms for describing the perpendicular dimensions of a space are its *axes, horizontal* and *vertical,* and the terms abscissa and ordinate refer to values located thereon.

variable, the latter would usually be found on the horizontal axis. Two decisions must be made with respect to the horizontal axis: What type of scale should be used and how long it should be.

The scale selected will ordinarily be of the equal-interval type such that addition of a constant value is represented by a constant distance along the scale. Familiar examples include number of training sessions, amount of reinforcement available, and time. Occasionally, the independent variable in the experiment will be varied in accordance with a geometric progression (2, 4, 8, 16, etc.), and this poses a display problem. If an equal interval scale is used, the first few points will be tightly bunched whereas the last ones will be widely spaced, giving less visual emphasis to the change accompanying each increment in the independent variable near the high end.

A common solution involves using a logarithmic scale that is, again, equal interval, but the intervals represent powers of values in the original dimension. Figure 16.1 shows the same data displayed against the alternate horizontal axes. The reader is invited to ignore the scales and interpret each relation as though the scale information were not available. Clearly, one sees very different patterns depending on which scale is chosen, yet the data remain the same. Will the interpretation be the same?

If a logarithmic scale is selected, how should that fact be communicated? One can identify points along the scale in terms of their actual values (Fig. 16.2, Panel A) and hope the viewer detects the absence of correspondence between equal visual and quantitative intervals, or one can label the units as log values (Panel B) and rely on the viewer's history of high school algebra to implement the translation back to "real" values. There is a possibility of misinterpretation either way, but, assuming nothing about the viewer's specialized history, it is probably wiser to exhibit the values in actual rather than logarithmic terms. The logarithmic property has been displayed by equal

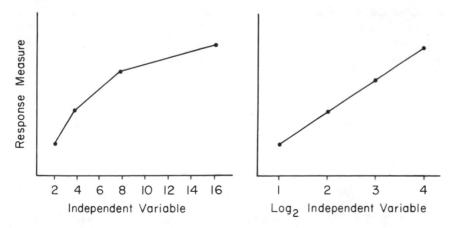

FIG. 16.1. Identical hypothetical data plotted against equal inverval and power-scaled *x*-axis.

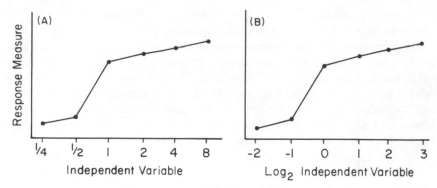

FIG. 16.2.   Labeling logarithmic *x*-axes.

interval positioning of the real values and need not be displayed twice,
whereas not displaying the real values at all is more nearly akin to omitting
information.

Special and serious problems arise when time is the dimension exhibited on
the horizontal axis. Not only is time a continuum, it is a parameter of every
experiment that cannot be arbitrarily lengthened or shortened. Moreover,
any change that is observed in the dependent variable must occur as a
function of time, no matter what else may have been responsible.
Consequently, representing the temporal dimension of an experiment *should
involve only decisions about the length of time line and the unit represented
by each interval,* nothing more. The importance of the decision concerning
the length of the line is illustrated in Fig. 16.3 in which, again, the amount of
change represented can be made to appear large or small, depending on the
unit selected and the space afforded it.

A common though totally unjustified practice consists of putting
discontinuities or inequalities in the representation of time, possibly to
conserve space. As laudable as this intention may be in these days of

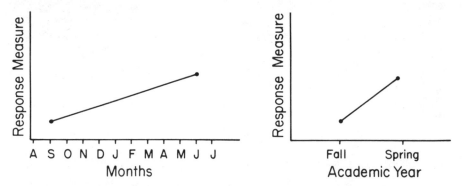

FIG. 16.3.   Contraction or expansion of time unit alters visual impact of
change.

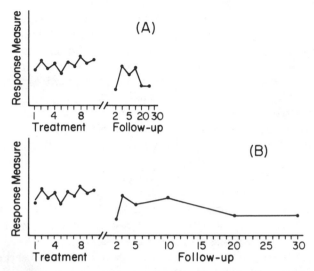

FIG. 16.4.   Discontinuity of time representation on the horizontal axis.

uncertainty concerning the ultimate role of forests in our society, such interests are often better served by the decision not to publish rather than to publish an unwitting distortion. Figure 16.4 shows how the subtle imposition of a discontinuity in the time line (Panel A) can influence interpretation of the course of behavioral change through time. The interpretation one is likely to render concerning the stability and trend evident in the follow-up data is considerably different depending on which version one encounters. The superiority of the version in Panel B shows time in the follow-up phase being represented as it actually passed, and a more accurate, though perhaps less persuasive, story is told.

A variation of this practice involves a far more subtle and difficult to detect source of distortion. Events that occurred in time but did not occur at equal temporal intervals are often presented along an x-axis scaled in terms of the cardinality of the events, ignoring the location of their occurrence in real time. Such dimensions as "Sessions," "Trials," and "Blocks" must necessarily occur serially in real time, yet the tacit assumption is often encouraged that variations in the real time intervals separating successive occurrences are of no importance in interpreting the nature of any observed variation. Though usually unintentional, presentation of such a display is tantamount to an act of almost unpardonable experimental grandiosity, for it implies that any time-dependent influences that could have been operating were either of such negligible consequence or so well controlled that no loss in interpretation could result from distortion of the represented time dimension. Put another way, the purveyor of such a display is asserting that the only variable with which the viewer need be concerned is the displayed treatment variable, variation in it being sufficient to account for all experimental variation that might be of interest. In the event that the viewer is also the investigator, this practice is likely to limit access to sources of variation that might prove instructive or illuminating. In the event the viewer is a member of the scientific community who has no other access to the data, this practice may properly be viewed as highly misleading, if not actually deceptive.

In its worst form, the practice of distorting the real time dimension is concealed by assigning a time unit to intervals along the x-axis and allowing the continuity of the dimension to impart the impression that obervation and measurement were continuous with respect to that unit. Thus, a horizontal axis labeled "Days" with the demarcations labeled consecutively and a data point presented corresponding to each almost demands the inference that measurement occurred every day throughout the period. Inspection of the text will often reveal that such was not the case and that a correct label for the axis would be "Successive days of observation" or a similar phrase, hinting at the fact that observation was not continuous, in spite of appearances to the contrary. Regardless of labels, however, presenting data distorted in this manner can only invite the interpretation that the investigator is either uncommonly careless or intent on prompting responses from the audience not warranted by the actual condition of the data. In either case, judgments concerning the findings should probably be suspended pending replotting against properly constructed axes.

Of considerable importance in relation to the issue of continuity of a temporal axis is selection of the unit of time by which the axis will be subdivided. Discontinuities can be made continuous by selecting a larger unit, the rule being that at least one period of observation must have occurred during each interval for continuity to be preserved. Thus, if observation occurs only on weekdays, but occurs at least once each week, the time dimension should be labeled "Weeks," not "Days," unless blank spaces are left in the records to correspond to weekends or any other days on which

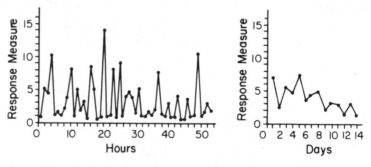

FIG. 16.5. Eliminating discontinuity among hourly measures (left) by replotting against the real time continuum of days (right). Note the appearance of the previously hidden decreasing trend.

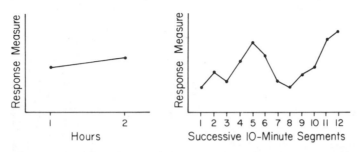

FIG. 16.6.   Hypothetical pattern of data revealed in plot against 10-minute periods that is obscured in the hourly plot.

measurement did not occur. Unfortunately, selecting a larger time unit carries an attendant loss in resolving power, because data will have to be pooled from the incomplete set of sampled smaller time units within each of the larger units.

The effect of such loss of resolution is illustrated in Fig. 16.5, in which the change from hours to days invites a vastly different interpretation. The hypothetical investigator's intent when presenting the data in the left-hand panel of Fig. 16.5 may have been to suggest the absence of any systematic trend over time as a result of efforts to establish steady state. Suppose that the hourly plots in Fig. 16.5 are based on four, spaced 1-hour observation sessions per day. Displaying them in the manner shown invites the conclusion that observation and recording were continuous over a 54-hour period, when, in fact, the only continuous dimensional unit available is days, because observation took place on 14 consecutive days. Replotting against the appropriate real time continuum was done by averaging the hourly measures for each day, and the data reveal a decreasing trend that is not obvious in the hourly plot. Had the investigator wished to retain the sensitivity of the hourly display, the hourly measures should have been plotted against a continuum of the 336 possibe hours of observation in the 14-day period depicted. The display would then reveal a decreasing trend despite the presence of what appear to be large gaps in the data. The practice of intermittently sampling behavior and then presenting the sample measures in a configuration that suggests continuity not only fails to restore completeness to the measurement procedure, but provides a false picture of what may actually have occurred over time. To the extent that concern is with measurement and analysis of behavior change over time, such practices are obviously self-defeating.

Data should initially be displayed against the smallest time unit that is likely to show systematic variability, even if accurate display requires that gaps be left corresponding to periods of nonobservation. Figure 16.6 shows how a systematic, orderly relation emerges when the scale is shifted from hours to 10-minute periods. Although these data are hypothetical, they illustrate the manner in which orderly variation can be detected by an

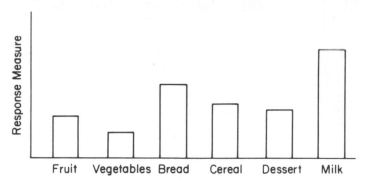

FIG. 16.7. Plot of hypothetical data showing correct designation of a horizontal axis that has no obvious underlying dimension.

adjustment in the resolving power of the display format. This example also illustrates the use of arbitrary shifts in magnification of the temporal dimension. Shifting from one representation per hour to one every 10 minutes increases the sensitivity by a factor of six, a smaller step than would be taken if a smaller unit such as the minute were selected.

In general, the time unit should be made smaller and smaller (the magnification increased) until either the white space becomes overwhelming or the variability observed appears essentially random. This process strongly suggests the metaphor of the microscope; increasing the power of the lens often reveals orderly phenomena that are not visible at lower powers, whereas further increases may not show anything at all. Of course, at any level of resolution, whether or not anything will be observed depends on the existence of something to be observed and the extent to which the original measurement procedure was sensitive enough to detect it. For this reason, it is recommended that whenever possible, continuous observing and recording of behavior be arranged so that the finest level of resolution will already exist to serve as a point of departure.

There are, of course, times when the horizontal axis of a graphic display corresponds to a discontinuous dimension, and that fact should be communicated clearly by the construction. For example, when performance in different tasks is being compared and there is no underlying dimension (such as difficulty) along which the tasks are ordered, they should be portrayed as separate, clearly disconnected pieces of the horizontal axis, as shown in Fig. 16.7. Having so constructed and labeled the axis, the investigator will be less likely to succumb to the temptation of connecting the symbols with straight lines, thus again suggesting continuity where it does not in fact exist.

Vertical Axis.   The series of decisions concerning how to display the dependent variable (behavioral) measures on the vertical or *y*-axis are no less

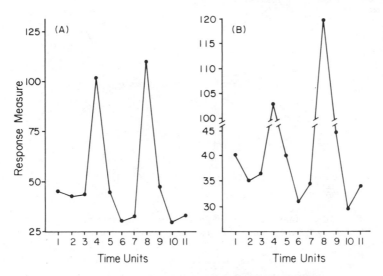

FIG. 16.8.   Comparison of two displays of variability.

important than those discussed previously for the horizontal axis. Selecting and designing the vertical axis determines to a great extent how clearly the variability, whether uncontrolled or imposed, is portrayed. Although a number of choices are available, by far the most common practice is to portray the dependent variable along an equal interval additive scale. The data set is usually inspected for minimum and maximum values, the range is computed, a line is drawn whose length stands in a 5:8 ratio to the length of the horizontal axis, the endpoints are labeled with a bracketing minimum at the origin and the maximum at the opposite end, and the scale is divided into equal units by some convenient additive factor. The data are then plotted and the display inspected. If it should happen that all but a few of the values lie at the low end of the scale, the scale may be "broken" and the resolution of the segments enlarged to provide a closer look at variability. Figure 16.8 illustrates this situation before and after such a fracture is made.

In Panel A of Fig. 16.8, the full scale is presented to encompass the range of values (28–117) represented in the data set. The two points corresponding to ordinate values of 103 and 117 deviate from the range of the remainder, which has 45 as the upper limit. The space required to accommodate these discrepant values is approximately five times that occupied by the others, hence the visual portrayal of the variability exhibited by the others is somewhat compressed. Breaking the vertical axis, as in Panel B, magnifies the lower portion of the figure, but destroys the relational portrayal of all values in the set. It is inherent in the nature of additive scales that compromises are often necessary between full-range display and local sensitivity. Frustrations engendered by this limitation should not be relieved by arbitrarily dissecting

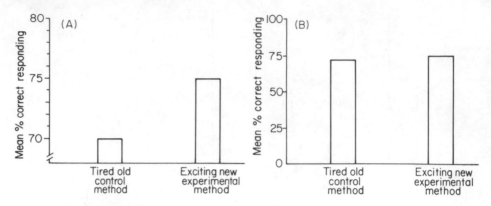

FIG. 16.9. Inappropriate magnification of an experimental result by restricting the range on the vertical axis (A) and representation against full percentage scale (B).

out "unnecessary" portions of the axis, as in Panel B, because the dimensional integrity of the dependent variable is requisite to an accurate portrayal of variability.

The reader should also note that the origin of Fig. 16.8 is the point $(t_1, 25)$. It is a common but unnecessary practice to locate the origin at the special point $(0, 0)$ and then "break" the y-axis to display the first value at the bracketing minimum. In fact, the origin of a two-dimensional Cartesian display can be drawn to coincide with any two-tuple in the space, and all other points may be automatically located in accordance with the metric of the space. In the usual case of two additive dimensions, the display portrays the *differences* among point coordinates, and the location of the origin is wholly arbitrary. Therefore, the practice of rigidly setting the origin at $(0, 0)$, then breaking the axes to induce sensitivity within the range of observed values should be discouraged in favor of direct portrayal of the chosen origin, whatever its coordinates (as in Fig. 16.8).

After a decision has been made as to what properties of the data are to be publicly displayed, the scale is often arbitrarily selected so that the difference of major interest appears almost to exhaust the capability of the scale to contain it. A common example of this mode of presentation is shown in the left panel of Fig. 16.9, which shows how the experimenter hopes the viewer will regard the benefit of the new teaching technique that is being propounded.

This practice is an extreme abuse of the experimenter's responsibility to select a scale that portrays obtained results with some reference to an external context of meaning and utility. An educational innovation that induces an improvement of only 5% should not be made to appear bigger than it is; in spite of the shortcomings of percentage measures discussed elsewhere, percentages do derive from a more or less standard scale and it can be argued that a 5% change should occupy 1/20 of the available dimension. In other contexts, a change of +5 in magnitude may warrant full-scale representation, particularly if that value approaches the upper limit of the possible increase.

The prevalence of display practices that rely on arbitrary and idiosyncratic selection of vertical axis ranges to magnify in an esthetically pleasing way experimental differences of any magnitude is closely related to the traditional manner by which such differences are evaluated. The finding that a particular difference is statistically significant says nothing whatsoever about either its magnitude (except that it exceeds 0) or its relevance. Lacking such constraints, the researcher may feel free to display such a difference to its maximum advantage in advocating some interpretation, usually without regard for the surrounding empirical context to which the findings may relate. However, as results accumulate in an area of research, their relative importance and generality become known, and, especially if measurement is performed with idemnotic units, it becomes desirable to portray findings in accordance with at least a crude relational metric that encompasses the entire area.

The most practical use of an equal interval additive scale in displaying the results of behavioral measurement arises in the case where the dimension is countability displayed cumulatively and the horizontal axis represents a continuous time record. This display is, of course, the well-known cumulative record (Fig. 16.10), and the problem of interval size on the scale corresponding to a single response is accommodated by the capability of the recorder to reset to the horizontal axis upon reaching the upper limit of the vertical axis. Thus, the interval is selected such that an increase in the desired number of responses (for maximal sensitivity, usually one) is easily detected by the viewer.

Each response leaves its trace on the record in the form of an upward step of one unit while displaying the exact location of every response in time relative to its predecessor. The slope of any segment of the record gives a good approximation of the frequency of responding during that segment, as shown in the inset. Changes in slope are more difficult to detect; hence, the cumulative record is not particularly useful for extracting measures of celeration.

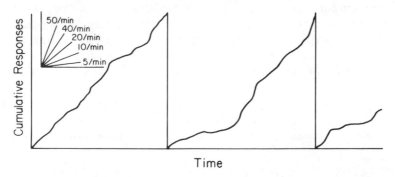

FIG. 16.10.   A hypothetical cumulative record.

Providing there is a known and constant relation between distance units on the *x*-axis and the passage of time, a cumulative record constitutes the first direct display of raw data we have encountered. All other displays discussed here and traditionally deposited in the literature (except for event records briefly described in Chapter 7) are summaries in one form or another and therefore reflect algebraic transformations of the observed responding. Displays of responses in the format of the cumulative record are the most directly descriptive that can be made; varying the physical distance on the *x*-axis corresponding to a unit of time permits representation of the temporal location of responses with whatever degree of magnification is desired. The benefits of such precision are sometimes accompanied by problems of excessive space required to display a small sample of behavior. Displays of this type must therefore usually be supplemented by more global summaries of larger portions of the data, leaving the cumulative record to serve its major function of revealing the fine-grained details of temporal patterning of single instances.

Before beginning a detailed discussion of displaying behavioral data against logarithmic vertical axes, it is useful to digress slightly and again consider variability in somewhat abstract terms. Earlier discussions of variability attempted to make the point that describing and analyzing variability is the major concern of any scientific endeavor. Variability is best described in terms of ratios (e.g., largest to smallest, males to females, Democrats to Republicans to Independents, etc.) for a variety of reasons. First, any units involved cancel when measures of like dimensional quantities are involved, and the description of variability is a pure scalar or dimensionless number (e.g., 30 cycles/minute $\div$ 6 cycles/minute = 5.0). This is as it should be, for the variability of a set of length measures, for example, is not a measure of the property of linear extent. Whatever the dimensional quantity appropriate to the description of variation, its unit is not the centimeter. Standard practice in the natural sciences reflects this insight when, for instance, the index used to describe measurement stability is the coefficient of variation ($\sigma/\bar{x} \times 100$; see chapter 17), which has no units, but exhibits the mean as a multiple of the standard deviation. Second, using ratio comparisons to describe variability renders these dimensionless quantites universal for purposes of comparison. With an appropriate quantitative index, the variability of a group of frequencies can be compared to that of another group of latencies, for example. Quantitative procedures for calculating such indexes are introduced in the next chapter.

In view of the foregoing, when we wish to use graphic displays for the purpose of examining variability, it is useful to select a scale in which equal units correspond to equal ratios, so that differing distances on the scale[2] will

---

[2]This use of the term "ratio scale" should not be confused with Stevens' (1951) use of the same term to refer to the results of measurement wherein the operations of addition and multiplication are preserved with respect to the dimension under investigation.

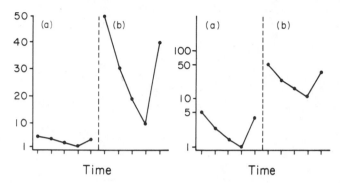

FIG. 16.11.   Comparison of interval and ratio plots of the same data.

be proportional to differing ratios and hence to differing measures of variability. For example, an equal ratio scale to the base 2 would have the same unit distances separating 1 and 2, 4 and 8, 16 and 32, etc. A common ratio scale uses the base 10, so that the distance from 1 to 10 is the same as the distance from 10 to 100 or 100 to 1000. It is true of all such scales, regardless of the base, that equal distances represent equal ratios. Such ratio scales are thus natural instruments for measuring variability.

To see the advantage visually, one need only consider two simple hypothetical sets of data: A: 5, 3, 2, 1, 4 and B: 50, 30, 20, 10, 40. Suppose these two sets of five observations each are collected serially such that A represents data before a treatment and B represents data during the treatment. Figure 16.11 shows these data plotted against both interval (left) and ratio (right) scales for purposes of comparison.

The left panel shows the two sets of data plotted against the familiar equal interval addition scale and invites the interpretation that great day-to-day variability was imposed by the introduction of the treatment along with the evident increase in level of responding. The same two sets of data are replotted on an equal ratio scale in the right panel, where the phase to phase variability now appears equivalent with respect to between-day changes. Not surprisingly, the quantitative index of variability computed from ratios described in the next chapter is the same for Phase A and Phase B; the right panel of Fig. 16.11 properly reflects this equivalence.

For purposes of magnifying sensitivity to variability, a single cycle ratio scale is often indicated. The ratio of the length of a single cycle on a multicycle axis to its length on the single cycle display gives a measure of the amount of magnification provided (see Fig. 16.12). If the axes are the same length, this magnification ratio is simply the ratio of the numbers of cycles on the two axes (i.e., 3:1 in the case of Fig. 16.12). Switching back and forth among scales of this type is like changing lenses on a microscope. Yet, there is always a fixed, reference value that is a known multiple of all of the others that defuses the feeling of arbitrariness that sometimes engulfs the viewer of most idiosyncratically devised scales.

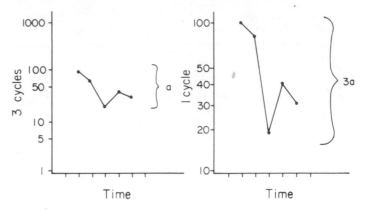

FIG. 16.12.   Comparisons of data on two ratio scales in ratio 3:1.

Ratio scales have other advantages as well, including the representation of celeration measures as simple linear functions. This results from the fact that behavior frequencies tend to change exponentially over time (Koenig, 1972; White & Haring, 1976). These are offset only by the lack of familiarity with their properties exhibited by most students and professionals in the social and behavioral sciences. Among these advantages is the capability of portraying a large range without sacrificing sensitivity, thus inviting useful standardization. Lindsley (1968) and his associates (Pennypacker, Koenig, & Lindsley, 1972) have promulgated a "Standard Behavior Chart" that displays frequency measures ranging from one per day to 1000 per minute in ratio form against real time in days.

There are also a number of commercially available, special purpose, preprinted graphs and charts for which the investigator may have occasional use. In almost all cases, these devices aid in detecting complex functional relations by yielding a display that is essentially linear. For example, if the nature of the function relating the dependent and independent variables of an experiment is of the general form $y = a^x$ (a power curve), plotting the data on log-log paper will yield a straight line whose slope is proportional to the constant, a. Data distributed in accordance with the function $y = e^{-x^2/2}$ will appear linear when plotted on normal probability coordinate paper. Various trigonometric transformations can similarly be detected by plotting against the appropriate grids. In general, special grids of the type mentioned should be used as analytical probes; if the investigator has reason to suspect that the relation between two variables is one of these complex types, that hunch can be quickly checked by observing the extent to which the resulting display conforms to simple linearity. As a rule, however, displays of this type should not be part of any dissemination effort unless the mathematical and/or theoretical sophistication of the intended audience is guaranteed or can be momentarily remediated by supplementary explanation.

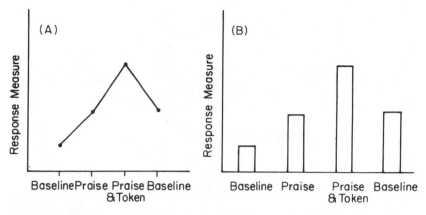

FIG. 16.13.   Improper (A) and proper (B) plotting against a discontinuous *x*-axis.

Plotting Technique.   After the scales of any graphic display have been chosen and labeled, there is still room for distortion and miscommunication as a result of the plotting conventions adopted. Perhaps the most widely practiced abuse is that of connecting dots representative of data summary points when the abscissa is clearly discontinuous. Figure 16.13 illustrates this error. The continuity in the display encourages interpretation of the values along the line as representative of predicted values of the dependent variable when, in fact, such values cannot exist because there can be no corresponding values of the independent variable. The preferable, unambiguous way to present such data is in the form of a bar graph, as shown in Panel B. Selecting this mode leaves the viewer certain that no continuum is implied.

Another practice to be encouraged involves including a graphic indication of the variability surrounding any summary data point. Moreover, the measure of variability represented (ratio, range, standard deviation, etc.) should be clearly identified in the legend, so the viewer can form an accurate impression of the extent of overlap in the distributions of raw data. Scrupulous adherence to this practice primarily benefits the researcher, who becomes less likely to let apparently large differences among measures of central tendency visually overwhelm the presence of equally large amounts of uncontrolled variability. Figure 16.14 illustrates this point. It is clear which set of results displays the greater degree of control over the behavioral phenomenon being described.

The same principle applies when a theoretical function is plotted representing a best-fitting curve describing the functional relation between two variables. Adding the indicator of variability allows the viewer to form an impression of how well the theoretical function predicts the contributing measures as well as the selected measures of central tendency. In both cases, the same principle is being urged: Whenever a single value is displayed as

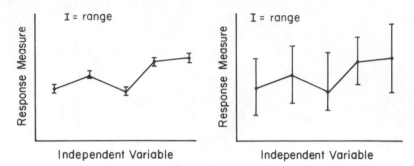

FIG. 16.14.   Hypothetical data showing the influence of range indicators on interpretations of the same central tendency data.

representative of all members of a set, some indication of the extent of its representativeness is called for as protection against mistaking statistical artifact for real experimental control.

Other Graphic Methods.   The reader is no doubt well aware that the range of graphic techniques by which relations can be displayed is almost limitless. Leafing through any newspaper or popular magazine will almost always uncover an example or two of pie charts or pictorial graphics of the types shown in Fig. 16.15.

It is instructive to analyze our reactions to these displays in light of the actual data represented, if they are available. Differences among the data are almost invariably represented by the heights of the figures, but we innocently respond to the areas and thus infer larger differences than are present. Pie charts present the reverse problem in that proportions are represented as areas, not linear values, and we are not accustomed to interpreting area representations. In the event a serious interpretation of such a display must be made, the cautious viewer takes the trouble to recast the information in a

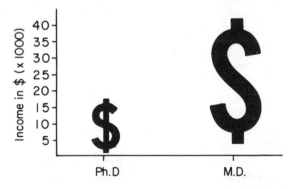

FIG. 16.15.   Average starting salary for terminal degree holders in the mental health professions.

familiar format before allowing the display to control any interpretative responses. Whenever displays of this type are incorporated into a scientific presentation (which is rare), extreme caution should precede accepting the purveyor's interpretations; there is often a good reason why the conventional modes of scientific data display have been avoided in favor of the more flamboyant and entertaining style.

In a similar vein, the use of color can suggest interpretations that may be unwarranted, even though all display cautions have been carefully observed. For example, if a bar graph is designed to show contrast, using bright colors and vertical stripes on the larger bars and dark colors and horizontal stripes on the smaller ones will heighten the appearance of disparity. Similarly, two line functions will appear more different if colored in contrasting as opposed to similar hues. These and other perceptual effects are well known to professional graphic artists and should be viewed with caution by the naive spectator. When in doubt, one should always ask, "How are the elements of this display likely to control my interpretations?"

General Issues in Graphic Display

As with any other area of scientific technique, long established traditions of graphic display have evolved into a pattern of practices that is all but autonomous, there being little or no residual reflection of the basic considerations underlying the purpose of graphically displaying data in the first place. As a result, discussions arise from time to time that appear to center on issues of substantial import and around which polar positions are readily adopted. Whenever this happens, we have lost sight of some basic principle; when data are allowed to guide decisions, heated disputes are rare. In this section, we identify two issues surrounding graphic procedures and show how review of the basic considerations already outlined render them largely moot.

Sensitivity Versus Standardization.   Many investigators cling tenaciously to a spirit of entrepreneurial innovativeness when arranging their data for public display, arguing that the uniqueness of their results demands equivalent uniqueness in the format in which they are presented. In opposition to this view is the position that all behavioral data should be presented in a single standardized format, and no variation should be tolerated. As is often the case in such matters, a reasonable approach lies somewhere between these extremes.

There are strong arguments for using a standard format as a point of departure, particularly because standardized display makes the results of all investigations immediately comparable. The researcher should also feel free to depart from the standard format for supplementary displays, always making clear both the nature and reason for the departure. Adjusting scales for purposes of magnification, rearranging data to clarify hidden relations, etc., are quite acceptable practices if they are justified and fully described and if both the researcher and audience can clearly see the relation to the original format. To the extent that behavioral data consist exclusively of measures of the basic dimensional quantities of behavior, it is not unreasonable to foresee further development of standard, universal formats for displaying these measures that will enjoy widespread utility and acceptance and that will enhance, rather than limit, communication.

Displaying Stability Versus Change.   Related to the foregoing issue is a preference for displaying summary characteristics as opposed to measures of instability and change. Many laboratory investigators of animal behavior have been seduced by the properties of the cumulative record, which is not a particularly sensitive display of behavior change. Stability thus became synonymous with a straight line of fixed slope on the cumulative record, indicating a stable frequency over the period of time represented. When such stability is achieved, there is little reason to display it except to certify its existence. Thereafter, a numerical statement of the stable frequency value is sufficient and far less costly. The decline in the frequency of published cumulative records (Skinner, 1976) probably reflects widespread adoption of the tactics required for achieving stability, thus seemingly obviating the need for analysis of cumulative records. As Sidman (1960) and the present volume (e.g., Chapters 11 and 12) make clear, however, behavior is always in transition, however slight, and the study of transitions therefore has enormous generality.

Nonetheless, having adopted the stable baseline strategy, many researchers opted for presenting summary characteristics of the data within experimental phases, leaving tacit the implication that stability had been achieved. Nowadays, the practice of presenting summary data is widespread among those who have never even seen a cumulative record and have only a vague appreciation of the underlying requirement of demonstrating steady-state responding. Displaying sample cumulative records along with graphs of summary effects seems warranted if any doubt can be raised concerning the stability implied by the summary statement. At the same time, displays of celeration permit the same degree of descriptive precision of behavior in transition that the cumulative record provides for behavior in steady state. These formats will be of great value in facilitating analysis of behavior change.

17

Quantification of Data

I frame no hypotheses; for whatever is not deduced from the phenomena is to be called an hypothesis; and hypotheses, whether metaphysical or physical, whether of occult qualities or mechanical, have no place in experimental philosophy.

—Isaac Newton

INTRODUCTION

Quantification in science begins with the occurrence of measurement as a number and unit are assigned to designate the amount of a dimensional quantity attendant to the object or event being measured. The process does not end there, however; quantification methods are further used in treating and analyzing the collections of measures that result from any empirical investigation. The nature of these methods and their proper use with respect to behavioral data are our primary concern in this chapter.

The principle function of quantification in this context is as an aid to description. Just as various display tactics are selected and applied to sharpen the picture afforded by a collection of results, so may quantitative methods be applied to clarify even further the relational characteristics inherent in the results. Nonetheless, the results of quantitative methods, however elegant or abstract, should *never* be allowed to serve as substitutes for graphic representations of the data as the investigator formulates interpretations of the experimental outcomes. When properly used, quantitative procedures may add descriptive precision to the content of a display, but interpretations that rest solely on the result of quantitative manipulations have almost invariably lost their direct connection to the original results and are in danger of being artifactual or ambiguous and of limited empirical generality.

The most common quantitative procedures are used for purposes of summarization. As the last chapter stressed, any effort to summarize necessarily imparts a loss of information, and it is essential that the elements and extent of such loss be fully visualized by a series of displays. Contrary to some appearances, elegant quantitative methods of summarization do not avoid or restore such losses, although they frequently generate additional extraneous information that many investigators permit to play a substitute role in guiding their interpretations. This is especially true in the case of certain inferential procedures that impose the concept of statistical significance upon a set of results, thus contaminating the investigator's interpretative behavior with a set of considerations foreign to the data themselves.

Quantitative methods of summarization should thus be used only as an adjunct to and in conjunction with graphic displays at each step of the summarization process, as described in the previous chapter. It is impossible to interpret properly the effects of a quantitative distillation of a set of results without simultaneously seeing the resulting change in some graphic form. While viewing such a change, however, the experimenter may derive some interpretative assistance by the addition of a more exact quantitative statement of the extent and nature of the change. In order to evaluate the utility of such an addition, the investigator must carefully consider the fundamental characteristics of the data and be fully cognizant of the probable consequences of any transformation, whether graphic or algebraic, on the interpretative responses that will be made.

SUMMARY CHARACTERISTICS OF DATA

As soon as any collection of data has been displayed visually, it may be summarized quantitatively and the representation of the summarized parameters added to the visual display. Generally, data collections are summarized with respect to three parameters: the typical or central value, the dispersion or variability, and the size of the collection. Let us briefly consider the information conveyed by each of these indices.

Typical or Central Value

After viewing the data in raw form and arranging it pictorially in various ways, the investigator may find it useful either to select or to calculate one value that is representative of the entire collection or each subcollection of interest. Anyone familiar with elementary statistical procedures is aware that the mean, median, and mode are worthy claimants to the honor of being selected as representative. We will not dwell on the relative merits of each, because this information is available in any introductory statistics text. The important point is that if either the median or mode is selected as the single representative, one is assured that the representative probably exists in the collection. Often, the mode is the choice simply because it is the most frequently occurring value and therefore is exactly representative of the largest subset of the data. The mean, on the other hand, is the result of an algebraic manipulation of the data and is not necessarily equivalent to any of the actual measures. Whether or not this is important is a matter for the investigator to decide, but the decision should not be reached by default. The question should be, "What is to be the function of this representative datum and which of the three will best serve that function?"

Variability or Dispersion

At the level of summarizing a collection of data, the question of representativeness of the selected value immediately arises. Again, this question can be answered statistically by calculating an average deviation, standard deviation, median deviation, or some other measure of dispersion that incorporates some or all of the data. A more fundamental question is frequently overlooked by this tactic—"What are the extremes?" Anyone describing a collection of, for example, fossilized bird eggs would probably say something like, "Well, the largest is 14 cm in diameter, whereas the smallest is only 8 mm in diameter." Although the collection is finite, stating the range makes a stronger descriptive statement than does any other measure of dispersion. *All* of the cases fall within it, and *none* fall outside it. Although there may exist in the world values that are not within these bounds, none are in this set. Furthermore, any experimental operation that imposes control over the range of a set of observations is likely to be of greater generality than one that merely influences the typical value. Especially when the range is reduced, variation is concomitantly eliminated and control is demonstrated, a circumstance that occurs only when an orderly process is at work. The investigator is therefore well advised to plot and examine the *range* of the observations, particularly before laying claim to some degree of experimental control.

Size of Collection

This simple index (N) tends to serve two functions, one statistical and the other descriptive. Through statistical calculations, N determines how well a sample statistic would represent the outcomes of future samplings, useful if certain assumptions are met and one is concerned with predicting the outcomes of actual future samplings. For descriptive purposes, N serves in a slightly different way; collection size becomes a measure of thoroughness, completeness, or exhaustiveness and therefore determines confidence in the likelihood that the range actually brackets all possible values. If there are only three fossilized bird eggs in the collection, little generalizable information is conveyed by the dimensions of the largest and smallest, because those two cases constitute the majority. True, they describe the collection, but the collection is probably not large enough to generate much confidence in the claim that all fossilized bird eggs have diameters between these values. Accordingly, this particular collection does not tell much about the population of fossilized bird eggs. On the other hand, if the collection contains 300 fossilized bird eggs, we have a large collection and can assert with considerable confidence that anyone who brings in a fossilized egg that falls outside the observed range of values has either made a rare discovery or is perpetrating a hoax. The ability to discriminate the rare, and probably important, discovery from the misclassified artifact is greatly assisted by extensive catalogs of known observations with the range carefully documented. A few such deviant values can significantly alter a mean and yet escape detection when blended with true observations in a calculated standard deviation. If they fall outside the established range, however, they are very conspicuous. The range is, therefore, an extremely important summary characteristic of any collection of data, and its value to statements of generality grows in proportion to the size of the collection.

At some point, the investigator will have visually arranged and may have summarized the data in such a manner that they have become an effective stimulus for a binary decision: These data are valuable and should be subjected to further analysis or these data should be discarded and a new collection process begun. Assuming the decision favors retaining the data, the real quantitative process of descriptive science begins. The investigator now asks, "What is the extent of the variability in these data, and what are its causes?" Although the investigator may have already developed reasonably accurate and functional answers to these questions on the basis of well-prepared visual displays, they cannot be exhaustively answered without quantitative tools for precise description and measurement of variability.

QUANTITATIVE DESCRIPTION OF VARIABILITY

In earlier chapters, we discussed extensively the difficulties encountered in describing variability when basic measurement is done with scales that are themselves defined by variability. Idemnotic measurement of behavior avoids these difficulties, because the units involved are not derived from the variability in the phenomenon being measured. Furthermore, the referent dimensional quantities all possess the properties of a ratio scale; this means that the operations of addition and multiplication may be performed on the resulting measures without loss of dimensional integrity. Most important, ratios involving like dimensional quantities may be formed with the result that the units cancel (e.g., 6 cycles/ minute ÷ 2 cycles/ minute = 3.0). Because these ratios lack units, they may be ideal candidates for the description of variability, functioning as *coefficients* or multipliers that can describe change along a specified dimension without the addition of another system of units. What was viewed as a liability in Chapter 7 (loss of dimensional quantity in such measures as percentage when describing *behavior*) now becomes an asset, because variability has no obvious dimensional quantity.

Because description of variability is equivalent to description of change, a simple numerical system for accomplishing this is preferable to one that requires new, derived units, because the problem of trying to invent a dimensional quantity along which variability is measured is avoided. The operation, "multiply by the coefficient, 2" has the same meaning regardless of the dimensional quantity measures upon which it is performed. The relation between 2 pounds and 4 pounds is thus the same as the relation between 10 years and 20 years, and the amount of variability described is the same in both cases. Similarly, the sets (1 cm, 2 cm, 3 cm, 4 cm, 5 cm) and (10 sec., 20 sec., 30 sec., 40 sec., 50 sec.) possess equivalent variability as defined by an aggregate, unit-free coefficient. How, then, is the notion of the unit-free coefficient involved in calculation of a descriptor of variability?

Ratio Descriptors

Range as a Ratio.   We have already seen that a useful index of variability is furnished by the extreme cases in a sample, the largest and smallest. Subtracting the smaller from the larger gives a measure known as the range, which retains the original units. However, dividing the larger by the smaller yields a coefficient that tells only how many times the smaller is the larger, regardless of the units. We might define this value as the *range coefficient*—that is, the largest in sample divided by the smallest in sample. For example, if there are 75 measures of eating frequency ranging from 0.6 bites/minute to 7.2 bites/minute, the range coefficient would be 12.0. The range coefficient has no units and is therefore of more general use as an index of variability than is the range.[1]

One commonly mentioned limitation of the range, also applicable to the range coefficient, is that it ignores all but two of the measurements in the set. Measures of variability that incorporate all of the observations in the set are certainly available. One such can be constructed by considering the deviations of every observation from every other observation in the set. For convenience, let $d_{ij} = X_i - X_j$. There are $n(n - 1)$ such deviations obtainable from a set of n observations, because every value will have every other value substracted from it. The sum of these deviations would appear as follows: $\sum_{j=1}^{n}\sum_{i=1}^{n}d_{ij}/n(n - 1)$. But, $\sum_{j=1}^{n}\sum_{i=1}^{n}d_{ij} = \sum_{j=1}^{n}\sum_{i=1}^{n}X_i - \sum_{j=1}^{n}\sum_{i=1}^{n}X_j = 0$. In other words, the average deviation of every value from every other value is 0, an interesting but hardly useful result. The classical solution to this problem involves squaring every deviation and then averaging the squares: $\sum_{j=1}^{n}\sum_{i=1}^{n}(X_i - X_j)^2/n(n- 1)$. It can be shown by further algebra that this quantity is equivalent to $[2n/(n - 1)]s^2$, where s^2 is the *variance* of the sample. If the sample is large, $2n/(n - 1)$ approximates 2, so the average squared difference among all observations is proportional to the variance.

From this result, the variance could be quite useful as a standard descriptive index of variability, because it involves the deviation of every value from every other value. However, we are again plagued by the units. Variance must be expressed in squared units of the original dimensional quantity; extracting the square root to arrive at the *standard deviation* still does not rid us of the original units. The reader should note, however, that computing the standard deviation this way does not require knowledge of the mean, because it has just been shown that the standard deviation may be derived from an algebraic combination of all possible differences among the measured values themselves.

An expedient solution to the problem of eliminating the original units from a measure of variability has been developed in the natural sciences, where it is common practice to form a ratio between the standard deviation and the mean (σ/m) known as the *fractional standard deviation* or *coefficient of variation*. This quantity obviously lacks any unit, because the unit common to both m and σ cancels. The ratio may be multiplied by 100 to obtain a *percent standard deviation;* it is this quantity that we often see attached to measures as

---

[1]The range coefficent is readily visualized as proportional to the distance between the largest and the smallest values displayed on a logarithmic scale.

an index of precision (e.g., 14.83 gm ± 2.1%). This practice yields a useful ratio, but at the expense of involving the mean in the index of variability. There may be nothing wrong with this for establishing measurement precision, but as a more general index of variability, it is less than fully satisfying, particularly if there is any reason to suspect correlation between the mean and standard deviation. In other words, if the means and standard deviations of sets of measures of a particular dimensional quantity tend to be correlated, the variability in each set is partially determined by the average magnitude in the set. Comparisons in terms of variability thus become comparisons of means to an extent specified by the size of the correlation. This situation is not only unacceptable from the standpoint of statistical inference, it can be descriptively and analytically misleading.

Absolute Mean Ratio.   Let us, therefore, consider another approach to the problem of involving all the measures in a set in developing an index of variability. We have established that a desirable characteristic of such an index is that it be a ratio; because all behavioral dimensions have the multiplicative property of ratio scales, change (variability) generally can be expressed as a ratio. We begin by considering all possible ratios of the values in the set, taken two at a time, just as we considered earlier the possibility of forming all possible differences. We are simply changing the algebraic operation from subtraction to division. Our goal is to arrive at an expression of the average of all such ratios. We form the quantity $r_{ij} = X_i/X_j$, in which case $\ln r_{ij}$ is $(\ln X_i - \ln X_j)$, and $r_{ij} = $ antilog $(\ln X_i - \ln X_j)$. For every pair of values, there will be a fractional quantity $(r_{ij} < 1)$ if $X_j > X_i$. Any summing would thus involve these quantities as well as the $r_{ij} > 1$, so let us consider the absolute value $|\ln X^i - \ln X_j|$. As before, there are $n(n - 1)$ such quantities, and since the absolute value of $(\ln X_i - \ln X_j)$ is equal to the absolute value of $(\ln X_j - \ln X_i)$, we are justified in dividing the sum by two because every pair of values forming a ratio is represented twice. Performing the algebra, we get a quantity that we shall call Kappa (κ), which is defined as follows:

$$\text{Kappa} = \text{absolute mean ratio} = \text{antilog}\left[\frac{2\sum_{i<j}^{n}|\ln X_i - \ln X_j|}{n(n-1)}\right] \qquad (1)$$

For those accustomed to geometric computations that are readily approximated on semilogarithmic graph paper, the equivalent expression for κ is:

$$\left[\prod_{i<j}^{n} \max\left(\frac{X_i}{X_j}, \frac{X_j}{X_i}\right)\right]^{\frac{2}{n(n-1)}} \qquad (2)$$

This algebraic statement converts directly to the phrase, "geometric absolute mean ratio," which is an excellent alternative descriptor for κ. Equations (1) and (2) do not lend themselves to convenient computation; a computational formula for κ is presented, along with illustrations, in Appendix A. Appendix B includes the graphic solution of Eq. (2), which permits rapid approximation of κ for small data sets.

Kappa has the important properties that are required. First, it is a general descriptor of variability applicable to any data set and interpretable if the measurement dimension has equal ratio properties. The dimensional quantities of countability, latency, duration, IRT, frequency, and celeration all qualify. Second, it has no units of its own. As a general coefficient, it can therefore be used to compare variability among data sets arising from different dimensional quantities, just as is true of the fractional standard deviation discussed earlier. Unlike the fractional standard deviation, which involves comparison of the mean and standard deviation, no mean is involved directly, and therefore no assumptions about independence of mean and variance are required for descriptive generality. In other words, the magnitude of κ will not be affected by the magnitude of the observations, even if correlation is present between the mean and σ^2. The assumption of independence, as we have seen, can be justified only in the case of random measurement errors that approximate a symmetric Gaussian distribution. It has not been established that behavioral variability is random, symmetric, or Gaussian; indeed, the objective of experimental analysis is to gain control over those factors that might otherwise be thought to interact randomly so as to create variability. As this control is gained, the isolated variability can be examined quantitatively without loss of interpretability through assumption failure.

Values of Kappa are illustrated in Fig. 17.1 for two data sets with differing characteristics.[2] There is obviously more variability displayed in Set A of Fig. 17.1 than in Set B, and the respective values of κ reflect this fact. The logarithmic y-axis is proportionally the same in both cases, so any given *ratio* is represented by the same linear distance on both, even though the range of values in Set B is 10 times that of Set A. Figure 17.1 thus illustrates the convenience with which a ratio-based index of variability like κ can be visualized with the aid of a semilogarithmic display.

Descriptors of Time-Dependent Variability

It is characteristic of the data of most sound behavioral experiments for time to be a major parameter, because the entire strategy of experimentation depends on comparisons evaluated with the behavior of one or a few subjects

---

[2]These data are used to illustrate the computational procedures in Appendix A.

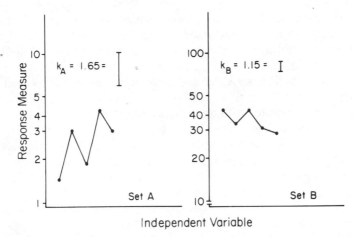

FIG. 17.1.   Display of two data sets showing calculated values of κ together with proportional vertical bars. Note the use of the logarithmic scale on the vertical axis, necessary for interpreting the vertical bar.

measured more or less continuously over substantial periods of time. Complex patterns of variation can almost always be discerned in any display of behavioral measures plotted against time. Describing such variation is a general problem that must be understood if reasonable interpretations of experimental effects are to be undertaken. Because the bulk of experimental reasoning is based on the temporal location and duration of imposed changes in some dimension of responding, all other time-related changes form the background against which the changes of interest are assessed. Methods of describing these background changes quantitatively may therefore be a useful supplement to their visual evaluation.

If an uncontrolled source of variation has some orderly pattern of occurrence in time, then its effect on responding can be expressed as some function of time. Accordingly, some function of the general form $y = f(t)$ can be said to describe the functional relation between responding and the uncontrolled source of variation. In other words, although the source may not be identified, its influence can be described with reference to its pattern in time. The simplest form of such a relational statement is $y = \beta_0 + \beta_1 t + \epsilon$, the equation of a straight line with an error term added to describe variation not related to the time-dependent variable. In this equation, β_0 is the so-called y-intercept, β_1 is the linear slope parameter, and ϵ is the error term.

Unfortunately, very few functions relating behavioral data to time are nicely fit by a straight line. Koenig (1972) has shown that the general function $y = a \times 10^{bt} + \epsilon$ provides a better description of changing behavior frequencies over time, regardless of the sources of additional extraneous variability that contribute to ϵ. As noted in the previous chapter, this function graphs as a straight line on semilogarithmic paper; it does not, however, describe the cyclic and frequently periodic patterns that remain highly visible after any linear or exponential trend is removed.

The methods that appear most powerful in their ability to describe such cyclic, time-dependent variation are grouped under the general rubric of *time series analysis*. A time series is any ordered series of values that, when exhibited as a function of time, display variation that depends on time (or a variable highly correlated with time). Thus, the mere fact that measurements are made serially in time does not necessarily mean they form a time series, because all variation might be explainable by independent variables whose only relation to time is marginal and/or accidental. However, if the value of every member of the series depends in some way on its location in time, then the series may be said to be a time series.

The general class of functions that adequately describes cyclic behavioral time series are known as Fourier series and are beyond the scope of this volume; however, techniques for determining a best-fitting Fourier function for a particular set of data are available (e.g., Box & Jenkins, 1970). Once the function has been determined, the residual variability can be described by the methods discussed in the following section, and interpretation can proceed in exactly the manner recommended throughout this volume for gaining understanding of the sources of variation in any natural phenomenon. Describing a time-dependent trend by means of a complex trigonometric equation (Fourier series) is no different in principle from describing a simple linear trend by a single valued slope coefficient, and it offers nothing more or less in the way of empirical explanation of the causes of the time-dependent variation. Explanation can be accomplished only by experimental analysis, and the vocabulary of time series may be expected to assist such an analysis to the extent that it provides a descriptive language worthy of the periodic variation that is widely observed in behavioral data. Efforts to subjugate the descriptive power of time series methods to the service of statistical inference as a basis for scientific judgment are completely contrary to the strategies of experimental analysis. The inappropriateness of the general approach of statistical inference in the science of behavior has already been raised in Chapter 5 and is examined at a broad level in the concluding section of this chapter.

USES OF QUANTITATIVE DESCRIPTION

The overall strategy that guides the treatment and analysis of data is to create stimuli that will influence interpretative responses of maximal generality on the part of both the investigator and the scientific audience. Such stimuli are primarily visual in nature and consist of representational displays of various characteristics of the data together with such quantitative refinements of the displayed characteristics as may be necessary to enhance the degree of exactness necessary for accurate interpretation. In this section, we describe the manner in which visual displays of data can be augmented by the results of appropriate quantitative procedures. Such results provide valuable information for addressing the central issues of any interpretative statement. Many of these issues have been fully explored and developed earlier in the volume (see especially Chapters 8, 10, and 11) and are reintroduced here only to the extent necessary to refresh the reader concerning the larger contexts in which display and quantification have an integrated function necessary to interpretation.

Uncontrolled Variability

Measurement Error.   In general, errors of this type are related to calibration of the transducing machine or observer and should be eliminated through periodic checking. Any transduction system, whether inanimate or biological, will generate an operating characteristic curve that describes the change in accuracy with which a calibration or test signal is transduced over time. By correcting observed values for the amount of operational error projected by the curve, true value estimates can be calculated that contain only residual "random" error generated by unknown, presumably canceling sources. Procedures for making such observations of human observers have been fully developed by workers in the area of human psychophysics and signal detection, and the interested reader is referred to that literature for detailed treatment of the subject (e.g., Green & Swets, 1966).

Extraneous Variation.   A persistent problem plaguing efforts to establish a coherent body of scientifically derived information about behavior has been the absence of a quantitative index of stability as an aid to identifying steady states. In Sidman's classic work (1960), the topic is treated as essentially an art form, faithfully reflecting the practices of nearly all laboratory investigators at the time. In the context of full reporting of complete, standardized response records, this nonquantitative practice was usually more than adequate for interpretative needs. However, in recent years, it has become commonplace to describe a set of baseline observations in terms of central value and some measure of dispersion and to assert that stability is achieved because the dispersion measure does not exceed some arbitrarily imposed value. Because there is little or no standardization of dispersion measures and because most are correlated over time with the magnitude of the behavioral measures under consideration, there has been no real advance toward a solution of the problem beyond that available through use and publication of standardized cumulative recordings.

The problem of describing the stability of a set of data should be understood as the problem of describing and summarizing the uncontrolled variability exhibited by the data. The use of available measures of dispersion, including Kappa, provides a conservative solution to the problem. In all cases, their definition and calculation does not exclude systematic variability that may be time dependent. In those instances in which time dependent variability is clearly either negligible or entirely absent, Kappa provides an appropriate index of variability that may be used to quantify stability.[3] However, steady states of this type are probably extremely rare in nature and usually require powerful laboratory control procedures for their demonstration.

A more general solution to the problem of describing stability emerges from reasserting the concept of stability as being inversely related to the presence of uncontrolled, unaccounted-for variability. If there is a time-dependent trend in the data, the source of this trend may be uncontrolled, but the result is clearly variation that is not unaccounted for. We account for it to some degree by noting its functional relation to time. Therefore, in assessing the amount of uncontrolled, extraneous variability present in a set of data, it is appropriate to remove that portion that is the result of a time-dependent process. This may be readily accomplished after the time-dependent trend has been described by a function of the general form $y' = f(t)$. To describe the variability not accounted for by this function requires that we form all possible ratios of the form y_i / y_i' and proceed with the calculation of a new value, which we will call Kappa prime (κ').[4] In other words, an average ratio is calculated on the basis of each value divided by its predicted counterpart in the time series. The result of this computation will be a numerical description of the variation of the data around the trend function, and its magnitude will vary inversely with the degree of obtained stability.

The process of computing and displaying κ' for a hypothetical set of data is presented in Fig. 17.2. We assume that the upward trending trigonometric function shown by the solid line has been determined by the method of time series analysis, and our task is to describe the variability in the data points not accounted for by the trigonometric function. The absolute distance by which each point deviates from its theoretical counterpart is expressed in ratio form and the nth root of the product of these ratios gives us the desired result. The actual computation for the values displayed in Fig. 17.2 is shown as an aid to

---

[3]Kappa has a theoretical lower limit of 1.0 and can range upward from that. Experience with its use will generate ranges of values that describe acceptable steady states under various conditions and with varying numbers of observations, much as rough standards exist for the value of (σ/m) as an index of measurement precision in the physical sciences.

[4]Technically, the computation of κ' involves the absolute ratios of y_i' and y_i, just as in the case of κ. The defining formula for κ' is therefore $\prod_{i=1}^{n} [\max (y_i/y_i', y_i'/y_i)]^{1/n}$. This formula differs from that for κ in that the ratios used to define κ involve only the empirical data points, not departures from values of a derived function.

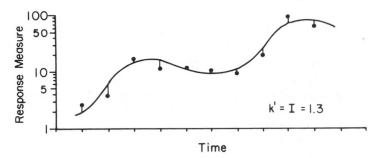

FIG. 17.2.   Hypothetical data and time function showing calculation and geometric representation of κ'.

the reader in interpreting the formula. Again, interpretation of the geometric representation of κ' by a vertical bar (I) depends on the semilogarithmic display format.

Values such as Kappa and Kappa' should be understood as only suggested tools to help the researcher gain some precision and generality in the measurement of variability. They should not be allowed to replace the judgment of the researcher, as statistical tools have in the past, in matters of timing of experimental manipulations, scientific merit of the findings, or scope of dissemination.

Imposed Variability

There is probably no more important role to be played by quantitative techniques in science than describing the results of experimental efforts to explain and control variability—that is, to describe treatment effects. Let us now consider the role of quantitative description and summarization in detecting and evaluating these effects.

Change in Central Tendency.   Whenever the introduction of an experimental variation causes a change in the dependent phenomenon of interest, this change will be reflected in each of the measurements made, providing measurement is sufficiently sensitive to detect the effects imposed. If the effect is evident in each of the measures, it will necessarily be evident in any aggregate. The converse is not true, of course; an effect may appear in an aggregate measure even though it pertains to only a fraction of the individual measures. For this reason, prior inspection of the data in graphic form is a prerequisite to any quantitative description of effects based on summary measures. Assuming a satisfactory outcome of this examination, a convenient way of quantifying such an effect is to measure its extent in the case of the typical or central value of the set. For example, we may observe that the median frequency of lever pressing for 10 sessions prior to introducing a particular drug is 30 cycles per minute; after the drug has been administered, the median frequency over the next 10 sessions drops to 10 cycles per minute.

It is obvious that variability has been imposed on the overall set of data by introducing the drug. How do we quantify this variability? The reasoning that led to the development of Kappa applies with equal cogency here. The ratio of the predrug to postdrug median response frequency is 3 to 1, so we may say that the effect of the drug on the median frequency of lever pressing is given by the coefficient .33. In keeping with our general contention that variation is best expressed in ratio terms, the respective pre- and postdrug measures should not be added to or subtracted from each other because to do so would attach the original response units to the measure of change and restrict the generality of that measure to observations made in terms of those units.

Change in central tendency can be expressed as a ratio regardless of the measure of central tendency employed. Clarity of presentation suggests that the same measure be used in comparing any group of two or more data sets, so that means are always compared with means, medians with medians, etc. Although this practice is convenient and conventional, it is by no means necessary; as long as the measures being compared have the same units, the ratio will be interpretable. One could compute the ratio between median predrug frequency and mean postdrug frequency and use that ratio as a measure of drug-induced change. This would appear to be a particularly good tactic if the data in the predrug sessions included some highly discrepant values that may have occurred during early training. Notice that the measure of change, a ratio, is strictly descriptive; no statements are made about its likelihood of occurrence in the future based upon the variability of available observations in the present.

Change in Variability.   The effect on behavior of introducing an experimental treatment is not limited to multiplication or division of all measures by a constant, as may have been implied in the previous section. More often than not, an operation that induces a change in the central tendency will also induce change in the variability around that value. It is this fact that makes conventional analytic statistical procedures particularly ill-suited to describing and analyzing behavioral phenomena, because these procedures usually require an assumption (or demonstration) of "homogeneity of variance" for their interpretation. At a more basic level, however, demonstrating a functional relation between an independent variable and changes in behavioral variability should be viewed not as an analytical inconvenience, but as a fact of potentially great scientific importance. Discovering a variable that exerts control over variability is a highly prized occurrence, for it may widen the window through which the natural phenomena of concern are viewed. This is particularly true of any operation that increases variability, providing the increase is reliable and reproducible rather than accidental. We have found, for example, that increasing the number of items a student responds to on a repeatable test increases the variability of performance from test to test. This increase in variability magnifies the complexity of the relations controlling performance and gives us more opportunity to observe the operation of unusual instances and perhaps understand them better. We can then ask, "What are the causes of these discrepant values?" and "Can we gain control over them so as to change the behavior to this level?"

Conversely, operations that reliably decrease variability in responding are indispensible in demonstrating experimental control, a necessity in detecting the effects of weak or subtle independent variables. Without the ability to generate a tight and stable baseline, we would lose such weak effects in the "noise" of uncontrolled variability, and although their presence might be detected statistically, the details of their functional effects on behavior would not.

It is therefore important to be able, when necessary, to describe accurately and quantitatively changes in variability that are caused by deliberate experimental operations, whether or not these operations produce a concomitant change in central tendency. Consistent with past discussion, it is a simple matter to describe a change in variability as the *ratio* between two values of Kappa. By convention, the reference value of κ is placed in the denominator and the value being compared in the numerator. For example, in the hypothetical drug study, the investigator may observe that along with a change in central tendency, introducing the drug induces greater variability. The value of Kappa computed for the treatment phase would be divided by the value of Kappa in the baseline phase in order to quantify this effect. The baseline phase serves as a meaningful referent against which to compare the drug effect and should be used accordingly, regardless of which value of Kappa is larger. To the extent that no change in variability is observed, the ratio of the two Kappas will approximate 1.0. Only with experience in various experimental contexts can experimenters develop sensitivity to the degree to which the ratio must depart from 1.0 in either direction before it is considered meaningful. Unlike the conventional F-statistic, which compares two independent variances, the ratio of two Kappas may be interpreted without reference to a sampling distribution, because the assumption of random variability is not required by the descriptive function of Kappa.

Change in Trend.   One of the most subtle, yet practically important, effects of the controlled introduction of an independent variable may be the imposition of variation in trend. That is, the nature of behavioral change over time may be altered as a consequence of a deliberate modification of major controlling variables, such as a teacher adjusting a curriculum in an effort to increase the rate at which a pupil approaches some mastery criterion. If the adjustment is sucessful, the slope of the function describing the relation of the behavioral measure to time should be increased. We have already noted the existence of mathematical techniques for describing time-dependent effects in data. Basically, these techniques serve to derive the function that relates the maximum amount of observed variability to the time parameter. Given that such a function can be obtained, the trend function is simply the first derivative of this function taken with respect to time. Evaluating a change in trend, then, becomes a matter of comparing two derivatives. In the linear case, slopes or derivatives are constants, and the matter of comparing trends reduces to forming a ratio of two such constants. This strategy will also work in the case of more complex derivatives that will arise if the trend functions are periodic or exponential. A solution to this problem in the case of trends among the logs of behavior frequencies displayed over time has been worked out by Lindsley and his associates (Pennypacker, Koenig, & Lindsley, 1972; see also Kazdin, 1976).

The researcher is again cautioned about premature reliance on the calculus to provide ad hoc descriptions of trend changes that are not reliable (i.e., reproducible). The elaborate mathematization of unstable data that occupied the efforts of a generation of psychologists influenced by Hull (1943) should serve to remind us that quantitative elegance will only temporarily conceal the effects of inadequate or incomplete experimental control. Failure to reproduce results should send us to the laboratory, not to a mathematics text. On the other hand, methodological sophistication and the proven reliability of certain portions of the data base underlying the science of behavior are now seen as justification for efforts to supplement graphic displays with formal quantification (Skinner, 1950).

THE ROLE OF INFERENTIAL STATISTICS
IN BEHAVIORAL RESEARCH

As every student of the subject is keenly aware, there are two general types of statistical procedures, descriptive and inferential. Descriptive statistical procedures play an important role in the conduct of any science that has advanced beyond the level of pure taxonomy, if only to provide estimates of the error associated with measurement. Throughout this chapter, we have tried to outline a strategy and some tactics for developing statistical descriptors of behavioral data that are consonant with the basic nature of the data and the needs of experimenters for quantification. These are intended to guide the experimenter through the process of data management and analysis in a fashion that allows the data to exert appropriate stimulus control over interpretative behavior. Crude tactical errors like averaging data from different subjects in the belief that something representative of a typical subject will emerge should no longer be a temptation to the reader.

There remains the necessity of dealing with the use of statistics in an inferential or evaluative mode in the science of behavior. The tradition of vaganotic measurement has had a major impact on the disciplines of psychology and education, not only with respect to defining and measuring otherwise obscure or inaccessible concepts, but in terms of fundamental decision making about the soundness or importance of experimental results that may otherwise be methodologically acceptable. Chapter 4 pointed out that the various procedures of statistical hypothesis testing are based on the vaganotic strategy because they compare an obtained deviation or difference with some standard value calculated on the basis of variability observed in the data. Thus, the data are asked to perform an impossible task, that of evaluating themselves against standards that are supplied by their own existence. To be sure, assistance is provided by the logical litany of the proof-by-contradiction structure of the deductive reasoning in hypothesis testing, but there are two fundamental deficiencies that are not rescued by logical elegance alone.

First, interpreting the outcome of any distribution-based statistical test requires that the data conform to assumptions underlying the distribution of the test statistic. Usually, these assumptions derive from the Normal Law of Error, which asserts (quite correctly for truly random events like dice throw outcomes) that as a result of random determination, errors will be distributed evenly around a central value and will tend to cancel. Furthermore, the assumption is often required that multiple distributions of such errors are roughly equivalent so that they can be pooled. The difficulty with these assumptions is that they are rarely met in the case of behavioral data, save for the case of truly random errors of measurement. The effects of uncontrolled variables on behavior cannot be assumed to resemble independent, random occurrences, because behavior is a continuous process, and the effects of any variable, uncontrolled or not, are more likely to exhibit serial dependence than independence. Attempting to remove such influences statistically by inferential application of time series methods prior to performing an analysis of variance does not diminish their effects in nature. Statistical control is never a substitute for experimental control, whether the variability at issue is random or serially time dependent. The only way to determine whether or not uncontrolled variables are influencing the data is to inspect the data at the finest available level of decomposition, usually point-by-point for each individual subject. No purpose is served by combining the data statistically to obscure such effects, except that of deceiving the experimenter and eventually the scientific audience. One does not transform uncontrolled variability into random error by a mere act of assumption, although the illusion that this is possible has persisted for some time in the social sciences. Statistical concepts of chance predicated on randomness and independence of sampling should not be used to cloak scientific ignorance (Boring, 1920). The appearance of reporting significance levels as a sort of descriptive index, and it is not uncommon to see "$p < .05$" and "$p < .001$" in the same set of results, certifying only that the author is unaware of the binary character of the accept–reject regions of the density function by which the test statistic is distributed. The same logic that permits designation of such regions in the first place demands that any point is exactly equivalent to any other within the same region. Of course, the investigator is supposed to decide the area of the rejection region *before* undertaking the analysis, presumably on the basis of the utility associated with an error of either the first or second type; then, the investigator is expected to perform the test and either accept or reject the null hypothesis on the basis of the outcome. The null hypothesis is either rejected or not, and it is no more or less rejectable because a particularly unlikely value of the test statistic happened to emerge (Fisher, 1956).

Except at the earliest stages of preliminary investigation, knowledge of whether or not a particular operation makes a difference is almost uselessly crude. The Bayesian movement in statistical inference attempted to provide some relief for this limitation by developing procedures for testing significance against null hypothesis distributions based on other than the simple expectation of no difference. Using these procedures, it is possible in principle to aggregate past results in formulating the null expectation and thereby evaluate each outcome against a more profound alternative than the mere operation of chance sampling differences in a population of equivalent parameters. In practice, however, Bayesian methods have enjoyed little use outside of certain business and military simulation activities, probably because the development of prior expectancy distributions is a highly subjective and inexact process occasioning justification through argument. The game is easier to play if everybody has to cross the same goal line.

From time to time, serious thinkers in experimental psychology have voiced misgivings concerning the future of a science that accumulates its results in the form of a series of binary hypothesis rejections (e.g., Grant, 1956). Among the alternatives suggested has been applying goodness-of-fit techniques to compare empirically derived data with expectancy based on either theory or aggregated past results. An obvious benefit of this practice would be the gradual, collective approximation of reliable functional relations, providing enough investigators collected data under sufficiently similar conditions to permit meaningful serial evaluation. Unfortunately, the evaluation process is again couched in terms of a series of binary hypothesis rejections; either the fit is acceptable or it is not by some statistical criterion. The basic deficiencies arising out of vaganotic measurement are not corrected.

A system of comparing and evaluating results serially is a fundamental need of any scientific enterprise extending beyond the limits of a single laboratory or an individual's life work. This need has been met in the case of the exact sciences by adoption of idemnotic measurement procedures to serve all descriptive functions and reliance on replication to support generality. This is the strategy recommended in the present volume for the natural science of behavior. Using standard units of behavioral measurement and deploying such entities as Kappa for quantifying variability should serve the quantitative needs of the science for the immediate future. Such a system of measures permits discussion and comparison of findings in a language that transcends the results of each separate collection of observations. In either the scientific or practical sense, the significance of experimental results can never be established by an appeal to a probability statement. Scientific significance must always be predicted on a condition of repeatability; a result that cannot be controlled and reproduced at will is at best a natural curiosity, yet nothing in the tactics of traditional statistical evaluation by inference excludes such curiosities from the accepted data base of the discipline.

Replication in the systematic sense (Sidman, 1960) achieves its loftiest state in the process of application. Any functional relation that emerges from an experiment is a statement of a relation between behavior and its determining variables and setting conditions that is ultimately a description of a natural phenomenon. A complete specification of the controlling variables and boundary conditions permits statements to be made concerning the conditions of reproducibility in a less controlled setting and allows outcome predictions to be attempted. Verifying such predictions in precise, idemnotic terms supplies confirmation of the original relation that cannot be approximated by a significance statement, no matter how small the alpha level. The understanding required for replication through application can come only from thorough and exhaustive experimental analysis of the determinants of effects, not the mere demonstration of their existence.

It has been argued that research in applied settings is so fraught with sources of uncontrollable variation that statistical procedures are required in order to detect effects that are partially obscured by such variation. This is a subtle but dangerous *non sequitur*; we have shown that the solution to uncontrolled variation does not lie with statistical inference, regardless of the setting. However, it may be best to suspend discussion of this situation pending the outcome of efforts to apply the full range of idemnotic measurement practices as advocated in this volume to the problems peculiar to applied settings. It is likely that sound measurement and design procedures will reduce the impact of the uncontrolled complexities of most applied settings. Furthermore, if the researcher still finds the environment uncontrollable to the extent of justifying statistical "controls" while attempting to conduct research, how is the environment to become less uncontrolled when the time for application arrives? Certainly not from the results of research, because effects whose only significance is statistical are notoriously impotent as influencers of the behavior of those charged with the unacceptable, uncontrolled variability in a set of experimental data should serve as a signal to redesign or repeat the experiment in an attempt to isolate and control the cause of the variability and thus reduce ignorance. It should never be a signal to enlarge the sample size and pray for cancellation through inexorable operation of the Law of Large Numbers.

The second, and perhaps more severe, deficiency associated with the practice of hypothesis testing is that the results are of dubious value, even if the assumptions are met. The evaluative decision afforded the experimenter is of a simple binary type: Either the difference is significant or it is not. A certain chafing under this limitation can be detected in the practice of responsibility of managing the environment. The lack of correspondence between the fruits of 50 years of such research in education and current classroom practice should suffice to illustrate this point.

It seems to us that the conscientious investigator will withdraw from such a setting, at least temporarily, in favor of one that affords a better opportunity to exercise the necessary control over relevant variables. This will be done in recognition that one's time and skills are finite and that little advancement of the goals of science will be possible under such circumstances. In fact, continued efforts in that environment may actually retard the emergence of widespread benefit to the extent that failures justify prolonging policies predicated on the invented knowledge that was not effectively challenged.

18 Critical Interpretation

The great tragedy of science—the slaying of a beautiful hypothesis by an ugly fact.

—T. H. Huxley

INTRODUCTION

One of the themes that has appeared in all of the previous chapters will now become the focus of an entire chapter. We have been looking closely at the scientist as a behaving organism whose actions are described and controlled by the same kind of environment–organism interactions that are the subject of his or her endeavors. Our special concern in this chapter is the various interpretative behaviors emitted by experimenters and their scientific peers and the sources of control over such responding. We think that a methodological treatise for a science of behavior not only must embody this perspective to be consistent but can profit enormously from doing so. A scientific approach to the study of scientific behavior can augment the quality of research method, producing two immediate and invaluable byproducts: marked increases in the effectiveness of methodological training and substantial increment in the reliability and generality of the discovered knowledge of the science. Such an approach must be empirical and inductive and will, therefore, be at some variance with the efforts of those who write from historical, sociological, philosophical and logical perspectives (see Mahoney, 1976).

INTERPRETATIVE RESPONSES

In general terms, the task of either the experimenter or the audience is to evaluate. More particularly, each must make many individually small decisions as the experiment is conducted or as the reported experiment is examined. These decisions concern whether or not or how different facets of the experiment should influence the transformation of experimental data into verbal statements about dependent–independent variable relations that are characterized by a high degree of generality. Interpreting the "meaning" of a study, then, is a matter of identifying the sources of potential influence on interpretative responses and making numerous judgments about whether or not those influences will augment or limit the generality of the resulting verbal statements. Interpretation is thus distinguished from experimental analysis in that the latter is a form of empirical activity whereas the former is exclusively a verbal activity that is properly influenced by the products of analysis. This is a useful distinction, because it calls attention to the sources of control over different classes of responding by experimenters. Though the line of demarcation is often a fine one, the researcher should be sensitive to the different influences that distinguish analytical activities from purely interpretative ones.

Like any other behavioral phenomenon, the interpretative behavior of a scientist is influenced by two broad classes of environmental events: antecedents and consequences. A scientific understanding of interpretative behavior cannot be expected in the absence of controlled experimental analysis wherein selected members of these environmental classes are imposed as independent variables in deliberate fashion and their effects on interpretative behavior examined. For the moment, we offer the following discussion of selected probable sources of control over interpretative behavior both for didactic purposes and as a guide to future investigators. The bulk of this discussion centers on antecedent influences immediately available in the details of the experimental protocol, in addition to those with more remote origins in the preexperimental history of the researcher. More. extended discussions of the influences of consequences on various interpretative actions are in the latter portion of this chapter and in the following chapter on generality. To a considerable extent, however, the reader should already be aware of many of the determinants of interpretative responding, because each and every discussion of tactical matters has been couched in the interpretative possibilities allowed by the various options. Interpretation thus becomes the ultimate scientific act for which all previous decisions and actions are preparatory. The goal of efforts to understand interpretative behaviors is to become fully aware of and to approve or eliminate each influence over this crucial category of scientific behavior, rather than to remain ignorant of and thus completely subservient to influences that may not always be functionally related to interpretations of maximal accuracy and generality.

SOURCES OF CONTROL

Preexperimental

Theory. Both the general theoretical perspective of the experimenter and the particular theory under investigation (if any) exert an influence on the interpretative responses of the scientist in at least two basic ways. First, by restricting many decisions at the stages of phrasing the experimental question, arranging measurement procedures, and designing and implementing the independent variable arrangements, the experimenter's theoretical history places numerous limitations on the nature of the data eventually available for interpretation. These influences are examined under subsequent headings. Second, theory exerts an influence directly when the experimenter or the reader examines the data and generates verbal descriptions designed to control their subsequent behavior or that of others. An acknowledged function of experimental data is to provide a source of binding arbitration among rival theories such that the vanquished retreat from view and their former adherents realign their beliefs in accordance with fact. Unfortunately, the theoretical factionalism that pervades the social sciences (documented by various writers, e.g., Mahoney, 1976) does not encourage this practice. This is probably partly the result of differentially rich personal histories of reinforcement for theoretical verbal behavior as opposed to objective, inductive descriptions of natural phenomena.

Literature. The published literature regarding the phenomenon of interest looms large as an influence on the interpretative behavior of the scientist. The necessity for more than passing familiarity with this material is obvious. It allows both experimenter and audience to compare the present results with those generated under conditions of varying similarity to the experiment being evaluated. The same data might lead to different interpretations if they stood in opposition to an established literature instead of confirming the findings already convincingly suggested in numerous studies. For example, a study that clearly showed that a seemingly standard use of the timeout paradigm produced increases in responding would merit a very careful examination and considerable scepticism given the conclusions so well established in the literature summarized in Chapter 15.

However, the interpreting scientist does not use the literature only to evaluate functional relations arising from the data. It is also necessary to compare methodological similarities and differences among published studies to the one under examination as a way of assessing how its many methodological features should affect any conclusions. It may be that a procedural deviation in the present experiment suggests that a particular interpretative consideration be entertained.

These uses of experimental literature make clear the necessity of thorough knowledge of relevant studes as a source of influence on any interpretations. The reader in particular must be aware of the possibility that the experiments referenced in the published study may be (intentionally or unintentionally) a biased and self-serving selection from a larger literature, designed to lead or mislead the reader to conclusions matching those advocated by the experimenter. The ability to assess this possibility can come only from sufficient training and background on the part of the reader so that any such deficiencies and prejudices are easily detected.

Experimenters.   One of the variables influencing interpretation of experiments is knowledge about the experimenter and research program from which the effort came. Although such a consideration might seem embarrassingly unprofessional and subjective, it is a realistic admission that the reputation of an experimenter and a program is sometimes useful information in the interpretation of any resulting work.

It is quite common to read research articles in which some pieces of information are omitted, forcing the reader to make assumptions about what was done or what happened. For example, it may be that multiple observers were used, but no mention was made about how the independence of observer judgments was ensured. In such situations, the reader has only the choice of giving the experimenter the benefit of the doubt or making a more conservative assumption. Similarly, all experienced investigators are aware that the necessities of editorial policy and the contingencies governing the experimenter's writing sometimes produce a lack of congruence between the actual details of experimental procedures and results and their published description. This discrepancy requires the same choice of assumptions referred to previously, although the decision here can be pervasive in its effects on the believability that the reader attributes to the study as a whole.

Selecting between the optimistic or the conservative assumptions is dictated partly by the consequences of the decisions for the reader and partly by what the reader knows about the experimenter, whether personally, by hearsay, or from the style of the experimenter as communicated in the article. The reputation of an individual as an experimenter comes from many sources. Personal interactions at professional meetings, comments by other researchers, reactions from the experimenter's students and colleagues, presentations, and other publications all contribute to a personal opinion about an experimenter's skill and thoroughness. These opinions may be strongly held in some instances, but are more likely only tentative. Such predispositions may improve the accurary of a reader's interpretations, but they can just as easily result in a well-known author's receiving too much license or an unknown experimenter's getting too little credit.

The experimenter's reputation is available as an interpretative influence prior to reading a report, but the style in which the manuscript is written can also contribute to this kind of bias. The reader is naturally somewhat reassured by a style of description and interpretation that is particularly thorough and conservative or is put on guard by a style that is sloppy and strongly advocative.

These influences on the reader augment or detract from the believability of the study aside from any other considerations. An experimenter's reputation is gradually developed over an extended period of time through all professional contacts as well as through published work. It is probably a variable in the evaluation of an individual's work that once established is very difficult to change, although it should be subject to reassessment with each professional offering. The careful cultivation of the respect of colleagues for one's professional efforts is thus an important and continuing consideration from the very beginning of a research career.

Extraexperimental Contingencies. Experimental activities are not conducted in the sterile environment that prevalent mythology describes. In fact, there are a great many potential sources of influence beyond those directly pertaining to the conduct of the experiment. Both experimenter and peers must be aware of what these influences may be in each case and must be prepared to assess their role in interpretation. The experimenter needs this objectivity in order to improve the accuracy of his or her own interpretations by minimizing those influences that impart less generality of conclusions. Readers of scientific literature need not only assess such influences on the experimenter, but on their own interpretative behavior as well. It is useful to describe these influences in terms of if–then contingencies. If I interpret the experiment this way, then what will be the result? There are a number of such extraexperimental consequences.

One source of influence comes from the fact that the experimenter has usually invested much time, money, effort, and professional reputation on the research program. Beyond other effects of interpreting the outcome of a particular experiment, it may be as punishing to draw a conclusion unfavorable to the program as it is reinforcing to draw a favorable conclusion. These contingencies can easily lead to a style of investigation best described as advocacy research, in which the experimenter takes a strong advocacy position from conception through interpretation of the study. It is admittedly difficult not to do this in some moderate degree, and the wise reader is naturally alert to these motives. However, as a general practice, such propensities can generate a literature consisting of poorly conceived studies that do not ask questions about nature and that offer conclusions of little generality. This is a major reason why replication across experimenters and programs is such a valuable source of information about the generality of conclusions.

Another controlling variable is related to the degree of fame and fortune that may accrue to the purveyor of the right kind of experimental results. That scientists are usually severely deprived of both and have fairly low personal criteria for what constitutes fame and wealth means only that such deprivations are easily satisfied. This is especially true in the case of those working with human behavior in applied settings, because there may be greater professional and public interest and economic potential in the implications of experimental findings. At the very least, publication of the results in professional journals sometimes brings a small and temporary measure of valued recognition for those in academia. Sometimes, the resulting riches are not personal but institutional. The continuation of external funding for a project is often contingent upon a certain experimental outcome. It may be that nonmonetary influences on the viability of the program are similarly affected through continuation of access to a setting or subjects or the cooperation of important individuals.

A third kind of influence stems from the social uses to which experimental answers may be put, independent of any personal effects on the investigator. For example, if the only function of certain experimental conclusions is to encourage further research, interpretations might not be as conservative as when the results will lead to the nationwide dissemination of a new vaccine or the multimillion dollar expenditure required to reorganize a state welfare system. The social uses of experimental results may temper interpretations in valuable ways as long as the experimenter does not improperly bias the findings in order to proselytize for social change in which there is any kind of personal or professional investment.

Experimental Question. Chapter 2 discussed various aspects of the experimental question, which is translated into independent variable manipulations and dependent variable measurement. By phrasing the question in the first place, the experimenter has presumably already exercised all available skills in this area to best advantage, and now the reader must make an assessment. It is deceptively easy to accept the premises upon which an experimental question is based without formally evaluating them, while proceeding to interpret other dimensions of the study. The reader should not feel bound by this most crucial experimental decision because the first and most important responsibility is to examine critically all assumptions and implications of the question being addressed. It may often seem to the reader that some facets of the question preclude giving serious attention to the resulting experiment; there should be no hesitation in ignoring the experimenter's conclusions from otherwise adequate experimental method and defendable results. Although such cases are probably rare because poorly phrased questions are not usually followed by carefully conducted research, they should occasion an active effort at proper interpretation in the light of any relevant and established body of fact.

Usually, poor experimental questions arise as part of a strong advocacy position and are phrased in a way that presupposes the answer or does not permit a true test or comparison. It might be that a question is premature because other more fundamental questions have not yet been addressed. The question may be unimportant, irrelevant, or capable of begetting only results with poor generality. It may only be stated in a form that precludes any theoretical or practical utility of the answer, or worse, in a form to which nature cannot possibly supply an unambiguous answer, no matter how careful and precise the investigation. Whatever the particular problem, a great many questions should probably not survive this stringent examination.

Measurement

Having considered preexperimental influences on interpretative behavior, we can now proceed to the influences of different facets of the conduct of the study itself. A clear prerequisite to an interpretation of the meaning of the data must be confidence in what the data are describing and how that description was created. It is often the case that very convincing data are generated by measurement procedures that have serious strategic inadequacies. The task for those interpreting experiments is to examine separately the various elements of measurement in order to make independent judgments regarding how each component should influence interpretation.

Response Class Definition.   Chapter 6 discussed the many considerations underlying response class definition, and those points are quite relevant here. Keeping those arguments in mind, the reader must be satisfied with the answers to such questions as: Does the study use primarily functional or topographical definitions? Is the definition of individual or group responding? Is the type of definition appropriate to other requirements of the study? Is the definition in terms of discrete movements? What level of specificity is aimed for? Is the transduction made automatically or manually? It may be that a study using a broad and poorly defined topographical definition of group responses can only leave the reader so strongly questioning what the measured data represent that the believability of any conclusions is severely limited. In addition, there is the more strategic question of whether or not the response classes, however adequately defined, were appropriately chosen for the announced purpose of the study.

Validity of measurement is automatically assured when functional response definitions are properly used, but the use of topographical definitions raises a legitimate issue as to what is really being measured. Some serious questions may be examined in this regard: Are multiple responses (topographically defined) recorded collectively and treated as the same response class? Do defined response classes cut across functional classes? Would different functional classes react differently to the independent variable manipulations? How might this possibility affect data interpretations? How might the generality of conclusions be affected by this problem? The reader must usually decide all of these issues without the assistance of any special evidence that would aid in interpreting the experimental approach to response definition.

Dimensional Quantities and Units.   Another source of control over interpretative behavior is the dimensional quantities and the units of measurement that the observation process uses to describe responding. The details of these considerations are discussed in Chapter 7; in general, the reader must consider how these experimental decisions may influence the way data are described and interpreted. Selecting idemnotic versus vaganotic measurement strategies is obviously crucial, and the choice of any dimensional quantity must satisfy the reader's judgment of the resulting unit's sensitivity to the effects of the independent variable. Does the dimensional quantity (or lack thereof) place any limits on the nature of the description that may be misleading (as percentage does)? Are the origins of any derived dimensionless quantities clearly traceable to natural properties of behavior in a manner that lends generality to their use? Does the dimensional quantity reflect variation that is of experimental interest or was it selected for observational convenience? The answers to these and similar questions may cast some degree of doubt on what aspect of the phenomenon the describe data actually represent.

Observing and Recording. The procedures by which behavioral facts are transduced into data are an obvious and powerful source of influence on interpretation, for the believability of the data is depreciated to the extent that the procedures used result in measurement error. A sampling of the important questions to answer in this context are: Did the observation procedures take account of the kind of response definition used? Was the frequency and duration of observation adequate? Were human observers properly trained? How well designed was the observer's task? Was independence among multiple observers ensured? What steps were taken to facilitate accuracy with human observers? Were automatic measurement devices properly calibrated and monitored? Was manual recording compatible with human observation?

Each observational situation is a unique treatment of these and related issues, and the reader must decide how the manner in which the experimenter addressed them affected the data. Unfortunately, the reader of a published article usually is not provided with enough of the necessary information required to make these judgments confidently, so it is usually necessary to make some assumptions about the missing observational details. The reader is forced to do this based on personal knowledge about the experimenter, any previously published and related work, and the research style of the investigator, which is communicated in and between the lines of the article. The investigator may or may not have earned the benefit of any doubt with each reader.

Stability and Accuracy of Measurement. Finally, the interpreter of an experiment must be satisfied as to the stability and accuracy of the data from the reported measurement procedures. There must be convincing evidence of the adequacy of efforts to calibrate human or automatic transducers. Furthermore, the reader must be persuaded that whatever stability is reported is not the spurious result of grossness or insensitivity of scale categories. The procedures used both in training and under experimental conditions should be fully described along with empirical information regarding the resulting accuracy of measurement. In the case of multiple observers, the degree of correspondence between observers' judgments must be properly described and the resulting believability evaluated.

Design

Experimental Reasoning. After carefully examining measurement procedures and deciding that they justify further consideration of the study, but before proceeding to examine the data, the interpreting scientist should look closely at the experimental design itself. The first task is to determine the experimental reasoning that the investigator would have had available assuming the obtained data showed ideal variations under the different conditions. Here, the interpreter will be looking at the arrangement of the three basic elements of design—the behavior, the experimental setting, and the independent variable changes—to see what consequents of different antecedent statements can be experimentally affirmed. One should be able to analyze a design in this fashion and list each proposition and the consequent that can affirm it, thus creating a clear picture of the reasoning that will be available under ideal data conditions. There may be a number of different propositions offered with one or several consequents examined for each. The experimenter or reader will have to decide if logical sufficiency and/or necessity statements are constructed by the design, as well as if the proper consequents afforded by the element arrangements can support believable arguments on behalf of the assertions. The design will also have to provide for examination of alternative explanations of independent variable effects by evaluating the effectiveness of the controls, the reasoning from which can clarify the conclusions permitted by the experiment. This kind of analysis of experimental reasoning must be a potent source of control over interpretative behavior and should always be undertaken *prior* to any examination of the data.

Replication.   In a similar fashion, the interpreting scientist must consider the evidence that the design will generate pertaining to the reliability and generality of the effect. One should be able to detect the different levels of replication that can provide information on the reliability of the functional relations. In addition, the presence of certain kinds of replications may suggest some degree of generality of the relations studied. A convincing treatment of replication in a design can strongly supplement a favorable interpretation by easing doubts raised by other aspects of the study.

At this point, the interpreting scientist is about to confront the evidence. He or she has evaluated the experimental question, is satisfied as to the tactical adequacy of the measurement procedures, and understands the logic of the empirical argument that can be advanced on the basis of the requirements of the design. The interpreter should now pause momentarily and ask, "What must be the nature of the evidence if I am to be convinced?" On this basis of a thorough familiarity with the details of the experiment and prior experience with the same or similar behavioral phenomena, it should be possible to formulate a standard that the evidence must meet to be convincing. It is important to take this step explicitly before encountering the data so as to be less susceptible to the numerous tactics of persuasion that are likely to be manifest in the data presentation.

Data

Display and Quantification.   Although we have finally reached the topic of experimental data as an influence on our interpretations, the experimenter and the audience must still force themselves to consider the influence on their interpretations of the format in which the data are presented. It is difficult to examine the details of graphs and other displays without drawing conclusions from the information they describe, and it is probably impossible to assess the appropriateness of a graph without considering the characteristics of the data it contains and the purpose it is intended to serve. However, it is most enlightening to examine the ways in which the display can encourage or even dictate certain interpretative responses; Chapter 16 was an extensive discussion of such matters. The present section only reiterates and summarizes certain points.

In attempting to ferret out any unwanted influences that have clear potential for deception, it is useful to start by evaluating the experimenter's goals in choosing any particular display. What is the experimenter trying to show with the data? Are certain kinds of interpretations being discouraged? What biases or perspectives are fostered by the display? A careful evaluation of the researchers's display decisions may uncover problems for interpretation. The choice of tabular versus graphic formats for certain information is crucial because of the many limitations of tables for certain interpretative functions. How were the axes selected? Is there appropriate consistency across graphs describing similar information? Are there any obviously deceptive elements that must be dealt with?

A major test of display formats concerns any possible losses of information. Although certain reasons for omitting data or displaying less detailed information are practical and innocuous, that is an evaluation that the reader must make by at least being able to identify such instances. Here, the reader must look for and evaluate summarizing, breaking axes, discontinuous time scales, and any other features that preclude seeing a complete and unexpurgated picture.

The display problems created by the experimenter may be sufficient to make it profitable for the reader to display some of the data in a different format in order to view the evidence from a better perspective. There is certainly no reason why the reader should be limited by the experimenter's display decisions as long as the necessary information is still available. Of course, important data is often omitted by a display format, and the reader is once again forced to judge how the believability of the remaining data is affected.

Previous chapters have discussed the various limitations of inferential statistics, and it is important to restate here their disadvantages as a means of providing information to either the experimenter or the reader. The significance statements that result from hypothesis tests are blatantly interpretative and, taken alone, preempt the reader's right to exercise his or her own judgment. In most cases, the detailed data that are consumed by statistical formulae are not presented in favor of the end products of various mathematical digestive operations. The consequent loss of information is enormous and is of no benefit to anyone except the journal editor concerned with brevity. The reader who never had access to the full data is at a particular disadvantage and may find it safest to insist that a sufficiently detailed picture of what happened is not available, precluding any interpretations at all.

Variability.   We now move to consideration of the data themselves, but before beginning to evaluate functional relations, it is important to examine the nature of the exhibited variability. This is a prerequisite step because of the possibility that the characteristics of the variability may prevent an unambiguous assessment of reliable organism–environment interactions.

The first judgment required is based on an opinion cumulated from analyzing all facets of described measurement operations. The question to be answered concerns how much of the displayed variability is illusory, having been created by measurment, versus real, having been imposed either by experimenter-controlled independent variable manipulations or uncontrolled extraneous factors. This is no less crucial a question when the amount and nature of variability is within acceptable limits. The difficulty of this decision is that beyond any empirical evidence the experimenter may present regarding stability and accuracy of measurement, there is no precise means of determining the amount of illusory variability represented. The judgment must be made by the reader after evaluating all of the measurement tactics that the experimenter designed.

A subsequent judgment requires an assessment of how much of the displayed real variability is a function of extraneous sources versus a function of the independent variable. The decision here may be somewhat less blind than the one previously described, because variation in responding may bear some degree of orderliness in relation to known or suspected extraneous events. However, there may also have been multiple, concurrent extraneous influences whose occurrences were not clear, thus leaving the viewer to the fundamental considerations discussed next.

A further question concerns the degree to which steady-state responding was achieved under each condition. As Chapter 12 pointed out, it is necessary to show stable responding in each phase in order to argue convincingly the effect of each treatment, as well as to permit unambiguous comparison of changes across phases. A careful examination of any trends in the data and the range of variability within phases is required to judge if the controlling variables were held sufficiently constant to permit a clear picture of the full and uncontaminated effects of treatment conditions. This decision is far from dichotomous, and answers to a number of questions are necessary: Are phase lengths sufficiently long to establish steady-state responding and to allow for the termination of possible transitory states? Are phase changes made while trends are in progress? Are the local ranges of variability within phases relatively constant? Are there plausible explanations for unusual patterns of responding? Are any cyclical patterns of responding properly accommodated by the design? As before, the reader must consider the impact of answers to these and other questions on the believability that will be assigned to the evidence for functional relations.

Functional Relations.   At some point before considering the functional relations described by the data, the critical scientist may have already decided that there are so many limiting factors as to preclude reliable and general interpretations. It is very difficult to begin reading a study and to stop short of looking at the data because measurement procedures have practically guaranteed that they will be misleading. The reader's interpretations are greatly controlled by graphic displays, and it is all too tempting to assume that a clear functional relation as shown has an unambiguous meaning, even though other influences equally clearly ensure ambiguity or worse. Yet, this kind of interpretative self-censorship is exactly what the reader's training and experience must impose.

However, let us assume that the reader's concerns are not yet fatal. An attempt must then be made to balance the believability of the functional relations with any special areas of hesitation. Each study is unique in this regard. The strength and clarity of the functional relations between independent variable changes and the dependent variable measures will often be less than unequivocal, and the degree of confidence in the effect itself must be considered in light of the influence of all of the previously discussed factors. The reader is, to some extent, in the position of making trade-offs between different sources of interpretative influence that suggest conflicting conclusions. For example, response definition or observation procedures may have been weak, but calibration data and treatment effects may be excellent. The design of elemental arrangements may have made stringent requirements on experimental control but the functional relations may be less than exciting. In other words, *the task is not just to interpret the data, but to interpret the entire experiment.*

In examining the described responding under different experimental conditions, it is important to look not just at molar differences between phases, but to examine in a molecular fashion the ebb and flow of responding under all conditions. There is a natural tendency to read overall patterns created by the data and in the process to ignore the scales of the axes or the details of changes within phases. This is particularly risky in the case of semilog graphs or with other axis scales that may contrast with the reader's history. It is helpful to regard the data points in terms of the numerical coordinates that they represent. One technique for encouraging this perspective was suggested in Chapter 12. If a piece of paper is placed over the chart and slowly moved to gradually uncover data points one by one, the reader will see the data in the same sequence the experimenter did (perhaps helping to explain some experimental decisions) and will be more likely to pay proper attention to individual data points as well as the larger patterns that are created.

In examining the data within and across phases for the purpose of generating a verbal translation of its meaning, it is imperative to keep such statements consistent with the limitations of the experimental reasoning that the design permits. The basic question that this reasoning and the obtained data address concerns the effects of the independent variable on the dependent variable. The word "effects" is plural because the reader should be looking for more than evidence of whether the treatment simply increases or decreases responding relative to baseline levels. Effects should include all details of changes that are associated with implementation of the treatment condition, including transitions states, variability, duration of changes, unexpected effects, etc., and interpretative statements should acknowledge all of these effects.

Finally, interpreting experimental data involves not just aspects of the immediate study but relating interpretive statements to the experimental and theoretical literature. That is, given the existence of good method and a clear treatment effect, what do the results mean in terms of past experimental findings, any theory or systematization of data, future research directions, technological application, and so forth? This is the acme of interpretative skill and is the font of whatever coherence and directional integration may be said to characterize a body of knowledge at any particular time.

CRITERIA

In light of this complex variety of sources of control over our interpretative behavior, it may be seriously asked how we ever draw the proper conclusions from experiments. It seems that there are so many influences that compromise accurate descriptions of nature that the cumulation of a useful literature would be difficult. In fact, it *is* difficult, and even the most sympathetic reviewer of experimental literature in the social sciences cannot avoid confronting the consequences of this problem. Relief will not come until the methodological standards of human behavioral research are considerably improved across all relevant disciplines. If we are not sufficiently aware of the problems with vaganotic measurement or groups-comparison designs to avoid such tactics, then we surely will not be sagacious enough in our interpretations to limit our conclusions properly. The inductive interpretations of experiments made within a discipline can certainly be no better than the quality of its scientific method.

Many thoughtful people have reacted to this state of affairs by arguing for policing of experimentation in the context of a set of rules, conventions, procedures, formulae, etc., to which all investigators are expected to adhere.

Research quality is then certified by presenting evidence that these codes have been complied with. Thus, an often unspoken rationale for requiring multiple observers, measures of interobserver agreement, certain generic classes of experimental design with their own interpretative regulations, and specific levels of statistical significance is that they furnish an automatic and presumably objective guarantee of valid conclusions.

There are a number of glaring deficiencies with this approach. First, it tends to restrict the tactical options open to the experimenter. Rather than being governed solely by the exigencies of nature in formulating questions and designing experiments, the researcher is further constrained by the necessity to follow rules that are not unambiguously applicable in every situation, much less appropriate. Second, this approach narrows the range of allowable interpretative responses to those that are subsumed by the codes. Rich implications of empirical findings are thus likely to be excluded from consideration. Third, as long as the rules are followed, bad data may be afforded undue attention and importance. The reliability and generality of an effect simply bears no relation to how well such rules and conventions were followed in demonstrating the effect, so good rule-following leaves open the question of how reliable and general the effect actually is. Finally, the inadequate methodological practices that seem to necessitate these codes either are not identified or are tolerated, regardless of the ambiguity of the resulting data, as long as the rules are followed. One temptation is to conclude that a given level of chaos is intrinsic if it cannot (or need not) be reduced in compliance with the rules. Scientific progress thus comes to depend on the evolution of the rule system, which, of course, will not occur unless someone shows a deficiency by violating them with beneficial effect.

Even as we reject codifications of scientific practice, we certainly cannot be complacent about the quality of research methods and the interpretation of experiments, for it is not as if there is no cost attached to interpretative actions. The consequences of interpretations can have significant professional, financial, and social effects, and in this sense, they dictate obvious criteria by which interpretations can be evaluated. In addition, applied research is conducted with special vigor in areas of considerable social need, and the demand for immediate answers to social problems is matched by the financial, social, and professional rewards for the scientist-technologist who is (or at least who appears to be) successful. The history of the interface between the social sciences and society clearly shows that many of these rewards were bestowed upon individuals making interpretations that were ultimately shown to be erroneous in some serious degree, independent of the goodness of scientists' intentions. These contingencies only exacerbate the difficulties of analyzing, training, and maintaining proper interpretative behavior. Fortunately, in matters of scientific interpretation, one person's opinion is not necessarily as good as another's, for an objective reality exists to serve as the final arbiter.

This argument suggests that the propriety of interpretations stemming from human behavioral research can only be placed upon the shoulders of the scientist, because only such individuals are properly trained for the task. This responsibility carries with it an unavoidable accountability that should be encouraged by the science and demanded by society. One of the necessities for such an accountability system is that there be some criterion for evaluation that reliably differentiates between good and poor interpretations. There is such a criterion that has always served that function, but whose role in this regard has never been properly clarified. This standard is the *generality* that our interpretations have. Generality refers to universality or replicability; the following chapter discusses this topic in detail. For now, it is important to understand its role as the criterion by which to judge interpretations of experiments.

Every time we make a verbal transformation of experimental procedures and results under the unavoidable control of the influences reviewed in this chapter, the resulting statement is characterized by some degree of accuracy and completeness probably short of absolute truth. The circumstances under which the statement will retain some degree of accuracy are not usually clear and certain, and the extent to which the interpretation is useful (universal, replicable, applicable, etc.) beyond the conditions of its origin is of primary interest and importance. This is what we are referring to when we ask what the generality of our conclusions are, and every interpretation can be characterized as to its generality. For example, it may be that problems with some aspect of measurement yield data that inaccurately describe what really happened, and if the resulting interpretations are not properly limited, they will not only poorly describe what happened but limit the applicability of the findings beyond the circumstances of the study. Of course, this deficiency will eventually be discovered in the process of further research and application, although the costs of such errors can be substantial. However, it is only through further investigation that the generality of interpretations is established and extended, as the replicative history of the timeout paradigm showed in Chapter 15. In other words, the criterion by which we are held accountable for our interpretations at any stage of experimentation is, fittingly enough, an empirical one, and this is a canon on which the self-corrective nature of science depends.

SCIENTIFIC COMMUNICATION

After weighing all of the considerations previously discussed, the researcher is faced with the most crucial decision a scientist can make: whether and how to make the findings public. As we have continually stressed, the issue may be stated in terms of attempts to influence the behavior of others who will undoubtedly lack equivalent access to the full details of procedures and results. The decision is not an easy one, because many factors of an essentially extrascientific nature will inevitably be involved. Nevertheless, we can highlight some of the basic considerations and outline certain options facing the investigator in such a way that the basic interests of the science are not likely to be severely compromised.

The first decision is probably the most difficult. The experimenter must demand an honest personal answer to the question, "Am I persuaded beyond reasonable doubt?" Only after being convinced of the basic veracity of the findings and their interpretation should one even consider attempting to convince others. The experimenter alone has access to all the information; even when the methodological quality of the experiment is unimpeachable, anyone else occupies a less tenable position from which to make this evaluation. There is a tendency, particularly among some younger researchers, to submit their findings to their professional superiors, usually editors and reviewers, in hopes of a positive or at least definitive evaluation of their work. This tendency has been recognized in the editorial policies of some journals, which make it an explicit part of their mission to educate the contributors through more than the usual amount of critical commentary from reviewers. Without questioning the nobility of purpose underlying this policy, we must point out that this is not the proper function of scientific journals. Although underdeveloped methodological practices in certain fields may temporarily justify such educational activity, a mature science relies on its journal system for dissemination and archival storage of its knowledge base. Furthermore, such policies encourage some researchers to substitute this pedagogical service for their own critical judgment. There can be no delegation of the basic responsibility of every scientist to decide the primary meaning and importance of his or her work. Ideally, the experimenter will be his or her own most severe critic, not releasing for public consumption any findings of which he or she is not completely convinced.

Everyone is aware that a complex set of contingencies influences the behavior of every scientist, and success at wresting secrets from nature may not be the most powerful. In a better world, the ratio of effective experiments to publications would be substantially greater than unity with only the most penetrating methods and integrative results being committed to print. Although it has probably always been tenuous, the relation between good experimentation and publication frequency is now badly ruptured, particularly in academic science. A system of contingencies has evolved wherein payoffs are for publications *per se* and only secondarily for their content. More or less explicit consequences in the form of professional, scholarly, and financial advancement are arranged on the basis of *number* of published items, thereby forcing the academic scientist to behave accordingly. There are several byproducts of this policy that merit examination.

It is clear that the purpose of publishing is no longer solely, or even primarily, to convince others of the signifcance and veracity of one's findings. Announcing solutions to long-standing problems has not only become a rarity, but training conditions have evolved to mitigate against its occurrence. It is customary to tell students that a good research endeavor raises more questions than it answers and then to look the other way as the student attempts to secure a public outlet for a manuscript that answers no questions at all. As a result, we are inundated by an "information explosion" that strains the capabilities of our most advanced electronic information storage and retrieval systems. No one is naive enough to think that each published article reports a significant finding, yet no one seems willing to place the responsibility squarely where it belongs: on the scientific conscience of each investigator. In order for each to discharge this obligation, ways must be found to arrange different contingencies for academic advancement so that the future of the sciences is not further compromised by what has become a highly cynical and wasteful process. The most unbearable cost is in lost opportunities to gain knowledge; workers under the control of the contingencies of publishing rather than discovery can be expected to make genuine advances only infrequently. Furthermore, in a system that discourages critical judgments of experiments, they are less likely to recognize a major finding should they or others happen to make one. This likelihood is even further reduced by the sheer bulk of the resulting literature.

Another unfortunate byproduct of the operation of publishing contingencies that stress frequency over quality has been the inevitable contraction of space allotted to each contribution. In order to publish as many titles as possible within the limitations of their financial resources, editors severely limit the amount of material an author can expect to have printed. Accordingly, productive and exhaustive interpretation by the scientific audience has become nearly impossible, forcing a degree of subjectivity in interpretation that severely strains and compromises the self-corrective nature of the scientific enterprise. No member of the eventual audience can properly interpret the data of an experiment unless furnished with a complete description of the procedure under which it was collected. Details of response definition, observational tactics, data recording, empirical definition of independent variables, and the sequence of experimental operations are as much a part of the report of a scientific experiment as are the actual data displays. Notwithstanding present editorial policies to the contrary, incomplete descriptions of procedural details are practically the equivalent of no description at all and, in the case of archival journals, should not be accepted. This is not to discourage the practice of occasional publication of extensive methodological statements that can be cross referenced, but future readers of today's journals will only be able to wonder at the details of procedure and will have no basis for comparison of today's results with theirs. Replication, the life blood of a systematic science, is all but impossible on the basis of contemporary archival journal reports.

Part of the solution of these problems lies in the fuller development and utilization of dissemination outlets other than the archival journals. Bulletins, newsletters, conference proceedings, and technical reports serve the useful function of disseminating progress reports and results of intentionally limited generality. These outlets should become the topic of an educational effort aimed at upgrading their status in the eyes of administrators who feel compelled to rely on publication frequency to certify activity.

There is another dimension of scientific communication that is vital to the well being of the enterprise—informing the patron of progress and accomplishments. From the beginnings of modern science in the Renaissance to the early 20th century, this was a relatively simple matter because scientific support was initially the function of a handful of wealthy patrons and, eventually, industrial concerns and foundations. Nowadays, however, science is increasingly supported by government, which is necessarily responsive to the will of the people. It becomes the duty of the scientist to help ensure that all expressions of that will are informed to the best extent possible. Fortunately, channels of communication now exist that make it possible for the scientist to discharge that obligation in a relatively painless fashion; the popular press and electronic media provide convenient outlets for communicating to the surrounding culture. The jocularity with which some prominent elected officials publicly castigate basic research efforts directly reflects the failure of the scientific community to take seriously its obligation to inform the sponsoring public. In the case of the natural science of behavior, this function must be performed especially well if the discipline is to have any hope of abbreviating the period of conflict between the proponents of traditional wisdom and the purveyors of discovered knowledge that inevitably accompanies any major scientific reformulation. Our discipline is especially vulnerable to misrepresentation and distortion by poorly informed popular writers who eagerly fill the public's demand for information about a subject with which they are vitally concerned, their own behavior. Forestalling needless controversies can be assured only if knowledgeable, competent researchers accept their obligation to present the public with a correct accounting in a style and through media with which the public is comfortable.

Because of the subject matter, scientific students of human behavior are in a unique position to offer exemplary leadership in developing solutions to the problems of scientific communication. By attending constantly to the variety of functional purposes served by communication and then tailoring tactics to the empirical requirements of these functions, they will be deploying their scientific knowledge in a way that benefits not only the discipline but the culture at large.

19 Generality

There is no worse lie than a truth misunderstood by those who hear it.

—William James

INTRODUCTION

In the previous chapter, generality was introduced as a standard by which the correctness of interpretations of experimental procedures and data is unavoidably judged. However, the concept of generality has broader usage than as an arbiter of experimental conclusions; this chapter explores its several meanings thoroughly. The synonyms already used include universality, replicability, and applicability; formally, generality may be defined in the context of scientific method as the characteristic of numerical data or verbal interpretations of data that describes some meaning or relevance beyond the circumstances of their origin. It must be distinguished from the concern for reliability of experimental effect, which simply raises the question, "If I repeat certain procedures, will I get the same result?" A broad statement of the question raised by generality is, "If I take part or all of a certain result and apply part or all of the procedures that produced it under circumstances that are in some degree different, will I get the same kind of effect?"

DATA VERSUS INTERPRETATIONS

A distinction must be made between references to generality of data and generality of *interpretations* of data. Although the former phrase is the more frequently used, the latter is more often appropriate. It may be argued that experimental data (functional relations) usually have some degree of inherent generality. That is, whether or not it is known or even of interest, the results of the independent variable manipulations on the subject's responding may have some applicability or universality under other conditions that are in some way different. When we render interpretations of the meaning of those results, we are in part and in some way attempting to describe the generality of the data. To the extent that we are at all in error, our interpretations will have limitations in generality that are not characteristic of the data's true generality. Thus, the difference refers to the fact that we usually interpose our description of the data and its meaning between the data themselves and efforts to examine generality. In other words, efforts to probe the generality of a set of data are really evaluations of the generality of our interpretations of the data, not of the data *per se*. Most of the time, we are primarily interested in the extent to which our interpretations of an experiment apply beyond the confines of their particular origin. We want to be able to assert that a finding will hold in another setting, that other subjects will react in the same manner to similar circumstances, that a certain variable will produce the same effects under somewhat changed conditions, or that a procedure will show the same controlling influence even though some parameters are modified.

These all involve questions regarding the generality of our interpretations of experimental data rather than the generality of the actual data themselves, and the distinction is more than academic. Its importance lies in the not at all unlikely possibility that the true generality of the data and our interpretation of it will be less than congruent. Given the nature of the many influences on our interpretations and especially the contingencies for us as experimenters, the tendency is for interpretations to err in a lenient or generous rather than stringent or conservative direction. To the extent that this is true, we will be in the position of pursuing and examining the generality not of data, but of optimistic estimates of the generality of the data for a particular question. Under such conditions, we should not be disappointed to find evidence of more severe limits on the universality of our conclusions than we had wished.

The reasons for such disappointments are in a sense not the fault of poor data, but poor experimental tactics. We have stated before that a question properly asked about nature always yields useful and interesting information. However, regardless of the adequacy of the question, queries of nature that are badly translated methodologically will always result in answers that are misleading or confusing to some degree. With such a data base, poor generality is guaranteed and incautious interpretations only compound the problem. Accurate interpretations of such data will recognize the necessity of avoiding any conclusions at all.

In the case of truly good data, it is clearly interpretations that are the cause of poor generality. Data that reliably describe a functional relation in nature will always have some utility beyond the particular case, whether or not the experimenter or reader recognizes the extant message. If an accurate verbal transduction is made, good data will speak clearly without distortion, and the result will be rewarding to those who attend to it. If the translation is in some way inaccurate, pursuit of poor conclusions about good data will lead to misdirected efforts and unnecessary frustration.

ORIGINS OF GENERALITY

The evidence that is available from the various manipulations in an experiment should constitute much of the influence on the experimenter's postulations about the generality of the findings. In addition to findings from earlier literature, there is often good support from the different independent variable conditions in the present experiment that, together with acceptable method, encourage reasonable speculations about the effects of other variables that might be arranged in the future. Except in abbreviated studies containing only one treatment condition, experiments that explore the effects of a number of changes in independent variables generate valuable information for purposes of making statements about the generality of the findings. The greater the number of independent variables and their parameters examined in the course of an experiment or series of experiments, the more secure the basis for predictions about independent variable effects under still different conditions.

This information about the generality of a functional relation is available from such a thorough and searching style of experimentation because it is based on an empirical knowledge of the variables that have any influence on the functional relation under study. As controlling variables and limiting parameters are identified and more precisely specified through experimental manipulations, the ability to reliably and accurately describe the necessary and sufficient conditions for producing the same kind of effect under specifiably different conditions is greatly increased. The more fully we can explain a phenomenon or effect, the more accurate will be any extrapolations to further experimental or applied situations.

To say that generality is a normal byproduct of good experimentation should not suggest that it automatically accrues to every research project, however. An examination of much contemporary human behavioral research in light of the strategies and tactics expounded in previous chapters should convince the rigorous reader that there are many popular practices that injure the possibilities for such benefits. We must attend to the molecular details of experimental method so that general design strategies and series of experimental manipulations are not prevented from yielding the broadly useful information that their conceptualization might otherwise deserve. For example, inadequate measurement procedures can severely limit the generality of the data that result from a powerful and informative experimental design.

Finally, methodologically acceptable experiments thematically guided by efforts to establish the generality of organism–environment interactions are crucial as a systematizing influence in a literature. This kind of literature tends toward an easy and natural integration that encourages a healthy, inductively constructed theoretical structure with all the benefits thereof. The literature reviewed in Chapter 15 is, to a limited extent, an example of this process.

DIMENSIONS OF GENERALITY

We are now ready to elaborate more fully the generic meaning of generality defined earlier. There are at least five distinguishable emphases in meaning that can be described, although the differences are to some extent more didactic than practical.[1] These differences are in the kinds of information about generality that are the object of experimental efforts. Because the investigator does not usually approach the quest for generality in quite the formal fashion that textbooks describe, it should be clear that these distinctions are not cleanly delineated. Actually, the typical process of experimentation provides information on a number of dimensions of generality simultaneously, although particular manipulations can be directed at specific dimensions of interest.

Across Subjects

Traditionally, the strongest concern with generality has undoubtedly been with the universality or representativeness of a finding across different subjects. It is interesting that in good behavioral research, the question is of relatively minor concern, is not regarded with special attention, and is easily answered in the normal course of experimentation. The strategic emphases here, in contrast with those of groups comparison research, highlight some of the inherent disadvantages of group formats. The between-group design deals with the question of the representativeness of effect in a way that precludes discovering a functional relation to test the generality of. In a phrase, the cart

---

[1]These different types of generality are discussed in an excellent chapter by Sidman (1960), and many of the central points in the following section are his.

is put before the horse. The tactic of exposing different levels of the independent variable to different groups composed of large numbers of subjects and treating their responses collectively by asking if they are representative of the untested portion of the population provides experimental comparisons that are descriptive of or applicable to *no* member of any of the groups, let alone any unmeasured individuals in the larger population. Attempts to extract functional relations from such comparisons can, as Grice and Hunter (1964) have shown, yield results that simply are not reproduced when tested with individuals, even if the individual data are grouped and averaged. Grice and Hunter examined the effects of varying the intensity of the conditioned stimulus on Pavlovian conditioning of the human eyeblink. Using the traditional groups comparison procedure wherein each subject was exposed to a single intensity of the conditioned stimulus, these investigators replicated the usual finding of no functional effect. However, when they exposed individual subjects to all levels of conditioned stimulus intensity, they found that conditioning performance was an increasing function of that variable. Thus, the effect of exposing a subject to all levels of the independent variable is usually not the same as the effect obtained when different subjects are exposed to each level of the variable. This should come as no surprise, because the experimental histories of subjects in these two types of experiments will be radically different. Yet, many investigators continue to behave as though results obtained from between-groups comparisons should automatically generalize to the single case (see Chapter 5). This strategy at least partly stems from assumptions of intrinsic variability, which are seen as necessary because of the large amounts of intersubject variability that attend the use of between-group designs. Because functional relations applicable to the individual are not uncovered, thus precluding attention to their generality, interest naturally gravitates to the representativeness of all that is left, the quantitative characteristics of group data.

Subject generality is not markedly improved by averaging the measures of responding of a large number of subjects to all values of the experimental variables. The cause of the problem has to do with the tactic of grouping individual data and the associated measurement and design decisions. As a result, individual functions are not usually examined, even if available, although the independent variable has its effects independently on each separate subject, not on the group. There is no reason to suspect that all aspects of the independent variable effect will be the same for each subject, even though the same kind of relation may be consistently present. For example, Fig. 19.1 from Sidman (1960) shows responding from four hypothetical subjects as a function of values of the independent variable.

In describing the problem posed by this particular example, Sidman (1960) points out that:

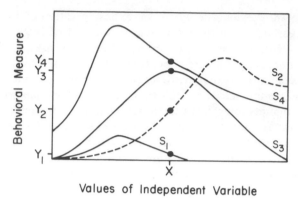

Values of Independent Variable

FIG. 19.1.   A set of curves from a hypothetical population of experimental subjects. The behavior of each subject passes through a maximum value as the independent variable increases magnitude, but each subject reacts maximally at a different value of the independent variable. (From Sidman, 1960, p. 50.)

Subjects S_3 and S_4 will show very similar quantitative responses to the value, X, of the experimental variable. In fact, however, this value of the independent variable catches Subjects S_3 and S_4 at markedly different phases of the process that is represented by the curvilinear function. Traditional group design will not reveal this fact, because the individual functions are not examined nor even obtained. We have here a case in which generality will falsely be attributed to the data. The quantitative similarity of the subjects' behavior is an artifact of an experimental design which does not permit analysis of the causes of variability. Quantitative differences or similarities among subjects at single isolated points of a functional relation do not provide appropriate criteria for evaluating the representativeness of experimental data [pp. 50–51].

There are many patterns of data that can be used to make this point graphically, all of which have in common the obscuring of functional relations at the individual organism–environment level by focusing attention on the generality of various quantitative aspects of group data (e.g., the shape of the distribution or the mean value). This argument should make clear the falsity of the belief that the larger the group, the greater the generality of the data.[2] The only certainty about a larger group is that intersubject variability will make it harder to understand what happened at the level of the individual organism where the actual effects of the manipulations occurred—the only level where the laws of behavior can be discovered. Individual versus any form of group data actually constitute two entirely different subject matters,

[2] The absurdity of this general strategy was charmingly noted by Claude Bernard in 1865 when he referred to "a physiologist who took urine from a railroad station urinal where people of all nations passed, and who believed he could thus present an analysis of *average* European urine! [pp. 134–135; italics his]."

with true interest in the quantitative effects of a treatment on a collection of different individuals being very infrequent (except in large-scale evaluation research). Even if the forms of individual and group curves are identical, they cannot provide the same kind of generality because they represent entirely different kinds of behavioral phenomena, and this creates considerable problems in attempting to integrate any two literatures separately dominated by these two different strategies.

What about those instances when the problem is difficult to approach with individual subjects or when the interest is clearly with "group behavior"? First, such instances are far fewer than many would suspect, and the flexibility of single-subject designs is much greater than many are probably aware of. For instance, the irreversibility of an effect is not a barrier in most applied studies, especially because the limitations on reversibility are usually of a logistical or practical nature. In the case of true irreversibility, Sidman (1960) correctly points out that the only solution is to study the processes as they occur in nature; group analyses will not be enlightening when the behavioral process exists only in the individual. Regardless of the source of the irreversibility, the design strategies discussed in Chapter 14 are quite capable of accommodating experimental inference in these situations. In other words, true irreversibility can only be verified by experimental demonstration showing that proper control of extraneous variables (sequence effects, etc.) fails to relieve the problem. When that is done, a fact about behavior has been established—under specifiable conditions, a particular phenomena is irreversible. That fact then constitutes an addition to the subject matter of the science and must be dealt with as such. For instance, its determinants can be fully explored in the usual ways be investigating the parametric influence of the controlling variables, the intersubject generality of the effect, the role of experimental history, etc. In no case should it be ignored or cancelled by statistical manipulation, just as no other fact of behavior should be so abused.

In those instances when someone wants to know what proportion of a population will show a certain treatment effect, the question is usually the wrong one, or at least premature. For example, instead of asking how many children in the 6-year-old population will learn to read to a certain criterion using a new reading skills program, we should be asking what prerequisite skills are necessary for program effectiveness with every child and what variations in style of management are necessary under what conditions. In other words, an understanding of the generality of a procedure comes not from blindly testing larger and larger proportions of the population, but from a thorough understanding of the variables controlling its effecs under any circumstances. It is not that the question of "how many" is irrelevant; it is simply asked well in advance of other more basic questions concerning the existence, and nature, and determinants of an effect. It is likely that the question of actuarial representativeness would be approached differently if the phenomenon were thoroughly understood in the first place.

If not quantitative aspects of collected individual data, then what characteristics of the data do we have a legitimate interest in the generality of across subjects? The functional relations between environmental manipulations and individual responding that are the grail of our efforts in an experiment should also be the object of extensions to additional subjects. If we can show that a particular treatment yields the same *kind* of orderliness in different individuals in the population, then the result has good subject generality. Detailed quantitative differences among subjects should be distinctly secondary in interest to the universality of the *form* of functional relations. Any quantitative variability may or may not warrant special attempts to identify controlling variables; at a certain point in our knowledge about a phenomenon, such differences will be of practical insignificance and beyond reasonable efforts to explain. The role of uncontrolled, unique environmental histories will always loom large as a component of such explanations.

The relative utility of this strategy in the larger scheme of things should not go unnoted. Attempting to demonstrate the generality of a functional relation across subjects leads directly to additional within-subject manipulations with new subjects that assist in clarifying the roles of variables requisite to an effect. These replicative experiments add to our useful knowledge about organism-environment interactions, because the questions are asked about lawful relations in nature and are posed in a way that nature's answer may be clearly detected. With this strategy, we avoid the disappointments of asking bad questions about the nonexistent organism called "group."

Across Species

A second and related meaning of generality concerns the applicability of a finding across species. Some of the most valuable human behavioral research results from efforts to extend the generality of findings in the animal laboratory to *homo sapiens*. Less common, but equally valid, are attempts to extend generality in the opposite direction—from human studies to other animals. A dramatic example of such an extension is the analysis of linguistic phenomena in chimpanzees (e.g., Gardner & Gardner, 1969; Premack, 1971), which appears to establish that phenomena once thought peculiar to humans are shared, at least by other primates. Extending generality in this direction augments the overall systematization of our behavioral knowledge.

The two meanings of generality discussed thus far refer to dimensions across which we investigate the generality of functional relations between variations in an organism's responding and the experimental environment. This sense of generality may be contrasted with the sense in which the three

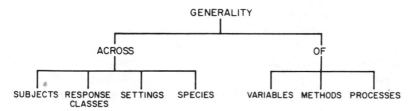

FIG. 19.2.   Dimensions of generality.

meanings discussed later are used. These have in common a detailed specification of the aspects of the functional relations that we want to clarify the generality of. In sum, the difference is between "generality across" versus "generality of"; in any experimental instance, emphasis may be on one kind of dimension or the other, if not both.

We can further subdivide the question of the generality of some facets of the functional relation into those meanings of generality having primarily to do with the independent variable and those having primarily to do with the dependent variable. We have chosen for further discussion two of the former (generality of variables and methods) and one of the latter (generality of processes), which Sidman (1960) emphasizes, but it must be pointed out that it is possible to fractionate both subcategories further, if desired. For example, we could examine the generality of any number of data characteristics or we could investigate parametric values of some variable in a search for generality. However, whatever the particular interest, we are always assessing the generality of both sides of a functional relation. We can look at variables and methods only through their associated effect, and a behavioral process cannot be studied independently of its environmental determinants. As an organizational aid to the reader, the relations among these various dimensions of generality are schematically depicted in Fig. 19.2.

Of Variables

Crucial to the healthy growth of a natural science of behavior is a strong interest in the generality of variables. This is an aspect of generality that serves an important role in integrating and systematizing a diverse literature. When we can show that a particular variable is relevant beyond the confines of a certain experiment, experimental program, or even an area of literature, then we have made an outstanding advance in our knowledge of behavior. Science progresses most with the discovery of similarities; differences, although easier to find, are only signs of our ignorance.

Information about the generality of a variable derives from using that variable in different ways in different experiments conducted for different purposes. In some studies, the variable may be the central focus of numerous manipulations. In other experiments, the variable may be used in a heuristic fashion to study some other phenomenon. But, in all cases, the purposes behind the use of the variable in different arrangements may range from basic research to purely practical development of methods of behavior control. It is this variety that is so useful in proving the consistency of effect from which we infer generality.

A good example of such a variable is conditioned reinforcement or reinforcement by stimuli that have acquired reinforcing properties through pairings with other reinforcers. This variable has excellent generality as a result of extensive investigation in and outside of the laboratory, across subjects and species, and under a very wide range of experimental conditions. The subject index of the *Cumulative Index* of a basic research journal, such as *Journal of the Experimental Analysis of Behavior,* provides a long list of variables that have accrued varying degrees of generality.

Of Methods

Most applied human behavioral research is, intentionally or not, directed toward the generality of methods of behavioral control. This is understandable, because the contingencies surrounding the conduct of experimentation in field settings discourage serious efforts to identify and pursue fundamental behavioral phenomena. Unfortunately, efforts to assess the generality of methods can, under the effects of those same contingencies, become premature drives to establish the universal efficacy of methodological "packages." This apparent inconsistency results from inadequate specification and understanding of the relevance and irrelevance of the variables that constitute such packages (the term is advisedly used in a marketing sense), with the result that honestly pursued generality will remain disconcertingly elusive. Methodological generality should be pursued by sound empirical development of the subcomponent parts of variables of a procedure, with the form of the finally assembled procedure being primarily determined by this kind of experimental evidence, rather than by theoretical, marketing, or personal preconceptions.

The lengthy replicative history of the timeout procedure (see Chapter 15) is an excellent example of the proper approach to establishing method generality. The breadth of knowledge supporting the eventual development of a useful behavior-management tool was considerable. Numerous facets of the general procedure had been thoroughly probed in many different experimental programs, and the final format that evolved was not a single method but a homogeneous collection of specific procedures with the necessary flexibility for the wide range of applications that are required. The functional similarity of procedural variations in the generic category was assured by empirically identifying and verifying the critical features of the method.

Of Processes

Interest with the generality of behavioral processes is an instance of a meaning of generality more concerned with the dependent variable side of the functional relation. Sidman (1960) has described two meanings of the phrase "behavioral process." First, we can call behavior that results from the interactions of two or more different variables or procedures a behavioral process. Perhaps the clearest example here is the process we term "discrimination," which results from a combination of reinforcement and extinction procedures. When an organism emits a response of a certain class only when a specific stimulus is present and never, or rarely, when that stimulus is absent, we say the organism "discriminates" the presence or absence of the stimulus. To produce such behavior, it is sufficient to arrange reinforcement of the response only in the presence of the stimulus, never in its absence. Thus, a combination of reinforcement and extinction, each correlated with specific aspects of the stimulating environment defines the process known as discrimination. Of course, there are other methods of producing the desired characteristics of responding (e.g., Terrace, 1966), and the comparative analysis of all such methods is a continuing effort to establish process generality.

Second, we can characterize as a behavioral process behavior that results from applying a wide range of quantitative values of a particular variable. An example here might be the decreasing number of presentations of a new word necessary to meet a criterion for verbal imitation by a schizophrenic child as a function of the number of presentations of other new words already mastered (see Lovaas, Berberich, Perloff, & Schaeffer, 1974). That the number of imitations of new words necessary to meet criterion is a decreasing function of the total number of presentations of already acquired words can be called a behavioral process.[3] As before, achieving some standard of generality of behavioral process can be easy or difficult depending on the complexity of the problem, but it is most successfully approached by developing and building on a careful knowledge of the smaller functional relations that make up the larger phenomenon.

It must be emphasized that unequivocal distinctions among these several or additional meanings of generality may often be somewhat elusive. In fact, all

---

[3]It should be clear that neither of the discussed meanings of "behavioral process" is intended to invite imposition of any explanatory device beyond the explicit statement of the functional relations involved. Thus, a behavioral process is described by functional relations but is not to be construed as a higher order cause of them.

methods are made up of variables, all variables are delivered under some procedural protocol that could be called a method, and all processes are the result of certain variables or operations. What is intended with these definitions is that we fully understand what generality can mean, its role in research strategies, how we go about achieving it, and how we evaluate the extent to which it has been demonstrated. The remainder of the chapter is devoted to this last issue.

EVALUATION OF GENERALITY

The question raised in evaluating generality is, "When has generality been established in any particular case?" As usual, no formula is available to guide an answer, but a discussion of some important strategic considerations will be helpful. Evaluating the generality of some phenomenon first invoves the cumulated interpretation of all relevant experiments in accordance with the many points made in the last chapter. Generality accrues to a functional relation only through improvements in the understanding of the variables that influence it, so the experiments that investigate these influences must be properly and cohesively interpreted in order to reach any clear picture of generality.

It is also important to consider the kinds of generality that are of primary concern. Generality of a functional relation across subjects can be established in part by repeating the same experimental conditions for a number of subjects, and the number of such successful reproductions becomes a straightforward index. Of course, methodological quality is a crucial consideration; a handful of methodologically powerful studies evidencing powerful results can easily outweigh whole areas of literatures showing equivocal results from inferior methods. Assessing the generality of variables, methods, and processes is more difficult in that all of the relevant experiments are necessarily different in some way. Even if we assumed, for the sake of argument, that all were methodologically excellent and properly interpreted, it should be clear that they will not be equal in the extent to which they contribute meaningful information about generality. Because of the areas of ignorance about the phenomenon and the particular manipulations arranged by a single experiment, that experiment may be far more or far less enlightening than another that approaches the phenomenon differently. A careful examination of the many different studies establishing the generality of the timeout procedure will make this problem clear; it would be impossible to rank order even crudely the experiments according to their contributions.

Still assuming flawless method and interpretation, there is a further problem in that in each experiment, the degree to which the extension of the functional relation to a new circumstance is successful is always different.

This raises the question of how exactly must the replicative manipulation reproduce the results of previous experimentation in order to contribute some generality. In addition to the considerations touched on in the chapter on replication, it is clear that the precision of the existing literature is at least a guideline. Certainly, one would not want to apply lower standards to this evaluation than are already available from completed studies. Whereas in one area, simple changes in response frequency in the right direction may be sufficiently encouraging to prompt further studies, in other areas, certain functional relations may be so well understood that their form must be reproduced almost exactly in order to offer convincing evidence. However, the fledgling science of human behavior is far from the stage of demanding precise quantitative duplication in order to contribute to generality.

Indeed, there is no particular point at which one can say that the generality of a functional relation is established, even though one may find or conduct some study that is especially convincing. It is not through any formal process, but through the behavioral process of inductive inference that we evaluate generality. Sidman (1960) expresses the point beautifully:

> Whether or not we make an inductive inference, and the degree of tenacity with which we cling to that inference, will depend on our behavioral history (experience). I refer to this history when I say that the evaluation of generality is a matter of judgement. From an act of induction based upon our own accumulated experience, we judge the amount of generality to be added to a variable when it proves effective in experiments that have little or no operational connection with each other [p. 59].

Thus, according to Sidman (1960), "the degree of confidence that prevails in a scientific community with respect to any particular induction will be a function of the extent to which the members of that community share a common history of experience [p. 61]."

Although the rules for assessing generality may be indefinite, there is at least a criterion for evaluating the propriety of our judgments, much as generality is the standard for evaluating the goodness of interpretations. Although generality is one of the guiding influences on the design of replicative manipulations, reproducibility is the ultimate gauge of generality. The reason why this is true becomes clear when we remember that reproducibility results from being able to specify and control all of the sources of variability that can influence a functional relation. Thus, if as a result of experimentation, we can describe the conditions that are required to reproduce or that limit the effect under varying circumstances, then replications of all kinds will yield successful reproductions of relations, and their generality is thereby affirmed.

Perhaps this principle can be more clearly seen if we suppose a situation in which generality is falsely attributed (or at least overenthusiastically assigned) to the findings of a particular study. Then, applications of that finding under different circumstances will likely yield some degree of failure to obtain the same results because unidentified factors (the importance of which are still unknown) were changed or otherwise not properly treated in the new application. The message that such a failure should carry is that the original findings are not yet generalizable (to the extent of the attempt) because of limitations in knowledge about sources of control. For the experimenter who is willing to assume responsibility for the risk of optimistic generalizing, a negative outcome of this type may eventually be quite informative. To the extent that it directs attention toward insufficiently examined sources of control, a failure of this type can contribute to the overall efficiency of the research enterprise by clearly delineating the areas of greatest ignorance. However, the implied responsibility is personal; no investigator should intentionally rely on others to perform the research necessary to illuminate and correct known shortcomings in the generality of his or her interpretations.

Reproducibility as a criterion for the evaluation of generality is a natural consequence for our extrapolations in that it constitutes an inevitable test. If we are even reasonably well trained and honest in our interpretations of experiments, the readiness of our conclusions for generalization to other circumstances will be more apparent than the didactic cautions of this chapter suggest. However, if we are not so experienced and conservative, then repeated failures to reproduce results will eventually be noticed by everyone else.

Part V TOWARD A MATURE SCIENCE OF BEHAVIOR

20 Behavioral Science and Scientific Behavior

```
I. Introduction
II. Some basic definitions
III. Continua of behavioral research
IV. Relations within behavioral research
V. Styles of behavioral research
   A. Thematic
   B. Independent
   C. Demonstration
   D. Advocacy
   E. Pilot
   F. In-house
VI. Toward an analysis of scientific behavior
```

No, a thousand times no; there does not exist a category of science to which one can give the name applied science. There are science and the applications of science, bound together as the fruit of the tree which bears it.

—Louis Pasteur

INTRODUCTION

Previous chapters have examined the methods by which we attempt to view human activity through a microscope of moderately high magnification. We are now in a position to step back and consider behavioral research from a broader perspective. Strategies at this general level are most important in developing our knowledge in an area; because of the special perspectives that human beings hold of their own behavior as a scientific subject matter, a fledgling science of human behavior may need all of this kind of consideration that can be mustered.

SOME BASIC DEFINITIONS

First, we would like to offer some definitions, as is *de rigueur* for volumes such as this. Unlike other volumes, ours places them in the last chapter on the presumption that exposure to the entirety of the foregoing material is

411

prerequisite to developing an appreciation of their contextual significance. There is probably some finite limit to the benefits of discussing the denotations and connotations of terms such as science, research, and experiment, but we shall persist, if only to give the reader something in the book that can be disagreed with. Actually, the perspective underlying this discussion is discriminably different from most of its genre, as well as being useful in the balance of the chapter.

We define *science* as the collection of human activities for which the consequences are statements of contingencies that allow prediction and control of natural phenomena. This is obviously a broadly inclusive definition and will require some elaboration. It is phrased to include many very different kinds of behavior related in a functional sense only by the common effect to which they all contribute. Thus, such diverse activities as securing funding to support research, arranging for access to the research setting and subjects, maintaining a favorable political climate for research, and communicating with others on professional topics are included along with the obvious activities more directly related to actually conducting experiments. However, any exhaustive analysis should take account of these somewhat peripheral activities that are in the long run necessary although not sufficient for scientific progress.

It is common to summarily classify numbers of related responses by referring to certain scientific attitudes (e.g., parsimony, empiricism, objectivity, etc.), and this is harmless as long as we do not forget that we are using only a kind of imprecise, shorthand reference to classes of human behavior that are no different in kind than any other human activity. In this regard, it should be clear that if science is a collection of responses that generate a certain consequence, then it is erroneous to refer to science as knowledge, because knowledge is only the result or byproduct of science (Skinner, 1974).

Describing the results of scientific activities as statements of contingencies may seen confusing to those unfamiliar with the behavioristic perspective. First, as the past two chapters pointed out, the data resulting from experimental manipulation are described in the language of our culture. These verbal statements are rules summarizing "if–then" relations in nature or contingencies that govern our actions in arranging parts of the environment of ourselves or others for which the rules have generality. Thus, these are statements describing the contingencies of nature that, if accommodated, will lead to effective actions. The enormous savings facilitated by this kind of discovered knowledge is that others who have not themselves experienced the contingencies personally can use the statements (knowledge) to behave successfully. In other words, according to Skinner (1974):

> By learning the laws of science, a person is able to behave effectively under the contingencies of an extraordinarily complex world. Science carries him beyond

experience and beyond the defective sampling of nature inevitable in a single lifetime. It also brings him under the control of conditions which could play no part in shaping and maintaining his behavior. He may stop smoking because of a rule derived from a statistical study of the consequences, although the consequences themselves are too deferred to have any reinforcing effect [p. 124].

As a corollary to this definiton of science, it is clear that there can be no Method of science in the sense of a structurally formal scientific method or methods. The failure of philosophers to understand this fact will continue to frustrate their efforts to explain scientific behavior. This volume does not describe *a* method, in spite of the fact that some will attempt to so characterize it by crudely summarizing certain described tactics in order to compare them to other similarly summarized "methods." In fact, there are many actions that can assist in discovering knowledge, and humanity learned much about nature long before there was any discussion of science and scientific method. Any actions that lead to accurate statements about nature must be considered as having some methodological legitimacy; the characterizations of contrasting methods are simply arguments that some scientific actions are more effective than others at producing statements of good generality. These chapters constitute one such argument, and there is no intention to imply that procedures that have been criticized here or omitted entirely cannot under some circumstances at least lead in the right direction. In a sense, our argument is for a kind of scientific efficiency in which researchers engage in investigative activities that minimize error, confusion, and misinterpretation and that maximize progress in understanding human behavior. If there are differences of opinion between ourselves and others, we are fortunate that arbitration lies in the success with which prediction and control of the subject matter is demonstrated. In other words, we are all equally susceptible to the behavioral law that states that the consequences of our present scientific actions will shape our future scientific actions, and hence the science itself.

Research may be generally defined as that subset of scientific activities that includes direct contact with the phenomena as well as closely related preparation for that contact and subsequent evaluation of its effects. In other words, the more peripheral scientific activities mentioned previously are not included in this domain in favor of those activities more closely related to learning about the phenomenon. These include reading the literature, constructing apparatus, talking with colleagues about the study, analyzing data, and, of course, actually conducting experiments. Also included are certain kinds of investigatory activities (excluded from the definition of experimentation offered below), such as observation and measurement procedures under relatively natural conditions, especially conditions not under the control of the experimenter, conditions that do not change in a predictable manner, or conditions that change predictably due to unknown causes.

Experiment refers to that subset of research activities involving measurement under more than one set of conditions that are either under the direct control of the experimenter or that naturally vary in a predictable fashion due to known sources of control. This includes the full variety of activities necessary to carry out measurement of a dependent variable directly under two or more independent variable arrangements.

In light of some traditional usages, these distinctions probably have the effect of pushing the descriptions of the investigatory style of some investigators from the narrow category of experiment to the broader category of research. There are certainly many research activities that can be quite enlightening and directive for experimental purposes, although sometimes nonexperimental pursuits may be sufficient in themselves to solve important problems. For instance, virtually all forms of demographic or actuarial research are adequate for purposes of description and detecting degrees of association, and this is sufficient for establishing insurance rates or articulating public policy. More often, however, information produced at this stage is only preliminary in its utility, and we must eventually turn to the precision of knowledge that experimentation can afford in order to isolate controlling relations.[1]

CONTINUA OF BEHAVIORAL RESEARCH

It is important to examine the full range of research efforts that contribute to a science of behavior. A useful way of introducing a number of important topics is to examine the interactions of a few continua that touch all research activities. One obvious continuum of central importance is defined by the degree of experimental control that can be arranged. The need for a certain degree of control is one of the most common reasons for selecting a certain kind of subject and setting. The state of present knowledge on the research topic, the nature of the questions being addressed, and the nature of the manipulations that will be implemented are all considerations in the decision about the precision of control that will be necessary over experimental and extraneous variables.

Related to experimental control is the continuum of precision of behavioral measurement. At one end, laboratory settings typically offer an opportunity to observe and record behavior with the highest degree of stability and accuracy that the state of the art allows. To widely varying degrees, many features of applied settings may interfere with optimum precision of measurement, although if the precision of measurement available

---

[1]We find it appropriate that the eighth edition of *Webster's New Collegiate Dictionary* (1976) references B. F. Skinner in its definition of "experimental."

is consistent with the nature of the question and the uses of the answers, then any loss of precision in nonlaboratory settings may be inconsequential.

Another continuum concerns the nature of the question to be addressed and the answer that will be required—in more general terms, the goals of the study. The question may state a fundamental concern regarding the most basic facts of vertebrate behavior or it may address purely technological issues. The question may focus on the role of variables, the effect of a method, or the determinants of a behavioral process, all in the context of either learning something basic about behavior or solving a major social problem. The immediate purpose to which an answer may be put may range from merely guiding further experimental questions to the other extreme of developing a practical policy for implementing an expensive social program.

A fourth continuum concerns the generality of experimental effects to human behavior in applied settings. Note that without specifying the kind of generality of interest, there is no inherent difference in the generality of methodologically sound results produced by any experimental situation. However, when the cardinal interest is in generalizing to human behavior in applied settings, then we can speak of a continuum of generality ranging from nonhuman species in the lab to humans in nonlaboratory circumstances.

There are other continua common to all experimental programs, but these will be sufficient to create by their interactions distinctions among the different forms of research activities that today constitute the effort of modern science to understand human behavior and to apply that understanding to the solution of individual and societal problems. At one extreme of the possible range of research activities are laboratory investigations using nonhuman species (most frequently nonhuman primates, pigeons, and rats). Under such circumstances, a very high degree of control is available over a wide range of both experimental and extraneous variables, including the histories of the subjects, their physiological functioning, and their 24-hour-a-day environment. Many conditions can be arranged in these situations that would not be ethical with humans, such as arranging for various deprivations, making surgical interventions, or using aversive stimuli, and the behavior of the subjects can be measured with any degree of precision that available instrumentation will allow. The goals of such experimental programs are to learn about the most basic principles of behavior, and the questions that are addressed often appear undecipherable or at least irrelevant to the uninitiated. The data from most isolated experiments have direct meaning only to the progress of research in a particular area of animal behavior, although the results of whole research programs or the accumulated findings in entire areas have enormous implications for a fuller explanation of human behavior. (The early years of the timeout literature summarized in Chapter 15 illustrate how a series of animal laboratory studies can lead to applied utility.) Establishing the generality of findings from this kind of experimentation to human behavior is still less than immediate and requires specific investigation toward that end. This form of behavioral research is the basic science for all behavioral technologies and has the strength of being able to ask and answer any fundamental questions about behavior having relevance to human behavior unfettered by almost any influences except our own ignorance.

Moving further along our complex of continua, the next discriminably different form of behavioral research comes from retaining the highly artificial setting of the laboratory while using human subjects. Thus, within the limits of ethical guidelines regulating the treatment of human subjects, a maximum degree of control over important variables is available and can be complemented with high accuracy of measurement. The human laboratory is the only setting in which to pursue major research enterprises for which the experimenter does not wish to make any sacrifices in methodological rigor. This experimental situation is also useful for addressing questions stemming either from the animal laboratory or from applied settings whenever the control of the laboratory is necessary or desirable to uncover answers with sufficient clarity. The goals might range from probing the generality of findings from animal research to searching for immediately usable solutions to practical problems in the field. Thus, such research efforts range widely along the experimental question continuum. They are all alike, however, in that species is not a consideration in establishing the generality of findings to nonlaboratory settings, although some studies may involve subjects from the target population of ultimate interest whereas others may not.

This form of research is an important component of the behavioral research picture because the advantages of the laboratory can be used to pursue questions with widely ranging goals using the species of primary interest. With a more active and effective human laboratory research speciality than now exists, we could expect a richer source of questions and problems amenable only to investigation with nonhuman species. The vast data base resulting from human psychophysical research in the 19th and early 20th centuries provided the empirical and methodological impetus for a major contemporary effort in the area of animal psychophysics, which has, in turn, broadened our understanding of the evolution of human sensory capacities (Masterton, Heffner, & Ravizza, 1969). Similar symbiotic stimulation in the exploration of other basic behavioral processes awaits only an overdue revival of interest in the unique potential of the human behavioral laboratory.

Still further along the collection of continua, it can be argued that an important format of behavioral research investigates human behavior in a variety of natural settings that have to some extent been modified in an artificial direction for the purpose of experimentation. In some cases, a natural setting may be created for research purposes that incorporates a number of relatively minor elements of artificiality necessary for experimental purposes. For example, a special preschool playroom in a university-affiliated school could be constructed to appear like a typical playroom to children serving as subjects. However, it might be designed so that many of the usual games, objects, and features of the room are wired into a control apparatus in the adjoining room so that various stimuli can be experimentally controlled and a number of responses automatically measured. Already existing environments are often modified with similar results for experimental purposes. The changes that are engineered may vary widely from merely rearranging furniture and objects to introducing measuring instrumentations, and they may include behavioral departures from the routine, such as experimenter-induced changes in the behavior of existing personnel or the introduction of new personnel (e.g., observers).

The resulting experimental environments are relatively standard field settings occasioning typical behavior from subjects indigenous to the setting but having the important advantage of augmenting experimental control and/or measurement through relatively nondisruptive modifications in some aspects of the situation. The kinds of questions addressed in such environments tend to be those of importance to the particular applied setting or subject population behaving in that setting. That is, the goals are usually restricted to solving a certain practical problem of some kind, as opposed to discovering some fundamental fact of behavior. Establishing the generality of experimental results to the appropriate population and setting is less of a chore than with the other forms of behavioral research discussed thus far because this format already uses both subjects and setting of target interest. Of course, well-designed settings of this type can also be used to address more basic behavioral questions, and results may always have broader generality than the question at hand suggests.

Finally, at the opposite extreme on all continua from the animal laboratory is the research format using the untampered with natural setting populated by its usual behavers. Here, naturalness of the setting and relative noninterference of experimental interests is the primary concern, and subjects are more likely to be included as normal circumstances dictate rather than chosen by the experimenter. The questions addressed are purely technological in nature, and the utility of the answers is potentially immediate, even though their origin may be the basic literature, the applied literature, or someone's experienced guess. The issue of generality is relevant here only insofar as there are elements stemming from research arrangements (measurement or control of variables) that could affect responding in some way different than in a nonresearch application.

These distinctions among forms of behavioral research are really just convenient divisions of contiguous ranges along true continua, and this can be verified merely by locating a number of actual studies at appropriate points and watching the gaps being filled. However, this activity misconstrues the importance of the breadth of this conception of the behavioral research enterprise. The following section probes this point further.

RELATIONS WITHIN BEHAVIORAL RESEARCH

The issue here concerns the symbiotic possibilities to be derived from the full scope of behavioral research. Among the foremost of these is the fact that there is both unanimity and complementary variety in the contributions of the different areas of research. There is variety in that the different formats ask different kinds of questions of different species in settings with importantly different characteristics for control, measurement, and generality and arrive at different answers with a wide range of immediate purposes and utility. At the same time, all of these approaches to the study of behavior have in common the goal of explaining the behavioral elements of the interface between organism and environment. The evidence is overwhelmingly clear that the laws of nature do not change across species and settings. Behavior is behavior, and progress in our understanding resulting from investigation at one point on the above collection of continua has meaning for interpretation at all other points. Questions raised and answered within the context of one format may suggest related inquiries in another format. For example, why is it that some institutionalized children and adults engage in high rates of seriously self-destructive behaviors, such as headbanging, hitting, etc.? Is the explanation in any way related to the contingencies that can be arranged to cause monkeys to regularly administer electric shock to themselves (Kelleher & Morse, 1968)? The different facets of the larger research picture can continually draw from each other through their questions and their answers. This kind of attack can lead to a more accurate, complete, and systematized body of discovered knowledge than could be produced by a narrower spectrum of research efforts, and this broad perspective validates the observation that science makes the most progress when it discovers similarities, not differences.

Another area of benefit from an integrated range of research formats comes from the resulting facilitation of communalities in language, experimental method, and training. Describing behavioral and environmental events in the same terms across all research formats is a major prerequisite to sharing the complementary contributions already discussed and to any useful communication at all. To the extent that phenomena are differently described, research questions will be differently phrased and methodologically addressed, and the answers will consequently be to some extent untranslatable. Moreover, this volume has already lamented the effects of different and conflicting strategies underlying experimental method. The completely different subject matters arising from vaganotic versus idemnotic measurement are one kind of particularly devastating result.

Finally, a certain degree of communality in professional training is a major benefit of this unifying conception of behavioral research. Some basic training in the full range of content across the entire spectrum of research formats along with fundamental preparation in experimental method for *all* who engage in any kind of behavioral research can be a potent influence on the progress of a science of behavior. Any serious student of human behavior is scientifically unprepared to address the subject matter without a basic grounding in the issues, problems, and results of contemporaneous research on animal behavior. Conversely, the exponent of laboratory analysis of behavior (nonhuman or human) overlooks a rich source of both questions and confirmations by failing to become and stay informed of developments in the more applied areas. Furthermore, adherents to disciplines such as sociology, economics, political science, and education, who profess explanations of the phenomena of human behavior on a regular basis, will find their enterprises far more productive and rewarding to the extent that they maintain contact with the methodological and factual advances of the natural science of behavior. As provision for such contact becomes a matter of prerequisite scientific training, the utility of the special designation "social sciences" will vanish from the lexicon.

One way to consider the benefits of a fully integrated behavioral research discipline across laboratory and nonlaboratory settings is to examine similar relations in an older area such as physics or chemistry and their related engineering disciplines. Although some internal problems of the type we have been discussing may be irritating to researchers in those areas, more notable are the fundamental similarities in the conception of the subject matter, description of events, experimental method, professional training, and general level of interaction across a broad span of research formats and interests. It is this kind of background that spawned P. W. Bridgeman's interest in the engineering problems posed by the collapse of the Tacoma Narrows Bridge in 1919, which led to his (1927) Nobel Prize winning work in the basic area of high pressure physics. Similar examples could be offered in other fields, such as biological and medical research.

Another way to examine the benefits of a fully integrated research enterprise is to consider the probable effects of one or more schisms at arbitrary points on the continua. For example, what might be the results of independence of nonhuman versus human research or laboratory versus applied research just in the sense of general communication between areas? It would seem likely that a specialized animal literature would evolve that was largely insensitive to its relevance and generality to nonlaboratory settings and that was insensitive to important questions being raised by more technological research. The effects of such a division on applied investigations would seem to be even more serious, leading to the development of principles and procedures inadequately related to empirical findings generalized from research in more controlled settings and leading further to a gradual separation from its source of basic scientific nourishment. Although the resulting behavioral technology would continue to change and develop, its potential technological capabilities would eventually be stunted as it became increasingly divorced from its supporting science, both basic and applied.[2]

This is a dismal picture; where does the science of behavior find itself? It can be argued that if we take into consideration all research on human behavior, this is an honest characterization. Across all of the social sciences, education, business, and the many other disciplines in which some investigation of human activity is commonplace, there is a most obvious absence of integration in a number of ways. The most conspicuous divisions have their origins in academic departmentalization. This late 19th-century movement in higher education resulted from a real growth in knowledge requiring greater specialization in graduate training and undergraduate teaching, the sheer increase in the size of colleges and universities and their faculties, and, once begun, the political and economic contingencies of academe. One historian (Rudolph, 1962) laments:

> Departmentalization was not only a method of organizing an otherwise unwieldly number of academic specialists into the framework of univeristy government; it was also a development that unleashed all of that competitiveness, that currying of favor, to hold attention to public relations, that scrambling for students, that pettiness and jealousy which in some of its manifestations made the university and college indistinguishable from other organizations [pp. 399–400].

The influence of such specialization has progressed in this century far beyond the formalities of higher education to our very conception of knowledge, especially behavioral knowledge. Across subdisciplines, departments, groups of disciplines, or any divisions whether apparently functional along some dimension or not, there are major and minor differences in the fundamental view of human behavior, in the kinds of questions that are asked, in the language with which events are described, in the procedures by which behavior is measured, in the methods by which research is conducted, and in the training that prospective investigators are given. Nature is not likely to be convinced.

The scope of research inquiries in most such specialities is quite narrow, being concentrated at the human behavior/applied setting ends of the

---

[2]Although the supporting science is a major and crucial source of technological development, the determinants of technological progress are multiple and the related issues are complex. This volume's emphasis on research designed to improve our understanding of behavior precludes adequate consideration of many matters more narrowly related to practical control of human behavior; the nature of technological development is one such topic.

continua. Yet, most specialities approach their territory of experimental questions and social problems with a proud desire for exclusiveness that promotes either ignorance of or indifference to the basic facts of all behavior that have already attained the status of scientific law. There are a number of unhealthy side effects of this scholastic chauvinism, not the least of which is a staggering inefficiency in our collective rate of acquiring basic knowledge of human behavior.

One result of these problems is a continuing erosion of public respect and support for the social sciences that may have been originally attracted by the early adoption of the superficial trappings of scientific method. The particulars of the various reasons for this increasingly depleted patience are beyond this volume, but they may be summarized with the argument that such public affection has not met with appropriate reinforcement. The failure of the social sciences, education, and related fields has been a failure to augment significantly our understanding of human behavior, with the resulting failure to provide any powerfully effective technological solutions to social problems. The discrepancy between this shortfall and the successes of the natural sciences in this century could hardly go unnoticed for very long.

This is not an original indictment but a restated description of one already rendered by society. As a generality, it is necessarily inaccurate and unfair in application to many individuals, programs, and some subspecialties. In fact, the past five decades have witnessed the emergence of an immature but true natural science of behavior, and its early achievements suggest much promise. Unfortunately, recognition and acceptance of these efforts have been doubly delayed, not only by the inevitable resistance to valid discovered knowledge conflicting with the wisdom of the surrounding culture, but also by the inability of those otherwise receptive to distinguish this undertaking from the social scientific context in which it is customarily located. The discrimination will be assisted, however, by any efforts to associate the legitimate technological achievements of this infant enterprise with its distinctive research strategies and tactics so that eventually it may be hoped that a mature and integrated discipline will occupy its rightful place among the sciences.

STYLES OF BEHAVIORAL RESEARCH

Having examined the range of formats of behavioral research along several continua, we are now in a position to discuss several research styles. Our use of the word "style" relates to the nature of the research question that guides many of the methodological decisions made by the experimenter. The research question can be examined as to the sources of influences over the experimenter's phrasing of it and the related effects characterizing the contributions to the literature of the data collected in answering it. Thus, loosely speaking, the style of an investigation refers to the functions it serves for the experimenter, and it is an important dimension in evaluating behavioral research because of the collective effects it has on the scientific and technological literature. We invite the reader to consider the relative distribution of these various styles in the literature of his or her own specialty.

Thematic

One such style can be described as thematic. Individual experiments with a thematic style fit into a carefully predetermined position in a larger research program. The functions these single studies serve may include developing method, establishing some kind of generality, assessing reliability, probing an uncertain lead, or further clarifying an experimental effect. Whatever the immediate use of the experiment, it fits into an organized and strategically meaningful sequence of other such individual efforts and contributes to a cohesive research program. The program may be directed by one person or a collaborative team, or it may exist as a program only thorough the complementary but independent efforts of scientists whose contact is primarily through the formal channels of communication. The themes to which each experimental effort is subservient may include developing a behavior change technology, specifying the role of a class of variables, describing the deteminants of a behavioral process, explaining a behavior pattern, examining a theoretical position, and many others.

The value of a thematic style underlying a number of separate experiments resides in the integration of the resulting data. Data produced under this influence are likely to have collectively greater utility than data from the same number of independent experiments addressing the same topic but that are otherwise relatable only in a *post hoc* manner. The difference lies in the redundancies and gaps typical of a nonthematic literature versus the thorough and efficient probing of all necessary questions in a thematic literature.

The contingencies controlling a researcher's decision to arrange experiments in a thematic manner seem to come more from professional training (which makes the results of such studies reinforcing) than from external contingencies in the research setting or surrounding community. This professional training should encourage the researcher to acquire such a thorough intimacy with the literature regarding a problem that the questions phrased are precisely those that are demanded by the gestalt of the theme. Upon occasion, the investigator may identify a known phenomenon that has been almost totally ignored by the literature and thereafter launch a thematic research enterprise to correct that deficiency. Finally, discovery of a new phenomenon or process invites a thematic undertaking to not only explore the phenomenon fully but to integrate it into the known subject matter. All of these clearly require a mastery of the literature that provides thematic direction to a researcher's efforts, and attaining that familiarity almost always presupposes proper professional training.

Independent

In many ways, the independent style is the opposite of the thematic style. Such experiments are not conducted in the context of any ongoing research program and perhaps only generally in the context of a published literature. They are not systematically preceded or followed by other studies to which a direct and meaningful relation can be traced. Such studies often originate from an opportunistic situation having to do with the availability of a particular problem, subject population, setting, or source of funding, but it must also be acknowledged that this style can be less demanding than designing and maintaining a thematic research program. And, it doesn't stretch a fable too much, it is for many probably more fun to play the grasshopper, jumping independently from one enticing morsel to another, than it is to be the ant who cooperatively labors with others to build a sound but sometimes inadequately appreciated foundation that supports the entire colony.

Studies conducted under this independent influence may be above reproach in every other way and may tender important contributions to an area of knowledge. However, a problem is created when this style comes to characterize too great a proportion of the studies in a literature, which may then have serious weaknesses in generality because of lack of cohesion among its studies. The predominance of this style in a literature can ensure a lack of direction to its growth, and there is already abundant evidence that sheer size of a literature is not directly related to its overall scientific and technological value.

Demonstration

Another style of behavioral research can be described as demonstration research. Whether this style is combined with thematic or, more typically, independent styles, any demonstration emphasizes showing that a method or variable controls responding, and this takes precedence over other goals, such as showing why the control is effective, what the roles of component elements are, or other kinds of more detailed explanations. This style of experiment may take the form of the final result of a series of sound manipulations, the public report following unpublished pilot work, or a single application of new or old procedure to a new or old problem (population, setting, behavior, etc.).

Such studies are especially important in directing new light on a problem or in opening entire areas of research, and any coherent literature has many such shining examples. Again, however, the weakness of this style can lie in its popularity (which in turn lies the many rewards for such results). A literature constituted of too many demonstration studies is lacking in a foundation of sufficient explanation of the demonstrations. In the early stages, many technological literatures are dominated by this research style; however, a healthy, flexible, and evolving technology must eventually be supported by a substantive base of fundamental facts. The predominance of this style in technological research can forecast a less reliable and weaker technology with insufficient explanation of technique, its limitations and excesses, and its generality. Technological growth must in the long run originate from a complementary balance of the efforts of theme-oriented researchers and creative and experienced technologists.

Advocacy

It is not unusual for demonstration studies (being assertive of their results from the beginning and usually not very illuminating if unsuccessful) to be characterized by a strong advocacy style as well. However, this influence can be seen in any format or area of research. It refers to the results of the many methodological decisions made during the project and the literary style of its published description that together show too active a bias in favor of certain results. We all have such prejudices, and it is the rare scientist who can scrupulously ignore all of them, but when the influence of such partialities begins to interfere with the conduct and description of an experiment to the significant detriment of the generality of its findings, then the experimenter has taken on the role of an advocate who defends a cause, not a scientist who searches for understanding.

The origins of this style again lie in the contingencies for the experimenter who produces certain results. A theoretical position may be too strong and public a conviction, requiring equally fervent empirical support. Funding, political support, or other experimental necessities may be at stake. The vested interested of a long personal involvement in developing a procedure may be too great. These and other contingencies surrounding experimental results can encourage investigators to make the wrong decisions at many stages of the investigation, so that "what will happen if?" becomes "this should happen when." This perspective can have the effect of encouraging the investigator to phrase the wrong question, select the wrong subjects or behaviors in the wrong setting, design facilitating (not accurate) measurement procedures, arrange a misleading presentation of data, and be less than fully honest (intentionally or not) in describing procedures and results. The consequence is data and interpretations of poor generality, making clear the disadvantages of this style of research for a literature.

Pilot

A different kind of style has been called pilot research by Sidman (1960). There is a long tradition of describing any experimental appetizers prior to the investigatory main course as exploratory or pilot studies. The argument has been that such preliminary efforts are useful to "pretest" a hypothesis to see if further study is warranted, a kind of feasibility or efficiency study. Being only preliminary, it is typical to make some shortcuts to keep costs and time to a minimum, so a number of sacrifices in normal experimental rigor may be made. Subjects may not be properly chosen, the controls exerted may not be adequate, apparatus may be unreliable or absent, measurement may be sloppy, design decisions may be weak, etc. The results of such efforts are unavoidably a poor guide to any decision-making about the value of further studies, because it is unclear whether or not their meanings support any hypothesis or suspicion. If a certain level of methodological clarity is necessary to communicate results clearly in a "real" experiment, then any methodological errors in a pilot study must only preclude clear interpretation. Still worse is when a pilot study supports the position of the experimenter and is then offered to the literature as a legitimate experiment. In this tradition then, a study is called a pilot study only after it is conducted and only if it does not support a hypothesis.

This contrasting rule must be clear (Sidman, 1960):

> If an experiment is technically adequate, its data must be accepted, regardless of whether or not they are appropriate to the investigator's purpose in carrying out the study. If, on the other hand, an experiment is technically inadequate, its data are unacceptable, even if they bolster the investigator's preconceptions [p. 219].

The pilot study as a style of research should only result from the experimenter's honest ignorance of important variables that go uncontrolled and that then create problems in an otherwise serious and major research project, thereby necessitating a halt to the study until the problems have been solved. The unanticipated difficulty may merely be corrected before starting anew or it may become the focus of a new experimental direction that may be more interesting and important than the original problem.

In-House

An unfortunate similarity to the pilot study style of research is often seen in in-house research projects. This style of research is one in which experiments are conducted to solve a particular local problem that is creating difficulties in a certain setting for some subject or staff. The goals are held to be strictly parochial problem solving, with results to be used *ad hoc* to ameliorate a special, one-time-only situation.

There is certainly nothing wrong with this motivation, and the results can sometimes be interesting and useful. However, the narrowness of the task is often used as a justification for the pilot study style criticized above. Such sloppiness is typically excused by arguing that methodological purity is not necessary, because professional publication is not intended. It may be contended that the results do not have to convince others but merely provide a guide for behavioral management under relatively private circumstances. This reasoning is most likely to be exercised in applied settings in which it may be argued that the need for successful and immediate modification of behavior must take precedence over the niceties of scientific measurement and experimental design, or that the realities of logistical or social pressures must dominate when they are in conflict with the demands of research.

The rejoinders to these excuses for proper investigation are strong, and the same arguments posed against the traditional use of pilot studies fully apply. If the immediate problem is sufficiently irritating to someone to justify an experimental solution, then it should be important enough for the accuracy of the answer to also be a serious concern. A little "informal" experimentation is likely to necessitate a little more and a little more still as inadequate data lead to insufficient solutions that require further efforts. Furthermore, it is a myth that such projects are really private. At the very least, the results will be communicated to others locally and may become a part of a written or oral folklore for an institution or setting. The experimenters may certainly be prone to apply any techniques or findings again if a similar situation arises. It is not unusual, moreover, for such in-house projects to be presented at institutional, area, state, regional, and even national professional meetings. If at least some minimum standards are met, reports may even be submitted to professional journals. These arguments suggest that the interests of efficiency and effectiveness of application, as well as the behavioral literature, will be better served by making serious experimental efforts to address even simple in-house questions.

All of these research styles may be conceptualized as overlaying the range of research formats discussed earlier to yield in concert a supraordinate cross-sectioning of behavioral research not revealed in the preceding chapters. This broader perspective is a crucial dimension of analysis because of its impact on the strength, progress, and direction of a science of behavior.

TOWARD AN ANALYSIS OF SCIENTIFIC BEHAVIOR

It is fitting that this book should conclude with a section on scientific behavior because that—and not behavioral research—is the best characterization of its theme. In every chapter, we have discussed experimental method in terms of various actions of the experimenter. As a matter of fact, methodology should be thought of not as the study of method, but as the study of the behavior of scientists. More specifically, it should be the empirical investigation of the controlling relations between the environment and scientist as behaver, and, as such, would become a subspecialty of the natural science of behavior.

There are many ways to describe scientific activities, and we have used some of them more for literary variety than for scrupulous accuracy. The actions of the experimenter could be described as responses or answers to a lengthy and detailed series of questions raised in the course of investigation. It would not be difficult to construct such a list, but we would like to discourage that simplification as quickly as we bring it up, lest someone seriously attempt it. The problem is that such systematizing or flow-charting of the exceedingly complex scientist–environment relations would result in nothing more than a form of methodological cookbook, and any cookbook will inevitably miss important themes; gloss over, distort, or omit subtle but crucial points; or in some way contribute to a less than thorough understanding of scientific behavior.

In any case, the questions the researcher must answer are not the proper dimension of analysis, and neither are decisions, reasoning, attitudes, or similar themes. Yes, the experimenter does make decisions (and we have exploited this metaphor for expository purposes), but this is just another way of describing the controlling effects of subtle and complex environmental contingencies, and decision theory will not enlighten us because that is not the fundamental level of analysis. The scientist also engages in what is popularly called reasoning, but an explanation in these terms will also be misleading if it is different in any way from the explanation of all other activities. Reasoning is a misleading way of describing scientific behavior because it encourages the creation of circular cognitive constructs whose explanatory utility is not subject to empirical verification. Finally, we have earlier pointed out the risks of an explanation of scientific activities (or any other behavior) in terms of attitudes.

The prevalence of such descriptions has played a part in encouraging a number of myths about science and scientists. For example, only by way of contrast to the crudest of nonscientific pursuits can scientific behavior be described as objective, systematic, logical, and so forth. All of the chapters have attempted to make clear the highly personal, subjective nature of the actions of every experimenter who is limited by a unique personal and professional history and the contingencies of the present situation. Although professional training may increase somewhat the likelihood that a few of the more blatant biases will be controlled, most scientific actions remain far from objective even in contrast to those of laymen. Neither does the scientist necessarily behave in a manner that is remarkably systematic or logical; great advances may be made by highly unsystematic and illogical leaps. Good replicative designs may involve bypassing systematic steps in favor of large and risky changes from existing procedures. The core of experimental reasoning even contains a logical fallacy and is very much inductive behavior rather than a logical process.[3]

If these are myths, what is the truth about scientific activities that results in the discovery of a cumulating and technologically useful body of knowledge about nature? What do scientists do that distinguishes their actions from those of nonscientists? What variables influence their actions? How can scientific behavior be accurately and usefully described? How can we improve scientific behavior? How do we go about training better scientists? How can we teach scientific strategies of inquiry to nonprofessionals?

The answers to these and similar questions can only come from the scientific investigation of scientific behavior, part of the unique purview of the science of behavior methodologically described in this book. The descriptions and explanations of logicians and philosophers will remain entertaining and even appealing but only rarely enlightening because the events and relations to be described and explained are natural (behavioral) phenomena that will only be revealed by the same strategies and tactics used so successfully to understand other natural phenomena. This kind of experimental scientific introspection has only a very modest and recent history, and it will probably always receive less attention than major social problems. However, this may be a serious error in the priorities that society's contingencies dictate, because the scientific competence with which we approach social problems will have much to do with the effectiveness of the solutions that result.

The perspective of this volume provides an important beginning to this effort in that we have talked about observable responses of the experimenter and some of their effects in the research environment. However, this orientation must be refined to a research mission to describe what behavior is emitted by experimenters under what controlling relations. In all areas of experimental activity, research should identify what actions of the researcher produce what kinds of consequences and the nature of the control that these effects have on subsequent experimental activities. For example, in the area of response definition, how do different kinds of definitions affect the reliability and validity of the data and subsequent interpretations, and how does this knowledge influence the kind of definition chosen? In another area, an experimental investigation of deductive and inductive reasoning that probed controlling antecedent influences and consequent effects would be of enormous value in understanding how experimental questions are constructed and how interpretations are generated.

Every chapter can be examined for numerous experimental questions whose answers can be used to improve the effectiveness of the scientific

---

[3]A charming expansion of this general perspective has been offered by Mahoney (1976).

enterprise. In addition to improving the quality of present efforts to understand human behavior, a major benefit of such a research program would be to facilitate scientific training throughout all levels of formal education. When we can disseminate that widely an understanding of the scientific basis for understanding human behavior, then the revolution in humanities' view of it which Copernicus initiated, Darwin advanced, Freud encouraged, and Skinner brought forth will be fully underway.

Tell me if anything ever was done.
                        —Leonardo da Vinci

APPENDIXES

APPENDIX A:
Rapid Methods for Computing *Kappa*

Grant A. Ritter[1]

In Chapter 17, the authors introduce a new statistic κ, which they argue is a far superior quantifier of variability than any of the commonly used measures such as the range or standard deviation. The one disadvantage of κ is that its defining formula (see p. 359) is rather intractable for computational purposes. This appendix presents two simple methods for finding κ with only a hand calculator. One method uses logs, and the other does not, permitting the researcher a choice depending on the type of calculator available. The first method requires a y^x key; the second requires $\ln x$ and e^x keys. Also, an example is given showing how advantageous κ is, once the problem of computing is remedied.

In examining the formula for κ, we see that each x_i value in the data appears many times, sometimes as a numerator and sometimes as a denominator. To some extent, cancellation takes place, and these easier methods for finding κ merely exploit a simple way of determining the net effect. Our first method begins by rearranging the data in descending order. Using as an example the two sets of data from Fig. 17.1 (p. 361), we have:

Set A	Set B
4.2	41
3.0	41
3.0	35
1.8	34
1.4	28

---

[1]Dr. Ritter is assistant professor of mathematics at the University of Florida.

If n is the number of values in the data set, begin a second vertical column with $n - 1$ at the top and decreasing each entry by two until either one or zero is reached. If one is reached, repeat it below and then increase the entries by two until you get back to $n - 1$. If zero is reached, the next entry will be two and again the ensuing entries increase by two until $n - 1$ is again obtained. We call the values in this column dummy values (v). Thus a set of data with eight values will have as its column of dummy values:

$$
\begin{array}{c}
7 \\
5 \\
3 \\
1 \\
1 \\
3 \\
5 \\
7
\end{array}
$$

whereas a data set of seven values has as its dummy value column:

$$
\begin{array}{c}
6 \\
4 \\
2 \\
0 \\
2 \\
4 \\
6
\end{array}
$$

Our example with sets of five values will appear as:

Set A		Set B	
x	v	x	v
4.2	4	41	4
3.0	2	41	2
3.0	0	35	0
1.8	2	34	2
1.4	4	28	4

We now use a calculator to form a third column by raising the number in the first column to the power in the second column:

	Set A			Set B	
x	v	x^v	x	v	x^v
4.2	4	$\left[\,3.1 \times 10^2\,\right]$	41	4	2.8×10^6
3.0	2	$\left[\begin{array}{c}9.0\end{array}\right.$	41	2	1.6×10^3
3.0	0	1.0	35	0	1.0
1.8	2	3.2	34	2	1.2×10^3
1.4	4	$\left.\begin{array}{c}3.8\end{array}\right]$	28	4	6.1×10^5

Now form a fraction with numerator the product of the values in the top half of the third column and with denominator the product of the values in the lower half of the third column (if n is odd, there will be a 1 exactly half way down the column, which may be ignored). In our example:

	Set A		
x	v	x^v	
4.2	4	3.1×10^2	} product is the numerator
3.0	2	9.0	
3.0	0	1.0	
1.8	2	3.2	} product is the denominator
1.4	4	3.8	

Set A's fraction is

$$\frac{3.1 \times 10^2 \times 9.0}{3.2 \times 3.8} = 2.3 \times 10^2.$$

	Set B		
x	v	x^v	
41	4	2.8×10^6	} product is the numerator
41	2	1.6×10^3	
35	0	1.0	
34	2	1.2×10^3	} product is the denominator
28	4	6.1×10^5	

Set B's fraction is

$$\frac{2.8 \times 10^6 \times 1.6 \times 10^3}{1.2 \times 10^3 \times 6.1 \times 10^5} = 6.7.$$

κ will be the $n(n-1)/2$-th root of this fraction. In our example,

$$\kappa_A = (230)^{\frac{1}{n(n-1)/2}} = 230^{1/10} = 1.7.$$

Similarly, $\kappa_B = 1.2$, indicating that set B varies a good deal less than Set A.

Our second method for computing κ is really just the logarithmic equivalent of the first. Begin with the same column displaying the data in descending order. In a second vertical column, enter the natural log of each value in the first column. Using the data sets from Fig. 17.1, we would have:

Set A		Set B	
x	$\log x$	x	$\log x$
4.2	1.4	41	3.7
3.0	1.1	41	3.7
3.0	1.1	35	3.5
1.8	.58	34	3.5
1.4	.34	28	3.3

Now, create a third column by the same method as was used to create the second column under the previous method—start at $n-1$ and descend in increments of two down to zero or one and then climb back up to $n-1$. The fourth column is just the product of the values in the second and third columns:

Set A			
x	$\log x$	dummy value	$(2) \times (3)$
4.2	1.4	4	5.6
3.0	1.1	2	2.2
3.0	1.1	0	0
1.8	.58	2	1.2
1.4	.34	4	1.4
Set B			
41	3.7	4	14.8
41	3.7	2	7.4
35	3.5	0	0
34	3.5	2	7.0
28	3.3	4	13.2

Now add the values in the top half of Column 4 to form one sum and the values in the bottom half to form another (if n is odd, there will be a zero exactly in the middle, which may be ignored). Subtract the second sum from the first:

				Set A		
4.2	1.4	4	5.8 }		sum is 8.0
3.0	1.1	2	2.2 }		
3.0	1.1	0	0		
1.8	.58	2	1.2 }		sum is 2.6
1.4	.34	4	1.4 }		

The difference for Set A is 5.4.

				Set B		
41	3.7	4	14.8 }		sum is 22.2
41	3.7	2	7.4 }		
35	3.5	0	0		
34	3.5	2	7.0 }		sum is 20.2
28	3.3	4	13.2 }		

The difference for Set B is 2.0.

Finally, κ is obtained by dividing this difference $n(n-1)/2$ and taking the antilog. In our example, we find the same values as before:

$$\kappa_A = \text{antilog}\left(\frac{5.4}{10}\right) = e^{.54} = 1.7$$

$$\kappa_B = \text{antilog}\left(\frac{2.0}{10}\right) = e^{.2} = 1.2$$

(The reader should note that all values have been rounded off to two significant figures because the original data are only this accurate.)

Set A's higher κ value indicates its greater variability. Comparison of these sets' standard deviations ($\sigma_A = 1.0$ and $\sigma_B = 4.9$) or ranges ($r_A = 2.8$ and $r_B = 13$) might mistakenly lead to the opposite conclusion. The reason for this discrepancy, of course, is that statistics such as the range and standard deviation are dependent on scale. For proper interpretation, the effect of this dependence must be taken into account. Unfortunately there is no obvious way to do this. The usual remedy of dividing by the mean is problematic, based on assumptions that are often hard to justify in practice. The statistic κ on the other hand is independent of scale. No normalization is necessary for either interpretation or comparisons. Once the problem of its computability is solved, it is obviously the preferred statistic for quantifying variability.

APPENDIX B:
Graphic Estimation of *Kappa* on Semilogarithmic Paper

William M. Hartman

It is possible to estimate accurately the κ measure with a straightedge and a piece of semilogarithmic chart paper. Given that all observations (X_i) in a set have been ordered from smallest to largest,

$$\kappa = \left[\prod_{i > j}^{n} \left(\frac{X_i}{X_j} \right) \right]^{1/n}$$

That is, κ is the geometric mean of all possible ratios greater than 1.0 in the set of interest, or the nth root of the product of these ratios. On a logarithmic scale, linear addition is analogous to the algebraic operation of multiplication. The product of all ratios is therefore displayed as a distance on the logarithmic scale (y-axis) and the number of ratios, n, on the equal interval scale (x-axis). A right triangle ($\triangle ABC$) is formed as shown in Fig. B.1, with $\overline{AB}$ = product of ratios, and $\overline{BC} = n$. In Fig. B.1, $\overline{AB}$ = ratio product = 200; $\overline{BC} = n = 6$. Because $\triangle CBA \sim \triangle CDE$, $\overline{OC} : \overline{BC} :: \overline{DE} :$

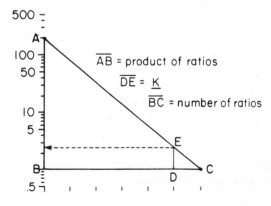

FIG. B.1. Graphic estimation of κ where $[\Pi_{i > j} (X_i / X_j)] = 200$ and $n = 6$.

441

$\overline{BA}$. Because length $\overline{CD} = 1$, and $\overline{BC} = 6$, $\overline{DE} = 1/6$ $\overline{AB} = (200)^{1/6} =$ 2.42 = κ.

Here is a simple method for estimating κ using a pencil, straightedge, and one semilogarithmic chart. Suppose the sample data set has four values, 2, 4, 7, and 10:

1. Mark all values on the y-axis of the chart. This automatically arranges them in ascending order. Align the straightedge parallel to this display with the bottom of the straightedge next to the lowest value, 2. Place a mark on the straightedge next to the second value, 4, in the set, as shown in Fig. B.2, Panel A.

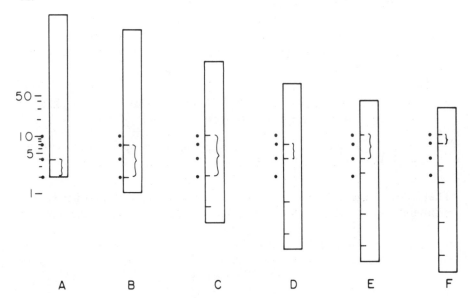

FIG. B.2. Steps in obtaining graphic representation of the product of all ratios.

2. Slide the straightedge down and align the mark next to the lowest value, 2. Place a new mark next to the third value, 7 (Panel B).

3. Again slide the straightedge down to align the newest mark with the lowest value, and place another mark next to the fourth value, 10 (Panel C). All possible ratios using the lowest value are now plotted in a line.

4. The process is repeated for the second value in the set, 4, as follows: Slide the straightedge down to align the newest mark with the second value, and make a mark next to the third value (Panel D). Again, align the newest mark next to the second value, and make a mark next to the fourth value (Panel E). All ratios using the second value are now plotted.

5. Plot the remaining comparison, between the third and fourth values (7 and 10) in the same manner: Align the newest mark with the 7 and make a final mark next to the 10 (Panel F). All possible ratios in the set of interest are plotted; their product is the logarithmic distance from the bottom of the straightedge to the highest mark. This distance and the number of ratios ($n = 6$; obtained by counting the number of marks on the straightedge) are used to form a right triangle similar to that in Fig. B.1, as follows:

6. Place the straightedge on the y-axis (or any parallel) with the bottom of the straightedge at the value, 1.0. Place a dot on the y-axis next to the highest mark of the straightedge. Place another dot at the intersection of the 1.0 line and the vertical line corresponding to the number of ratios (6). Connect the two dots, and read $\kappa = 2.45$ at the intersection of the diagonal and the fifth vertical line, as shown in Fig. B.3.

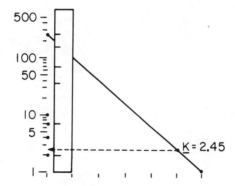

FIG. B.3. Use of the straightedge with the plotted ratios and a semilogarithmic chart to estimate κ.

References

Adams, C. K., Goldstein, M. K., Hench, L., Hall, D. C., Madden, M., Pennypacker, H. S., Stein, G. H., & Catania, A. C. Lump detection in a simulated human breast. *Perception and Psychophysics,* 1976, *20*(3), 163–167.

Adams, C. K., Hall, D., Rice, P., Wood, K., & Willis, R. *Stimulus control problems in developing an animal model for prosthetic vision.* Presented at the 16th annual meeting of the Psychonomic Society, Denver, November 1975.

Allen, K. E., & Harris, F. R. Eliminating a child' scratching by training the mother in reinforcement procedures. *Behavior Research and Therapy,* 1966, *4,* 79–84.

Appel, J. B. Aversive aspects of a schedule of positive reinforcement. *Journal of Experimental Analysis of Behavior,* 1963, *6,* 423–428.

Ayllon, T. Intensive treatment of psychotic behavior by stimulus satiation and food reinforcement. *Behavior Research and Therapy,* 1963, *1,* 53–61.

Ayllon, T., & Azrin, N. *The token economy: A motivational system for therapy and rehabilitation.* New York: Appleton-Century-Crofts, 1968.

Ayllon, T., & Michael, J. The psychiatric nurse as a behavioral engineer. *Journal of the Experimental Analysis of Behavior,* 1959, *2,* 323–334.

Azrin, N. H. Time-out from positive reinforcement. *Science,* 1961, *133,* 382–383.

Azrin, N. H., Hutchinson, R. R., & Hake, D. F. Extinction-induced aggression. *Journal of the Experimental Analysis of Behavior,* 1966, *9,* 191–204.

Azrin, N. H., Rubin, H., O'Brien, F., Ayllon, T., & Roll, D. Behavioral engineering; postural control by a portable operant apparatus. *Journal of Applied Behavior Analysis,* 1968, *1,* 99–108.

Baer, A. M., Rowbury, T., & Baer, D. M. The development of instructional control over classroom activities of deviant preschool children. *Journal of Applied Behavior Analysis,* 1973, *6,* 289–298.

Baer, D. M. Escape and avoidance responses of pre-school children to two schedules of reinforcement withdrawal. *Journal of the Experimental Analysis of Behavior,* 1960, *3,* 155–159.

Baer, D. M. Effect of withdrawal of positive reinforcement on an extinguishing response in young children. *Child Development,* 1961, *32,* 67–74.

445

Baer, D. M. Laboratory control of thumbsucking by withdrawal and representation of reinforcement. *Journal of the Experimental Analysis of Behavior*, 1962, *5*, 525–528.

Barrett, B. H. Reduction in rate of multiple tics by free operant conditioning methods. *Journal of Nervous and Mental Disease*, 1962, *135*, 187–195.

Barton, E. S. Inappropriate speech in a severely retarded child: A case study in language conditioning and generalization. *Journal of Applied Behavior Analysis*, 1970, *3*, 299–307.

Barton, E. S., Guess, D., Garcia, E., & Baer, D. M. Improvement of retardates' mealtime behaviors by timeout procedures using multiple baseline techniques. *Journal of Applied Behavior Analysis*, 1970, *3*, 77–84.

Bernard, C. *An introduction to the study of experimental medicine*. New York: Dover, 1957. (Originally published, 1865.)

Birnbrauer, J. S., Wolf, M. M., Kidder, J. D., & Tague, C. E. Classroom behavior of retarded pupils with token reinforcement. *Journal of Experimental Child Psychology*, 1965, *2*, 219–235.

Blackwood, R. O., Horrocks, J. E., Keele, T. F., Hundziak, M., & Rettig, J. H. Operant conditioning of social behavior in severely retarded patients. In A. M. Graziano (Ed.), *Behavior therapy with children*. Chicago: Aldine, 1971.

Blough, D. S. The study of animal sensory processes by operant methods. In W. K. Honig (Ed.), *Operant behavior: Areas of research and application*. New York: Appleton-Century-Crofts, 1966.

Boring, E. G. The logic of the normal law of error in mental measurement. *American Journal of Psychology*, 1920, *31*, 1–33.

Boring, E. G. *Sensation and perception in the history of experimental psychology*. New York: Appelton-Century-Crofts, 1942.

Boring, E. G. *A history of experimental psychology* (2nd ed.). New York: Appleton-Century-Crofts, 1950.

Boring, E. G. Measurement in psychology. In H. Woolf (Ed.), *Quantification*. New York: Bobbs-Merrill, 1961.

Bostow, D. E., & Bailey, J. Modification of severe disruptive and aggressive behavior using brief timeout and reinforcement procedures. *Journal of Applied Behavior Analysis*, 1969, *2*, 31–37.

Box, G. E. P., & Jenkins, G. M. *Time series analysis: Forecasting and control*. San Francisco: Holden-Day, 1970.

Bridgeman, P. W. *The logic of modern physics*. New York: Macmillan, 1927.

Brown, P., & Elliott, R. Control of aggression in a nursery school class. *Journal of Experimental Child Psychology*, 1965, *2*, 103–107.

Burchard, J. D. Systematic socialization: A programmed environment for the habilitation of antisocial retardates. *The Psychological Record*, 1967, *17*, 461–476.

Burchard, J., & Tyler, V., Jr. The modification of delinquent behavior through operant conditioning. *Behavior Research and Therapy*, 1965, *2*, 245–250.

Campbell, D. T., & Stanley, J. C. *Experimental and quasi-experimental designs for research*. Chicago: Rand McNally, 1966.

Carlin, G. *Occupation: Foole*. New York: Little David Records, 1973.

Carr, A. Adaptation aspects of the scheduled travel of *Chelonia*. In *Annual orientation and navigation*. Corvallis: Oregon State University Press, 1966.

Clark, H. B., Rowbury, T., Baer, A. M., & Baer, D. M. Timeout as a punishing stimulus in continuous and intermittent schedules. *Journal of Applied Behavior Analysis*, 1973, *6*, 443–456.

Cochran, W., & Cox, G. *Experimental designs*. New York: Wiley, 1950.

Crombie, A. C. Quantification in medieval physics. In H. Woolf (Ed.), *Quantification*. New York: Bobbs-Merrill, 1961.

Cumming, W. W. A bird's eye glimpse of men and machines. In R. Ulrich, T. Stachnik, & J. Mabry (Eds.), *Control of human behavior* (Vol. 1). Glenview, Ill.: Scott, Foresman, 1966.

Dampier, W. C. *A history of science and its relations with philosophy and religion.* New York: Macmillan, 1942.

Darwin, C. *On the origin of species by means of natural selection.* London: J. Murray, 1859.

Dews, P. B. Studies on behavior. I. Differential sensitivity to pentobarbital of pecking performance in pigeons depending on the schedule of reward. *Journal of Pharmacology and Experimental Therapeutics,* 1955, *113,* 393–401.

Ferster, C. B. The use of the free operant in the analysis of behavior. *Psychological Bulletin,* 1953, *50,*(4), 263–274.

Ferster, C. B. Control of behavior in chimpanzees and pigeons by time out from positive reinforcement. *Psychology Monographs,* 1958, *72*(8, Whole No. 461).

Ferster, C. B. Suppression of performance under differential reinforcement of low rates by a pre-timeout stimulus. *Journal of the Experimental Analysis of Behavior,* 1960, *3,* 143–153.

Ferster, C. B., & Appel, J. B. Punishment of *S*-delta responding in matching-to-sample by timeout from positive reinforcement. *Journal of the Experimental Analysis of Behavior,* 1961, *4,* 45–56.

Ferster, C. B., Appel, J. B., & Hiss, R. A. Effect of drugs on a fixed ratio performance suppressed by a pre-timeout stimulus. *Journal of the Experimental Analysis of Behavior,* 1962, *5,* 73–88.

Ferster, C. B., & Skinner, B. F. *Schedules of reinforcement.* New York: Appleton-Century-Crofts, 1957.

Fisher, R. *Design of experiments.* London: Oliver & Boyd, Ltd., 1942.

Fisher, R. *Statistical methods and scientific inference.* London: Oliver & Boyd, Ltd., 1956.

Fisher, R. A. *Statistical methods for research workers.* London: Oliver & Boyd, 1925.

Galton, F. *Natural inheritance.* London: McMillan, 1889.

Gardner, R. A., & Gardner, B. T. Teaching sign language to a chimpanzee. *Science,* 1969, *165,* 664–672.

Goldstein, M. K., Stein, G. H., Smolen, D. M., & Perlini, W. S. Bio-behavioral monitoring: A method for remote health measurement. *Archives of Physical Medicine and Rehabilitation,* 1976, *57,* 253–258.

Grant, D. A. A sensitized eyelid reaction related to the conditioned eyelid response. *Journal of Experimental Psychology,* 1945, *35,* 393–402.

Grant, D. A. Analysis-of-variance tests in the analysis and comparison of curves. *Psychological Bulletin,* 1956, *53*(2), 141–154.

Green, D. M., & Swets, J. A. *Signal detection theory and psychophysics.* New York: Wiley, 1966.

Grice, G. R., & Hunter, J. J. Stimulus intensity effects depend upon the type of experimental design. *Psychological Review,* 1964, *71,* 247–256.

Hall, D., Goldstein, M. K., & Stein, G. H. Progress in manual breast examination. *Cancer,* 1977, *40,* 364–370.

Hall, R. V. *Managing behavior, part 1: The measurement of behavior.* Lawrence, Ks.: H & H Enterprises, 1974.

Hamilton, J., & Allen, P. Ward programming for severely retarded institutionalized residents. *Mental Retardation,* 1967, *5,* 22–24.

Hamilton, J., Stephens, L., & Allen, P. Controlling aggressive and destructive behavior in severely retarded institutionalized residents. *American Journal of Mental Deficiency,* 1967, *7,* 852–856.

Harris, F. R., Johnston, M. K., Kelley, C. S., & Wolf, M. M. Effects of positive reinforcement on regressed crawling of a nursery school child. *Journal of Educational Psychology,* 1964, *55,* 35–41.

Hawkins, R. P., & Dotson, V. A. Reliability scores that delude: An Alice in Wonderland Trip through the misleading characteristics of interobserver agreement scores in interval recording. In E. Ramp & G. Semb (Eds.), *Behavior analysis: Areas of research and application.* Englewood Cliffs, N.J.: Prentice-Hall, 1975.

Hawkins, R. P., Peterson, R. F., Schweid, E., & Bijou, S. Behavior therapy in the home: Amelioration of problem parent–child relations with the parent in a therapeutic role. *Journal of Experimental Child Psychology,* 1966, *4,* 99–107.

Herrnstein, R. J. *Behavior consequences of the removal of a discriminative stimulus associated with variable interval reinforcement.* Unpublished doctoral dissertation, Harvard University, 1955.

Herson, M., & Barlow, D. *Single case experimental designs.* New York: Pergamon Press, 1976.

Hilgard, E. R. *Theories of learning.* New York: Appleton-Century-Crofts, 1940.

Holz, W. C., Azrin, H. H., & Ayllon, T. Elimination of behavior of mental patients by response-produced extinction. *Journal of the Experimental Analysis of Behavior,* 1963, *6,* 407–412.

Honig, W. K., & Staddon, J. E. R. *Handbook of operant behavior.* Englewood Cliffs, N.J.: Prentice-Hall, 1977.

Hull, C. L. *Mathematico-deductive theory of rote learning: A study in scientific methodology.* New York: Appleton-Century-Crofts, 1940.

Hull, C. L. *Principles of behavior: An introduction to behavior theory.* New York: Appleton-Century-Crofts, 1943.

Johnson, S. M., & Bolstad, O. D. Methodological issues in naturalistic observation: Some problems and solutions for field research. In L. A. Hamerlynck, L. C. Handy, & E. J. Mash (Eds.), *Behavioral change: Methodology, concepts, and practice.* Champagne, Ill.: Research Press, 1973.

Johnston, J. M., O'Neill, G. W., Walters, W. M., & Rasheed, T. A. The measurement and analysis of college student study behavior: Tactics for research. In J. M. Johnston (Ed.), *Behavior research and technology in higher education.* Springfield, Ill.: Thomas, 1975.

Johnston, J. M., & Pennypacker, H. S. A behavioral approach to college teaching. *American Psychologist,* 1971, *43,* 219–244.

Jones, W. T. *A history of western philosophy* (Vol. II). New York: Harcourt, Brace, 1952.

Kazdin, A. Statistical analysis for single case experimental designs. In M. Hersen & D. Barlow (Eds.), *Single case experimental designs.* New York: Pergamon Press, 1976.

Kelleher, R. G., & Morse, W. H. Schedules using noxious stimuli, III: Responding maintained with response-produced electric shocks. *Journal of the Experimental Analysis of Behavior,* 1968, *11,* 819–838.

Knight, M. F., & McKenzie, H. S. Elimination of behavior of mental patients by response-produced extinction. *Journal of Applied Behavior Analysis,* 1974, *7,* 33–38.

Koch, S. Clark L. Hull. In W. K. Estes, S. Koch, K. MacCorquodale, P. Meehl, C. Mueller, W. Schoenfeld, & W. Verplanck (Eds.), *Modern learning theory: A critical analysis of five examples.* New York: Appleton-Century-Crofts, 1954.

Koch, S. (Ed.). *Psychology: A study of science* (Vol. 1). New York: McGraw-Hill, 1959.

Koenig, C. *Charting the future course of behavior.* Kansas City: Precision Media, 1972.

Krantz, D. L. Schools and systems: The mutual isolation of operant and non-operant psychology as a case study. *Journal of the History of the Behavioral Sciences,* 1972, *8,* 86–102.

Lahey, B. B., McNees, M. P., & McNees, M. C. Control of an obscene verbal tic through timeout in an elementary school classroom. *Journal of Applied Behavior Analysis,* 1973, *6,* 101–104.

Lashley, K. S. *Brain mechanisms and intelligence.* Chicago: University of Chicago Press, 1929.

Lazarfeld, P. F. Quantification in sociology. In H. Woolf (Ed.), *Quantification.* New York: Bobbs-Merrill, 1961.

LeBlanc, J. M., Busby, K. H., & Thompson, C. L. The function of time-out for changing the aggressive behaviors of a preschool child: A multiple-baseline analysis. In R. Ulrich, T. Stachnik, & J. Mabry (Eds.), *Control of human behavior* (Vol. III). Glenview, Ill.: Scott, Foresman, 1974.

Liberman, R. P., Teigen, J., Patterson, R., & Baker, V. Reducing delusional speech in chronic, paranoid schizophrenics. *Journal of Applied Behavior Analysis,* 1973, *6,* 57–64.

Lindquist, E. F. *Design and analysis of experiments in psychology and education.* Boston: Houghton Mifflin, 1953.

Lindsley, O. R. Operant conditioning methods in chronic schizophrenia. *Psychiatric Research Reports,* 1956, *5,* 118–139.

Lindsley, O. R. Geriatric behavior prosthetics. In R. Kastenbaum (Ed.), *New thoughts on old age.* New York: Springer, 1964.

Lindsley, O. R. Advertisement in *Journal of Applied Behavior Analysis,* 1968, *1,* back cover.

Lindsley, O. R. Personal communication, 1969.

Lindsley, O. R., & Lindsley, M. *The reinforcing effect of auditory stimuli on operant behavior in the human infant.* Paper read at the meeting of the Eastern Psychological Association, Atlantic City, N.J., March 1951.

Lovaas, I. O., Berberich, J. P., Perloff, B. F., & Schaeffer, B. Acquisition of imitative speech by schizophrenic children. In I. O. Lovaas & B. D. Bucher (Eds.), *Perspectives in behavior modification with deviant children.* Englewood Cliffs, N.J.: Prentice-Hall, 1974.

Lovaas, I. O., & Simmons, J. Q. Manipulation of self-destruction in three retarded children. *Journal of Applied Behavior Analysis,* 1969, *2,* 143–158.

Lyon, D. O. Frequency of reinforcement as a parameter of conditioned suppression. *Journal of the Experimental Analysis of Behavior,* 1963, *6,* 95–98.

MacPherson, E. M., Candee, B. L., & Hohman, R. J. A comparison of three methods for eliminating disruptive lunchroom behavior. *Journal of Applied Behavior Analysis,* 1974, *7,* 287–298.

Mahoney, M. J. *Scientist as subject: The psychological imperative.* Cambridge, Mass.: Ballinger, 1976.

Malagodi, E. F. Fixed ratio schedules of token reinforcement. *Psychonomic Science,* 1967, *8,* 469–470.

Mann, H. *Analysis and design of experiments.* New York: Dover, 1949.

Mason, S. F. *Main currents of scientific thought.* New York: Henry Schuman, 1953.

Masters, W. H., & Johnson, V. E. *Human sexual response.* Boston: Little, Brown, 1966.

Masterton, R. B., Heffner, H., & Ravizza, R. The evolution of human hearing. *Journal of the Acoustical Society of America,* 1969, *45,* 966–985.

McArthur, M., & Hawkins, R. P. The modification of several classroom behaviors of an emotionally disturbed child in a regular classroom. In R. Ulrich, T. Stachnik, & J. Mabry (Eds.), *Control of human behavior* (Vol. III). Glenview, Ill.: Scott, Foresman, 1974.

McNemar, Q. *Psychological statistics.* New York: Wiley, 1949.

McReynolds, L. Application of timeout from positive reinforcement for increasing the efficiency of speech training. *Journal of Applied Behavior Analysis,* 1969, *2,* 199–205.

Mechner, F., & Ray, R. Avoidance of time out from fixed-interval reinforcement. *Journal of the Experimental Analysis of Behavior,* 1959, *2,* 261.

Miller, F. *College physics.* New York: Harcourt, Brace, 1972.

Mood, O. *Introduction to the theory of statistics.* New York: McGraw-Hill, 1950.

Moore, K. Gideon Ariel and his magic machine. *Sports Illustrated,* 1977, *47*(8), 52–60.

Morse, W. H., & Kelleher, R. T. Determinants of reinforcement and punishment. In W. K. Honig & J. E. R. Staddon (Eds.), *Handbook of operant behavior.* Englewood Cliffs, N.J.: Prentice-Hall, 1977.

Nordquist, V. M., & Wahler, R. G. Naturalistic treatment of an autistic child. *Journal of Applied Behavior Analysis,* 1973, *6,* 79–88.

O'Neill, G. W., Walters, W. M., Rasheed, J. A., & Johnston, J. M. Validity of the study report form. II. In J. M. Johnston (Ed.), *Behavior research and technology in higher education.* Springfield, Ill.: Thomas, 1975.

Pavlov, I. P. *Conditioned reflexes* (G. Aurup, trans.). London: Oxford University Press, 1927.

Pennypacker, H. S., Koenig, C., & Lindsley, O. *Handbook of the standard behavior chart.* Kansas City: Precision Media, 1972.

Peterson, R. F., & Peterson, L. R. The use of positive reinforcement in the control of self-destructive behavior in a retarded boy. *Journal of Experimental Child Psychology,* 1968, *6,* 351–360.

Polya, G. *Mathematics and plausible reasoning* (Vol. 1): *Induction and analogy in mathematics.* Princeton, N.J.: Princeton University Press, 1954.

Premack, D. Language in chimpanzees? *Science,* 1971, *172,* 808–822.

Quetelet, A. *Sur l'homme et le développement de ses facultés.* Paris: Bachelier, 1835.

Ramp, E., Ulrich, R., & Dulaney, S. Delayed timeout as a procedure for reducing disruptive classroom behavior: A case study. *Journal of Applied Behavior Analysis,* 1971, *4,* 235–239.

Reynolds, G. S. *A primer of operant conditioning* (rev. ed.). Glenview, Ill.: Scott, Foresman, 1975.

Richard, H. C., Dignam, P. J., & Horner, R. F. Verbal manipulation in a psychotherepeutic relationship. *Journal of Clinical Psychology,* 1960, *16,* 364–367.

Risley, T. R. The effects and side effects of punishing the autistic behaviors of a deviant child. *Journal of Applied Behavior Analysis,* 1968, *1,* 21–34.

Risley, T. R., & Wolf, M. Establishing functional speech in echolalic children. *Behavior Research and Therapy,* 1967, *5,* 73–88.

Rudolph, F. *The American college and university.* New York: Random House (Vintage Books), 1962.

Salmon, W. C. *The foundations of scientific inference.* Pittsburgh: University of Pittsburgh Press, 1966.

Schwitzgebel, R. L. Behavioral technology. In H. Leitenberg (Ed.), *Handbook of behavior modification and behavior therapy.* Englewood Cliffs, N.J.: Prentice-Hall, 1976.

Sidman, M. *Tactics of scientific research.* New York: Basic Books, 1960.

Skinner, B. F. The generic nature of the concepts of stimulus and response. *The Journal of General Psychology,* 1935, *12,* 40–65.

Skinner, B. F. *The behavior of organisms.* New York: Appleton-Century-Crofts, 1938.

Skinner, B. F. Are theories of learning necessary? *Psychological Review,* 1950, *57,* 193–216.

Skinner, B. F. *Science and human behavior.* New York: Macmillan, 1953. (a)

Skinner, B. F. Some contributions of experimental analysis of behavior to psychology as a whole. *American Psychologist,* 1953, *8,* 69–79. (b)

Skinner, B. F. A case history in scientific method. *American Psychologist,* 1956, *11,* 221–233.

Skinner, B. F. *Verbal behavior.* New York: Appleton-Century-Crofts, 1957.

Skinner, B. F. *Cumulative record.* New York: Appleton-Century-Crofts, 1961.

Skinner, B. F. The phylogency and ontogeny of behavior. *Science,* 1966, *153,* 1205–1213.

Skinner, B. F. *The technology of teaching.* New York: Appleton-Century-Crofts, 1968.

Skinner, B. F. B. F. Skinner...an autobiography. In P. B. Dews (Ed.), *Festschrift for B. F. Skinner.* New York: Appleton-Century-Crofts, 1970.

Skinner, B. F. *Beyond freedom and dignity.* New York: Knopf, 1973.

Skinner, B. F. *About behaviorism.* New York: Knopf, 1974.

Skinner, B. F. The shaping of phylogenic behavior. *Journal of the Experimental Analysis of Behavior,* 1975, *24,* 117.

Skinner, B. F. Farewell, my lovely! *Journal of the Experimental Analysis of Behavior,* 1976, *25,* 218.

Snedecor, G. W. *Calculation and interpretation of analysis of variance and covariance.* Ames, Iowa: Collegiate Press, 1934.

Snedecor, G. W. *Statistical methods.* Ames, Iowa: Iowa State University Press, 1937.

Spence, K. W. Personal communication. Gainesville, Florida, 1962.

Stein, G. H., Goldstein, M. K., & Smolen, D. M. Remote medical-behavioral monitoring: An alternative for ambulatory health assessment. In J. W. Cullen, B. H. Fox, & R. N. Isom (Eds.), *Cancer: The behavioral dimensions.* New York: Raven Press, 1976.

Stevens, S. S. Mathematics, measurement, and psychophysics. In S. S. Stevens (Ed.), *Handbook of experimental psychology.* New York: Wiley, 1951.

Stevens, S. S. On the psychophysical law. *Psychological Review,* 1957, *64,* 153–187.

Tate, B. G., & Baroff, G. S. Aversive control of self-injurious behavior in a psychotic boy. *Behavior Research and Therapy,* 1966, *4,* 281–287.

Teitelbaum, P. Levels of integration of the operant. In W. K. Honig & J. E. R. Staddon (Eds.), *Handbook of operant behavior.* Englewood Cliffs, N.J.: Prentice-Hall, 1977.

Terrace, H. S. Stimulus control. In W. K. Honig (Ed.), *Operant behavior: Areas of research and application.* New York: Appleton-Century-Crofts, 1966.

Thomas, J. R. Avoidance of time-out from two VI schedules of positive reinforcement. *Journal of the Experimental Analysis of Behavior,* 1964, *7,* 168.

Thompson, D. M. Escape from S^D associated with fixed-ratio reinforcement. *Journal of the Experimental Analysis of Behavior,* 1964, *7,* 1–8.

Thorndike, E. L. *Animal intelligence.* New York: Macmillan, 1898.

Tyler, V. O., & Brown, G. D. The use of swift, brief isolation as a group control device for institutionalized delinquents. *Behavior Research and Therapy,* 1967, *5,* 1–9.

Verhave, T. The pigeon as a quality-control inspector. In R. Ulrich, T. Stachnik, & J. Mabry (Eds.), *Control of human behavior.* Glenview, Ill.: Scott, Foresman, 1966.

Wahler, R. G. Oppositional children: A quest for parental reinforcement and controls. *Journal of Applied Behavior Analysis,* 1969, *2,* 129–170. (a)

Wahler, R. G. Setting generality: Some specific and general effects of child behavior therapy. *Journal of Applied Behavior Analysis,* 1969, *2,* 239–246. (b)

Walker, H. *Studies in the history of statistical method.* Baltimore: Williams & Wilkins, 1929.

Walters, W. M., O'Neill, G. W., Rasheed, J. A., & Johnston, J. M. Validity of the study report form. I. In J. M. Johnston (Ed.), *Behavior research and technology in higher education.* Springfield, Ill.: Thomas, 1975.

Wasik, B. H., Senn, K., Welch, R. H., & Cooper, B. R. Behavior modification with culturally deprived school children: Two case studies. *Journal of Applied Behavior Analysis,* 1969, *2,* 181–194.

Watson, J. D. *The double helix.* New York: Atheneum, 1968.

Webster's new collegiate dictionary (8th ed.). Springfield, Mass.: Merriam, 1976.

White, O. R. The "split middle"—A "quickie" method of trend estimation. Experimental Education Unit, Child Development and Mental Retardation Center, University of Washington, 1974.

White, O. R., & Haring, N. G. *Exceptional teaching.* Columbus, Ohio: Merrill, 1976.

Wilson, E. O. *Sociobiology: The new synthesis.* Cambridge: Belknap Press of Harvard University Press, 1975.

Wilson, E. O. *On human nature.* Cambridge: Harvard University Press, 1978.

Wolf, M., Risley, T., & Mees, H. Application of operant conditioning procedures to the behavior problems of an autistic child. *Behavior Research and Therapy,* 1964, *1,* 305–312.

Wolfe, J. B. Effectiveness of token rewards for chimpanzees. *Comparative Psychology Monographs,* 1936, *12*(60), 1–72.

Woolf, H. (Ed.). *Quantification.* New York: Bobbs-Merrill, 1961.

Wulbert, M., Nyman, B. A., Snow, D., & Owen, Y. The efficacy of stimulus fading and contingency management in the treatment of elective mutism: A case study. *Journal of Applied Behavior Analysis,* 1973, *6,* 435–442.

Zeilberger, J., Sampen, S. E., & Sloane, H. N., Jr. Modification of a child's problem behavior in the home with the mother as therapist. *Journal of Applied Behavior Analysis,* 1968, *1,* 47–53.

Zimmerman, E. H., & Zimmerman, J. The alteration of behavior in a special classroom situation. *Journal of the Experimental Analysis of Behavior,* 1962, *5,* 59–60.

Zimmerman, J., & Ferster, C. B. Intermittent punishment of S-delta responding in matching-to-sample. *Journal of the Experimental Analysis of Behavior,* 1963, *6,* 349–356.

Index

Variability *(cont.)*
  increases in, 368–369
  inherent, 45n, 74
  and interpretation, 386–387
  intersubject (*see* Intersubject variability)
  intrinsic (*see* Intrinsic variability)
  measurement induced, 149, 365
  and measurement strategy, 74–75
  quantification of, 355–356
  expressed in ratios, 348–350
  real extraneous (*see* Real extraneous
    variability)
  residual, 218
  influenced by response definition, 97
  treatment imposed, 115, 149, 203
  uncontrolled, 365–367
  units of, 87–88
Variability, sources of, 210–224, 248 (*see
    also* Variability)
  developmental, 211–212
  dimensional quantity, 217–218
  display, 223–224
  experimental design, 220–223
  independent variable, 224
  measurement, 215–220
  observing, 218–220
  organism, 211–213
  quantification, 223–224
  recording, 218–220
  response class definition, 216–217
  setting, 213–215
Variance, 89, 360
Verbal behavior, relation to scientific
    behavior, 100, 330, 376, 390
Verhave, T., 153n
Visual display (*see* Display of data)
Visual inspection, 239–240

Voice operated relay, 154
Volta, A., 81

W

Wahler, R. G., 323
Walker, H., 82, 83, 84
Wallace, 44
Walters, W. M., 184, 185, 186 fig
Wasik, B. H., 323
Watson, 13, 14, 32, 46
Weber, E., 63
Weight management, 287–288
Welch, R. H., 323
White, O. R., 139, 350
Wilberforce, S., 6, 7
William of Occam, 80
Willis, R., 177
Wilson, E. O., 44n
Within subject comparison notation, 265 fig
Wolf, M., 321, 322, 323
Wolfe, J. B., 308
Wood, K., 177
Woolfe, H., 62
Wrist counter, 182
Writing style as source of control, 379
Wulbert, M., 323
Wundt, w., 69, 70, 172

Z

Zeilberger, J., 323
Zimmerman, E. H., 321
Zimmerman, J., 317, 321
Zero rate behavior, 113–114